MCDOUGAL LITTELL

The

AMERICANS

Reading Study Guide

 McDougal Littell

A HOUGHTON MIFFLIN COMPANY

Evanston, Illinois • Boston • Dallas

Contents

The Living Constitution

Chapter 6   Launching the New Nation, 1789–1816

Chapter 7   Balancing Nationalism and Sectionalism, 1815–1840

Chapter 8   Reforming American Society, 1820–1850

UNIT 3   An Era of Growth and Disunion, 1825–1877

Chapter 9   Expanding Markets and Moving West, 1825–1847

Chapter 10   The Union in Peril, 1850–1861

UNIT 4   Migration and Industrialization, 1877–1917

UNIT 9 Passage to a New Century, 1968–2001

Being a Strategic Reader

Strategies for Reading Your History Book

UNDERSTANDING THE BIG PICTURE

History is filled with people, events, facts, and details. Sometimes you can get lost in all the details. This is why the most important strategy to remember as you read a history textbook is to form the "big picture" of history. As you read, keep asking yourself, "What is the main idea?" When you do this, the details will make more sense.

Use the strategies shown here to help you read *The Americans*.

Strategy: Look for key terms and names, which are in dark type in the section. The text gives clues to the important terms and names in the section.
Try This: Read the terms. Then look at pages 468 and 469. Which of the terms appear on these pages? How did you recognize them?

Strategy: Read the Main Idea and Why it Matters Now to begin forming the "big picture" of the section.
Try This: What do you think will be the subject of this section?

Strategy: Look closely at the photographs, art, and other illustrations in the text. Be sure to read the captions.
Try This: Look at the photograph. What does it show about life in American cities in the 1800s?

Strategy: Look at the heads and subheads in each section to get a general understanding of the subject.
Try This: Preview the head and subheads on pages 468 and 469. What do you expect to learn in this section?

SECTION 2

The Challenges of Urbanization

MAIN IDEA	WHY IT MATTERS NOW	Terms & Names
The rapid growth of cities forced people to contend with problems of housing, transportation, water, and sanitation.	Consequently, residents of U.S. cities today enjoy vastly improved living conditions.	• urbanization • Americanization movement • tenement • mass transit • Social Gospel movement • settlement house • Jane Addams

One American's Story

In 1870, at age 21, Jacob Riis left his native Denmark for the United States. Riis found work as a police reporter, a job that took him into some of New York City's worst slums, where he was shocked at the conditions in the overcrowded, airless, filthy tenements. Riis used his talents to expose the hardships of New York City's poor.

A PERSONAL VOICE JACOB RIIS

" Be a little careful, please! The hall is dark and you might stumble over the children pitching pennies back there. Not that it would hurt them; kicks and cuffs are their daily diet. They have little else. . . . Close [stuffy]? Yes! What would you have? All the fresh air that ever enters these stairs comes from the hall-door that is forever slamming. . . . Here is a door. Listen! That short hacking cough, that tiny, helpless wail—what do they mean? . . . The child is dying with measles. With half a chance it might have lived; but it had none. That dark bedroom killed it. "

—*How the Other Half Lives*

Making a living in the late 19th and early 20th centuries was not easy. Natural and economic disasters had hit farmers hard in Europe and in the United States, and the promise of industrial jobs drew millions of people to American cities. The urban population exploded from 10 million to 54 million between 1870 and 1920. This growth revitalized the cities but also created serious problems that, as Riis observed, had a powerful impact on the new urban poor.

As many as 12 people slept in rooms such as this one in New York City, photographed by Jacob Riis around 1889.

Urban Opportunities

The technological boom in the 19th century contributed to the growing industrial strength of the United States. The result was rapid **urbanization,** or growth of cities, mostly in the regions of the Northeast and Midwest.

468 CHAPTER 15

IMMIGRANTS SETTLE IN CITIES
Most of the immigrants who streamed into the United States in the late 19th century became city dwellers because cities were the cheapest and most convenient places to live. Cities also offered unskilled laborers steady jobs in mills and factories. By 1890, there were twice as many Irish residents in New York City as in Dublin, Ireland. By 1910, immigrant families made up more than half the total population of 18 major American cities.

The **Americanization movement** was designed to assimilate people of wide-ranging cultures into the dominant culture. This social campaign was sponsored by the government and by concerned citizens. Schools and voluntary associations provided programs to teach immigrants skills needed for citizenship, such as English literacy and American history and government. Subjects such as cooking and social etiquette were included in the curriculum to help the newcomers learn the ways of native-born Americans. Ⓐ

Despite these efforts, many immigrants did not wish to abandon their traditions. Ethnic communities provided the social support of other immigrants from the same country. This enabled them to speak their own language and practice their customs and religion. However, these neighborhoods soon became overcrowded, a problem that was intensified by the arrival of new transplants from America's rural areas.

MAIN IDEA

Analyzing Motives
Ⓐ Why did native-born Americans start the Americanization movement?

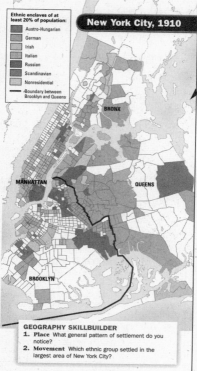

Ethnic enclaves of at least 20% of population:
- Austro-Hungarian
- German
- Irish
- Italian
- Russian
- Scandinavian
- Nonresidential
- — Boundary between Brooklyn and Queens

New York City, 1910

BRONX

MANHATTAN

QUEENS

BROOKLYN

GEOGRAPHY SKILLBUILDER
1. **Place** What general pattern of settlement do you notice?
2. **Movement** Which ethnic group settled in the largest area of New York City?

MIGRATION FROM COUNTRY TO CITY Rapid improvements in farming technology during the second half of the 19th century were good news for some farmers but bad news for others. Inventions such as the McCormick reaper and the steel plow made farming more efficient but meant that fewer laborers were needed to work the land. As more and more farms merged, many rural people moved to cities to find whatever work they could.

Many of the Southern farmers who lost their livelihoods were African Americans. Between 1890 and 1910, about 200,000 African Americans moved north and west, to cities such as Chicago and Detroit, in an effort to escape racial violence, economic hardship, and political oppression. Many found conditions only somewhat better than those they had left behind. Segregation and discrimination were often the reality in Northern cities. Job competition between blacks and white immigrants caused further racial tension.

Immigrants and Urbanization **469**

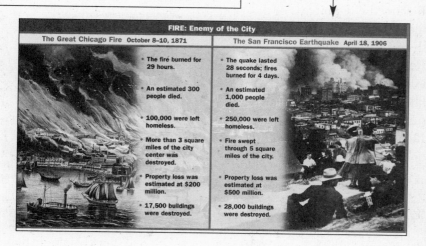

FIRE: Enemy of the City

The Great Chicago Fire October 8–10, 1871	The San Francisco Earthquake April 18, 1906
• The fire burned for 29 hours.	• The quake lasted 28 seconds; fires burned for 4 days.
• An estimated 300 people died.	• An estimated 1,000 people died.
• 100,000 were left homeless.	• 250,000 were left homeless.
• More than 3 square miles of the city center was destroyed.	• Fire swept through 5 square miles of the city.
• Property loss was estimated at $200 million.	• Property loss was estimated at $500 million.
• 17,500 buildings were destroyed.	• 28,000 buildings were destroyed.

Strategy: Preview the maps in each section. Think about how geography affected historical events.
Try This: Look closely at the map. What is the map about?

Strategy: Look at charts and graphs that present ideas in visual ways.
Try This: Study the chart below. What two events are being compared?

Strategy: Use the Main Idea questions to check your understanding as you read.
Try This: Read Question A. How would the details in the text help you answer the question?

Being a Strategic Reader

How to Use This Reading Study Guide

The purpose of this *Reading Study Guide* is to help you read and understand your history textbook, *The Americans.* You can use this *Reading Study Guide* in two ways.

1. Use the *Reading Study Guide* side-by-side with your history book.

- Turn to the section that you are going to read in the textbook. Then, next to the book, put the pages from the *Reading Study Guide* that accompany that section. All of the heads in the *Reading Study Guide* match the heads in the textbook.
- Use the *Reading Study Guide* to help you read and organize the information in the textbook.

2. Use the *Reading Study Guide* to study for tests on the textbook.

- Reread the summary of every chapter.
- Review the definitions of the Terms and Names in the *Reading Study Guide*.
- Review the diagram of information that you filled out as you read the summaries.
- Review your answers to questions.

Strategy: Read the Terms and Names and the definition of each. The Terms and Names are in dark type in the section.
Try This: What are the definitions of "Ellis Island" and "melting pot"?

Name _____ Date _____

CHAPTER 15 Section 1 (pages 460–465)

The New Immigrants

BEFORE YOU READ

In the last section, you read about the nation's labor union movement.

In this section, you will read how millions of immigrants entered the United States, where they faced culture shock, prejudice, and opportunity.

AS YOU READ

Use this diagram to take notes on the anti-immigration measures that the United States took.

MEASURE	DESCRIPTION
Chinese Exclusion Act	
Gentlemen's Agreement	

TERMS AND NAMES

Ellis Island Inspection station for immigrants arriving on the East Coast
Angel Island Inspection station for immigrants arriving on the West Coast
melting pot A mixture of different cultures living together
nativism Overt favoritism toward native-born Americans
Chinese Exclusion Act Act that limited Chinese immigration
Gentlemen's Agreement Agreement that limited Japanese emigration to U.S.

Through the "Golden Door"
(pages 460–462)

Where did the immigrants come from?

Between 1870 and 1920, about 20 million Europeans *immigrated* to the United States. Many of them came from eastern and southern Europe.

Some immigrants came to escape religious *persecution*. Many others were poor and looking to improve their economic situation. Still others came to experience greater freedom in the United States. Most European immigrants arrived on the East Coast.

A smaller number of immigrants came from Asia. They arrived on the West Coast. About 200,000 Chinese immigrants came between 1851 to 1883. Many Chinese immigrants helped build the nation's first transcontinental railroad. When the United States *annexed* Hawaii in 1898, several thousand Japanese immigrants came to the United States.

From 1880 to 1920, about 260,000 immigrants arrived from various islands in the Caribbean Sea. They came from Jamaica, Cuba, Puerto Rico, and other islands. Many left their homelands because jobs were *scarce.*

Many Mexicans came to the United States as well. Some became U.S. citizens when the nation

CHAPTER 15 IMMIGRANTS AND URBANIZATION **151**

Strategy: Fill in the diagram as you read. The diagram will help you organize information in the section.
Try This: What is the purpose of this diagram?

Strategy: Read the summary. It contains the main ideas and the key information under the head.
Try This: What do you think this section will be about?

---

acquired Mexican territory in 1848 as a result of the Mexican War. About a million Mexicans arrived between 1910 to 1930 to escape *turmoil* in their country.

1. Name two regions of the world where immigrants to the U.S. came from.

_____

_____

Life in the New Land (pages 462–464)

How did immigrants cope in America?

Many immigrants traveled to the United States by steamship. On board the ship they shared a cramped, unsanitary space. Under these harsh conditions, disease spread quickly. As a result, some immigrants died before they reached America.

Most European immigrants to the United States arrived in New York. There, they had to pass through an immigration station located on **Ellis Island** in New York Harbor. Officials at the station decided whether the immigrants could enter the country or had to return. Any immigrant with serious health problems or a *contagious* disease was sent home. Inspectors also made sure that immigrants met the legal requirements for entering the United States.

Asian immigrants arriving on the West Coast went through **Angel Island** in San Francisco. The inspection process on Angel Island was more difficult than on Ellis Island.

Getting along in a new country with a different language and culture was a great challenge for new immigrants. Many immigrants settled in communities with other immigrants from the same country. This made them feel more at home. They also formed organizations to help each other.

2. Name two ways immigrants dealt with adjusting to life in the United States.

_____

_____

Immigration Restrictions
(pages 464–465)

How did some Americans react to immigration?

By the turn of the century, some observers called America a **melting pot.** This term referred to the fact that many different cultures and races had blended in the United States.

However, this was not always the case. Many new immigrants refused to give up their culture to become part of American society.

Some Americans also preferred not to live in a melting pot. They did not like the idea of so many immigrants living in their country. The arrival of so many immigrants led to the growth of **nativism.** Nativism is an obvious preference for native-born Americans. Nativism gave rise to anti-immigrant groups. It also led to a demand for immigration restrictions.

On the West Coast, *prejudice* against Asians was first directed at the Chinese. During the depression of the 1870s, many Chinese immigrants agreed to work for low wages. Many American workers feared they would lose their jobs to the Chinese. As a result, labor groups pressured politicians to restrict Asian immigration. In 1882, Congress passed the **Chinese Exclusion Act.** This law banned all but a few Chinese immigrants. The ban was not lifted until 1943.

Americans showed prejudice against Japanese immigrants as well. In San Francisco, the local school board put all Chinese, Japanese, and Korean children in special Asian schools. This led to anti-American riots in Japan. President Theodore Roosevelt persuaded San Francisco officials to stop their separation policy. In exchange, Japan agreed to limit *emigration* to the United States under the **Gentlemen's Agreement** of 1907–1908.

3. Give two examples of anti-immigration measures in the U.S.

_____

_____

Strategy: When you see a word in italic type, read the definition in the Glossary at the end of the chapter.
Try This: What does *prejudice* mean? Look at the Glossary on the next page to find the definition.

Strategy: Answer the question at the end of each part.
Try This: Write an answer to Question 3.

Strategy: Underline main ideas and key information as you read.
Try This: Read the summary under the head "Life in the New Land." Underline information that you think is important. One important idea is already underlined.

Being a Strategic Reader

How to Use This Reading Study Guide

At the end of every chapter in the *Reading Study Guide*, you will find a Glossary and a section called After You Read. The Glossary gives definitions of all the words in italic type in the chapter summaries.

After You Read is a two-page chapter review. Use After You Read to identify those parts of the chapter that you need to study more for the test on the chapter.

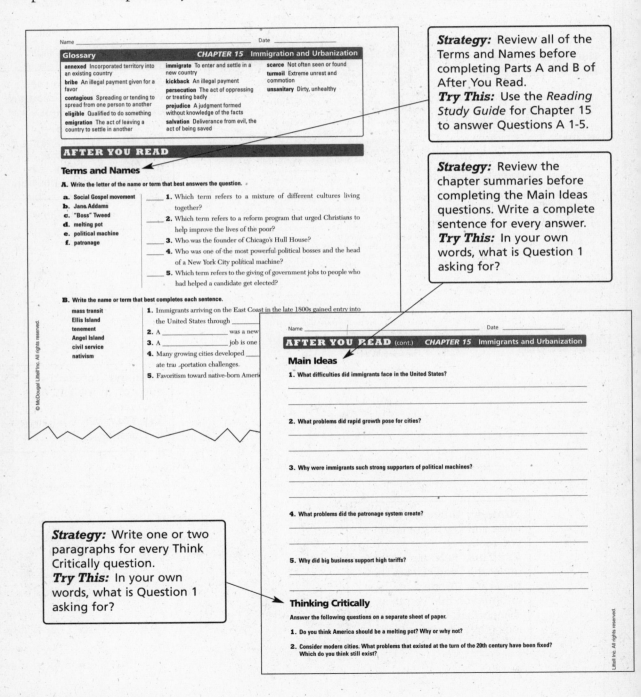

Name _____   Date _____

Glossary   **CHAPTER 15** Immigration and Urbanization

annexed Incorporated territory into an existing country
bribe An illegal payment given for a favor
contagious Spreading or tending to spread from one person to another
eligible Qualified to do something
emigration The act of leaving a country to settle in another

immigrate To enter and settle in a new country
kickback An illegal payment
persecution The act of oppressing or treating badly
prejudice A judgment formed without knowledge of the facts
salvation Deliverance from evil, the act of being saved

scarce Not often seen or found
turmoil Extreme unrest and commotion
unsanitary Dirty, unhealthy

AFTER YOU READ

Terms and Names

A. Write the letter of the name or term that best answers the question.

a. Social Gospel movement
b. Jane Addams
c. "Boss" Tweed
d. melting pot
e. political machine
f. patronage

_____ **1.** Which term refers to a mixture of different cultures living together?
_____ **2.** Which term refers to a reform program that urged Christians to help improve the lives of the poor?
_____ **3.** Who was the founder of Chicago's Hull House?
_____ **4.** Who was one of the most powerful political bosses and the head of a New York City political machine?
_____ **5.** Which term refers to the giving of government jobs to people who had helped a candidate get elected?

B. Write the name or term that best completes each sentence.

mass transit
Ellis Island
tenement
Angel Island
civil service
nativism

1. Immigrants arriving on the East Coast in the late 1800s gained entry into the United States through _____
2. A _____ was a new
3. A _____ job is one
4. Many growing cities developed _____ ate tra..portation challenges.
5. Favoritism toward native-born Americ

Name _____   Date _____

AFTER YOU READ (cont.)   **CHAPTER 15** Immigrants and Urbanization

Main Ideas

1. What difficulties did immigrants face in the United States?

_____

_____

2. What problems did rapid growth pose for cities?

_____

_____

3. Why were immigrants such strong supporters of political machines?

_____

_____

4. What problems did the patronage system create?

_____

_____

5. Why did big business support high tariffs?

_____

_____

Thinking Critically

Answer the following questions on a separate sheet of paper.

1. Do you think America should be a melting pot? Why or why not?

2. Consider modern cities. What problems that existed at the turn of the 20th century have been fixed? Which do you think still exist?

Strategy: Review all of the Terms and Names before completing Parts A and B of After You Read.
Try This: Use the *Reading Study Guide* for Chapter 15 to answer Questions A 1-5.

Strategy: Review the chapter summaries before completing the Main Ideas questions. Write a complete sentence for every answer.
Try This: In your own words, what is Question 1 asking for?

Strategy: Write one or two paragraphs for every Think Critically question.
Try This: In your own words, what is Question 1 asking for?

CHAPTER 1 Section 1 (pages 4–7)

Peopling the Americas

BEFORE YOU READ

In this section, you will learn about early peoples who first settled in the Americas.

In the next section, you will learn about the different Native American groups who lived in North America.

AS YOU READ

Use the chart below to take notes about the early civilizations of the Americas.

TERMS AND NAMES

nomadic Moving one's home

Olmec People who created a civilization along the coast of the Gulf of Mexico, beginning around 1200 B.C.

Maya People who created a civilization in Guatemala and the Yucatan Peninsula, about A.D. 250 to 900

Aztec People who built an empire in Mexico, beginning in the 1200s

Inca People who built an empire along the west coast of South America, beginning in the 1400s

Hohokam Native Americans who lived in the Southwest from about 300 B.C. to A.D. 1300

Anasazi Native Americans who lived in the Southwest from about A.D. 300 to 1300

Adena Mound-building people who lived in the Ohio River valley

Hopewell Mound-building people who lived in the Ohio River valley

Mississippian Mound-building people who lived in the Ohio and Mississippi river valleys

LOCATION	CIVILIZATIONS / DATES
Middle and South America	Olmec 1200 to 400 B.C.
Southwest North America	
Ohio and Mississippi river valleys	

Ancient Peoples Come to the Americas (pages 4–5)

How did people first arrive in the Americas?

The first people in *the Americas* may have arrived 22,000 years ago. Ice age *glaciers* had frozen vast amounts of water. This lowered sea levels enough to expose a land bridge between Asia and Alaska called *Beringia*. Ancient hunters came across the land bridge from Asia to Alaska. These early people most likely hunted large animals. Over thousands of years, these people spread out across North and South America.

Changes occurred when the Ice Age ended around 12,000 to 10,000 years ago. The sea once again covered the land bridge. People no longer came to the Americas across this bridge. The climate grew warmer. Large animals began to dissappear and people switched to hunting smaller animals. They also began to fish and to gather nuts and berries.

Many groups of people settled in North America. Other groups continued south into present-day Mexico and South America. Wherever these people settled, they *adapted* to the *environment* in which they lived.

Between 10,000 and 5,000 years ago (3000 to 800 B.C.), people living in Mexico discovered a new way to get food. They began to raise plants or to farm. They first grew *maize*. Soon they raised other crops. The practice of farming spread throughout the Americas.

People who farmed no longer had to search for plant foods. They could stay in one place. They had more time to learn new skills and to build settled communities. In this way, farming made possible the growth of complex *cultures*. Some Native American groups never gave up their **nomadic** way of life and continued to move from place to place in search of food and water.

1. How did people first come to the Americas?

_____

_____

Complex Societies Flourish in the Americas (pages 5–7)

Where did civilizations develop in the Americas?

Beginning about 3,000 years ago, many advanced Native American *civilizations* arose. The **Olmec** peoples began their civilization in Mexico around 1200 B.C. They created a thriving civilization in the humid rain forests. Other civilizations influenced by the Olmec appeared after their mysterious collapse around 400 B.C. They included the **Maya.** The Maya built their civilization between A.D. 250 and 900. It was located in what is today Guatemala and the Yucatan Peninsula.

The **Aztec** people built their empire in central Mexico in the 1200s. Starting around 1400, the **Inca** created a large, rich empire. It stretched along the western coast of South America.

All of these empires had achievements that were as great as those of other ancient cultures. All had great skills at mining and working precious metals, such as gold and silver. All built great cities or ceremonial centers with huge palaces, pyramids with temples, and central plazas. To record their histories, some of the later groups invented some form of writing that used symbols or images to express words or ideas.

In North America, the **Hohokam** and **Anasazi** built their civilizations in desert areas. Both groups settled in the Southwest. By 300 B.C. to A.D. 1400, each group had grown large enough to carve out its own civilization. The Hohokam settled in the river valleys in Central Arizona. The Anasazi lived in the canyon bottoms of the Four Corner region. This is an area where the present-day states of Utah, Colorado, Arizona, and New Mexico meet.

The **Adena, Hopewell,** and **Mississippian** civilizations developed east of the Mississippi River. These civilizations are called the Mound Builders. They created large burial *mounds*. The Mississipian also built huge pyramids.

2. What civilizations started in the desert areas of southwestern North America?

_____

_____

Name ______________________________ Date ______________

Native American Societies Around 1492

TERMS AND NAMES

Kashaya Pomo Native American group that lived in what is now California

Kwakiutl Native American group that lived on the Northwest coast

Pueblo Native American group in the Southwest

Iroquois Native American group in Eastern North America

kinship The ties between members of a family

division of labor The assignment of different jobs to different individuals

BEFORE YOU READ

In the last section, you learned about early peoples who first settled in the Americas.

In this section, you will learn about later Native American groups who lived in North America.

AS YOU READ

Use the diagram below to take notes on how Native American groups adapted to various regions.

REGION	WAYS OF ADAPTING TO ENVIRONMENT
Northwest Coast	The Kwakiutl hunted whales and seals.
California	
Southwest	
Eastern Woodlands	

Native Americans Live in Diverse Societies (pages 8–10)

How did Native Americans live?

Native American people lived in many kinds of settings. The cultures that they developed depended on how they adapted to their environments. For example, some Native American people lived in what is now California. This region was made up of a long coastline, a rain forest, and a desert. The **Kashaya Pomo** lived along the central coast of California. They hunted water birds for food.

The Northwest Coast was made up of ocean, waterways, and forests. The **Kwakiutl** and other Native American groups lived here. The ocean was their source of food. They hunted for whales and seals. They fished for salmon. The Kwakiutl used the trees from the forests to make *totem poles.*

The **Pueblo** people lived in the dry Southwest (today's Arizona and New Mexico). They built *adobe* houses. They grew corn and beans.

Forests made up the Eastern Woodlands. This region stretched from the Great Lakes and the St. Lawrence River in the North to the Gulf of Mexico in the South. Native Americans who lived in the colder Northeast depended on hunting. Those who lived in the warmer Southeast depended more on farming. The **Iroquois** lived in the forests of the Northeast (today's New York state). They hunted, fished, and gathered fruits and nuts.

1. How did the Native American people in different environments get their food?

_____

_____

Native Americans Share Cultural Patterns (pages 10–13)

What practices and beliefs did Native Americans have in common?

Although Native American societies had many differences, they did share certain cultural traits. These traits included trade patterns, attitudes toward the land and its use, and some religious and social values.

Trade routes across North America brought many Native American peoples into contact with one another. As tribes established permanent settlements, many of these settlements became known for certain products or skills. Elaborate trade routes allowed North American groups that lived far apart to exchange both goods and ideas with one another.

All Native American groups respected the land. They thought that it could not be bought or sold. They treated the land as a *resource* that belonged to all groups. Native Americans changed the land very little. They used it for the most important activities, such as farming. This attitude would lead to clashes with the Europeans who believed in private ownership of the land.

Most Native American groups believed that *spirits* lived in the world. For example, the spirit of a relative who had died might still serve as a guide to the living. Some groups believed in one spirit as the most powerful being.

The family was the basic unit. Native Americans had strong feelings of **kinship,** or family ties. Older family members were valued. They passed on their knowledge to the younger family members. In exchange, the young honored their elders and departed ancestors.

Most Native American groups practiced a **division of labor.** In this system, different jobs were assigned. The type of work someone did depended on *gender,* age, or social position.

The basic unit of organization among all Native American groups was the family, which included aunts, uncles, cousins, and other relatives. Some tribes also organized the families into clans, or groups of families descended from a common ancestor. Not all Native American groups lived together for long periods of time. Groups who hunted and gathered often broke up into smaller groups. The small groups came together for just important occasions.

2. What views did Native Americans hold about the land?

_____

_____

CHAPTER 1 **Section 3** (pages 14–19)

West African Societies Around 1492

TERMS AND NAMES

Islam Religion founded by the prophet Muhammad in the 600s

plantation A huge farm on which slaves or other workers grow a single crop

Songhai Large African kingdom known for trading

savanna A dry grassland with trees and bushes

Benin African kingdom around the Niger River known for metalworking

Kongo Small kingdoms on the lower Congo River united under one ruler

lineage Descent from a common ancestor

BEFORE YOU READ

In the last section, you learned about Native American groups who lived in North America during the 1400s.

In this section, you will learn about people who lived in West Africa in the 1400s.

AS YOU READ

Use this diagram to take notes about three West African kingdoms of the 1400s.

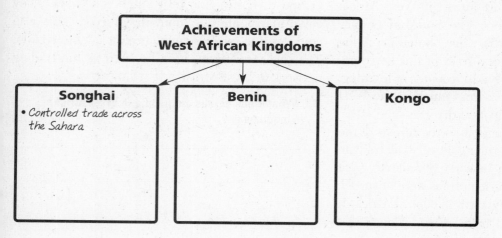

Achievements of West African Kingdoms → Songhai / Benin / Kongo

Songhai
• Controlled trade across the Sahara

Benin

Kongo

West Africa and the Wider World (pages 14–16)

What influenced the way of life in West Africa?

Africa was isolated from Europe and Asia by geography. But for centuries, trade routes throughout Africa had connected different regions in the exchange of goods, ideas, and beliefs.

Timbuktu was the hub of a well-established trading network that connected most of West Africa to the coastal ports of North Africa. These trade routes crossed the Sahara Desert. Cities at the crossroads of these trading routes like Timbuktu, Gao, and Jenne grew wealthy and powerful.

Traders from North Africa also brought a new religion—**Islam**—to West Africa. Islam was founded by the prophet Muhammad in Arabia in 622. It quickly spread across the Middle East and North Africa. By the 1200s, Islam became the official religion of the empires in West Africa.

In the 1400s, traders from Portugal arrived off West Africa. Within 50 years, they claimed two islands. They also began **plantations,** or large farms, to grow sugar cane. The Portuguese bought slaves from the African *mainland.* The slaves worked on these plantations. This practice would later be copied on a larger scale in the Americas. The Portuguese did not use the trade routes across the Sahara. Instead, they traded directly with the coastal people of West Africa.

1. Why did African cities grow wealthy and powerful?

_____

_____

Three African Kingdoms Flourish (pages 16–17)

What three powerful kingdoms existed in West Africa in the 1400s and 1500s?

Three powerful kingdoms arose in West Africa. They all had strong rulers. The **Songhai** empire controlled trade across the Sahara. Askia Muhammad was the second ruler of this kingdom. He made the city of Timbuktu a center of learning. Songhai power extended across much of the West African **savanna,** the region of dry grassland.

Benin was a great kingdom in the forests of the southern coast. A mighty ruler controlled all trade in the kingdom. Benin metalworkers created great works of art. Their bronze sculptures were beautiful.

The kingdom of **Kongo** was in central Africa. It arose along the Zaire (Congo) River. Kongo was made up of small kingdoms. These were held together under one ruler.

2. What three kingdoms controlled West Africa in the 1400s and 1500s?

_____

_____

West African Culture (pages 18–19)

What was life like in a West African kingdom?

Most West Africans lived with their families in small villages. Each family traced its **lineage,** or line of descent. These family ties helped to decide *inheritances* and marriage partners.

Age was very important to West African families. The oldest people influenced other family members. They also represented the family in large group meetings.

West African people valued religion. Religious *rituals* were part of daily life. West Africans respected the spirits of living and nonliving things. Many also believed in a single creator.

West African people divided jobs. Work was done by men and women of different ages and social positions. Throughout West Africa, people farmed and herded. Many hunted and fished. Some also mined and traded. Most groups in West Africa believed that land belonged to all people.

People on the dry savanna depended on rivers, such as the Niger, to nourish their crops and water their livestock. Some groups in West Africa held slaves. In Africa, however, slavery did not always mean a lifetime without freedom. Slaves could escape their situation in a number of ways. They could marry into the family they served. They also could escape into the familiar African countryside. The slave trade became a key part of the trading network in West Africa.

3. What kinds of jobs did people in West African kingdoms do?

_____

_____

European Societies Around 1492

BEFORE YOU READ

In the last section, you learned about kingdoms in West Africa around the 1400s.

In this section, you will learn about life in Europe during the 1300s and 1400s.

AS YOU READ

Use the web below to take notes on the changes in Western Europe that led to the Age of Exploration.

> ### TERMS AND NAMES
>
> **Renaissance** Period when Europeans began investigating all aspects of the physical world
>
> **hierarchy** Social ordering by rank or class
>
> **nuclear family** Household made up of a mother and father and their children
>
> **Crusades** Series of wars started by Europeans to win back the Holy Land from the Muslims
>
> **Reformation** Split in the Christian Church that led to Protestantism
>
> **Prince Henry** Portuguese prince who started a school for sailors and sponsored early voyages of exploration

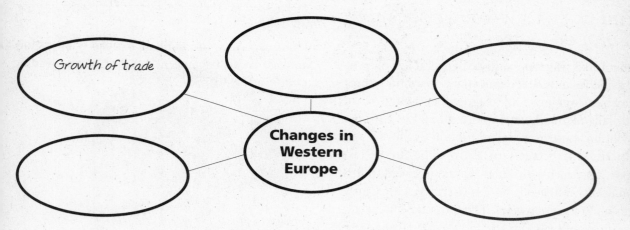

The European Social Order
(pages 20–21)

How were European societies arranged in the 1400s?

European societies were arranged in a **hierarchy,** that is by order of rank or position. Rulers and nobles were at the top. They owned the most land and were the most powerful. *Peasants* were at the bottom. They made up most of the people in European society.

In Europe, kinship did not play as an important role as it did in Native American and African societies. Life in Europe centered around the **nuclear family.** This kind of household was made up of a mother and father and their children.

1. Who made up the highest and lowest levels of society in Europe during the 1400s?

_____

_____

Christianity Shapes the European Outlook (page 22)

How did the Crusades affect Europe?

The Roman Catholic Church was important in Europe. It played a central role in people's daily lives.

The Church encouraged Christians to take Spain from the Muslims, who were followers of Islam. The Church also wanted Muslims to leave the Holy Land. From 1096 to 1270, Europeans took part in the **Crusades.** These were series of wars to retake the Holy Land. The Crusades failed to achieve this goal.

The Crusades still had a big impact, though. Trade increased. Europeans wanted the goods they saw in Asia. The Crusades helped to make European rulers stronger and to make nobles and the Church weaker.

In the early 1500s, *reformers* called for changes in the Church. This movement was called the **Reformation.**

2. What were two results of the Crusades?

_____

_____

_____

Changes Come to Europe (pages 23–24)

What changes were happening in Europe?

In the 1300s, Europe suffered several serious setbacks. Thousands died from starvation after a crop failure. An epidemic of plagues beginning in the 1340s killed 25 million people, a quarter of Europe's population. Long wars killed thousands more.

In the 1400s, modern Europe began to take shape. The Crusades had opened trade routes. Population increased, and towns and cities grew larger and more powerful. The Crusades had weakened the nobility and made *monarchs* more powerful. By the late 1400s, four major nations were taking shape in western Europe: Portugal, Spain, France, and England.

The Renaissance led to a more secular spirit, an interest in worldly pleasures, and a new confidence in human achievement. People began to regard themselves as individuals.

3. What were two important changes in Europe?

_____

_____

Europe Enters a New Age of Expansion (page 25)

Why did Europeans become interested in exploration?

Europeans looked for new routes to the East. The introduction of the compass and astrolabe allowed ship captains to *navigate* better. New ships such as the *caravel* allowed sailors to sail against the wind.

Prince Henry of Portugal, often called "Henry the Navigator," developed and *employed* these new innovations. He sent his captains to explore the coast of Africa. Bartolomeu Dias rounded the southern tip of Africa in 1488. Ten years later, Vasco da Gama reached India.

4. What contributed to more interest in exploration during the 1400s?

_____

_____

Skillbuilder

Use the picture to answer the questions.

1. What class of people are shown here?

_____

_____

2. What does the picture reveal about their daily life?

_____

_____

Name _____   Date _____

Transatlantic Encounters

TERMS AND NAMES

Christopher Columbus Italian explorer who sailed to North America for Spain

Taino Native Americans who lived where Columbus first landed

colonization The establishment of outlying settlements that are controlled by a parent country

Columbian Exchange Early trade across the Atlantic Ocean

Treaty of Tordesillas Agreement between Spain and Portugal to explore different lands

BEFORE YOU READ

In the last section, you learned about the changes that happened in Europe by the late 1400s.

In this section, you will learn how Christopher Columbus's voyages changed the world.

AS YOU READ

Use the diagram below to take notes on the effects of Columbus's voyages.

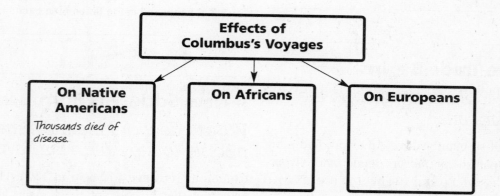

Columbus Crosses the Atlantic
(pages 26–27)

What were Christopher Columbus's goals?

Christopher Columbus was an Italian sailor. He thought he could find a new trade route to Asia. He wanted to sail west across the Atlantic. Columbus asked the rulers of Spain to give him money and supplies. In return, he would claim new lands for Spain. He would also *convert* the people he found to Christianity.

In 1492, Columbus sailed across the Atlantic. He landed on an island between North and South America. The people he met there called themselves the **Taino,** from their word for "noble ones."

Columbus renamed their island San Salvador. He claimed it for Spain.

Columbus returned to Spain in 1493. He mistakenly thought that he had reached islands off Asia. These were known to the Europeans as the Indies. So Columbus called the people that he saw there *los indios*—"Indians." This name was used for all the people who lived in the Americas.

The Spanish rulers funded three more voyages to the Americas. On these voyages, Columbus brought soldiers, priests, and people to settle the land.

1. What deal did Christopher Columbus strike with the Spanish monarchs?

_____

_____

The Impact on Native Americans

(page 28)

How did Columbus change the lives of Native Americans?

By the time Columbus came to Hispaniola, Europeans had developed a way of **colonization.** They set up areas controlled by the parent country. Europeans started plantations. They forced people to work there. Europeans also used new weapons to threaten people. Such methods were used on the Native Americans. But Native Americans fought back.

Still, many Native Americans caught diseases brought by Europeans. Thousands of Native Americans died from disease and brutality.

2. How did Columbus's voyages affect Native American lives?

_____

The Slave Trade Begins (page 29)

How did Columbus change the lives of Africans?

The deaths of so many Native American had a big effect. The Spanish conquerors needed more workers. Spanish rulers did want to use Native Americans as slaves. The Spanish began to bring Africans to the Americas as slaves.

The price of enslaved Africans increased. More Europeans took part in the slave trade. Slaves were brought from Africa, across the Atlantic Ocean, to the Americas.

The Atlantic slave trade destroyed many African societies, especially in West Africa. Many of these societies lost their fittest people. By the 1800s, about 12 million enslaved Africans were taken to the Americas.

3. How did the Atlantic slave trade affect Africa?

_____

_____

The Impact on Europeans (pages 29–30)

What was the Columbian Exchange?

After Columbus's voyage, ships carried trade goods to various regions. These were the Americas, Africa, Asia, and Europe. This transfer of goods came to be known as the **Columbian Exchange.** The Americas introduced crops to Europe and Africa. European goods were brought to the Americas. African foods were carried to the Americas on the slave ships.

Many European countries wanted to claim American land for themselves. In 1494, Spain and Portugal signed the **Treaty of Tordesillas.** It divided the Western Hemisphere along a north-south line. Spain could explore areas west of the line. It could also start colonies there. Portugal could have lands to the east.

4. What happened in the Columbian Exchange?

_____

_____

A New Society Is Born (pages 30–31)

What effect did the movement of people to the Americas have?

Columbus returned to Spain in 1504. He felt discouraged that he did not reach Asia. He did not know how his voyages would change the world.

In time, settlers from England would bring their culture to colonies in North America. These colonies would later form a new nation.

The history of the United States began with a meeting of Native Americans, Europeans, and Africans. These people helped create a *diverse* society. The United States today is still a society of diverse peoples.

5. How did the movement of people to the Americas create a new kind of society?

_____

_____

Name _____ Date _____

adapted Changed to fit in

adobe Sun-dried bricks

caravel A ship that allowed sailors to sail against the wind

civilization Society with highly developed culture, including arts, politics, writing, and science

convert To persuade someone to accept a particular religion

culture The traditions and way of life shared by people

diverse Different from one another

employed Put to use

environment Natural surroundings, including weather, plants, and animals

gender Being male or female

glacier Large sheets of ice

inheritance Something that is passed on to an individual from an ancestor at his or her death

mainland The main part of a continent

maize A kind of corn

monarch A ruler, such as a king or queen

mound A hill made of earth or stone

navigate To direct the course of a ship

peasants People who work in fields for rich landowners

reformers People who work to improve the way things are done

resource A natural source of something useful, like water

ritual Repeated ceremony that gives meaning to events

spirit The soul or consciousness of a being

the Americas North, South, and Central America

totem pole Tall, hand-carved pole that often told about a family

AFTER YOU READ

Terms and Names

A. Write the letter of the name or term next to the statement that describes it best.

a. Anasazi

b. Kwakiutl

c. Benin

d. peasant

e. Christopher Columbus

f. Prince Henry

_____ **1.** The Italian explorer who found the Americas instead of a westward route to Asia

_____ **2.** A Native American group of the Northwest Coast of North America

_____ **3.** The bottom of the European hierarchy around 1400

_____ **4.** An ancient Native American people of the Southwest

_____ **5.** A kingdom of West Africa, famous for its metalwork

B. Circle the name or term that best completes each sentence.

1. The _____ society was the last of the Mound Builder societies.
   Mississippian   **Hohokam**   **Maya**

2. The _____ lived in the forests of the Eastern Woodlands.
   Hohokam   **Iroquois**   **Aztec**

3. In the 1400s, the Portuguese started _____ to grow sugar on two islands off the African coast.
   savannas   **kinship**   **plantations**

AFTER YOU READ (continued)　　　CHAPTER 1　Three Worlds Meet

4. The _____ was a split in the Christian Church that led to Protestantism.
Renaissance　　　　　**Crusades**　　　　　**Reformation**

5. The voyages of Columbus led to the transfer of goods between the Americas, Europe, Asia, and Africa known as the _____.
Columbian Exchange　　　　　**kinship**　　　　　**joint-stock company**

Main Ideas

1. How did the invention of farming lead to the development of civilizations?

_____

_____

2. What were two practices or beliefs that Native American groups had in common?

_____

_____

3. How did the Portuguese change the established trading methods in West Africa in the 1400s?

_____

_____

4. What were two reasons that the power of the Roman Catholic Church began to weaken around the 1400s?

_____

_____

5. How did disease affect European colonization?

_____

_____

Thinking Critically

Answer the following questions on a separate sheet of paper.

1. Explain how one Native American group of North America adapted to its environment.

2. What two factors led to the European interest in overseas expansion?

CHAPTER 2 Section 1 (pages 36–41)

Spain's Empire in the Americas

BEFORE YOU READ

In the last section, you learned about the people living in North America, West Africa, and Europe.

In this section, you will learn about how the Spanish became the first Europeans to settle Central and North America.

AS YOU READ

Use this web diagram to take notes. Fill it with details about how Spain established an empire in the Americas.

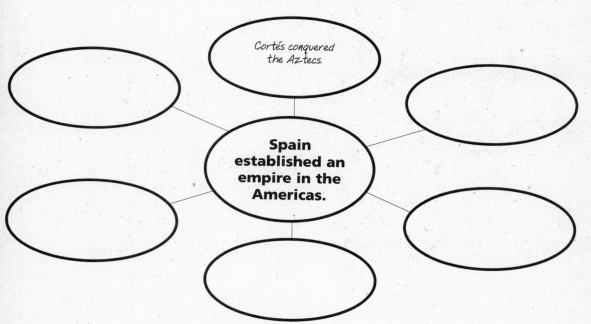

TERMS AND NAMES

conquistador Spanish explorer

Hernándo Cortés Conquistador who defeated the Aztecs

New Spain Spanish colony in the New World

mestizo Person of mixed Spanish and Native American descent

encomienda Brutal Spanish system of using Native Americans for labor

Juan Ponce de León Conquistador who explored present-day Florida

New Mexico Spanish colonies in North America

Popé Pueblo religious leader who led an uprising against the Spanish

The Spanish Claim a New Empire (pages 36–38)

Who were the conquistadores?

In the years after Columbus's voyages, many Spanish explorers sailed to the Americas. They were known as **conquistadores,** or conquerors. They came in search of gold and silver.

The conquistador **Hernándo Cortés** landed in Mexico in 1519. He soon heard about the rich Aztec empire. Cortés's army conquered the Aztecs and took their gold. The Aztecs regrouped and rebelled. However, by this time many Aztecs had died from European diseases. As a result, they did not have enough forces to put up a strong fight. In 1521, the Spanish defeated the Aztecs again and claimed their land for Spain.

Cortés marched 200 miles to the Aztec capital, Tenochtitlan. The Spanish marveled at the Aztec capital. Cortés was a skilled diplomat as well as a

In the web diagram: *Cortés conquered the Aztecs.* / **Spain established an empire in the Americas.**

solider. The Aztec Emperor, Montezuma, believed the Spanish leader to be a god and gave him gold. But the Spanish kept demanding more. Finally the Aztec rebelled. While they were successful at first, the Aztec were weakened by disease and Spanish arms. Cortés launched a counterattack in 1521. After several months of fighting, the invaders conquered Tenochtitlan and burned the capital. Cortés then laid plans for the colony of **New Spain** whose capital he called Mexico City.

Most of the Spanish who settled in the Americas were men. They often married Native American women. This created a large population of *mestizos.* These are people who were part Spanish and part Native American. Their descendants live today in Mexico, other Latin American countries, and the United States.

Spanish settlers forced native workers to work under the *encomienda* system. They made Native Americans farm, ranch, or mine the land. The settlers treated their workers badly. Many workers died from disease and abuse. In 1542, Spain ended the *encomienda* system because it was so brutal. Soon after that, Spanish settlers began to use African slaves.

1. **Why did Montezuma give the Spanish gold?**

_____

_____

_____

The Conquistadores Push North
(pages 38–40)

Who settled New Mexico?

The Spanish eventually moved into the present-day United States. **Juan Ponce de León** explored the area that is present-day Florida. The Spanish also explored the southwestern United States. Throughout the late 1500s and early 1600s, Spain sent mostly Catholic priests to settle this region. The colony became known as **New Mexico.**

The priests' mission was to convert Native Americans to the Roman Catholic faith. To do this,

the priests moved the Native Americans into large communities called *congregaciónes.* In addition to converting Native Americans, Spanish *missionaries* taught them European styles and ways.

The Spanish rulers saw the scattered missions, forts, and small ranches that dotted the lands of New Mexico as headquarters for spreading the Catholic religion.

2. **What was the duty of the Spanish priests in New Mexico?**

_____

_____

_____

Resistance to the Spanish (pages 40–41)

Why did the Native Americans rebel?

Spanish settlers in New Mexico tried to *impose* Spanish culture on the Native Americans. The settlers destroyed objects that the Native Americans considered *sacred.* The settlers also did not allow the Native Americans to perform their ancient ceremonies and rituals. In addition, the Spanish forced the Native Americans to work for them. Sometimes they abused workers physically.

One Native American who suffered such abuse was the Pueblo religious leader, **Popé.** The Spanish priests viewed Popé's religious practices as witchcraft. As a result, they beat and whipped him.

In 1680, Popé led a large rebellion against the Spanish. The uprising involved 17,000 Native Americans from all over New Mexico. The fighters drove the Spaniards back into Mexico. It would be another 14 years before the Spanish reconquered New Mexico.

3. **Why did the Native Americans of New Mexico rebel against the Spanish?**

_____

_____

_____

Name _____   Date _____

An English Settlement at Jamestown

TERMS AND NAMES

John Smith Leader of Jamestown

joint-stock companies Companies in which investors pooled their wealth with the hope of yielding a profit

Jamestown First permanent English settlement in North America

Powhatan Native Americans who lived in the area that became Jamestown

headright system The Virginia Company's system in which settlers and the family members who came with them each received 50 acres of land

indentured servants Workers who exchanged their labor for help getting started in America

royal colony A colony under the direct control of a monarch

Nathaniel Bacon Planter who led a rebellion in 1676 against the governor of the Virginia Colony

BEFORE YOU READ

In the last section, you learned how the Spanish claimed an empire in the Americas.

In this section, you will learn how the English came to North America and founded their own colonies.

AS YOU READ

Use this time line to take notes. Fill it with important events in the colonization of Virginia.

1607 Jamestown founded.	1618

1619	1622

English Settlers Struggle in North America (pages 42–46)

What happened at Jamestown?

John Smith was a soldier and adventurer. In 1606, he joined the Virginia Company. It was a **joint-stock company** which allowed *investors* to pool their wealth to fund a colony. In 1607, the Virginia Company sent 150 colonists aboard three ships to North America. The colonists built a settlement along the coast of modern-day Virginia. They called the colony **Jamestown** in honor of King James I. It was the first permanent English colony in the Americas.

Many English colonists wanted to get rich quick by finding gold. They did not take time to grow food. As a result, many colonists at Jamestown died. By the winter of 1607, only 39 colonists remained alive. Then John Smith took control of the settlement. He forced the colonists to farm. He received help from the **Powhatan** inhabitants of the area, who offered the colonists food. Under Smith's leadership, the colony slowly recovered.

An injury forced Smith to return to England. After he left, the settlement grew disorganized. Again, many colonists starved to death. The colony was saved when more colonists and supplies arrived from England.

The new settlers restored order to Jamestown. They also began to grow tobacco. The colonists discovered that they could sell this crop in Europe for a great profit. The colony needed more settlers to grow more tobacco. To lure more settlers to Jamestown, the Virginia Company started the **headright system** in 1618. Under this system, each new person who came to the colony received 50 acres of land and another 50 acres for each family member who came.

Most of the people who arrived, however, did not come under the headright system. Most came as **indentured servants.** In exchange for passage to North America, as well as food and shelter, an indentured servant agreed to work on a farm for several years. After that time, the indentured servant would be free. Most indentured servants were poor English citizens in search of a new life.

In 1619, the first Africans arrived in North America. They were treated as indentured servants. After several years of labor, they gained their freedom. In the decades to come, more and more Africans would arrive in North America—not as indentured servants, but as slaves.

1. How did tobacco help save the settlement at Jamestown?

_____

_____

The Settlers Clash with Native Americans
(pages 46–47)

How did English colonists treat the Native Americans?

Unlike the Spanish, English settlers had no desire to live among or intermarry with Native Americans. Instead, they struggled to drive the Native Americans away.

As Jamestown grew, the colony needed more land for farming. As a result, the English settlers seized Powhatan land. In 1622, the Native Americans fought back. They attacked numerous colonial villages. More than 340 colonists were killed. The Native American attack forced the Virginia Company to send in more troops and sup-

plies. This left the company nearly *bankrupt*. The *turmoil* in Virginia angered the English government. As a result, the king took over the colony from the Virginia Company. Virginia became a **royal colony**—a colony under the control of the king.

England sent in more settlers to strengthen the colony. The government also sent in more troops to conquer the Native Americans. By 1644, nearly 10,000 English settlers lived in Virginia. The native population continued to decrease.

2. How did becoming a royal colony help Virginia?

_____

_____

Economic Differences Split Virginia (pages 47–48)

Who held the power in Virginia?

In addition to fighting Native Americans, the English settlers fought among themselves. Wealthy landowners controlled life in the colony. Freed indentured servants had little money to buy land. Because they did not own land, they could not vote and had almost no rights. They were forced to live on the western edge of Virginia. Out there, they constantly fought with the Native Americans for land.

Virginia's government refused to help these poor settlers in their battles with Native Americans. **Nathaniel Bacon,** a wealthy planter, came to the settlers' rescue. He raised an army to fight the Native Americans. The governor of Virginia declared that army illegal. When Bacon heard this, he led a group of marchers into Jamestown. They protested the government's treatment of poor settlers. The march turned violent. The government eventually put down the *rebellion*.

3. Why did Nathaniel Bacon lead a rebellion against the governor of Virginia?

_____

_____

CHAPTER 2 Section 3 (pages 49–54)

Puritan New England

BEFORE YOU READ

In the last section, you learned about England's first permanent settlement in the Americas.

In this section, you will learn why the Puritans settled in North America.

AS YOU READ

Use this chart to take notes. These notes will help you see the effects of events that occurred in the New England colonies in the 1600s.

TERMS AND NAMES

Puritans Members of a religious group known for its strict beliefs

John Winthrop Leader of the first settlers at Massachusetts Bay Colony

Separatists Members of a Puritan group who established their own congregations

Plymouth Colony Second permanent English colony in North America founded by the Pilgrims

Massachusetts Bay Colony Colony founded by Puritans in 1630

Roger Williams Puritan dissenter who set up a new colony in Rhode Island

Anne Hutchinson Puritan dissenter banished from the Massachusetts Bay Colony who fled to Rhode Island in 1638

Pequot War A 1637 conflict in which the Pequots battled Connecticut colonists

Metacom Native American chief who fought against English colonists in the King Philip's War

King Philip's War Conflict between settlers and Native Americans

CAUSE	EFFECT
Puritans are persecuted in England	Puritans move to New England
Puritans believed in hard work	
Roger Williams held different views from the Puritans in Massachusetts Bay	
The colonies in New England grew rapidly	
Native Americans were defeated in King Philip's War	

Puritans Create a "New England" (pages 49–52)

Why did the Puritans come to America?

A different group of English people settled north of Jamestown. They were members of a religious group that wanted to *purify* the Church of England by removing some of its Catholic practices. Because of this, they were known as **Puritans.**

Puritans believed in the idea of a "priesthood of all believers." This meant that every worshipper should experience God directly through faith, prayer, and study of the Bible—instead of through services conducted by church priests.

Some Puritans believed in trying to change the Church of England. Other Puritans chose to leave the church and form their own *congregations.* They were known as **Separatists.**

The English king punished anyone who broke away from the Church of England. One Separatist group, known today as Pilgrims, decided to leave England. In 1620, they arrived in North America and founded **Plymouth Colony.**

In 1630, another group of Puritans sailed to North America. Like the Pilgrims, they came to practice their religion without fear of punishment. They started a settlement called the **Massachusetts Bay Colony.** By 1640, more than 20,000 English settlers lived there. The region would become known as New England.

Unlike the settlers in Jamestown, the Puritans were well prepared to live in this new land. They were organized and had many supplies. **John Winthrop** was the settlement's first governor.

The Puritans wanted to create a society that all people would look up to. All adult male members of the Puritan Church could vote. The Puritans also placed great importance on families and church authority.

They also stressed hard work. No matter what one's duties were, Puritans believed that God required men and women to work long and hard at them. This "Puritan work ethic" helped lead to the rapid growth and success of the New England colonies.

1. Why did the colonists at Massachusetts Bay fare better at the beginning than the colonists in Virginia?

Dissent in the Puritan Community (page 52)

Why did some Puritans leave the Massachusetts Bay Colony?

The Puritans came to America to practice their religion in freedom. However, they did not like dissent, or the expression of other points of view.

A minister named **Roger Williams** preached that the settlers should buy—not take—land from Native Americans. He also said that government officials should not punish those with different religious views. Williams's views angered Puritan leaders. They soon ordered his arrest. In 1636, Williams fled Massachusetts Bay. He settled a new colony in what is now Rhode Island.

Anne Hutchinson also angered Church leaders with her beliefs. She argued that worshipers should interpret the Bible on their own—without the help of the church or its ministers. Puritan leaders *banished* Hutchinson from the colony in 1638. She and her family went to Rhode Island.

2. Why did Puritan leaders force Roger Williams and Anne Hutchinson to leave the colony?

Native Americans Resist Colonial Expansion (pages 53–54)

How did Puritans treat Native Americans?

At first, Puritans and the local Native Americans helped each other. As New England grew, however, settlers began to seize Native American lands. In addition, the settlers tried to force the Native Americans to accept Puritan laws and religion.

Many Native Americans saw the Puritans as a threat to their way of life. The tense relationship between the two groups soon led to war. In 1637, the Pequot tribe, who lived in what is now Connecticut, went to war with the colonists. The **Pequot War** ended in total defeat for the Native Americans. Most of the Pequot civilization was wiped out.

War between Native Americans and colonists broke out again in 1675. Chief **Metacom,** whom the English called King Philip, led an alliance of Native Americans against the settlers. **King Philip's War** lasted over a year. In the end, the English won.

3. Why did Native Americans fight the Puritans?

CHAPTER 2   Section 4 (pages 55–59)

Settlement of the Middle Colonies

TERMS AND NAMES

New Netherland Colony founded by the Dutch in 1621

proprietor Owner of a colony

William Penn Founder of Pennsylvania

Quakers Members of a religious group known for tolerance

BEFORE YOU READ

In the last section, you learned how the New England colonies were formed.

In this section, you will learn how the Middle Colonies were settled.

AS YOU READ

Use this chart to take notes about the settlement of New Netherland and Pennsylvania.

COLONY	WHEN STARTED?	WHO CAME?	WHY DID THEY COME?
New Netherland	1621	Dutch, Germans, French, Scandinavians, and other Europeans; Africans; people of many faiths	
Pennsylvania			

The Dutch Found New Netherland (pages 58–59)

Who settled in New Netherland?

England and Spain were not the only nations to establish colonies in North America. The Dutch founded settlements on the shores of what is now the United States. In 1621, the Dutch founded the colony of **New Netherland** (present day Albany and New York City). They also took over a Swedish settlement along the Delaware River.

New Netherland was a diverse colony. People from many different European nations lived in the settlement. In addition, Africans—free as well as enslaved—lived there. By the 1660s, about one-fifth of the population was of African descent.

The leaders of New Netherland allowed people the freedom to practice their own religion. As a result, people of many different religious faiths settled there.

The Dutch had mostly friendly relations with the Native Americans. Unlike the English colonists, the Dutch settlers did not wish to take the Native Americans' land. They were more interested in trading with the Native Americans.

The Dutch settlement stood in the way of England's plan to unite its Northern and Southern colonies. As a result, the English seized control of the Dutch colony. England's Duke of York became the new **proprietor,** or owner, of New Netherland. He renamed it New York. In addition, he separated the southern part of the colony and named it New Jersey.

1. Why did people of many faiths settle in New Netherland?

_____

_____

The Quakers Settle Pennsylvania

(pages 59–61)

Why was Pennsylvania founded?

During the late 1600s, England enlarged its North American settlements. To repay a debt, King Charles II gave Englishman **William Penn** a piece of land to the west of New Jersey. Penn was a mem-

ber of a religious group called **Quakers.** Quakers believed God's "inner light" burned inside everyone. Quakers were pacifists, persons who oppose war or violence for any reason. Because of their different beliefs, Quakers suffered *persecution* in England.

Penn's settlement allowed freedom of religion. The colony also granted the right to vote to all adult male settlers and sought friendly relations with Native Americans. Penn believed that settlers had to buy land from the Native Americans. He formed a court that included colonists and Native Americans to help settle differences between the two groups.

To encourage people to live in Pennsylvania, Penn advertised his colony in western Europe. As a result, numerous Germans, Dutch, and French settled there.

Other British colonies were founded in the 1600s and 1700s. George Calvert, the first Lord Baltimore, founded the colony of Maryland. James Oglethorpe founded Georgia as a colony for debtors.

2. What ideals characterized Pennsylvania?

_____

_____

Geography Skillbuilder

Use the map and what you have read to answer the following questions.

1. What colonies made up New England in 1675?

_____

_____

2. Near what geographic feature were most of the early settlements in New England started?

_____

_____

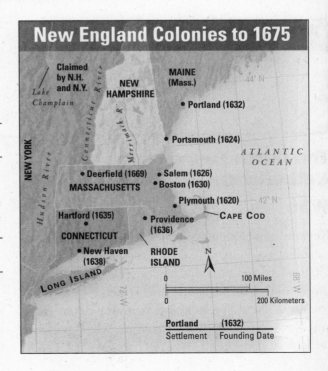

New England Colonies to 1675

Name _____ Date _____

banish To force to leave a country or place

bankrupt Having no money

congregations Groups of people who come together to worship

impose To force upon another

investor Someone who commits money to something in the hopes of making a profit

missionary Someone sent to convert others to a religion

persecution The act of treating harshly or oppressing

purify To make pure or to simplify

rebellion Revolt or opposition against a government or any authority

sacred Holy

turmoil Extreme confusion or commotion

AFTER YOU READ

Terms and Names

A. Write the name or term that best completes each sentence.

proprietor

Jamestown

Dutch

conquistador

Hernándo Cortés

Puritans

Popé

1. The Spanish explorer _____ explored Mexico and conquered the Aztecs.

2. In 1680, _____, a Pueblo religious leader, rebelled against Spanish rule in New Mexico.

3. The first permanent English colony in the Americas was _____.

4. In 1630, the _____ founded Massachusetts Bay Colony.

5. William Penn was the _____ of the Pennsylvania colony.

B. Write the letter of the name or term that matches the description.

a. Roger Williams

b. Powhatan

c. Quakers

d. Puritans

e. *mestizo*

f. John Winthrop

_____ **1.** A person of mixed Spanish and Native American blood

_____ **2.** Native Americans who helped the settlers at Jamestown

_____ **3.** First governor of the Massachusetts Bay Colony

_____ **4.** Founded the colony of Rhode Island

_____ **5.** Religious group that settled in the Pennsylvania colony

AFTER YOU READ (cont.) *CHAPTER 2* **The American Colonies Emerge**

Main Ideas

1. Why did Native Americans in New Mexico resist the Spanish?

_____

_____

2. Why did the settlement at Jamestown nearly fail?

_____

_____

3. Why did Nathaniel Bacon lead a rebellion against wealthy landowners in Virginia?

_____

_____

4. What did Puritans want to achieve in the Massachusetts Bay Colony?

_____

_____

5. What two things did New Netherland and Pennsylvania have in common?

_____

_____

Thinking Critically

Answer the following questions on a separate sheet of paper.

1. Compare the relations of the Spanish, the English, and the Dutch with Native Americans.

2. How did the reason for settling Jamestown differ from the reason for settling the Massachusetts Bay Colony?

CHAPTER 3 Section 1 (pages 66–71)

England and Its Colonies

BEFORE YOU READ

In the last section, you learned how the English established colonies in North America.

In this section, you will learn how the relationship between England and its colonies grew tense.

AS YOU READ

Use this web diagram to take notes on ways that England tried to keep control over the colonies.

TERMS AND NAMES

mercantilism Theory that countries should acquire gold and focus on exporting goods and owning colonies

Parliament The lawmaking body of England

Navigation Acts Laws passed by the British to control colonial trade

Dominion of New England A huge colony formed by the King of England, which included land from southern Maine to New Jersey

Sir Edmund Andros Governor appointed by the King of England to govern over the Dominion of England

Glorious Revolution Overthrow of James II

salutary neglect An English policy of not strictly enforcing laws in its colonies

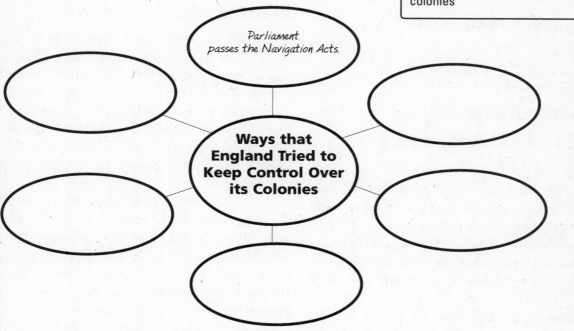

Parliament passes the Navigation Acts.

Ways that England Tried to Keep Control Over its Colonies

England and Its Colonies Prosper (pages 66–68)

What is mercantilism?

England's North American colonies existed mainly for the benefit of the home country—England. This idea was based on the theory of **mercantilism.** Under mercantilism, a nation could become rich and powerful in two ways: (1) by obtaining gold and silver, and (2) by establishing a favorable *balance of trade* in which it sold more goods than it bought. A nation's ultimate goal under mercantilism was to become self-sufficient so that it did not have to depend on other countries for goods.

The key to achieving a favorable balance of trade was establishing colonies. Colonies provided *raw materials*, such as lumber, furs, grain, and tobacco to the home country. This meant that the home country did not have to buy these goods from other nations. With colonies, nations had a built-in market in which to sell the goods it produced.

Throughout the 1600s, the American colonies behaved as they were supposed to under the mercantilist system. They *exported* much of their raw materials to England. However, the colonies also sold raw materials to other countries. England saw this as a threat to their economic strength. Under mercantilism, a nation's colonies should not supply goods to other countries.

In 1651, England's **Parliament,** or lawmaking body, passed the **Navigation Acts.** The acts greatly *restricted* colonial trade. They declared that the colonies could export certain products only to England. They also required that goods traded between the colonies and other nations first had to be unloaded in England. This allowed England to tax the goods—and thus make money off the trade.

1. **What did the Navigation Acts do?**

_____

_____

Tensions Emerge (pages 68–69)

What was the Dominion of New England?

Despite the Navigation Acts, some colonial merchants continued to trade goods with other countries illegally. In 1684, the English King, Charles II, responded by punishing Massachusetts, where much of the illegal trading occurred. The king took away the colony's *charter* and made it a royal colony.

In 1685, James II replaced Charles as king. He cracked down further on the American colonies. James placed the colonies from southern Maine to New Jersey under one large colony called the **Dominion of New England.** The king made **Sir Edmund Andros** the new royal governor of the Dominion. Andros angered the colonists by outlawing local government and by forcing new taxes on the colonists.

At about this time, England was experiencing great *turmoil.* The country's Parliament, which often fought with James, wanted to get rid of him.

In 1688, Parliament helped overthrow James. This event became known as the **Glorious Revolution.** In the aftermath of the revolution, Parliament passed laws that gave it greater power over the English king.

Parliament restored the original colonies that made up the Dominion of New England. In addition, Parliament gave Massachusetts its charter back. The new charter, however, called for the king to appoint the governor of Massachusetts. The charter also required Massachusetts be more tolerant of different religions.

2. **How did the Glorious Revolution affect the colonies?**

_____

_____

England Loosens the Reins
(pages 70–71)

What is salutary neglect?

After 1688, England turned its attention away from the colonies. It was more concerned with France which was competing with England for control of Europe.

In this period, the new English government followed a policy of **salutary neglect.** This meant that it rarely enforced the laws. Parliament did not think it was necessary to supervise the colonies closely.

Under this new policy, governors appointed by the king ruled each colony. However, colonial assemblies—lawmaking bodies comprised of elected colonists—held a good deal of power. The governor could veto the laws the assemblies passed. However, the assemblies had the power to raise taxes. This meant that they controlled the governor's salary. In this way, the colonies were able to practice an early form self-government.

3. **In what way did the colonists hold some political power in the colonies?**

_____

_____

The Agricultural South

BEFORE YOU READ

In the last section, you learned about the ways in which England tried to control its colonies.

In this section, you will learn about the characteristics of the Southern colonies.

AS YOU READ

Use this chart to take notes on Southern society. List and describe the different classes of people that made up Southern society. Start with the most powerful group on top and the least powerful at the bottom.

SOCIAL CLASS	DESCRIPTION
1. planters	Controlled the South's economic, social and political life
2.	
3.	
4.	
5.	

TERMS AND NAMES

cash crop A crop grown for sale rather than for the farmer's use

slave Person who is considered the property of another

triangular trade The pattern of shipping trade across the Atlantic

middle passage The voyage that brought slaves to America

Stono Rebellion A 1739 slave rebellion in Charleston, South Carolina

A Plantation Economy Arises
(pages 72–73)

What kind of economy developed in the South?

Throughout the 1600s and 1700s, the American colonies grew and prospered. They also grew into two distinct regions: North and South. Colonists in the South created a society based on farming. A typical large southern farm, or plantation, grew a single **cash crop**—a crop grown for sale rather than for the farmer's use. Cash crops included tobacco, rice, and *indigo*.

Few major cities developed in the South. One reason was that plantations usually were located along the rivers. This meant that farmers could transport their goods to the northern colonies and Europe without a need for city docks. Another reason for the absence of large towns in the South was that farmers could store their goods on their plantations. Thus, they did not need city warehouses. Furthermore, plantation owners produced much of what they needed, so there was no reason for shops or bakeries. There were a few major cities in the South, such as Charles Town (later called Charleston), in South Carolina. However, southern society was mostly *rural*.

1. Why were there so few cities in the South?

_____

Life in Southern Society (pages 73–75)

What was Southern life like?

Most Southerners worked small farms. The few wealthy plantation owners, or planters, controlled the economy. They also controlled much of the South's social and political life.

Southern women could not vote, attend school, or own property. They worked long hours on farms and in the house.

The South's many indentured servants also had few rights. Indentured servants were mainly white European males who exchanged a trip to North America for several years of farm labor. Many indentured servants hoped to start a new life once their servitude was over. However, once they completed their terms of labor, most indentured servants had a difficult time trying to survive.

2. Which group controlled most aspects of life in the South?

_____

Slavery Becomes Entrenched
(pages 75–77)

What was the triangular trade?

Throughout the late 1600s, the number of indentured servants in the South decreased. As a result, planters faced a labor shortage on their plantations. They soon turned to the use of African **slaves.**

Enslaved Africans had been working for years in the English colonies of the *West Indies*. During the 1600s, Africans had become part of a trade network called the **triangular trade.** This network had three main parts: (1) merchants carried rum and other goods from New England to Africa; (2) the merchants brought slaves from Africa to the West Indies, where they sold them for sugar and molasses; (3) the merchants then sold these goods

in New England to be distilled into rum. The network also included many minor routes that crisscrossed the Northern and Southern colonies, the West Indies, Europe, and Africa.

The part of the triangular trade that brought Africans to the West Indies and later to North America was called the **middle passage.** Africans made this trip on crowded, dirty ships. Nearly 20 percent of the Africans aboard each ship died from either cruel treatment or disease.

Those who survived the trip entered a hard life of labor in North America. About 90 percent of enslaved Africans worked in the fields. The rest worked in planters' houses. Some learned skills such as carpentry. Children began working at age 12.

Slaves were treated harshly. Slave owners whipped and beat slaves they considered disobedient or disrespectful.

3. What was life like for enslaved Africans in North America?

_____

Africans Cope in Their New World (pages 77–78)

How did slaves cope in the American colonies?

Once in America, slaves tried to hold onto their African culture. They wove baskets and created pottery as they had done in their homeland. Slaves also played African music and told traditional stories.

Many slaves resisted their position of *subservience*. Some slaves faked illness to get out of working. Others broke tools or worked slow on purpose. Some slaves pushed their resistance into open revolt. In the **Stono Rebellion** of 1739, a group of slaves killed several plantation owners. These slaves eventually were captured and executed. Many other slaves ran away. Some found a new home in Native American tribes.

4. How did enslaved Africans resist slavery?

_____

CHAPTER 3 Section 3 (pages 79–84)

The Commercial North

BEFORE YOU READ

In the last section, you learned about the growth of the Southern colonies.

In this section, you will learn about the development of the Northern colonies.

AS YOU READ

Use this diagram to take notes. List the ways that the Northern colonies were diverse.

The Northern Colonies Are Diverse

Diverse economies
several cash crops

Diverse population

Diverse religious groups

Commerce Grows in the North
(pages 79–80)

How did people earn a living in the North?

The economies of the New England and the Middle colonies were more diverse than that of the Southern colonies. While farmers in the South produced mainly one cash crop, Northern farmers normally grew several. Like the South, however, farming was important in the North, especially in Pennsylvania and New York.

However, the North's economy existed of more than just agriculture. Other industries, such as grinding wheat, fishing, and lumbering, were also important in the North. Shipbuilding became a major industry. By the 1770s, the Northern colonies built one third of all British ships. They also made more iron than England did.

Bustling port cities grew in the North. Boston and New York became important urban centers.

Philadelphia became the largest port in the British Empire. The growing cities resulted in some problems. Cities became overcrowded, and clean water was difficult to get. Fire and diseases spread rapidly. Also, many people living in cities faced poverty.

1. Name three types of industry in the North.

_____

_____

Northern Society Is Diverse
(pages 81–82)

What groups of people lived in the Northern colonies?

The Northern colonies were made up of diverse groups of people. Many *immigrants* from Europe settled in New England and the Middle colonies. Germans came to Pennsylvania in search of jobs and religious freedom. Another large immigrant group was the Scots-Irish. Other immigrant groups included the Dutch, Scandinavians, and Jews.

Africans, both enslaved and free, lived in the North. Unlike the South, The Northern economy did not depend on slave labor. However, slavery did exist in the Northern colonies. Most slaves in the North had greater legal standing than slaves elsewhere in the colonies. They could sue and be sued. They had the right to appeal to the highest colonial courts. They could also testify against white persons in cases not involving Africans.

Enslaved Africans in the North, however, were treated harshly, just as in the South. Furthermore, free Africans faced much *racial prejudice* in the North.

As in the South, women in the Northern colonies enjoyed few rights. They could not vote or buy or sell property. Women in the North handled many jobs in the home and in the fields.

The limited rights of women in the Northern colonies contributed to an outbreak of witch-hunting in the late 1600s. During the 1690s, in Salem, Massachusetts, many women were falsely accused of being witches—those who possess evil powers. Many of the accused women were considered too independent and rebellious. Several women were tried and executed. The courts finally put an end to the witch hunts.

2. **What five groups of people immigrated from Europe to the Northern colonies?**

_____

_____

New Ideas Influence the Colonists
(pages 80–82)

What new ideas and beliefs spread in the colonies?

Americans participated in several new intellectual movements during the 1700s that helped change the way of thinking throughout the colonies.

One such movement was known as the **Enlightenment.** This was a philosophical move-

ment that called for using reason and science to find truth. The Enlightenment began in Europe and spread to the colonies through books and pamphlets. **Benjamin Franklin,** a *prominent* colonist, was one of the movement's leaders. He conducted scientific experiments and made several practical inventions.

The Enlightenment also affected political thought. Colonial leaders used reason to conclude that individuals have natural rights which governments must respect.

The Enlightenment had two important effects: (1) the idea that people have natural rights that governments must respect challenged the authority of the British rulers; (2) the movement's emphasis on science as a source of truth weakened the authority of the church.

By the 1700s, the Puritan church had lost its grip on society. **Jonathan Edwards** was a Massachusetts preacher who sought to revive the intensity and commitment of the Puritan vision. Edwards preached that people must acknowledge their sinfulness and feel God's love for them. He started a religious revival that became known as the **Great Awakening**.

The Great Awakening brought many colonists, Native Americans, and African Americans into organized Christian churches for the first time. The movement challenged the authority of established churches. Some colonists abandoned their old Puritan or Anglican churches. At the same time, independent *denominations* such as Baptist and Methodist gained new members.

The Great Awakening and the Enlightenment emphasized some opposing ideas. The Great Awakening stressed emotion. The Enlightenment stressed reason. However, both also stressed the importance of the individual. In addition, both caused people to question authority.

3. **How did the Enlightenment and the Great Awakening help change people's beliefs?**

_____

_____

CHAPTER 3 Section 4 (pages 85–89)

The French and Indian War

BEFORE YOU READ

In the last section, you read about life in the Northern colonies.

In this section, you will learn about how Great Britain enlarged its holdings in North America.

AS YOU READ

Use this time line to take notes on the major events in the French and Indian War.

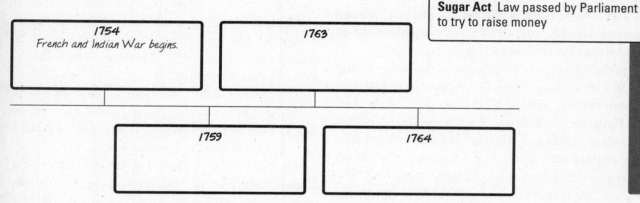

1754
French and Indian War begins.

1763

1759

1764

Rivals for an Empire (pages 85–86)

Why were the French in North America?

France was Great Britain's rival in North America. **New France,** France's colony included eastern Canada, the Great Lakes region, and the Mississippi River valley.

Most French settlers were not interested in establishing large, populated colonies in North America. Most French settlers were fur traders or Catholic priests who wanted to convert the Native Americans. Because the French settlers relied on the Native Americans for their fur trade, they established better relations with the Native Americans than the English did.

1. What were two main reasons that the French established colonies in the Americas?

_____

_____

Britain Defeats an Old Enemy
(pages 86–88)

What caused the French and Indian War?

As the French and British empires in North America grew, conflicts arose between the two nations. In 1754, fighting broke out between the British and French over western land around the Ohio River. That year, Virginia troops led by

George Washington marched to the Ohio River to drive out the French. The French and their Native American *allies* easily defeated the American troops. This battle marked the beginning of the **French and Indian War.**

For the next several years, fighting continued between British and French forces to determine who would rule North America. The French beat the British during much of the early fighting. Then, in 1757, the English king appointed **William Pitt** to the government. Under Pitt's leadership, the British began winning battles.

The British army's victories prompted the powerful Iroquois Indians to support them. This agreement gave Britain some Native American allies to balance those of France.

In 1759, British forces defeated the French at Quebec. With this victory the British had won the war. The two nations signed a peace treaty signed in 1763. As a result of the Treaty of Paris, France gave up Canada and all of North America east of the Mississippi to Britain.

Although Great Britain won the war, it still faced problems. Native Americans did not like British settlers moving west onto their lands. Led by **Pontiac,** an Ottawa chief, a group of Native Americans attacked British forts. During peace negotiations with the Native Americans, the British gave them blankets infected with small pox. The disease killed many in the group. As a result, the Native Americans surrendered.

To prevent further fighting with Native Americans, the British government issued the **Proclamation of 1763.** The proclamation forbid colonists from settling west of an imaginary line along the Appalachian Mountains. Many colonists were angered by the proclamation. They argued that it kept them from settling more land. Colonists ignored the proclamation and continued to settle west of the line.

2. How did Britain's victory in the war affect its colonial holdings in North America?

_____

_____

_____

The Colonies and Britain Grow Apart (pages 88–89)

What made the colonists angry at Britain?

Great Britain's financial crisis after the war resulted in new laws that angered the colonists. To crack down on smuggling in Massachusetts, British officials searched the homes of colonial merchants. This practice outraged the merchants.

After winning the French and Indian War, Britain left troops in North America to protect the colonists from Native Americans. However, many of the colonists disliked the presence of the troops. These colonists felt that Britain kept the troops there to keep them in line.

Maintaining troops in North America only added to Britain's economic woes. The British had spent a great amount of money to win the French and Indian War. As a result, the nation was heavily in *debt*. Hoping to lower the debt, King George III chose a financial expert, **George Grenville,** as Britain's prime minister.

Grenville wanted to raise money from the colonies to help pay off the war debt. His first act was to reduce smuggling or illegal trading—which hurt Britain in lost tax money.

In 1764, The British Parliament passed the **Sugar Act.** The act did three things. It cut the import taxes on foreign-made molasses. This was done with the hope that colonists would pay a lower tax rather than risk arrest by smuggling. Secondly, it placed a tax on certain imported goods that had not been taxed before. Thirdly, the act strengthened the enforcement of smuggling laws by establishing a new court—known as a vice-admiralty court. In this new court, a single judge—not a jury of sympathetic colonists—decided cases. This meant that accused smugglers faced a greater chance of being found guilty.

3. What made the colonists angry at the British government?

_____

_____

_____

Name _____ Date _____

allies People who have joined with another for a special purpose

balance of trade The difference between goods sold and goods bought

charter A written grant that gives certain rights to the people

debt Something that is owed to another

denominations A group of churches within one religion

export To deliver overseas for trade or sale

immigrants People who come to a foreign country to live

indigo A plant that gives a blue dye

prominent Well known

racial prejudice Dislike of people because of race

raw material Unprocessed natural resource such as timber or wool

restrict To limit or restrain

rural Relating to the countryside

subservience In a position of serving someone

turmoil Extreme confusion or disorganization

West Indies Area between North America and South America made up of islands in the Caribbean

AFTER YOU READ

Terms and Names

A. If the statement is true, write "true" on the line. If it is false, change the underlined word or words to make it true.

1. _____ The British Parliament passed the <u>Sugar Act</u> to control colonial trade.

2. _____ Typical large southern plantations grew a single <u>cash crop</u>.

3. _____ Africans were brought to the Americas along a trade network known as the <u>triangular trade.</u>

4. _____ The <u>Great Awakening</u> was a philosophical movement that emphasized science as a source of truth.

5. _____ Colonists in the mid-1700s were angry about <u>salutary neglect</u>, which banned them from settling west of a line along the Appalachian Mountains.

B. Write the letter of the name that matches the description.

a. Benjamin Franklin   b. Pontiac   c. George Grenville   d. Jonathan Edwards   e. Sir Edmund Andros   f. James II

_____ **1.** I was appointed the royal governor of the Dominion of New England in 1685.

_____ **2.** I am an important colonial leader of the Enlightenment.

_____ **3.** I am a powerful preacher during the Great Awakening in the 1730s and 1740s.

_____ **4.** I am a Native American leader who fought the British after they won the French and Indian War.

_____ **5.** I am the British prime minister who wanted the colonies to help pay the British debt after the French and Indian War.

AFTER YOU READ (continued) **CHAPTER 3** The Colonies Come of Age

Main Ideas

1. How did the colonies help make England wealthy?

_____

_____

_____

2. Why was the South basically a self-sufficient society?

_____

_____

_____

3. How was the economy of the South different from the economy of the North?

_____

_____

_____

4. What contributed to a diverse society in the Northern colonies?

_____

_____

_____

5. What was the geographic outcome of the French and Indian War?

_____

_____

_____

Thinking Critically

Answer the following questions on a separate sheet of paper.

1. How were women's lives similar in the Southern and Northern colonies?

2. Do you think the Enlightenment ideas are still important today? Give evidence for your opinion.

CHAPTER 4 Section 1 (pages 96–102)

The Stirrings of Rebellion

BEFORE YOU READ

In the last section, you learned how the British and their American colonists pushed the French out of North America.

In this section, you will learn about the conflicts that led to the start of the American Revolution.

AS YOU READ

Use this chart to take notes about the conflicts between Great Britain and the American colonies.

TERMS AND NAMES

Stamp Act Law passed by Parliament to make colonists buy a stamp to place on many items such as wills and newspapers

Samuel Adams One of the founders of the Sons of Liberty

Townshend Acts Laws passed by Parliament in 1767 that set taxes on imports to the colonies

Boston Massacre Conflict between colonists and British soldiers in which four colonists were killed

committees of correspondence A network of communication set up in Massachusetts and Virginia to inform other colonies of ways that Britain threatened colonial rights

Boston Tea Party Protest against increased tea prices in which colonists dumped British tea into Boston Harbor

King George III King of England during the American Revolution

Intolerable Acts A series of laws set up by Parliament to punish Massachusetts for its protests against the British

martial law Rule by the military

minutemen Civilian soldiers

BRITISH ACTIONS	COLONISTS' ACTIONS
Stamp Act	Boycotted British goods

The Colonies Organize to Resist Britain (pages 96–98)

Why did the colonists protest Britain's taxes?

Tension between Britain and the colonists continued to grow. In 1765, The British Parliament passed the **Stamp Act.** This act required colonists to buy and place stamps on items such as wills and playing cards. It was the first tax that affected the colonists directly because it was placed on the everyday goods they bought. Previous taxes had been placed only on goods coming into the country.

The new tax angered the colonists. Many *boycotted* British products in protest. A secret group called the Sons of Liberty played an active role in the boycott. The group was led by political activist **Samuel Adams.**

The colonists declared that Parliament could not tax them because they were not represented in Parliament. The colonists argued that only colonial lawmaking bodies had the right to tax them.

In March of 1766, Parliament *repealed* the Stamp Act. However, a year later, Parliament passed the **Townshend Acts.** These laws placed taxes on even more imports and on tea. Colonists in Boston protested the new taxes with boycotts and riots. The British sent more troops to America to prevent further riots.

1. Why did the colonists feel that Parliament had no right to tax them?

_____

_____

Tension Mounts in Massachusetts (pages 98–99)

Why did the king take control of Massachusetts?

In the winter of 1770, a group of Boston protesters gathered to harass some British soldiers. The soldiers fired into the group. Five Bostonians were killed. Colonial leaders called the event the **Boston Massacre.**

For a while after the shooting, both sides relaxed. Tensions, however, eventually increased again. As a result, the colonial assemblies established **committees of correspondence** to communicate with each other about various threats to American liberties.

In 1773, the British made yet another move that angered the colonists. The government gave a British company the right to all the trade in tea. Colonial merchants were angry at losing their tea business. One night, several colonists snuck aboard a British ship carrying tea in Boston Harbor. The colonists dumped all of the ship's tea into the harbor. This event became known as the **Boston Tea Party.**

The Boston Tea Party angered **King George III.** To punish Massachusetts, Parliament passed a set of laws called the **Intolerable Acts.** Acting under these acts, Britain closed Boston Harbor and placed Boston under **martial law,** or rule by the military.

Britain's actions prompted colonial leaders to form the First Continental Congress. The group met in 1774 and drew up a declaration of colonial rights. They demanded that the colonies be allowed to run their own affairs. They agreed to meet again in 1775 if their demands were not met.

2. How did the colonists react to the Intolerable Acts?

_____

_____

Fighting Erupts at Lexington and Concord (pages 100–102)

What happened at Concord and Lexington?

Some New England towns began to prepare for a war against Britain. **Minutemen,** or civilian soldiers, stored guns and ammunition in secret hideaways. In 1775, the British marched to Concord, Massachusetts, to seize these weapons. Colonists, including Paul Revere, watched the troops march out of Boston. Revere rode ahead of the troops on his horse. He warned people that the British were headed for Concord.

A group of armed minutemen met the British troops as they reached the town of Lexington, Massachusetts. Someone fired a shot. The British soldiers responded by shooting into the crowd of minutemen. Several minutemen were killed, while others were injured. The British suffered only one *casualty.* The Battle of Lexington lasted only 15 minutes.

The British soldiers then marched on to Concord, where they found no weapons. On their trip back to Boston, between 3,000 and 4,000 minutemen *ambushed* them. The colonial soldiers killed dozens of British soldiers. The rest of the defeated British troops returned to Boston that night.

3. How did the outcomes at Lexington and Concord differ?

_____

_____

CHAPTER 4 Section 2 (pages 103–108)

Ideas Help Start a Revolution

BEFORE YOU READ

In the last section, you learned about the conflicts that led to the start of the American Revolution.

In this section, you will learn why the colonists declared their independence.

AS YOU READ

Use this diagram to take notes. Fill in the boxes with the events that led to the signing of the Declaration of Independence.

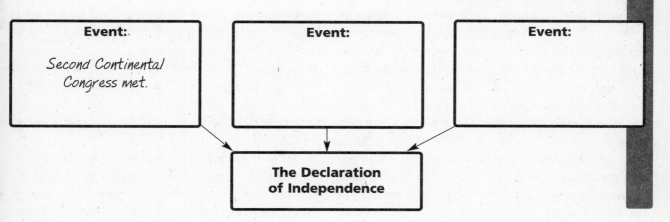

Event:

Second Continental Congress met.

Event:

Event:

The Declaration of Independence

The Colonies Hover Between Peace and War (pages 103–105)

What was the Olive Branch Petition?

In May of 1775, *delegates* from the First Continental Congress met again at what became known as the **Second Continental Congress.** During the meeting, some leaders urged independence from Great Britain. Others were not ready for independence. The Congress did create the Continental Army, however. Congressional leaders placed George Washington in charge of the army.

In June of 1775, British troops fought against colonial soldiers near Boston in the Battle of Bunker Hill. More than 1,000 British soldiers were killed. The colonists lost 311 men. This battle would be the deadliest of the war.

Although the colonists were preparing for war, they were hoping for peace. Most colonists still felt a deep loyalty to Britain's king, George III. They blamed the bloodshed in the colonies on the king's ministers. In July of 1775, the Continental Congress sent King George III a peace offer, called the **Olive Branch Petition.** This petition urged a return to "the former harmony" between Britain and the colonies.

King George III flatly rejected the petition. Furthermore, he issued a proclamation stating that the colonies were in rebellion. He urged Parliament to order a naval blockade of the American coast.

1. How did King George III react to the Olive Branch Petition?

_____

_____

_____

The Patriots Declare Independence (pages 105–106)

What ideas supported rebellion?

More colonists began to object to British rule and to call for independence. Many were influenced by a pamphlet titled ***Common Sense.*** Colonist Thomas Paine was the author. He argued that independence would lead to a better society.

In June 1776, the Continental Congress moved closer to declaring the colonies independent. The Congress asked **Thomas Jefferson** of Virginia to write a document stating the colonies' reasons for declaring their freedom. The document became known as the **Declaration of Independence.**

The Declaration of Independence was based on the ideas of English philosopher John Locke. Locke said that people have "natural rights" to life, liberty, and property. Locke also argued that citizens form a social contract, or an agreement, with their government. If the government tries to take away people's natural rights, the people can overthrow the government.

In the Declaration of Independence, Jefferson wrote that people's rights to life, liberty, and the pursuit of happiness cannot be taken away. Government gets its power from the people, and the people can remove a government that threatens their rights. He then listed in the document the many ways that Britain had taken away the colonists' rights.

The Declaration states that "all men are created equal." When this phrase was written, it expressed the common belief that free citizens were political equals. However, it did not claim that all people had the same ability or ought to have equal wealth. In addition, the Declaration did not include women,

Native Americans, and African American slaves. However, Jefferson's words presented ideals that would later help these groups challenge traditional attitudes.

The Second Continental Congress adopted the Declaration on July 4, 1776. The Declaration of Independence thrilled **Patriots**—colonists who supported independence.

2. How did the Declaration of Independence support the notion of rebelling against Britain?

_____

_____

_____

Americans Choose Sides (pages 106–108)

Who were the Loyalists and the Patriots?

Despite the growing atmosphere of rebellion in the colonies, many colonists opposed independence. These colonists were known as **Loyalists.** They supported the British and were loyal to the king. Some loyalists felt a special tie to the king because they had served as judges, councilors, or governors. Most Loyalists, however, were ordinary people. Some felt that the British could protect their rights better than a new colonial government could. Others simply did not want to be punished as rebels.

Those colonists who supported independence were called Patriots. This group included farmers, artisans, merchants, and landowners. They wanted to be free from British rule. Others saw great economic opportunity in a new and independent nation. Patriots made up a little less than half of the colonial population.

The conflict divided other groups as well. The Quakers generally supported the Patriots. However, they did not fight. They did not believe in war. Many African Americans joined the Patriots. Others joined the Loyalists because they were offered freedom from slavery. Most Native Americans supported the British. They viewed colonial settlers as a bigger threat to their land.

3. Why did some colonists remain loyal to Britain?

_____

CHAPTER 4 Section 3 (pages 113–117)

Struggling Toward Saratoga

TERMS AND NAMES

Trenton Battle won by the Americans in 1776

Saratoga Battle won by the Americans in 1777

Valley Forge Place where Washington's army spent the winter of 1777–1778

inflation Rise in the price of goods

profiteering Selling goods that are difficult to come by for a profit

BEFORE YOU READ

In the last section, you learned about the events that led to the signing of the Declaration of Independence.

In this section, you will learn about the important early battles in the War for Independence.

AS YOU READ

Use the chart below to take notes about the early battles of the American Revolution.

BATTLE	OUTCOME
New York	British win and force Continental Army to retreat.

The War Moves to the Middle States (pages 114–116)

What were the important early battles?

Shortly after the Continental Congress adopted the Declaration of Independence, the colonies suffered a major defeat at the hand of the British. In late August 1776, the British army seized New York City. Its aim was to *isolate* New England from the rest of the colonies. George Washington tried to resist the British troops, but his soldiers were poorly prepared and equipped. The British forced Washington's army to retreat into Pennsylvania.

On Christmas night of 1776, Washington and his army struck back. They crossed the Delaware River into **Trenton,** New Jersey. In a surprise attack, the colonial army captured almost 1,000 British soldiers. Shortly afterwards, Washington's troops attempted to retake Philadelphia—which the British also had seized. However, British troops forced the colonial army to retreat.

Late in 1777, British troops and Native Americans marched south from Canada. The

Continental Army met them at **Saratoga,** New York. The colonists won the battle. Saratoga was considered a turning point of the war. The colonists' victory proved that they could compete with the larger and better-equipped British army. The victory also convinced the French that the colonists had a chance to win the war. The French were longtime enemies of the British. After Saratoga, the French recognized American independence. They also agreed to send troops and supplies.

Meanwhile, Washington and his soldiers spent a miserable winter at **Valley Forge,** Pennsylvania, in the woods outside Philadelphia. The American soldiers camped there suffered from hunger and frostbite. More than 2,000 soldiers died.

1. Why was the Battle of Saratoga important?

_____

_____

Colonial Life During the Revolution (pages 116–117)

How did the war affect American society?

The war touched all Americans. For one thing, the nation's economy suffered. In an attempt to pay its troops, the Continental Congress printed more paper money. The more money Congress printed, the less it became worth. This caused **inflation,** which is a rise in the price of goods. In New York, for example, the price of beef and sugar doubled in one three-month period.

The Congress also struggled to supply its army with weapons. One problem was that Britain's powerful navy controlled the American coast. As a result, Americans had to smuggle arms in from Europe. Some *corrupt* government officials took part in **profiteering,** or selling hard-to-find weapons and goods for a high price.

As colonial men went to war, many women took their husbands' places running homes, farms, and businesses. Some women earned money washing and cooking for the troops. A few women even fought in battle.

The war also led to greater opportunity for African Americans. Thousands of slaves escaped to freedom during the war. About 5,000 African Americans served in the Continental Army. Their courage and loyalty impressed many white Americans.

2. How did the war affect different groups of Americans?

_____

_____

General Washington's troops march to Valley Forge.

Skillbuilder

Use the picture to answer the questions

1. What does this picture of American soldiers at Valley Forge tell you about conditions there?

_____

_____

2. How did these conditions affect the American soldiers?

_____

_____

CHAPTER 4   Section 4 (pages 118–123)

Winning the War

BEFORE YOU READ

In the last section, you learned about the early battles in the American Revolution.

In this section, you will learn how the Americans won the war.

AS YOU READ

Use the time line to take notes on the important battles and other events toward the end of the Revolutionary War.

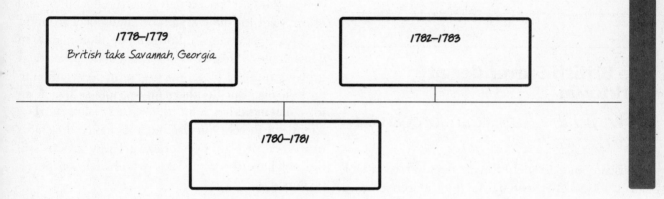

1778–1779
British take Savannah, Georgia.

1782–1783

1780–1781

European Allies Shift the Balance (pages 118–119)

What help did the Europeans offer?

During its miserable winter at Valley Forge, the Continental Army underwent a significant change. **Friedrich von Steuben,** a Prussian officer and expert drillmaster, began to train the American troops. He helped to turn the inexperienced soldiers into a strong fighting army.

In 1778, French help began to arrive for the colonists. **Marquis de Lafayette,** a Frenchman, also offered his help to Washington's army. Along with von Steuben, he helped improve the fighting ability of the Continental Army.

1. How did von Steuben and Lafayette help the Americans?

_____

_____

The British Move South (pages 119–121)

Why did the British forces move South?

In the summer of 1778, the British changed their war strategy. They shifted much of their operations to the South. British generals hoped to gain Loyalist support in the South and then fight their way back north.

At first, the British plan worked. British troops took Savannah, Georgia. The British Army, led by General **Charles Cornwallis,** then captured Charles Town, South Carolina. The British took 5,500 American soldiers as prisoners of war. The British soon had a firm hold on Georgia and South Carolina.

Washington sent General Nathanael Greene to stop the British in the South. A unit of Greene's army defeated the British at Cowpens, South Carolina, in January 1781. Meanwhile, Cornwallis continued moving north. He marched his army to Yorktown, Virginia. Yorktown lay along the Chesapeake Bay. From there, Cornwallis hoped to take Virginia and then meet up with British forces in the Northern colonies.

2. Why did the British move much of its military operations to the south?

_____

_____

The British Surrender at Yorktown (pages 121–122)

How did the American forces win at Yorktown?

American and French forces decided to attack Cornwallis at **Yorktown.** As they marched in, a French naval force defeated a British fleet on the Chesapeake Bay. As a result, the Americans and French were able to surround Cornwallis's troops—blocking both their land and sea routes. The colonial and French forces bombarded Yorktown for days. Finally, on October 19, 1781, the British surrendered. The Americans had won the war.

The next year, the Americans and British began to discuss peace terms. John Adams, Benjamin Franklin, and John Jay were the American delegates to the peace talks in Paris. The Treaty of Paris was signed in 1783. Under the agreement, Britain recognized the United States as an independent nation. The British also gave America all the land from the Atlantic Ocean to the Mississippi River. Some provisions of the treaty promised future trouble. The treaty, for example, did not specify when the British would evacuate their American forts.

3. What did Britain do as a result of the Treaty of Paris?

_____

_____

The War Becomes a Symbol of Liberty (pages 122–123)

What did the Revolution mean?

The American Revolution brought society's different classes together. During the war, rich and poor fought alongside each other. Military leaders grew to respect their men. This togetherness brought about a feeling of **egalitarianism**—a belief in the equality of all people. Egalitarianism taught that people should be valued for their ability and effort—not for their wealth or family background.

This egalitarianism, however, applied mainly to white males. Most Africans remained enslaved. A growing number of people urged the new nation to end slavery. But Southern states opposed such an idea. They did not want to lose their laborers. The American Revolution also did not change the status of women or Native Americans. These groups still did not have the rights that white male property-owners did.

Americans had rejected the British system of government, in which kings and nobles held power. In its place, they set out to build a stable republic, a government of the people. To create this republic, however, the colonists would have to address several key issues: Who should participate in government? How should the government answer to the people? How could all of the different groups' voices be heard?

4. How were the changes to American society brought on by the American Revolution limited?

_____

_____

Glossary	**CHAPTER 4** The War for Independence

ambush To attack from a hidden place

boycott To refuse to buy certain goods

casualty One who is injured or killed

corrupt Influenced by others to be dishonest

delegate A person given power to act for others; a representative to a convention

isolate To set apart from others

repeal To cancel

AFTER YOU READ

Terms and Names

A. Circle the name or term that best completes each sentence.

1. _____ led a secret group of colonists called the Sons of Liberty, who protested British actions.

Samuel Adams   **Thomas Jefferson**   **George Washington**

2. The Second Continental Congress sent King George III an offer for peace, called the _____.

Intolerable Acts   **Declaration of Independence**   **Olive Branch Petition**

3. In his pamphlet _____, Thomas Paine argued for the colonies' independence from Great Britain.

Declaration of Independence   *Common Sense*   **Olive Branch Petition**

4. The battle at _____ convinced the French to help the Americans.

Trenton   **Yorktown**   **Saratoga**

5. In 1781, the British General _____ surrendered to the Americans at Yorktown.

Nathanael Greene   **Charles Cornwallis**   **Friedrich von Steuben**

B. Write the letter of the name or term that matches the description.

a. Thomas Jefferson

b. Patriots

c. Marquis de Lafayette

d. Stamp Act

e. Valley Forge

f. Loyalists

g. Thomas Paine

_____**1.** A law that placed a tax on many items colonists used

_____**2.** Author of the Declaration of Independence

_____**3.** Colonists who supported the British and opposed independence

_____**4.** Place where George Washington's troops spent a miserable winter

_____**5.** French nobleman who helped the Continental Army

AFTER YOU READ (continued) **CHAPTER 4** The War for Independence

Main Ideas

1. Why did the colonists oppose Britain's attempts to tax them?

_____

_____

2. What was the Boston Tea Party?

_____

_____

3. How did the American Revolution lead to inflation in the colonies?

_____

_____

4. What was the result of the Treaty of Paris?

_____

_____

5. How did the American Revolution help bring about a feeling of egalitarianism in parts of American society?

_____

_____

Think Critically

Answer the following questions on a separate sheet of paper.

1. If you were living during the time of the Revolutionary War, would you be a Loyalist or a Patriot? Explain your position.

2. Do you think feelings of egalitarianism exist in the United States today? Explain.

CHAPTER 5 **Section 1** (pages 132–137)

Experimenting with Confederation

BEFORE YOU READ

In the last section, you learned how the American colonists won their independence from Great Britain.

In this section, you will learn how the colonists tried to create a new government.

AS YOU READ

Use this chart to take notes on the problems that the Continental Congress faced in setting up a new government and the weaknesses of the Articles of Confederation.

TERMS AND NAMES

republic A government in which the people elect representatives to govern

republicanism The idea that governments should be based on the consent of the people

Articles of Confederation The set of laws that established the first government of the United States

confederation A loose alliance of states

Land Ordinance of 1785 A law that set up a plan for surveying land west of the Appalachian Mountains

Northwest Ordinance of 1787 Law that organized the Northwest Territories

ISSUES FACING NEW GOVERNMENT	WEAKNESSES OF THE ARTICLES OF CONFEDERATION
How states should be represented	

Americans Debate Republicanism (pages 132–134)

What style of government did Americans favor?

After winning their independence from Great Britain, the American colonists turned to the question of how to govern themselves. Most Americans believed that a democracy, government directly by the people, gave too much power to the uneducated masses. They instead favored a **republic**—a government in which the people elect capable leaders to govern. The idea behind this style of rule is **republicanism,** the notion that government should be based on the consent of the people.

In the years following the Revolutionary War, the American states created their own constitutions. A constitution is a written system of laws and principles that spells out the functions and limits of a government. The states' constitutions were based largely on the ideals of republicanism. They limited the power of the government and guaranteed specific rights for its citizens. Some of these rights included freedom of speech, religion, and the press.

The states' constitutions also differed from one another. Some states granted voting rights to all adult males who paid taxes. Others continued to make property ownership a requirement for voting. Those who qualified to vote were generally white. With few exceptions, women were not allowed to vote.

1. What kind of government did the state constitutions create?

_____

_____

_____

The Continental Congress Debates (pages 134–135)

What issues did the Continental Congress face?

While the states developed their own constitutions, the Continental Congress sought to create a government for the entire nation. In doing so, the Congress had to address three basic issues. The first was how much representation each of the different-sized states would receive in Congress. The Congress decided that each state would have one vote, regardless of the number of people in the state.

The second issue dealt with how the states and federal government would share power. In addressing this issue, the Continental Congress proposed the **Articles of Confederation.** This set of laws established a two-tier government. State governments were supreme in some matters, while the national government was supreme in other matters. The delegates called this new form of government a **confederation,** or alliance. The Articles created no separate executive department to *enforce* the acts of Congress. In addition, they established no national court system to decide the meaning of laws. The Articles of Confederation went into effect in 1781.

By this time, Congress also had to address a third issue: how to govern the land west of the Appalachian Mountains. The **Land Ordinance of 1785** established a plan by which the federal government *surveyed* the land and sold it to settlers at affordable prices. The **Northwest Ordinance of 1787** organized the land into territories. It also established a procedure for how these *territories* eventually could become states.

2. How did Congress address the issue of state representation in the federal government?

_____

_____

The Confederation Encounters Problems (pages 136–137)

What were some of the Articles' weaknesses?

The Articles of Confederation had many weaknesses. First, the new government did little to unify the country. The states continued to act in their own interests, with little regard for other states or the nation as a whole. In addition, the one-vote per state policy created an imbalance of political power. With a population of 23,375, Georgia had the same power in the national government as Massachusetts with 235,000 people. Furthermore, all states had to agree to *amend* the Articles. As a result, changes in government were difficult to achieve. The Continental Congress also had no power to tax. This meant that it could not collect money.

The federal government's weakness *hindered* its efforts to deal with foreign-relations problems as well. After the Revolutionary War, Britain refused to evacuate its military forts on the Great Lakes. In addition, the Spanish attempted to strengthen their presence in the West by closing the Mississippi River to American navigation. Lacking money and support from the states, the Congress could do little to address these issues.

3. How did the one-vote per state policy lead to unequal political representation?

_____

_____

_____

CHAPTER 5 Section 2 (pages 140–144)

Drafting the Constitution

BEFORE YOU READ

In the last section, you learned about the weaknesses of the Articles of Confederation.

In this section, you will learn how the Constitution and a new federal government were created.

AS YOU READ

Use this chart to take notes on the problems that the Constitutional Convention faced and how they solved them.

PROBLEMS FACING CONSTITUTIONAL CONVENTION	HOW PROBLEM WAS SOLVED
Balancing the rights of the states with the rights of the federal government	

TERMS AND NAMES

Shays's Rebellion Anti-tax protest by farmers

James Madison One of the leaders of the Constitutional Convention

Roger Sherman Delegate who developed the Great Compromise

Great Compromise Compromise made by Constitutional Convention in which states would have equal representation in one house of the legislature and representation based on population in the other house

Three-Fifths Compromise Compromise that allowed states to count three-fifths of their slaves as part of the population

federalism The division of power between the federal and state governments

legislative branch The branch of government that makes laws

executive branch The branch of government that enforces the laws

judicial branch The branch of government that interprets the laws and the Constitution

checks and balances Powers given to separate branches of government to keep any one from getting too much power

electoral college A group selected to elect the president, in which each state's number of electors is equal to the number of its senators and representatives in Congress

Nationalists Strengthen the Government (pages 140–141)

What was Shays's Rebellion?

Americans feared giving too much power to the national government. As a result, the government was too weak to deal with the nation's problems. A frightening example of this occurred in 1787, when a group of Massachusetts farmers revolted against the state. The protestors were led by farmer Daniel Shays. They accused the state government of taxing them too much. The armed protesters clashed with the state *militia*. Four farmers were killed. The incident was known as **Shays's Rebellion.** It

caused panic throughout the nation. Many Americans feared their new country was sinking into *chaos* and violence.

Before Shays's Rebellion, leaders such as **James Madison** of Virginia had called for a meeting of delegates to discuss conflicts over interstate trade. Only five states sent representatives. After news spread of Shays's Rebellion, delegates from all states except Rhode Island came to the Philadelphia convention.

1. Why did Shays's Rebellion prompt a call for a stronger central government?

_____

_____

_____

Conflict Leads to Compromise

Pages (142–143)

What compromises did the delegates make?

Within five days of the meeting, the delegates gave up the idea of fixing the Articles of Confederation. They decided to form a new government.

An immediate issue facing the delegates was how to give fair representation to both large and small states. Political leader James Madison offered the Virginia Plan. It proposed that a state's representation be based on the size of its population. Under this plan, the larger the state, the more political power it would have. The smaller states objected to this plan. They supported the New Jersey Plan. It called for giving each state equal representation—no matter what its size.

The delegates finally settled on a compromise plan developed by delegate **Roger Sherman.** The plan became known as the **Great Compromise.** It called for a legislature with two houses—a House of Representatives and a Senate. Each state would have two members in the Senate. In the House, the number of representatives from each state would be based on the size of the state's population.

The delegates then debated whether slaves should be included in a state's population count. The Northern states had few slaves. As a result, they did not want slaves counted. The Southern states—which had numerous slaves—favored counting them. The delegates again compromised. Their agreement was known as the **Three-Fifths Compromise.** It allowed each state to count three-fifths of their slaves as part of the population.

2. How did the Great Compromise satisfy both small and large states?

_____

_____

Creating a New Government

(pages 143–144)

Who held power under the Constitution?

After agreeing on the difficult issue of representation, the delegates dealt with other issues somewhat more easily. The new system of government was a form of **federalism** in which power was divided between the national and state governments. Powers granted to the national government by the Constitution included control of foreign affairs, providing national defense, and regulating trade between the states. Powers reserved for the states included providing for and supervising education, establishing marriage laws, and trade within a state. Both levels of government shared such powers as the right to tax, borrow money, pay debts, and establish courts.

The delegates, however, made sure to limit the authority of the federal government. First, they separated powers within the national government. They gave the **legislative branch**—the Senate and House of Representatives—the power to make laws. The **executive branch** would carry out the laws. The **judicial branch** would interpret and settle disputes about the laws. The delegates also made sure that each branch had certain powers over the others. This was called a system of **checks and balances.** It ensured that no one branch became too powerful.

The delegates also feared placing too much power in the hands of the people. So instead of choosing a president directly, each state would choose a group of electors equal to the number of senators and representatives each state had in Congress. Together, these electors were known as the **electoral college.** They were the ones who cast ballots for the presidential candidates. The delegates at the Constitutional Convention also created a way to amend, or change, the Constitution.

3. For what reason did the delegates create a system of checks and balances within the federal government?

_____

_____

CHAPTER 5 Section 3 (pages 145–149)

Ratifying the Constitution

TERMS AND NAMES

ratification Official approval of the Constitution

Federalists Supporters of the new Constitution

Antifederalists People opposed to ratification of the new Constitution

The Federalist Essays written by the Federalist leaders that defended the Constitution

Bill of Rights Set of amendments passed to protect individual rights

BEFORE YOU READ

In the last section, you learned how the Constitutional Convention created the Constitution.

In this section, you will learn how the nation ratified the Constitution.

AS YOU READ

Use this chart to take notes on the differences between the Federalists and the Antifederalists regarding ratification of the Constitution.

LEADERS' VIEWS ON THE CONSTITUTION	
Federalists	*Antifederalists*
Supported it	

Federalists and Antifederalists

(pages 145–146)

What was the controversy over the Constitution?

The Constitutional Convention created a new government. But the new government could not become a reality until the nation's voters approved it. The delegates to the Constitutional Convention decided on a plan for **ratification,** or official approval. Each state would hold a special convention. Voters in the state would elect delegates to the convention. The delegates would then vote to accept or reject the Constitution. If at least nine states approved the Constitution, it would become the law of the land.

Supporters of the Constitution were known as **Federalists.** They were led by George Washington and James Madison. Opponents of the Constitution were known as **Antifederalists.** They included heroes of the American Revolution, such as Patrick Henry and Samuel Adams.

Federalists argued that the division of powers and the system of checks and balances would protect Americans from the abuses of a strong central government. Antifederalists disagreed. They offered a long list of abuses of power by a strong central government. These included a fear that the government would serve the interests of the privileged minority and ignore the rights of the majority.

Antifederalists also raised doubts that a single government could manage the affairs of a large country. Their leading argument, however, centered on the Constitution's lack of protection for individual rights.

Madison and other Federalists published **The Federalist,** a series of essays defending the Constitution. The essays provided an analysis and explanation of the Constitution that remain important today. These include the separation of powers.

Letters from the Federal Farmer was written by Richard Henry Lee. It was the most widely read Antifederalist publication. Lee listed the rights the Antifederalists believed should be protected. They included freedom of the press and of religion, guarantees against unreasonable searches of people and their homes, and the right to a trial by jury.

1. **Why did the Antifederalists oppose the Constitution?**

_____

_____

The Bill of Rights Leads to Ratification (pages 147–149)

What rights does the Bill of Rights protect?

Many Federalists eventually admitted that the Constitution needed a **Bill of Rights** to protect the nation's citizens. They promised to add a Bill of Rights if the states ratified the Constitution.

Delaware was the first state to ratify the Constitution, in December 1787. The following June, New Hampshire became the ninth state to ratify it. The Constitution officially had been approved. However, New York and Virginia had not voted yet. The government needed the support of these large and *influential* states in order for the Constitution to work. By July 1788, both states ratified the Constitution. The Constitution became the basis for the new government in 1789.

In several states, ratification had hinged on the Federalists' pledge to add a bill of rights. In September 1789, Congress approved 12 *amendments*. The government then sent them to the state legislatures for approval. By December 1791, the states ratified ten of the amendments. As a result, they became part of the Constitution.

The Bill of Rights guaranteed Americans such rights as freedom of religion, speech, and the press. They protected citizens against having their homes searched and property seized without a proper reason. They also protected the rights of people accused of crimes. Finally, the Bill of Rights gave all powers not granted to the federal government to the people and the states.

Not all Americans, however, enjoyed these rights. Women were not mentioned in the Constitution. Native Americans and slaves were *excluded*. A growing number of free blacks also did not receive adequate protection from the Constitution. Many states permitted free blacks the right to vote. However, the Bill of Rights offered them no protection against discrimination and hostility from whites. The expansion of democracy came with later amendments. The flexibility of the United States Constitution made it a model for governments around the world.

2. **How does the Bill of Rights help ensure that the central government does not become too strong?**

_____

_____

Name _____ Date _____

amend To change

amendment A formal change to the Constitution

chaos A state of disorder or confusion

enforce To make sure a law or order is obeyed

exclude To leave out or reject

hinder To prevent or delay the progress of

influential Able to affect other people or events

militia A group of citizens who receive military training and who are called in emergencies

survey To find out the measurements and boundaries of an area by measuring angles and distances

territories Areas of land that are owned and governed by the United States but that are not states

AFTER YOU READ

Terms and Names

A. Write the name or term that best completes each sentence.

Northwest Ordinance of 1787

James Madison

Three-Fifths Compromise

judicial branch

Federalists

Antifederalists

Bill of Rights

executive branch

1. People who supported the Constitution were called _____.

2. People who were opposed to the Constitution were called _____.

3. The _____ organized the land west of the Appalachian Mountains into territories.

4. The first ten amendments to the Constitution, are called the _____.

5. The branch of government that interprets the laws and the Constitution is the _____.

B. Write the letter of the name or term next to the description that explains it best.

a. Articles of Confederation

b. executive

c. republic

d. checks and balances

e. Great Compromise

f. ratification

g. Shays's Rebellion

h. Three-Fifths Compromise

i. legislative

_____ **1.** A government in which the people elect representatives to govern

_____ **2.** The first plan for governing the United States

_____ **3.** An anti-tax protest by farmers

_____ **4.** The compromise that solved the problem of how states would be represented in Congress

_____ **5.** Branch of government that makes the laws

_____ **6.** A system to prevent one branch of government from getting too much power

_____ **7.** Official approval

AFTER YOU READ (continued)   CHAPTER 5   Shaping a New Nation

Main Ideas

1. What three issues did the Continental Congress have to address?

_____

_____

2. What were three weaknesses of the Articles of Confederation?

_____

_____

3. How was power divided in the new Constitution?

_____

_____

4. How did the Federalists and Antifederalists feel about the Constitution?

_____

_____

5. What are three rights guaranteed in the Bill of Rights?

_____

_____

Think Critically

Answer the following questions on a separate sheet of paper.

1. How was the government created by the Constitution different from the one created by the Articles of Confederation?

2. Would you have voted to ratify the Constitution? Why or why not?

THE LIVING CONSTITUTION   Section 1 (pages 152–160)

The Preamble and Article 1: The Legislature

TERMS AND NAMES

Preamble Introduction to the Constitution

Congress National legislature

House of Representatives Lower house of the national legislature

Senate Upper house of the national legislature

checks and balances Provisions of the Constitution that keep one branch of the government from controlling the other two branches

enumerated powers Powers specifically granted in the Constitution

implied powers Powers not specifically stated in the Constitution

elastic clause Clause in the Constitution that allows Congress to pass laws necessary to carry out its enumerated powers

BEFORE YOU READ

In the last section, you saw how the new government began to work under the Constitution.

In this section, you will learn about the Constitution itself—how the Preamble introduces the Constitution and explains its purpose and how Article 1 sets up the Congress.

AS YOU READ

Use the informal outline below to take notes on the Preamble and on the powers of Congress.

Preamble	shows legitimacy created by people who will be governed
Article 1 Congress House of Representatives Senate	

Preamble. *Purpose of the Constitution* (page 154)

What does the Preamble do?

The **Preamble,** or introduction, sets out to do two things. The first is to show the *legitimacy* of the new government, or its right to rule. The Preamble shows that this government is based on the agreement of those who are to be governed. It is the people themselves who have the power to create a government. That is why the Constitution begins with, "We the people of the United States . . . do ordain and establish this Constitution."

This statement also shows that the legitimacy of this government does not come from the states. Instead, it comes from the people. The Confederation was an agreement among the states, and the national government was too weak.

The second purpose of the Preamble is to state why this new government is being formed:
- to improve the structure of the government,
- to create justice and peace within the nation,
- to protect the nation from outside attack,
- to ensure the well-being of the people,
- to keep citizens and their descendants free.

1. What are the two purposes of the Preamble?

_____

_____

Article 1. Sections 1–7: The Legislature (pages 154–157)

How are the House and Senate different?

The *framers* of the Constitution set up **Congress** first. It was to be the legislature, or law-making branch of government. The framers saw the Congress as the central branch of government because it represents the people most directly.

Congress is made up of two houses. The **House of Representatives** is sometimes called "the House" or "the lower house." Its members are most responsible to the people who elect them because they serve for only two years. Then they must run for reelection. The number of representatives each state can send to the House is based on population. Thus, the House reflects the will of the majority of the people of the nation.

The **Senate** is sometimes called the "upper house." To make the government more stable, the framers made the Senate more removed from the will of the people. To do this, they had Senators chosen by state legislatures. (They are now elected directly by the voters in each state [Amendment 17]). Senators are elected for longer terms than House members, six-years.

Only one-third of the Senate is elected every two years. That also adds stability. Each state, regardless of population, has two Senators. This equal representation gives small states more power in the Senate than they have in the House.

Section 2.5 of Article 1 gives the House the power of *impeachment*. It can bring charges of misbehavior in office against officials in other branches of government, including the president. When the House impeaches a federal official, the Senate tries the case. It takes a two-thirds vote of the Senate to convict the impeached person.

The power of impeachment means that the legislative and judicial branches can make sure that a president does not take too much power. It is part of the system of **checks and balances,** in which the Constitution prevents any branch from dominating the others.

2. What are two important differences between the House and the Senate?

Sections 8–10: *Powers of the Legislature*
(pages 158–160)

What power does Congress have?

Section 7 of Article 1 explains how new laws are passed. A *bill* may be introduced in either the House or the Senate. But it must be approved by a majority vote in both houses. To become a law, a bill needs the approval of the president. That is part of the system of checks and balances. It gives the president, who is elected by all of the people, a say in what becomes the law of the land. If the president does not sign, or approve, the bill, he is said to *veto* it. The bill can still become law if two-thirds of both houses vote to *override* the veto. This procedure ensures that the president does not have too much power.

Section 7 also states that all bills for raising money—such as taxes—must begin in the House of Representatives. That is the house most responsive to the people. The Senate may propose changes to the bill.

Section 8 lists particular powers of the Congress. They are often called the *federal* government's **enumerated powers.** They include the power to tax, to borrow money, and to set up courts. Clauses 11–16 in Section 8 make sure that the civilians control the military. This is designed to prevent the armed forces from staging a *coup*, or seizing control of the government.

The 18th clause is different. It gives Congress the power to do what is "necessary and proper" to carry out its other powers. This is the basis of the **implied powers** of the federal government. It is called the **elastic clause** because it can be used to stretch, or expand, the government's power.

Section 9 tells what powers the federal government does not have. Clauses 2 and 3 say the government cannot take away a citizen's right to a fair trial. Section 10 tells what powers the states do not have. It emphasizes that they cannot make treaties or war. Only a *sovereign* nation can do that.

3. How does Congress limit the power of the president and the military?

THE LIVING CONSTITUTION Section 2 (pages 160–163)

Articles 2 and 3:
The Executive and the Judiciary

TERMS AND NAMES

chief executive President of the United States

electoral college Electors chosen by the states to elect the president and vice president

succession Order in which the office of president is filled if it becomes vacant before an election

State of the Union Address Message delivered by the president once a year

Supreme Court Highest federal court in the United States

judicial power Authority to decide cases involving disputes over the law or behavior of people

judicial review Authority to decide whether a law is constitutional

BEFORE YOU READ

In the last section, you saw that the Preamble introduced the Constitution and that Article 1 dealt with the powers of Congress.

In this section, you will see that Article 2 covers the powers of the president and Article 3 lists the powers of the judiciary.

AS YOU READ

Continue to use the outline you began in the last section with the Preamble. Take notes on the powers of the executive and the judicial branches of government.

Article 2. The Executive	President is chief executive; sees that laws are carried out.

Article 2. *The Executive* (pages 160–162)

What are the powers of the president?

The president is the **chief executive,** or administrator of the nation. It is his or her responsibility to "take care that laws be faithfully executed," or carried out.

Section 1.2 sets up the **electoral college.** The president and vice-president are elected by electors chosen by the states. At first, this clause did not work well in practice. In 1800, when only one ballot was used to elect both president and vice-president, two candidates received the same number of votes. The election had to be settled by the House of Representatives. To prevent this from happening again, the Twelfth Amendment was passed in 1804. It calls for separate ballots for president and vice-president.

However, the electoral college is still important. Each state has as many electors as it has senators and representatives in Congress. That is why presidential candidates work hard to "carry," or get the majority of the popular vote in, the largest states. The candidate that gets the majority of votes in a state gets all the electoral votes of that state.

Section 1.6 explains **succession:** what happens if a president dies in office or leaves office for another reason. It is important that everyone understands who will assume the power of the president. That prevents a struggle for power or a time when no one is in charge. It also makes sure that power will be transferred in a peaceful and orderly manner.

The president's salary cannot be changed during his or her term of office. In other words, the president cannot be punished or rewarded by payment for particular policies or official acts.

Section 2.1 makes the president commander-in-chief of the armed forces. This authority is another way to ensure civilian control of the military. It is also another example of checks and balances, because only Congress has the power to declare war. In practice, this authority has caused some problems. Since the president has the power to give orders to American military forces, some presidents have taken military action against the wishes of Congress and without a declaration of war.

Presidential appointments are another example of the separation of powers. The president can appoint ambassadors, justices of the Supreme Court, and other officials only "with the advice and consent of the Senate." In other words, the Senate must approve these appointments. The president can also make treaties, but these must also be approved by the Senate.

"Heads of departments" are mentioned in Section 2.1. These departments actually carry out the functions of the executive branch of government under the direction of the president. The heads of important departments make up the president's *Cabinet*.

The framers included reporting to the Congress as one of the president's duties. This requirement has led to the president making a **State of the Union Address** once a year. It is a report to the other branches of government and to the people. Its subject is the condition, or state, of the nation. The address includes the president's plans and policies for the year.

1. What are two examples of checks and balances found in Article 2?

_____

_____

Article 3. *The Judiciary* (pages 162–163)

What are the powers of the federal courts?

Article 3 sets up the judicial branch of the federal government. It establishes one **Supreme Court** but leaves the rest of the "inferior," or lower, federal courts to be set up by Congress. District courts and federal courts of appeal are now part of the regular federal court system. (States have their own court systems that deal with state laws.) Federal judges are appointed by the president with the approval of the Senate.

Judges serve "during good behavior." In other words, they are appointed for life, unless they are found guilty of misbehavior, or inappropriate conduct. The salary of a judge cannot be lowered while the judge is in office.

The federal courts have jurisdiction, or authority, only in certain kinds of cases. These are listed in Section 2. The Constitution gives the courts **judicial power**—the authority to decide cases involving disputes over the law or behavior of people. It does not specifically grant the Supreme Court the power of **judicial review**—the authority to decide whether a law is constitutional. The Supreme Court claimed this authority in the famous case of *Marbury* v. *Madison* in 1803.

Clause 3 again protects citizens' rights to a trial by jury. (See Article 1, Section 9.) The framers' concern for this right is a result of the American colonists' experiences under British rule.

2. What does the federal judiciary do?

_____

_____

THE LIVING CONSTITUTION Section 3 (pages 164–165)

Articles 4–7: The States and the Federal Government; Amendments and Ratification

BEFORE YOU READ

In the last section, you saw how Articles 2 and 3 set forth the powers of the executive and judicial branches.

In this section, you will see how Articles 4–7 grant specific powers to the national and state governments. You will also learn how the Constitution assures the unity of the nation and the supremacy of the national government.

AS YOU READ

Continue your outline of the Constitution. Take notes on the relations among the states and between the states and the national government.

Relations among states	Must accept decisions that occur in other states

Article 4. *Relations Among States* (page 164)

Who *has more power—the states or the national government?*

Article 4 sets out many principles of the federal system. It describes the relations among the states. It also describes the relations between the national government and the states.

Sections 1 and 2 make it clear that the United States is one nation. The separate states must accept decisions, such as criminal convictions, that occur in other states. Section 2.2 allows for **extradition.** This means that if a person charged with a crime in one state flees to another state, he or she must be returned to the state where the crime was committed.

Section 2 also makes it clear that citizens of the United States are citizens of the whole nation.

They have the same rights and privileges of citizenship no matter which state they are in. However, slaves were not considered to be citizens and so did not have the rights of citizens.

Clause 3 provides for the return of runaway slaves to their masters, even if the slave escapes to another state. This shows that the Constitution recognized slavery as legitimate, even though the word "slave" is not used. When the Thirteenth Amendment abolished slavery in 1865, it effectively canceled this clause.

Section 3 describes the process for forming new states. It says that new states cannot be formed within any existing state without that state's approval. However, there is a case where something very close to that happened. During the Civil War, Virginia seceded, or separated, from the Union. However, the people of the western part of Virginia did not want to secede. They asked

Congress for permission to form the new state of West Virginia. They wanted West Virginia to be part of the Union. Congress agreed. After the Civil War, the legislature of Virginia gave its formal approval to the creation of West Virginia.

1. List two ways the framers made it clear that the United States is one nation, not a loose confederation of semi-independent states.

_____

_____

Articles 5–7. *Amending the Constitution; The Supremacy of the National Government; Ratification* (pages 164–165)

How can the Constitution be amended?

Article 5 sets up two ways of amending, or changing, the Constitution. In both cases, it takes more votes to **ratify,** or officially approve, than to propose an amendment. To propose an amendment takes two-thirds of Congress or two-thirds of state legislatures. To ratify takes three-fourths of state legislatures or state conventions.

The framers wanted it to be relatively easy to consider changes to the Constitution. Yet they wanted proposed changes to be carefully consid-

ered. They also wanted to be sure that Amendments had the full support of the nation. Therefore, it is more difficult to ratify an Amendment and make it into law than it is to propose, or suggest, it.

Article 6 makes the laws of the federal government, or national laws, the supreme law of the land. If a state law is in conflict with a national law, it is the national law which must be obeyed. States must then change their laws to agree with the national law. This article strengthens the national government. It again makes sure that the United States is one nation, not just a loose confederation of states.

Finally, Article 7 says that the Constitution was to go into effect as soon as nine states voted to accept it. It did not require agreement of all 13 states. The framers felt that it would be difficult to get all 13 states to agree right away. But they also felt that if nine states ratified, the others would follow. The Constitution was ratified on June 21, 1788, when the ninth state, New Hampshire, agreed. The last state, Rhode Island, finally ratified the Constitution in May of 1790. The first presidential election under the Constitution was to be in 1792.

2. Why is it harder to ratify an amendment than to propose it?

_____

_____

Amending the Constitution

PROPOSAL STAGE		RATIFICATION STAGE
• Two-thirds vote of members present in both houses of Congress (33 amendments proposed)		• Three-fourths of state legislatures (25 amendments ratified)
or		or
• National convention convened by Congress at request of two-thirds of state legislatures (no amendments proposed)		• Conventions in three-fourths of the states (one amendment, the 21st, ratified)

Skillbuilder

Use the chart to answer the questions.

1. In what two ways can a Constitutional amendment be proposed?

_____

_____

2. In what two ways is an amendment ratified?

_____

_____

THE LIVING CONSTITUTION   Section 4 (pages 166–173)

The Bill of Rights and the Other Amendments

TERMS AND NAMES

Bill of Rights First ten Amendments

double jeopardy Being tried more than once for the same crime

due process of law All the procedures for fair treatment must be carried out whenever a citizen is accused of a crime

reserved powers Powers not specifically granted to the federal government or denied to the states belong to the states and the people

suffrage Right to vote

BEFORE YOU READ

In the last section, you saw the process of amending the Constitution.

In this section, you will learn about the Bill of Rights and the other Amendments.

AS YOU READ

Continue your outline. Take notes on how Amendments added to or changed the government of the United States.

Amendments 1-10 (The Bill of Rights)	First Amendment—civil liberties:
	    freedom of religion
	    freedom of speech

The Bill of Rights (pages 166–167)

What liberties are protected by the Bill of Rights?

The first ten Amendments are called the **Bill of Rights.** They were added to the Constitution in 1791. The supporters of the Constitution had to promise to include these protections of citizens' rights in order to get the states to ratify the Constitution. Some of these rights are the ones that the colonists had under British rule. The framers wanted to be sure the people still had these rights under the new government. Some are the rights that the colonists felt Britain had taken away from them. That was one reason why they fought the Revolutionary War.

Amendment 1 protects basic civil liberties. It prevents the government from interfering with citizens' freedom of religion, speech, and press. It says that citizens can gather together, or assemble, freely. Citizens also have the right to ask the government to redress, or correct, injustices. Because

of this amendment, citizens can protest government action without fear of punishment.

Amendment 2 says the federal government cannot prevent states from having an armed militia. This was designed to make sure that states and citizens could protect themselves from the military power of a tyrannical government—as they did during the Revolution. The right of individual citizens to carry weapons has become controversial in modern times.

Amendment 3 says that citizens cannot be forced to let soldiers stay in their homes during peacetime. Amendment 4 extends the people's right to privacy. It is why a search warrant is required to look through a citizen's home or belongings. Such a warrant can be issued only if a judge decides that it is likely that evidence of a crime will be found. The warrant must state exactly what evidence the government is looking for.

Amendments 5 through 8 deal with the rights of citizens accused of crimes. Amendment 5 prevents double jeopardy, or being tried more than once for the same crime. In other words, if a citizen is found not guilty in a trial, the government cannot keep bringing the case to trial until it gets a conviction. (Citizens found guilty do have the right of appeal, however.)

This amendment is also the basis for "pleading the Fifth." That is the slang term for a citizen's right to refuse to testify when that testimony might *incriminate* him/her. It also guarantees **due process of law.** That means that all of the procedures for fair treatment (including the rights mentioned here) must be carried out whenever a citizen is accused of a crime.

Amendment 6 guarantees the right to a "speedy and public trial." It is intended to protect citizens from being kept in jail (in a sense, punished) for long periods of time before they are even brought to trial. The right to know the charges and to have legal counsel also prevents citizens from having to defend themselves in court. This amendment also makes sure the public is informed of what is going on in their courts.

Amendment 9 guarantees that rights are not denied simply because they have not been mentioned in the Constitution. And Amendment 10 establishes the so-called **reserved powers.** It states that the powers that are not specifically given to the federal government—as long as they are not specifically denied to the states—belong to the states and to the people.

1. **Name two ways the Bill of Rights protects citizens accused of crimes.**

_____

_____

Amendments 11–27 (pages 168–173)

How have Amendments changed American society?

The amendments ratified after 1791 have had a variety of purposes. Some are quite technical, such as the legal question decided in Amendment 11. This amendment said that citizens of another state or a foreign country cannot sue a state in federal court unless the state agrees to it. Other amendments changed American society.

Amendments 13, 14, and 15 were a result of the Union victory in the Civil War. Amendment 13 (ratified in 1865) abolishes slavery. Amendment 14 (1868) grants citizenship to African Americans by saying that all persons born or *naturalized* in the United States are citizens. Amendment 15 (1870) protects the voting rights of citizens, particularly former enslaved persons.

However, it was not until 1964 that Amendment 24 made the poll tax illegal. Some Southern states used this tax to keep African Americans from voting. Because many blacks could not afford to pay the tax required at the *polls,* they could not exercise their right to vote.

Voting is the subject of several other Amendments. Amendment 17 provides for direct election of Senators by the people (rather than by state legislatures as described in Article 1). Amendment 19 grants **suffrage,** or the right to vote, to women. And Amendment 26 lowers the age at which citizens can vote to 18.

Amendment 18 is known as Prohibition. It prohibited, or banned, the manufacture, sale, or shipment of alcoholic beverages. It was an attempt to change American society that failed. It was repealed by Amendment 21.

Amendment 22 sets limits on the number of terms a president may serve. No person may be elected president more than twice. Franklin Roosevelt was the first and only president to be elected to more than two terms. He was elected to four. Many people felt that was too long to be president. Today, the idea of *term limits* for other federal offices has some supporters.

2. **How did Amendments 15, 19, 24, and 26 change American society?**

_____

_____

Glossary

bills Drafts of proposed laws presented for approval to the legislature

Cabinet Official advisers appointed by a chief executive to head the executive departments of the government

coup Sudden overthrow of a government by a small group in positions of authority, such as military leaders

federal Relating to a political system in which authority is divided between a national government and its political subdivisions

framers Persons who wrote the U.S. Constitution

impeachment Judicial procedure whereby a government official is accused of wrongdoing and brought to trial before a legislative body

incriminate To cause to appear guilty of a crime

legitimacy Authority; in accordance with accepted standards

naturalized Granted full citizenship to one of foreign birth

override To declare null and void; to set aside

polls Voting places

sovereign Independent

term limits Legal restriction on how long a public official may serve

veto Power of a chief executive to reject a bill passed by the legislature and prevent it from becoming a law

AFTER YOU READ

Terms and Names

A. Write the letter of the name or term next to the description that explains it best.

a. Preamble
b. Senate
c. Supreme Court
d. Congress
e. chief executive
f. judicial power
g. House of Representatives

_____ **1.** The "lower" house of Congress whose membership is based on population

_____ **2.** The introduction to the Constitution

_____ **3.** The authority to decide cases involving disputes over law and behavior of people

_____ **4.** The legislative branch of government

_____ **5.** The "upper" house of Congress whose members are elected to six-year terms

_____ **6.** The president

_____ **7.** The highest federal court

B. Write the name or term that best completes each sentence.

| enumerated powers | elastic clause | Bill of Rights | double jeopardy |
| succession | State of the Union | due process of law | suffrage |

1. The Fifth Amendment protects citizens against _____, or being tried twice for the same crime.

2. Several Amendments expanded _____, or the right to vote.

3. The Amendments called the _____ protect the basic civil liberties of American citizens.

4. Particular powers of the Congress that are listed in Article 1 are often called the _____ of the federal government.

AFTER YOU READ (continued)   *THE LIVING CONSTITUTION*

5. The clause giving Congress the power to do whatever is "necessary and proper" to govern is called the _____.

6. The Constitution describes _____, or who assumes the power of the presidency if the president dies in office.

7. _____, ensured by the Fifth Amendment, protects the rights of citizens accused of a crime.

8. The president uses the yearly _____ to report on the condition of the nation to the Congress and the people.

Main Ideas

1. Why are there more House members than Senate members?

_____

_____

2. How can the president lose his or her job before election time?

_____

_____

3. How are Supreme Court justices appointed?

_____

4. Why is judicial review, although not mentioned in the Constitution, an important activity for the Supreme Court?

_____

_____

5. What did the 26th Amendment do?

_____

Thinking Critically

Answer the following questions on a separate sheet of paper.

1. How does the Constitution reflect the fear of making the country's leader too strong?

2. Why did the framers make it so difficult to amend the Constitution? Do you agree or disagree with their philosophy? Explain.

Name _____   Date _____

Washington Heads the New Government

BEFORE YOU READ

In the last section, you learned how the country ratified the Constitution.

In this section, you will see how the nation's leaders organized the new government.

AS YOU READ

Use this chart to take notes on the differences between Hamilton's and Jefferson's approach to government.

TERMS AND NAMES

Judiciary Act of 1789 Law that set up the national court system

Alexander Hamilton An early Federalist leader

Cabinet Chief advisers of the president

Bank of the United States A national bank funded by the federal government and wealthy investors

Democratic-Republicans Jefferson's political party and ancestors of today's Democratic Party

two-party system Political system where two political parties compete for power

protective tariff Tax on imported goods to protect domestic business

excise tax Tax on goods produced within the country

HAMILTON	JEFFERSON
believed in a strong central government	

The New Government Takes Shape (pages 182–183)

What steps did Washington and Congress take?

The first president of the country under the new government was George Washington. The task ahead of him and Congress was a difficult one. Although the Constitution provided a strong foundation, it was not a detailed blue print for governing. There was no precedent, or prior example, of how to make this new government work. That job was left up to the nation's leaders.

One of the first steps Washington and Congress took was to create a judicial system. **The Judiciary Act of 1789** established a national court system. This law allowed state court decisions to be *appealed* to a federal court when constitutional issues were raised.

Washington and Congress also created three

executive departments: the Department of State to deal with foreign affairs; the Department of War to handle military matters; and the Department of Treasury to manage finances. To head these departments, Washington chose strong leaders. He chose Thomas Jefferson as secretary of state. He picked Henry Knox as secretary of war, and **Alexander Hamilton** as secretary of the treasury. These department heads soon became the president's chief advisers, or **Cabinet.**

1. Why was the task of governing such a difficult one for Washington and Congress?

_____

_____

_____

Hamilton and Jefferson Debate
pages 184–186)

Why did Hamilton and Jefferson disagree?

Secretary of State Thomas Jefferson and Secretary of Treasury Alexander Hamilton disagreed on the direction the nation should take. Hamilton wanted a strong central government. He also called for an economy that helped trade and industry. Jefferson wanted a weak central government. He also wanted an economy that favored farmers. The industrial North backed Hamilton. The largely agricultural South backed Jefferson.

Hamilton wanted to set up the **Bank of the United States.** This bank would be funded by the federal government and wealthy *investors*. The bank would issue paper money. It also would handle tax receipts and other government funds. Hamilton believed that if wealthy people invested in the nation's bank, they would become more committed to helping the new government succeed. Thomas Jefferson and James Madison opposed the plan for a national bank. They argued that it would create an alliance between government and wealthy business interests.

In the end, Hamilton convinced Congress to pass his plan for a national bank. He won support from the Southern lawmakers by agreeing to build the nation's new capital in the South, in Washington, D.C.

2. How did Hamilton and Jefferson's views of government and the economy differ?

_____

_____

_____

The First Political Parties and Rebellion (pages 186–187)

Who led the first political parties?

The differences between Hamilton and Jefferson led to the nation's first political parties. Hamilton and supporters of a strong central government were called Federalists. Jefferson and those who believed that state governments should be stronger than the federal government were called Republicans. They later referred to themselves as **Democratic-Republicans.** (This party was the ancestor of today's Democratic party.) These groups served as the basis for the nations's **two-party system.** Under this system, two main political parties compete for power.

As the nation's two political parties formed, Congress passed two important taxes. One was a **protective tariff.** It placed a tax on goods *imported* from Europe. This tax brought in a great amount of revenue for the federal government. But Hamilton wanted more tax money. He pushed through an **excise tax,** or sales tax, on whiskey. Small frontier farmers produced most of the nation's whiskey. They became so angry about the tax that they attacked the tax collectors. Their actions became known as the Whiskey Rebellion.

Hamilton wanted to show the nation that the federal government could enforce the law on the frontier. As a result, he employed federal troops to put down the Whiskey Rebellion.

3. What action did Congress take that it had been unable to do under the Articles of Confederation?

_____

_____

_____

_____

CHAPTER 6 Section 2 (pages 190–196)

Foreign Affairs Trouble the Nation

TERMS AND NAMES

neutrality To support neither side

Edmond Genêt French diplomat who tried to get American support against the British

Thomas Pinckney Negotiated treaty with Spain over Spanish lands east of the Mississippi River

Little Turtle Native American leader who led Native American confederacy against Americans in the Battle of Fallen Timbers

John Jay Negotiated a treaty with Britain over territory

sectionalism Practice of placing the interests of one region over those of the nation as a whole

XYZ Affair American anger over bribes demanded by French diplomats

Alien and Sedition Acts Laws that made it harder to become a citizen and created harsh punishments for people who criticize the government

nullification The idea that states had the right to nullify or void any law they deemed unconstitutional

BEFORE YOU READ

In the last section, you learned how Washington and Congress set up the new government.

In this section, you will learn how the United States dealt with foreign affairs.

AS YOU READ

Use this chart to take notes about foreign-affairs issues the United States faced with each country shown in the chart.

FRANCE	GREAT BRITAIN	SPAIN
President Washington issues a declaration of neutrality.		

U.S. Response to Events in Europe (pages 190–192)

What were America's earliest foreign policy problems?

In 1789, the French overthrew their monarchy. Then the French went to war against Britain. The United States had a treaty with France. Democratic-Republicans wanted to honor the treaty and support France. Federalists wanted to back the British. Washington decided on **neutrality**—which is to support neither side.

In April 1793, the French sent a diplomat, **Edmond Genêt,** to the United States to win American support. Genêt, however, did not present himself to President Washington. Instead, he tried to get Americans to help the French against Great Britain. Washington was outraged that the French did not respect his country's neutrality.

Meanwhile, the United States and Spain worked to negotiate an agreement over lands west of the Appalachian Mountains. In 1795, U.S.

Ambassador **Thomas Pinckney** negotiated a treaty with Spain. Under the agreement, known as Pinckney's Treaty, Spain gave up its claims to the land east of the Mississippi River. Spain also agreed to open the Mississippi River to American traffic. This treaty paved the way for American expansion west of the Appalachian Mountains.

1. Why was Pinckney's Treaty favorable for the United States?

Native Americans Resist White Settlers (pages 192–194)

How did U.S. expansion affect Native Americans?

Even before Pinckney's Treaty in 1795, Americans had been moving west of the Appalachians in search of new lands to settle. One region many Americans streamed into was the Northwest Territory. This area included Ohio, Indiana, Illinois, Michigan, and Wisconsin.

American settlers encountered much trouble in this land, however. First, despite losing the Revolutionary War, the British still maintained forts in the area. In addition, numerous Native Americans inhabited the region.

As American settlers moved in, Native Americans there grew angry. Conflicts eventually broke out between the Native Americans and the white settlers. One *notable* clash occurred in 1790. Under the leadership of **Little Turtle,** a chieftain of the Miami Tribe, Native Americans defeated American troops as they fought for control of what would become Ohio. In 1794, the American general defeated Native Americans at the Battle of Fallen Timbers. This defeat ended Native American *resistance* in Ohio.

That same year, U.S. diplomat **John Jay** negotiated a treaty with Britain. Under the Jay Treaty, the British agreed to give up their forts in the Northwest Territory. Still, the British continued to bother American ships in the Caribbean. Thus, the treaty did not resolve this problem of British *harassment.*

2. Why did American expansion make Native Americans angry?

Adams Provokes Criticism
(pages 194–196)

What were the Alien and Sedition Acts?

George Washington retired from the presidency after two terms. In a close election, Federalist John Adams was elected president in 1796. Back then, the second-place finisher became vice-president. In this case, it was Thomas Jefferson, a Democratic-Republican.

The election highlighted the dangers of **sectionalism**—placing the interests of one region over those of the nation as a whole. Almost all the electors from Southern states voted for Jefferson. Nearly all the electors from Northern states voted for Adams.

Shortly after the election, America faced yet another foreign affairs crisis. France had begun to interfere with American shipping. During negotiations to *resolve* the matter, three French officials demanded *bribes* from the Americans in order to help them. This incident became knows as the **XYZ Affair.** Some Americans felt insulted and called for war against France. But Adams settled the matter through *diplomacy.*

Republicans cheered Adams's handling of the XYZ Affair. However, they criticized him on numerous other issues. As a result, Adams and his party considered Republicans a threat to the nation. The Federalists also viewed immigrants as a threat because many of them were active in the Republican Party.

Acting on their fears, the Federalists pushed through Congress the **Alien and Sedition Acts** of 1798. These acts made it harder for immigrants to become American citizens. The acts also handed out harsh punishments for people who criticized the government.

Democratic-Republicans loudly criticized the law. Two states, Kentucky and Virginia, passed resolutions refusing to obey the acts. They claimed to be acting on the principle of **nullification.** Under this principle, states could refuse to obey federal laws that they thought were unconstitutional.

3. Why might some states feel justified in refusing to obey the Alien and Sedition Acts?

Jefferson Alters the Nation's Course

BEFORE YOU READ

In the last section, you read how Washington and Adams led the young country.

In this section, you will learn about the presidency of Thomas Jefferson.

AS YOU READ

Use this diagram to take notes on the changes that Jefferson made during his presidency.

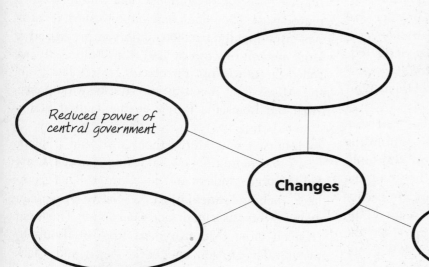

> **TERMS AND NAMES**
>
> **Aaron Burr** Democratic-Republican and running mate of Thomas Jefferson in the 1800 election
>
> **John Marshall** Chief Justice of the Supreme Court
>
> **Judiciary Act of 1801** Law the increased the number of federal judges by sixteen
>
> **midnight judge** Judge appointed to the Supreme Court by President Adams late on the last day of his administration
>
> **Marbury v. Madison** Court case that established the power of judicial review
>
> **judicial review** The power of judges to declare a law unconstitutional
>
> **Louisiana Purchase** Land bought from France in 1803
>
> **Lewis and Clark** Leaders of an expedition to explore the Louisiana Purchase
>
> **Sacajawea** Native American woman who served as a guide an interpreter for the Lewis and Clark expedition

Jefferson Wins Presidential Election of 1800 (pages 197–198)

How did Jefferson become president?

Thomas Jefferson and John Adams faced each other again in the presidential election of 1800. The election was close and bitter. Thomas Jefferson and his followers accused President Adams of making the federal government too pow-

erful. They also claimed he put the people's liberties in danger.

Jefferson defeated Adams by eight electoral votes. However, Jefferson and his running mate, **Aaron Burr,** received the same number of electoral votes. The House of Representatives had to decide the winner. Alexander Hamilton quickly stepped in. Hamilton, who disliked Burr, persuaded his supporters in the House to vote for Jefferson.

This controversy revealed a problem with the

election system. The nation solved it by passing the Twelfth Amendment. The amendment called for electors to vote separately for president and vice-president.

1. What were Jefferson's beliefs about government?

_____

_____

_____

The Jefferson Presidency
(pages 198–199)

What is judicial review?

Jefferson's *inauguration* signaled the first time in the new nation's history that power was transferred from one political party to another. Jefferson believed that the people should have greater control of the government. He also believed that government should be simple and small. As president, he got a chance to put his beliefs into practice. He took steps to limit the power of the central government. For example, he reduced the size of the federal army. He also rolled back Hamilton's economic program by reducing the influence of the national bank.

While they no longer ruled the executive branch, the Federalists remained powerful in the judicial branch. Adams appointed **John Marshall,** a Federalist, as Chief Justice of the Supreme Court. Just before he left office, President Adams pushed a law through Congress called the **Judiciary Act of 1801.** This law increased the number of justices on the Supreme Court to sixteen. Adams quickly filled the positions with Federalists. These judges were called **midnight judges** because Adams signed their appointments late on the last day of his presidency.

Adams' packing of the courts with Federalists angered Jefferson and the Democratic-Republicans. They argued that these appointments were not *valid.*

This debate led to one of the most important Supreme Court decisions of all time. The case revolved around an appointed judge's insistence that he receive his official papers from Congress. The judge claimed that Congress must hand them

over under the Judiciary Act of 1789. In *Marbury v. Madison,* however, the Supreme Court ruled that the Judiciary Act was unconstitutional. The Court ruled that the Constitution contained no provision for the Supreme Court to issue such orders as the act required. This decision established the principle of **judicial review.** This principle allows the Supreme Court to declare a law unconstitutional.

2. What was the importance of *Marbury* v. *Madison?*

_____

_____

_____

The United States Expands West
(pages 199–201)

What was the Louisiana Purchase?

During Jefferson's presidency, many more settlers moved west. The population in the western territories grew rapidly. In 1803, Jefferson purchased a large amount of western land from France. It was called the **Louisiana Purchase.** It stretched from the Mississippi River to the Rocky Mountains. With the Louisiana Purchase, the United States doubled in size.

Jefferson sent Meriwether Lewis and William Clark to explore the new land. **Lewis and CLark** led a team of soldiers and adventurers. This group later included **Sacajawea,** a Native American woman who was a guide and *interpreter.* The team traveled more than two years from St. Louis to present-day Oregon and back. Lewis and Clark kept a journal of their explorations. The Lewis and Clark expedition showed that people could travel across the continent. It paved the way for even greater settlement of the West.

3. How did the Louisiana Purchase affect the nation?

_____

_____

_____

CHAPTER 6 Section 4 (pages 202–205)

The War of 1812

BEFORE YOU READ

In the last section, you learned about the early years of the Jefferson presidency.

In this section, you will learn about the conflicts that led to war between the United States and Great Britain.

AS YOU READ

Use this diagram to take notes about the reasons the war hawks wanted war with Great Britain.

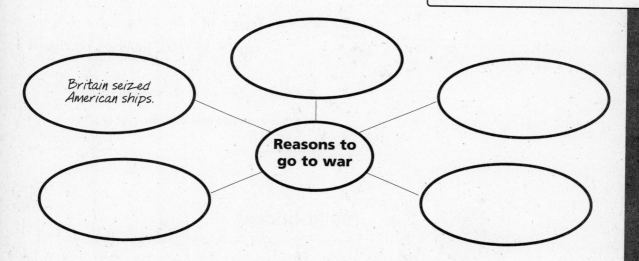

Britain seized American ships.

Reasons to go to war

The War Hawks Demand War

(pages 202–203)

Why did Americans want war with Britain?

In 1804, Jefferson won a second term as president. Shortly after his victory, Britain and France went to war. In 1806, France began refusing to allow British goods to come into Europe. In turn, Britain decided to **blockade** Europe—or prevent ships from entering or leaving its ports. By 1807, both Britain and France had seized more than 1,000 American ships.

The British also practiced **impressment.** This was a practice in which British forces seized American sailors and forced them to serve in the British navy. In 1807, Jefferson asked Congress to declare an **embargo,** a ban on exporting goods to other countries. Jefferson hoped the embargo would hurt Britain and other European countries and force them to respect American neutrality. Rather than hurting Britain, however, the embargo hurt American businesses. As a result, Congress ended the embargo.

The call for war against Britain grew louder in the wake of an incident involving Native Americans in the Northwest Territory. In 1809 General **William Henry Harrison,** the governor of the Indiana Territory, *persuaded* several Native American chiefs to sign away millions of acres of tribal land to the U.S. government. **Tecumseh,** a Native American leader, organized a confederacy of Native Americans to fight for these lands. American troops defeated the confederacy in 1811. After the battle, Americans discovered that the British had supplied the Native Americans arms. As a result, the two nations grew closer to war.

American anger at Britain steadily grew. Some leaders demanded war against Britain. They were known as **war hawks.** They were led by legislators John C. Calhoun and Henry Clay.

1. **What were two reasons that Americans wanted war with Great Britain?**

_____

_____

The War Brings Mixed Results
(pages 204–205)

What were the results of the war?

James Madison became president in 1808. By 1812, relations with Britain were more strained than ever. That year, Madison asked Congress to declare war on Britain. Congress approved the war declaration.

Soon afterward, U.S. forces attacked the British in Canada. The war did not go well for the Americans at first. Then a U.S. Navy fleet defeated the British on Lake Erie. The British took the upper hand again in 1814, however, when they launched a successful attack on Washington, D.C. President Madison had to flee the city.

The advantage swung back to the Americans in 1815, when U.S. General **Andrew Jackson** scored a victory in the Battle of New Orleans. This victory, however, came after British and American diplomats already had agreed on a peace treaty.

The **Treaty of Ghent,** signed in December 1814, declared an **armistice,** or end to the fighting. The War of 1812 showed that the United States was truly independent. The war also increased a feeling of national pride.

2. **What were two results of the War of 1812?**

_____

_____

Skillbuilder

Americans created the figure of Uncle Sam during the War of 1812. Shown here is an early depiction of his character. The Uncle Sam image later evolved into the one we know today—a man with white hair and a beard. Use the cartoon to help answer the questions.

1. **How would you describe this image of Uncle Sam?**

_____

_____

2. **Why might a war prompt Americans to create Uncle Sam?**

_____

_____

Name _____ Date _____

appeal To bring a legal case from a lower court to a higher court to be heard again

bribe Payment of money to persuade or influence

diplomacy Settling disagreements between nations by discussion and negotiation

harassment The act of disturbing or bothering

import Something brought in from an outside place

inauguration The official beginning of an office

interpreter Person who explains the meaning of something

investor One who commits money to something in order to gain a profit

notable Remarkable, significant

persuade To cause someone to do something by means of argument or reasoning

resistance Not giving in to

resolve To find a solution

valid Acceptable according to law or rules

AFTER YOU READ

Terms and Names

A. If the statement is true, write "true" on the line. If it is false, change the underlined word or words to make it true.

1. _____

2. _____

3. _____

4. _____

5. _____

George Washington appointed <u>Alexander Hamilton</u> secretary of the treasury.

During Washington's term, Congress passed an <u>excise tax</u> on goods produced in Europe.

President Washington issued a declaration of <u>nullification</u> during the conflict between France and Great Britain.

The court ruling in *Marbury v. Madison* established the power of <u>judicial review</u>.

Many Americans in the early 1800s were angry with the British for their policy of <u>impressment</u>.

B. Write the name or term that best completes each sentence.

Andrew Jackson

John Marshall

sectionalism

Judiciary Act of 1789

Marbury vs. Madison

Louisiana Purchase

nullification

1. The _____ provided for a federal court system.

2. The election of 1796 highlighted the rise of _____, or placing the interests of one region over those of the nation.

3. In 1801, President Adams appointed _____ as Chief Justice of the Supreme Court.

4. In the _____, Thomas Jefferson bought land from France.

5. General _____ led the American troops to victory in the Battle of New Orleans.

AFTER YOU READ (continued) *CHAPTER 6* Launching the New Nation

Main Ideas

1. What political parties helped establish the two-party system in the United States?

_____

_____

_____

2. What happened as a result of the Battle of Fallen Timbers?

_____

_____

_____

3. Why was President Jefferson's inauguration important?

_____

_____

_____

4. Why was the Lewis and Clark expedition important?

_____

_____

_____

5. What did the Treaty of Ghent do?

_____

_____

_____

Think Critically

Answer the following questions on a separate sheet of paper.

1. Would you have been a supporter of the Federalist or the Democratic-Republican party? Explain your choice.

2. What do you think was President Jefferson's greatest accomplishment? Why do you think so?

CHAPTER 7 Section 1 (pages 212–218)

Regional Economies Create Differences

BEFORE YOU READ

In the last section, you learned about President Madison's administration and the War of 1812.

In this section, you will learn about the different economies that developed in various sections of the country.

AS YOU READ

Use the chart to take notes on the different economies that developed in the North, the West, and the South.

THE NORTH	THE WEST	THE SOUTH
manufacturing		

Another Revolution Affects America; Two Economic Systems Develop (pages 212–216)

How did agriculture differ in the North and South?

America's government had transformed greatly by 1800. By then, other changes had taken place in America as well. The production of goods, for example, moved from small workshops to large factories that used machines. This change was partly due to **Eli Whitney.** In 1798, Whitney found a new way to make goods by using **interchangeable parts.** These are *standardized* parts that can be used in place of one another. In factories, power-driven machinery and many laborers made **mass production** possible. This is the production of goods in large amounts.

These changes in manufacturing brought about an **Industrial Revolution.** This was the name given to the massive changes—to both the economy and society—that resulted from the the growth of the factory system.

Industrialization in America took place primarily in the New England states. Farming was difficult in New England. As a result, people were willing to manufacture goods.

What farming there was in the North was changing by 1800. Farmers began to raise livestock and crops for sale. Farmers then used the cash to buy goods made in Northern factories. As a result, a market economy developed. This is an economy in which manufacturing and agriculture support the growth of each other. Due to manufacturing, the North did not depend on slave labor.

The South was an entirely different story. The South's economy had long been based on agriculture. In 1793, Eli Whitney helped to further promote agriculture by inventing the **cotton gin.** The machine helped to clean the cotton and increased cotton production, which led to the establishment of large cotton plantations.

Larger plantations called for more workers. As a result, the number of slaves in the South nearly doubled from 700,000 to 1,200,000 by the mid-1800s.

1. How did the agricultural systems in the North and South differ?

Clay Proposes the American System (pages 216–218)

What was the American System?

The North and South appeared to be growing apart.

As a result, the nation's leaders focused on making sure the country stayed unified. In 1815, President Madison presented a unification plan to Congress. It called for establishing protective tariffs. It also called for strengthening the national bank. In addition, the plan *promoted* the development of national transportation systems. The plan received support from many members of Congress, including Speaker of the House **Henry Clay.** He called the plan the **American System.**

The federal government also began improving the nation's transportation network. In 1811, the government began building the **National Road** to carry settlers west. The road extended from Cumberland, Maryland to Vandalia, Illinois. In the meantime, states continued to improve their own transportation systems. New York, for example, built the **Erie Canal.** The canal connected the Great Lakes with the Atlantic Ocean.

As part of the plan, President Madison proposed the **Tariff of 1816.** The tariff would increase the cost of foreign-made goods and thus make American goods more attractive.

Most people in the industrial North supported the tariff. But people in the South and the West opposed it. They resented the government's attempts to make inexpensive foreign goods more expensive. After much debate, the three regions approved the tariff.

People from all regions supported strengthening the national bank. A national bank would provide a national currency. In 1816, Congress voted to set up the Second Bank of the United States.

2. How did the American System help strengthen the nation's sense of unity?

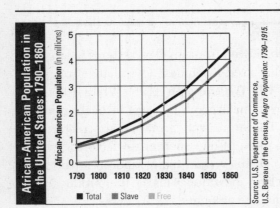

African-American Population in the United States: 1790–1860

African-American Population (in millions)

5 4 3 2 1 0

1790 1800 1810 1820 1830 1840 1850 1860

■ Total ■ Slave ■ Free

Source: U.S. Department of Commerce, U.S. Bureau of the Census, *Negro Population: 1790–1915.*

Skillbuilder

Use the graph to answer the questions.

1. In what year was the difference between enslaved African Americans and free African Americans the greatest?

2. Why do you think the number of slaves increased rapidly after 179(

CHAPTER 7 Section 2 (pages 219–223)

Nationalism at Center Stage

BEFORE YOU READ

In the last section, you read about the two distinct economies that developed in the country.

In this section, you will learn about the growth of nationalism in the United States.

AS YOU READ

Use the diagram to take notes about how nationalism affected the United States.

TERMS AND NAMES

McColloch v. Maryland Supreme Court case that denied Maryland the right to tax the Bank of the United States

John Quincy Adams Sixth president of the United States

nationalism A belief that national interests as a whole should be more important than what one region wants

Adams-Onís Treaty Treaty that secured the purchase of Florida from Spain

Monroe Doctrine Warning to European nations not to interfere in the Americas

Missouri Compromise Agreement that temporarily settled the issue of slavery in the territories

Supreme Court
Supreme Court rules that federal government has authority over commerce between states.

Westward Expansion

Foreign Affairs

Influence of Nationalism

The Supreme Court Boosts National Power
(pages 219–220)

Who strengthened the power of the federal government?

As the states were strengthening their economies, the federal government was increasing its power.

Two significant Supreme Court decisions paved the way. In 1819, the Supreme Court ruled in

McCulloch v. Maryland, that states cannot pass laws that end up overturning laws passed by Congress. In 1824, the Supreme Court ruled in, *Gibbons v. Ogden,* that Congress—not the states—had the power to regulate interstate trade.

1. In what ways did the Supreme Court boost federal power?

_____

_____

Nationalism Shapes Foreign Policy (pages 220–221)

What is nationalism?

On the international front, Secretary of State **John Quincy Adams** established a foreign policy that was based on **nationalism.** This is a belief that national interests as a whole should be more important than what one region wants. Adams believed that foreign affairs should be guided by this national interest.

In 1817, Adams worked out a treaty with Great Britain that reduced the number of both countries' navy ships on the Great Lakes. The United States and Great Britain also agreed to settle boundary disputes in North America.

Two years later, Adams turned his attention to Florida. By this time, most Americans assumed that Spanish Florida eventually would become part of the United States. As a result, settlers had begun moving in on their own. Adams convinced the Spanish minister to the United States that Spain should give up Florida before impatient Americans simply seized it. Spain responded by handing over Florida to the United States in the **Adams–Onís Treaty.** Under the terms of the treaty, Spain also gave up any claims it had to the Oregon Territory.

While the United States worked for peaceful relations with foreign nations, it also warned them against interfering with affairs in the Western Hemisphere. Spain and Portugal, for example, wanted to regain control of their former Latin American colonies. In addition, Russia tried to claim more land on the west coast of North America.

In 1823, President James Monroe warned European nations not to interfere with any nation in the Americas. In return, the United States would stay out of European affairs. This statement is called the **Monroe Doctrine.**

2. What was the purpose of the Monroe Doctrine?

_____

_____

Nationalism Pushes America West (pages 222–223)

What was the Missouri Compromise?

As the country dealt with important foreign issues, Americans continued to move west. Some settlers, such as the mountain man Jim Beckwourth, established a fur trade. Many settlers, however, moved west for the rich and plentiful land.

As a growing number of Americans settled there, the West became more populated. As a result, some territories were ready to become states. The issue of slavery made the process of becoming a new state difficult. In order to *appease* both the North and the South, Congress tried to keep an even number of slave and free states, or states where slavery was prohibited.

In 1819, Missouri asked to enter the union. At that time, the nation consisted of 11 free states and 10 slave states. Southerners expected Missouri to become the 11th slave state. However, the House of Representatives passed a statehood bill that would allow Missouri to gradually free its slaves. Southerners saw this as a threat to their power. As a result, they blocked the bill's passage in the Senate.

The debate over Missouri grew more intense after Alabama was admitted as a slave state. This meant that Missouri's admittance would tip the scales in favor of either the free or slave states. A crisis was averted when Henry Clay crafted a series of agreements known as the **Missouri Compromise.** Under the compromise, Maine was admitted as a free state and Missouri as a slave state. This preserved the balance between slave and free states. In addition, the rest of the Louisiana Purchase was divided into free and slave territory. South of the dividing line, slavery was legal. North of the line, slavery was banned.

3. How did the Missouri Compromise help settle the issue of slavery in the Western territories?

_____

_____

CHAPTER 7 Section 3 (pages 224–229)

The Age of Jackson

BEFORE YOU READ

In the last section, you learned about the growth of nationalism in the United States.

In this section, you will learn about the presidency of Andrew Jackson.

AS YOU READ

Use the time line to take notes about the political career of Andrew Jackson.

TERMS AND NAMES

Andrew Jackson Military hero and seventh president

Democratic-Republican Party Party started by Jackson's followers

spoils system System in which incoming political parties throw out former government workers and replace them with their own friends

Indian Removal Act Law that forced Native Americans to move west

Trail of Tears Path the Cherokee were forced to travel from Georgia to Indian Territory

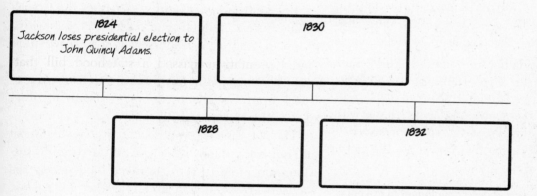

1824
Jackson loses presidential election to John Quincy Adams.

1830

1828

1832

Expanding Democracy Changes Politics (pages 224–225)

What led to the formation of the Democratic-Republican Party?

Andrew Jackson, a hero from the War of 1812, ran for president in 1824 against John Quincy Adams. Neither candidate received a majority of electoral votes and the House of Representatives had to decide the winner. Speaker of the House Henry Clay disliked Jackson. He used his influence to help Adams win the election. Jackson's followers accused Adams of stealing the election. They formed their own party—the **Democratic-Republican Party.** For the next four years, the new party attacked Adams's policies.

During Adams's presidency, most states had eased voting requirements a citizen had to fulfill to be able to vote. As a result, the voting population greatly increased. Fewer states had property qualifications for voting. This meant that many more individuals could vote.

The 1828 presidential election signaled how much the nation's voter rolls had grown. In the election of 1824, about 350,000 white males voted for the presidency. In 1828, more than three times that number voted. However, certain groups still lacked political power. Free blacks and women did not enjoy the freedoms and privileges of white males.

1. How did the voting population grow?

_____

_____

Jackson's New Presidential Style
(pages 225–226)

What is the spoils system?

Andrew Jackson appealed to many of these new voters. When Jackson ran for president again in 1828, these new voters supported him. With their help, Jackson won the presidency by a *landslide*.

Andrew Jackson also appealed to the common people. He was so popular that crowds of people came to Washington for his inauguration.

Jackson wanted common people to have a chance to participate in government. Once in office, he removed about 10 percent of federal workers from their jobs. He gave those jobs to friends and loyal followers. Jackson's friends also became his advisers. These advisers were known as his "kitchen cabinet" because they supposedly slipped into the White House through the kitchen.

The practice by incoming political parties of removing old workers and replacing them with their supporters is known as the **spoils system.** It comes from an old saying that in war "to the victor belong the spoils of the enemy."

2. How did Jackson show his commitment to the common people once in office?

_____

_____

Removal of Native Americans
(pages 226–229)

What was the Trail of Tears?

By the early 1800s, some Native American groups in the Southeast began to take on the culture of their white neighbors. These tribes—The Cherokee, Choctaw, Seminole, Creek, and Chickasaw—were called the Five Civilized Tribes.

Despite all this, white settlers did not wish to live with Native Americans. Instead, they wanted Native American land in the South and West for farms. As a result, President Jackson decided to remove the Native Americans from their lands.

Congress passed the **Indian Removal Act** in 1830. The law ordered all Native Americans to move west of the Mississippi River. In 1830, Jackson pressured the Chocktaw to sign a treaty that required them to move from Mississippi. In 1831, he ordered U.S. troops to forcibly remove the Sauk and Fox from their lands in Illinois and Missouri. In 1832, he forced the Chickasaw to leave their lands in Alabama and Mississippi.

The Cherokee Nation, however, fought the Indian Removal Act in court. Chief Justice Marshall ruled in their favor. The Court said that the United States had no right to take Cherokee land.

But Andrew Jackson refused to obey the Court's ruling. Instead, federal agents signed a treaty with a group of Cherokee leaders willing to leave their land. Beginning in October and November of 1838, U.S. Army troops began forcing the Cherokee to travel from Georgia to the new Indian territory west of the Mississippi River.

The 800-mile trip was made partly by steamboat and railroad but mostly on foot. As the winter came, more and more of the Cherokee died. Along the way, government officials stole the Cherokees' money, while outlaws made off with their livestock. The journey became known as the **Trail of Tears** because more than a quarter of the travelers died on it. When they reached their final destination, the Cherokee ended up on land far inferior to that which they had been forced to leave.

3. How did the removal of Native Americans cause a rift between the executive and judicial branches?

_____

_____

CHAPTER 7 Section 4 (pages 230–235)

States' Rights and the National Bank

BEFORE YOU READ

In the last section, you read about how Jackson dealt with Native Americans.

In this section, you will learn about Jackson's policies on other issues.

AS YOU READ

Use the chart below to take notes on how President Jackson responded to major issues facing his presidency.

ISSUES/EVENTS	JACKSON'S RESPONSE
South Carolina nullifies 1832 tariff passed by Congress	
The Bank of the United States	

A Tariff Raises the States' Rights Issue (pages 230–232)

What is the principle of nullification?

Jackson's vice-president was **John C. Calhoun** of South Carolina. The two men opposed each other over the Tariff of 1816. This was a tax that increased the price of foreign-made goods. By 1828, the tariff had been raised twice. Although Calhoun supported the tariff at first, he came to oppose it. He called it a **Tariff of Abominations,** because he believed that it hurt the South. Southerners had little industry of their own. They believed that they were paying more for goods in order to support industry in the North.

Calhoun believed the South had the right to disobey the tariff based on the principle of nullification. This principle held that states could *nullify* federal laws that they felt were unconstitutional. Calhoun went even further. He believed that if the government *forbid* a state from nullifying a federal law, that state had the right to leave the Union.

In 1830, the Senate debated the tariff—as well as the issue of nullification. Senator **Daniel Webster** of Massachusetts opposed states' efforts to nullify a federal law. Senator Robert Hayne of South Carolina defended nullification.

In 1832, Congress passed a new tariff. The issue of nullification erupted again. South Carolina declared the new tariff invalid. The state threatened to secede, or leave the Union. This made President Jackson furious. He threatened to send troops to make South Carolina obey the law. Henry Clay worked out a compromise that kept South Carolina in the union.

1. **Why did South Carolina threaten to leave the union?**

_____

_____

Jackson Attacks the National Bank (pages 232–234)

How did Jackson destroy the national bank?

South Carolina's action wasn't the only thing that stirred Andrew Jackson's anger. The President also took on the second national bank—the **Bank of the United States** (BUS) in Philadelphia. Jackson viewed the bank as an agent of the wealthy and *elite*—a group he deeply distrusted.

Jackson tried to shut the bank down by taking money out of it and putting it in other banks. In an attempt to save the bank, the bank's president called for all loans to be repaid. This caused many businesses to go *bankrupt*. As a result, the bank lost much support. In 1836 the national bank went out of business.

Jackson's actions against the bank angered a number of people—including some from his own party. They thought that the president had become too powerful. As a result, these people formed a new political party. Known as the **Whig Party,** it tried to limit the power of the presidency.

2. **What was a political consequence of Jackson's fight against the national bank?**

_____

_____

Van Buren Deals with Jackson's Legacy (pages 234–235)

What was the Panic of 1837?

Jackson's vice-president, **Martin Van Buren,** won the election in 1836. He inherited another Jackson *legacy:* a financial mess brought on by the bank fight.

By 1837, many of the banks Jackson had put money in during the bank fight had failed. This helped cause the **panic of 1837.** During this time, many banks closed and people lost their savings. As a result, the country sank into a *depression.*

In the 1840 presidential election, Van Buren lost to Whig candidate **William Henry Harrison.** Harrison died soon after taking office. His vice-president, **John Tyler,** became president. Tyler did not agree with many of the Whig policies. As a result, the party was unable to enact many of its programs.

3. **What helped caused the nation's depression during the Van Buren presidency?**

_____

_____

Name _____ Date _____

appease To satisfy or soothe

bankrupt Completely without money

depression A period when economic activity declines greatly

elite Superior or privileged

forbid To command not to do something, to prohibit

landslide A victory by a huge majority of votes

legacy Something handed down from an ancestor or predecessor

nullify To make ineffective or useless

promote To contribute to the progress or growth of

standardized Compared to something that is accepted as a basis for measuring

AFTER YOU READ

Terms and Names

A. Write the letter of the name or term next to the statement that describes it best.

a. **Henry Clay**

b. **Andrew Jackson**

c. **Martin Van Buren**

d. **Eli Whitney**

e. **William Henry Harrison**

f. **John Quincy Adams**

_____**1.** I am the inventor who developed interchangeable parts and the cotton gin.

_____**2.** I am the congressional leader who promoted the American System.

_____**3.** I am the secretary of state whose foreign policy was guided by a belief in nationalism

_____**4.** I am the President who defeated John Quincy Adams in a landslide in the 1828 presidential election.

_____**5.** I am the Whig Party candidate for president in 1840.

B. Circle the name or term that best completes each sentence.

1. The _____ was a plan to unite the regions of the country and to help create a healthy economy.

   National Road   **American System**   **Monroe Doctrine**

2. The _____ was a warning to European nations not to interfere in the Americas.

   American System   **Monroe Doctrine**   **Missouri Compromise**

3. The _____ was a series of agreements that temporarily settled the issue of slavery in the territories of the Louisiana Purchase.

   American System   **Monroe Doctrine**   **Missouri Compromise**

4. The Cherokee were forced to move to Indian territory along the _____.

   Trail of Tears   **National Road**   **American System**

5. _____ was the president who had to deal with the economic problems that President Jackson left behind.

   John C. Calhoun   **Martin Van Buren**   **John Tyler**

AFTER YOU READ (continued)   *CHAPTER 7*   Balancing Nationalism and Sectionalism

Main Ideas

1. How did the invention of the cotton gin affect the Southern economy?

_____

_____

2. How did the nation's regions—North, West, and South—feel about the Tariff of 1816?

_____

_____

3. How did Supreme Court decisions under Chief Justice Marshall increase national power?

_____

_____

4. What was President Andrew Jackson's policy toward Native Americans?

_____

_____

5. What did President Jackson do about the national bank?

_____

_____

Think Critically

Answer the following questions on a separate sheet of paper.

1. Compare the economies of the North and the South by the 1820s.

2. Nationalism grew in the United States by the 1820s. Do you think nationalism exists in the United States today? Explain.

CHAPTER 8 Section 1 (pages 240–245)

Religion Sparks Reform

BEFORE YOU READ

In the last section, you read about politics in the 1820s to the 1840s.

In this section, you will learn about religious and reform movements in the United States in the 1800s.

AS YOU READ

Use this chart to take notes on the aims of the religious and reform movements of the early 19th century.

TERMS AND NAMES

Second Great Awakening Widespread spiritual movement

revival A religious gathering that relied on emotional sermons to awaken religious feelings

Charles Grandison Finney An important preacher in the revivalist movement

Ralph Waldo Emerson Leading transcendental philosopher

transcendentalism Philosophy that emphasized the truth to be found in nature and intuition

Henry David Thoreau Author of *Walden* who practiced ideas of transcendentalism

civil disobedience The form of protest that calls on people to disobey unjust laws

utopian communities Experimental communities designed to be perfect societies

Dorothea Dix Reformer who worked for improved treatment of the mentally ill

---

TOPIC	AIMS
Second Great Awakening	bring more people to attend church
Unitarianism	
Transcendentalism	
The African-American Church	
School reform	
Utopian communities	

The Second Great Awakening

pages 240–242)

What was the Second Great Awakening?

The **Second Great Awakening** was a religious movement that swept across the United States after 1800. It relied on emotional sermons in meet-

ings called **revivals.** A revival might last several days. Its participants were known as revivalists. During the day, revival participants studied the Bible. In the evening, they heard emotional preaching that could make them cry or tremble with fear. Preachers, such as **Charles G. Finney,** gave exciting sermons to bring out emotional responses from their audiences. They preached that each person had the responsibility to find *salvation*. They also stressed that people could change themselves—and society. Charles Finney and other preaches influenced more people in the United States to attend church.

The revivalist movement—with its message of salvation—attracted numerous African Americans. In the South, slave owners feared that African-American slaves would use the message of salvation as a call to revolt. In Philadelphia, Richard Allen started the African Methodist Episcopal Church. The church became a political, cultural, and social center for many African Americans.

1. What was the appeal of revivalism?

_____

_____

Transcendentalism and Reforms

(pages 242–243)

What was transcendentalism?

Many people sought an alternative to traditional religion. One philosophical and literary movement was based on the ideas of **Ralph Waldo Emerson,** a New England writer and philosopher. Emerson led a group practicing **transcendentalism.**

According to transcendentalism, people could find truth by looking at nature and within themselves rather than in any organized system of beliefs.

Transcendentalists believed in the dignity of the individual. They fought for social changes such as getting rid of slavery and improving conditions in prisons. They also contributed to a *literary* movement that stressed freedom and *self-reliance*. Emerson's friend and fellow writer **Henry David Thoreau** practiced self-reliance. He left his regular life and built a cabin on the shore of Walden Pond, near Concord, Massachusetts. He lived alone there for two years.

Thoreau believed in **civil disobedience.** This meant he believed that people should protest and not obey laws they considered unjust.

The Unitarian movement was another spiritual movement that grew during this time. Unitarianism appealed to reason, not to emotion. It objected to revival meetings as too emotional. The movement attracted wealthy and educated people. Unitarian ministers, like revivalists, stressed the power of the individual.

2. What did transcendentalism emphasize?

_____

_____

Americans Form Ideal Communities; Schools and Prisons Undergo Reform

(pages 243–245)

What did Americans attempt to reform?

Some reformers wanted to create ideal living environments, or **utopian communities.** In these experimental communities, people tried to create a "perfect" place by living in harmony and self-sufficiency out in the country. Several utopian communities were established, but none of them succeeded.

Many Americans worked to reform society during the early 1800s. In the 1830s, Americans began to demand tax-supported public schools. By the 1850s, every state had a law that created an elementary school system.

Dorothea Dix worked for reform in the treatment of mentally ill people. She was successful in getting some states to pass laws aimed at improving conditions. She also persuaded some Southern states to set up public hospitals for the mentally ill. Other reformers worked to improve conditions in the nation's prisons and schools.

3. In what areas did Americans push for reforms?

_____

_____

Slavery and Abolition

TERMS AND NAMES

abolition Movement to outlaw slavery

William Lloyd Garrison Abolitionist leader

emancipation The freeing of slaves

David Walker A free African American who urged blacks to take their freedom by force

Frederick Douglass Escaped slave who became a noted abolitionist leader

Nat Turner Leader of a violent slave rebellion

antebellum Pre-Civil War

gag rule A rule limiting debate on an issue

BEFORE YOU READ

In the last section, you read about different religious movements in the United States in the 1800s.

In this section, you will learn about the movement to end slavery.

AS YOU READ

Use this chart to take notes about the antislavery and proslavery actions that happened from 1820 to 1850.

ANTISLAVERY ACTIONS	PROSLAVERY ACTIONS
William Lloyd Garrison publishes The Liberator.	

Abolitionists Speak Out
(pages 248–250)

What did abolitionists want?

Free African Americans had urged the end of slavery for years. Gradually, more and more whites began to support **abolition,** the movement to end slavery. Some were encouraged by Charles Finney and other preachers who called slavery a sin.

One of the more significant abolitionists was **William Lloyd Garrison,** a newspaper publisher. In his newspaper, *The Liberator,* Garrison called for immediate **emancipation,** or freeing of the slaves. He changed the abolitionists' goal from a gradual end of slavery to an immediate end.

David Walker was a free black who moved from the South to the North. He urged African Americans to fight for their freedom. Another important abolitionist was **Frederick Douglass,** a former slave. Born a slave in 1817, Douglass had been taught to read and write by the wife of one of his owners. In 1838, Douglass held a skilled job as a ship caulker in Baltimore. He excelled at his job and earned high wages. However, Douglass's slave owner took his pay each week. As a result, Douglass escaped and went to New York.

In New York, Douglass became an eager reader of *The Liberator,* and an admirer of William Lloyd Garrison. Soon, Douglass became a leader in the abolitionist cause. He wrote and spoke powerfully in favor of achieving emancipation through nonviolence. He founded an antislavery newspaper called *The North Star*.

1. How did Walker's and Douglass's views differ?

_____

_____

Life Under Slavery (pages 250–252)

What was life like under slavery?

As the debate over slavery grew, the number of slaves in the United States also increased. The nation's slave population doubled between 1810 and 1830—from 1.2 million to about 2 million.

The institution of slavery had changed substantially since the 18th century. In those days, most slaves were male. Most had recently arrived from the Caribbean or Africa and spoke one of several non-English languages. Most of these slaves worked on small farms.

By 1830, however, the majority of slaves had been born in America and spoke enough English to communicate with other slaves. The rise of the plantation system brought further changes to slaves' lives.

Most slaves worked on large plantations. They worked from dawn to dusk in the fields. Some slaves worked in the plantation owner's house as butlers, cooks, and maids.

Many African American slaves also supplied the labor needed in cities. They worked in textile mills, mines, and lumber yards. Some slaves were skilled workers, such as blacksmiths or carpenters.

In 1831, a Virginia slave named **Nat Turner** led a violent slave rebellion. He and his followers attacked five plantations. They killed several people. Turner and his followers eventually were captured and executed.

2. Where did most slaves work?

_____

_____

Slave Owners Defend Slavery

(pages 252–253)

How did Southerners react to the Turner rebellion?

The Turner rebellion frightened white Southerners. Some argued that the only way to prevent rebellions was to abolish slavery. Virginia lawmakers introduced a bill that abolished slavery in the state. After a heated debate, the bill was defeated by a close vote. That loss ended the debate on slavery in the **antebellum,** or pre-Civil War, South.

Others in the South argued that placing tighter restrictions on slaves would keep them from revolting. Across the South, state legislatures passed laws known as slave codes, restricting blacks' rights even further. Under these new laws, slaves could not preach, testify in court, own property, or learn to read.

Despite the *controversy* surrounding slavery, many Southerners defended it. They argued that slavery actually benefitted blacks by introducing them to Christianity. Southern white Christian churches gradually shifted their positions on slavery during this period. While some ministers had attacked slavery in the early 1800s, by the 1830s, most agreed that slavery and Christianity could coexist.

Southerners also invented the myth of the happy slave—a beloved member of the plantation family. They argued that, unlike Northerners who fired their slaves, Southerners cared for their slaves for a lifetime.

Despite these claims from Southerners, the abolitionist movement continued. Northern legislators tried to introduce bills in Congress to abolish slavery. Southern representatives responded by getting Congress to adopt a **gag rule** in 1836. Under this rule, legislators could limit or ban debate on any issue—including slavery. The rule was *repealed* in 1845. But until then, Southerners were able to limit the debate over slavery in Congress.

3. In what ways did Southerners further restrict slaves' rights?

_____

_____

CHAPTER 8 Section 3 (pages 254–258)

Women and Reform

BEFORE YOU READ

In the last section, you read about slavery and the abolitionist movement.

In this section, you will learn about women's roles in the country's various reform movements.

AS YOU READ

Use this diagram to take notes on 19th-century reform movements in which women participated.

TERMS AND NAMES

cult of domesticity Social customs that restricted women to caring for the house

Sarah and Angelina Grimké Leaders in the abolitionist movement

temperance movement Movement to ban the drinking of alcohol

Elizabeth Cady Stanton Leader in the abolitionist and women's rights movements

Lucretia Mott Leader in the abolitionist and women's rights movements

Seneca Falls convention Convention held in 1848 to argue for women's rights

Sojourner Truth Former slave who became an abolitionist and women's rights activist

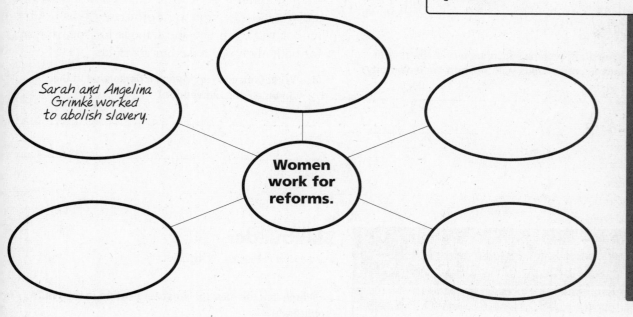

Sarah and Angelina Grimké worked to abolish slavery.

Women work for reforms.

Women's Roles in the Mid-1800s; Women Mobilize for Reform
(pages 254–257)

What reform movements did women participate in?

American women in the early 1800s had few rights. Social customs required women to restrict themselves to caring for the house. This idea came to be known as the **cult of domesticity.** About one in ten single women worked outside the home. They earned only half of what men earned for doing the same job. Women could not vote or serve on juries. In many states, wives had to give their property to their husbands.

Despite such limits, many women actively participated in the important reform movements of the nineteenth century. **Sarah and Angelina Grimké** worked for the abolition of slavery. Mary

Vaughan and other women joined the **temperance movement.** This was an effort to ban the drinking of alcohol.

Many women also worked to improve education—mainly for girls. Until the 1820s, American girls had little chance for education. Some female reformers opened schools of higher learning for girls. Emma Willard opened a school for girls in New York. Mary Lyon started Mount Holyoke in Massachusetts. It later became a college.

Some women worked to improve women's health. In the 1850's, Catherine Beecher, a respected educator, undertook a national survey of women's health. She found three sick women for every healthy one. One reason was that they wore clothing so restrictive that breathing sometimes was difficult. Amelia Bloomer, a newpaper publisher came up with a solution. She devised looser-fitting clothes known as "bloomers."

Elizabeth Blackwell became the first woman to graduate from medical college. She then opened a hospital for women.

1. Why were women's involvement in the reform movements at odds with the cult of domesticity?

_____

_____

_____

Women's Rights Movement Emerges (pages 257–258)

What *was the Seneca Falls convention?*

Women's work on behalf of others eventually *prompted* them to improve their own lives. Some women began to campaign for greater women's rights. Two such women were **Elizabeth Cady Stanton** and **Lucretia Mott.** Both had been abolitionists. In 1848, they organized a women's right convention in Seneca Falls, New York. It became known as the **Seneca Falls convention.** More than 300 women and men attended. They called for laws that guaranteed equal rights for women. One of the more controversial rights women called for was suffrage, or the right to vote.

The women's rights movement involved mostly whites. For the most part, African American women found it difficult to draw attention to their *plight*. One exception was **Sojourner Truth.** A former slave, Truth became famous for speaking out for both abolition and women's rights.

2. What was one right women demanded at the Seneca Falls convention?

_____

_____

_____

Changes in Women's Lives in the U.S., 1830–1850

CHANGES	1830	1840	1850
Percentage of women in labor force	6	8	10
Average number of children per white woman	7	6	5
White birthrate per 1000 population	51	48	43

Source: Nancy Woloch, *Women and the American Experience*

Skillbuilder
Use the table to help answer the questions.

1. Which decade saw the steepest decline in the white birthrate?

_____

_____

2. How did the nation's labor force change between 1830 and 1850?

_____

_____

Name _____ Date _____

The Changing Workplace

TERMS AND NAMES

cottage industry System in which manufacturers provided the materials for goods to be produced at home

master A skilled artisan who owned a business and employed others

journeyman Skilled worker employed by a master

apprentice A worker learning a trade or craft, usually under the supervision of a master

strike Work stoppages by workers

National Trades' Union Early national workers' organization

BEFORE YOU READ

In the last section, you read about the reform movements that women participated in.

In this section, you will read about changes in work and in working conditions.

AS YOU READ

Use this diagram to take notes on what workers did in response to worsening working conditions.

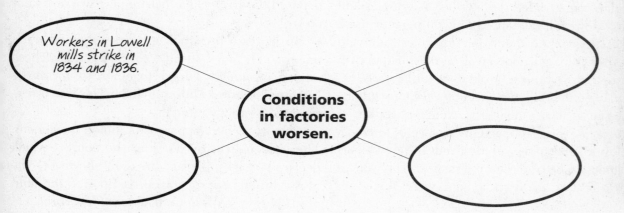

Workers in Lowell mills strike in 1834 and 1836.

Conditions in factories worsen.

Industry Changes Work
(pages 259–260)

How did work change?

The increase of factories in the 1800s changed the way Americans worked. Before the 1820s, textile, or cloth, makers spun thread in factories. Then they employed people working at home to make clothing from the thread. This was known as the **cottage industry** system in which manufacturers provided the materials for goods to be manufactured at home. By the 1830s, factories had replaced the cottage industry system. The thread as well as the clothes were made in the factories.

In the early 19th century, *artisans* made goods that a family could not make for itself. These included

such items as furniture and tools. The artisans usually worked in shops attached to their homes. The most experienced artisans were called **masters.** They were assisted by **journeymen.** These were skilled workers employed by the masters. **Apprentices** were young workers learning the craft.

This way of producing goods also changed with the growth of factories. New machines allowed unskilled factory workers to make goods that skilled artisans once made.

1. How did the growth of factories change the way Americans worked?

_____

_____

Farm Worker to Factory Worker
(pages 260–263)

Who were the "mill girls"?

In the mills of Lowell, Massachusetts, most factory workers were young, unmarried women. Factory owners hired mostly young women because they could pay them less than men. These women were known as "mill girls." They lived in boarding houses owned by the factory.

At first, the women felt lucky to have these jobs. Factory work paid better than other jobs for women—teaching, sewing, and being a servant. But throughout the early 1800s, working conditions in the textile mills steadily grew worse. The workday was more than 12 hours long. Factories were hot, noisy, and dirty. Many workers became ill.

In addition, managers forced workers to increase their pace. Between 1836 and 1850, Lowell owners tripled the number of spindles and looms. However, they hired only 50 percent more workers to operate them. Factory rules tightened too. After gulping a noon meal, workers had to rush back to their stations to avoid fines for lateness.

In 1834, the mill owners cut *wages* for workers. In response, 800 "mill girls" went on **strike.** A strike is a work stoppage in order to force an employer to respond to demands. The workers demanded to be paid their old salaries. The women eventually lost their strike and were forced to return to work.

Two years later, the "mill girls" struck again—over what amounted to another pay cut. Twice as many women participated as had two years earlier. Like the previous strike, however, the company prevailed.

The Lowell workers did not give up their fight for better working conditions after these setbacks. In the years that followed the strikes, the women worked to improve their situation through legislation.

2. Why did the "mill girls" go on strike in 1834?

_____

_____

_____

Workers Seek Better Conditions
(pages 263–265)

What did workers want?

There were dozens of strikes for shorter hours or higher pay in the 1830s and 1840s. Employers won most of them. One reason was that owners could hire strikebreakers, or replacement workers.

Many of these strikebreakers were European immigrants. Immigration from Europe to the United States increased between 1830 and 1860. Irish immigrants had come to escape the Great Potato Famine. In the 1840s, a disease killed most of the potato crop in Ireland. About 1 million Irish people starved. More than 1 million came to America. The Irish faced *prejudice* in the United States because they were poor and Roman Catholic. Because they were poor, the Irish were willing to work for low wages. As a result, employers used the Irish when their regular workers went on strike.

To increase their power, workers joined trade unions, or unions specific to each trade. These unions eventually joined together to form the **National Trades' Union** in 1834. This union represented a variety of trades.

Factory owners opposed the union movement. They had help early on from the courts—which declared strikes illegal. In 1842, however, the Massachusetts Supreme Court supported the right of workers to strike in *Commonwealth* v. *Hunt*.

By 1860, barely 5,000 workers were members of what would now be called labor unions. By this time, however, more than 20,000 workers participated in strikes for improved working conditions and wages.

3. Why was the ruling in *Commonwealth* v. *Hunt* important for workers?

_____

_____

Glossary　　　　　　　　　　CHAPTER 8　Reforming American Society

artisan Skilled worker who make products by hand

controversy a major dispute or disagreement

literary Relating to books

plight A condition of difficulty or adversity

prejudice Irrational suspicion or hatred of a particular group

prompt To press into action or cause to do

repeal To officially withdraw or annul

salvation The deliverance of a person's soul from sin, redemption

self-reliance Confidence in one's own abilities and resources

wage Payment for a job, a salary

AFTER YOU READ

Terms and Names

A. Fill in the blanks with the letter of the name or term that best completes the sentence.

a. abolition

b. Nat Turner

c. temperance movement

d. transcendentalism

e. strike

f. Dorothea Dix

g. Sojourner Truth

1. _____ is a philosophy that says that people could find truth by looking at nature and within themselves.

2. _____ worked for reform in the treatment of mentally ill people.

3. In the 1800s, more and more whites began to support _____, or the movement to end slavery.

4. _____ led a slave rebellion that failed.

5. Some women in the 1800s joined the _____, the effort to ban the drinking of alcohol.

6. _____, a former slave, spoke out for abolition and women's rights.

7. In a _____, workers stop working in order to improve their working conditions.

B. Write the letter of the name or term next to the description that explains it best.

a. Ralph Waldo Emerson

b. Elizabeth Cady Stanton

c. cottage industry

d. Charles G. Finney

e. transcendentalism

f. Frederick Douglass

_____ **1.** Religious leader who preached in revivals

_____ **2.** A New England writer and philosopher who started transcendentalism

_____ **3.** A former slave who became an important abolitionist

_____ **4.** Worked for abolition and women's rights

_____ **5.** A way of making goods in which manufacturers provide materials for goods to be made in the home

AFTER YOU READ (continued) *CHAPTER 8* Reforming American Society

Main Ideas

1. What was the Second Great Awakening?

_____

_____

2. How was life different for urban and rural slaves?

_____

_____

3. How did some Southern slave owners defend slavery?

_____

_____

4. For which reform movements did women work?

_____

_____

5. What brought an end to cottage industries?

_____

_____

Think Critically

Answer the following questions on a separate sheet of paper.

1. Which reform movement in the 1800s do you think was most important? Why do you think so?

2. What problems resulted from the changes in the American workplace?

Name _____ Date _____

The Market Revolution

BEFORE YOU READ

In the last section, you read about the changes in working conditions in the United States.

In this section, you will learn about changes in the American economy.

AS YOU READ

Use this diagram to take notes on the market revolution. Use the boxes on the left to write about the causes of the market revolution. Write the effects of the market revolution in the boxes on the right.

TERMS AND NAMES

specialization In farming, the raising of one or two crops for sale rather than a variety of foods for personal use

market revolution Economic changes where people buy and sell goods rather than make them themselves

capitalism Economic system in which individuals and businesses control the means of production

entrepreneur Business owner

Samuel F. B. Morse Inventor of the telegraph

telegraph Device that sends messages by wires

John Deere Inventor of the steel plow

Cyrus McCormick Inventor of the mechanical reaper

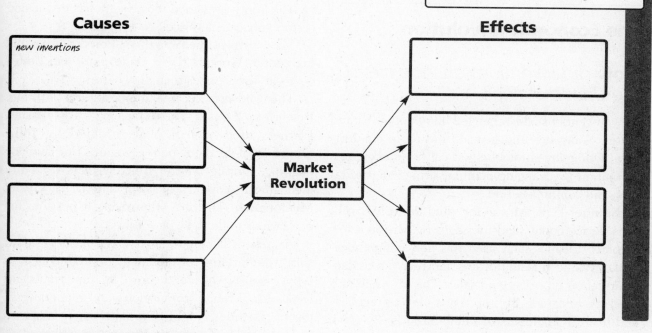

Causes

new inventions

Market Revolution

Effects

U.S. Markets Expand (pages 274–276)

What was the Market Revolution?

The United States experienced great economic changes during the first half of the 1800s. For one thing, the country became more industrialized. One result of this was that workers spent the money they earned on goods made by others. This led many farmers to change their practices. Before,

farmers raised a variety crops for their own families. Now they turned to **specialization,** raising one or two crops that they could sell.

These changes brought about a **market revolution,** in which people bought and sold goods rather than making them for themselves. This new process depended on **capitalism.** Capitalism is an economic system in which private businesses and individuals control production in order to make a profit. Under capitalism, **entrepreneurs,** or business owners, invested their money in new industries. If the industries failed, these entrepreneurs lost their money. If the businesses succeeded, they grew wealthy.

Inventor-entrepreneurs began making goods to make life more comfortable. Vulcanized rubber and sewing machines were two such important inventions.

Farmers also did well. The growing populations in the cities needed more and more food. Farmers used machines to plant and harvest the crops that they then sold to the cities. With their cash, farmers bought manufactured goods. As technology improved, many of these goods grew less expensive. Soon, many Americans could afford to buy a variety of manufactured goods.

1. What was the market revolution?

_____

_____

The Economic Revolution
(pages 276–278)

How did inventions change life in the United States?

New inventions also changed life in the United States. Some inventions made life more comfortable. Other inventions helped cause an economic revolution by changing manufacturing, transportation, and communication.

Samuel F. B. Morse invented the **telegraph.** This device could send messages by wire in a few seconds. Businessmen used this new communication device to transmit orders and relay up-to-date information on prices and sales. The new railroads used the telegraph to keep trains moving regularly and to warn engineers of safety hazards. By 1854, 23,000 miles of telegraph wire crossed the country.

Inventions also improved transportation. Steamboats made river travel quicker and cheaper. In places that didn't have passable rivers, people dug canals, which cut the cost of shipping goods. The Erie Canal reduced freight charges and transportation times

Soon, people began building railroads to move goods. Transporting goods by railroads was more expensive than by canals. However, railroads moved goods faster. Eventually, the cost of shipping goods by railroad became less expensive. By 1850, almost 10,000 miles of railroad track had been laid in the United States. By 1859, railroads carried 2 billion tons of freight a year.

2. What areas did inventions help to improve?

_____

_____

New Markets Link Regions
(pages 278–279)

How did farming improve?

By the 1840s, improved transportation made America's regions *interdependent*. America's regions developed regional specialties. The South exported its cotton to England as well as New England. The West sent grain and livestock to the East. The East manufactured textiles and machinery.

The South remained mostly agricultural, raising cotton, tobacco, and rice.

The Northeast became the nation's manufacturing center. Workers there made more and better goods at lower prices than ever before.

The Midwest became important for farming. Inventions helped make farmers' lives easier. Farmers used a steel plow invented by **John Deere** to help them better prepare the land for planting. During *harvest* time, farmers used the mechanical reaper a new invention by **Cyrus McCormick.** This invention made it possible for one farmer to do the work of five.

Armed with plows and reapers, farmers could shift from farming for the family to producing cash crops, such as wheat and corn. The same trains and canals that brought them plows and reapers from distant factories would then carry their crops to markets in the East and in Europe.

3. What two inventions helped to improve farming?

_____

_____

Name _____ Date _____

Manifest Destiny

BEFORE YOU READ

In the last section, you learned about changes in the American economy.

In this section, you will learn why Americans continued to move westward.

AS YOU READ

Use this chart to take notes on the reasons why people used the Santa Fe Trail and the Oregon Trail to move westward.

TERMS AND NAMES

manifest destiny Belief that the United States would expand across the continent

Treaty of Fort Laramie Treaty that gave Native Americans control of the central plains

Santa Fe Trail Trail from Missouri to Santa Fe, New Mexico

Oregon Trail Trail from Missouri to Oregon

Mormons Religious group that settled near present-day Salt Lake City

Joseph Smith Founder and leader of the Mormons

Brigham Young Leader of the Mormons who decided to move the group west to Utah

"Fifty-Four Forty or Fight!" Slogan used in the 1844 presidential election as a call for U.S. annexation of the Oregon Territory

---

TRAILS WESTWARD	REASONS FOR MOVEMENT ON TRAIL
Santa Fe Trail	to trade,
Oregon Trail	

The Frontier Draws Settlers
(pages 280–281)

Why did settlers continue moving westward?

Many Americans believed that God wanted the United States to expand across the continent. They felt that Americans were meant to control the West. This belief was called **manifest destiny.**

As a result of this belief, many people began moving west. Some moved because of the cheap land. Others—such as business owners—hoped to start trade with Asia. Some fled west to escape economic problems in the east. The Panic of 1837—in which many of the nation's banks failed—caused many people to lose their jobs and savings. As a result, some Americans wanted a fresh start on the *frontier.*

1. What was manifest destiny?

_____

_____

Settlers and Native Americans
(pages 281–282)

How did westward expansion affect Native Americans?

The westward movement caused conflicts between Native Americans and white settlers. In the early 1830s, Chief Black Hawk and members of the Sauk and Fox tribes led a rebellion against settlers in Illinois and Wisconsin territories. The battle ended when the Illinois militia killed 200 Sauk and Fox people. As a result of their defeat, these tribes were forced to move west of the Mississippi River.

In 1851, the United States government signed the **Treaty of Fort Laramie** with many Native American groups. The treaty gave Native Americans control of much of the Great Plains. In return, the Native Americans agreed not to attack settlers as they moved west. The Native Americans also allowed the government to build forts and roads. The United States promised that settlers would stay out of the Native American lands. But the U.S. government did not honor this treaty.

2. What was the agreement made in the Fort Laramie Treaty?

_____

_____

Trails West (pages 282–285)

What routes did the settlers take?

Settlers used several major routes as they moved west. They were a series of old Native American trails and new routes. The **Santa Fe Trail** was a trade route between Independence, Missouri, and Santa Fe, New Mexico. Traders traveled this route to Santa Fe, where they sold cloth, guns, and knives. In return, they bought silver, gold, and furs.

The **Oregon Trail** stretched from Independence to Portland, Oregon. By 1844, about 5,000 Americans had settled in Oregon.

One group that migrated west along the Oregon Trail was the **Mormons.** The Mormons were a religious group, started by **Joseph Smith.** Because of their different views, Mormons had been *persecuted* for their beliefs. **Brigham Young** was the Mormon leader who followed Smith. Young decided that the Mormons would be safer if they lived apart from society.

In 1847, thousands of Mormons settled near the edge of the Great Salt Lake in Utah. They shared water and timberland and built a community around present-day Salt Lake City.

Both the United States and Britain claimed the Oregon Territory. In 1844, James K. Polk, the Democratic presidential candidate, called for the entire Oregon Territory to be part of the United States. His campaign slogan was **"Fifty-Four Forty or Fight!"** This referred to the northern limit of the territory—the latitude 54°40'.

Britain was interested in the Oregon Territory mainly for its many beaver furs. Eventually, beaver hats went out of style. As a result, the British lost interest in the Oregon Territory. The United States claimed the region as theirs. This established the current border between the United States and Canada.

3. What two trails did Americans take to move West?

_____

_____

In this painting by William Henry Jackson, Mormon wagons wait to ferry across the Missouri River at Council Bluffs, Iowa, in 1846.

Skillbuilder

Use the picture to answer the questions.

1. How did many people travel westward during the 1800s?

_____

_____

2. How does this picture show that the population of the West grew in the 1800s?

_____

_____

Expansion in Texas

BEFORE YOU READ

In the last section, you read about American expansion to the West.

In this section, you will learn about the conflict between the United States and Mexico over Texas.

AS YOU READ

Use this chart to take notes about the struggle between Mexico and the Anglo settlers in Texas.

ACTION	OUTCOME
Mexico offers land grants to settlers to settle Texas.	Many Americans start farms in Texas.

Americans Settle in the Southwest (pages 288–290)

What were Mexico's land grants?

In the early 1800s, Mexico's northern provinces included present-day Texas, New Mexico, and California. Texas had few settlers. Although its land was good for farming, people feared attacks by Native Americans.

Mexico won its independence from Spain in 1821. In the years that followed, Mexico sought to improve its economy. As a result, Mexico loosened its trade *restrictions* between its northern provinces and the United States.

Mexico also encouraged American farmers to settle in Texas. In the early 1820s, Mexico offered huge **land grants** to American settlers. Under these land grants, Americans bought land in Mexico for a low price. In exchange, they promised to obey Mexican laws and practice Roman Catholicism. Many Americans rushed at the chance. The same restless determination that produced new inventions and manufactured goods fed the American urge to settle the west. American settlers in Texas were called Anglos. They soon out-numbered the Tejanos, or Spanish-speaking Texans.

The Americans in Texas eventually established a colony in Texas. The American **Stephen F. Austin** was the colony's leader. The number of Anglos in Texas steadily grew and their colony thrived. As a result, many people in the United States considered making Texas part of their country.

President John Quincy Adams had offered to buy Texas for $1 million. President Andrew Jackson later offered $5 million. Mexico refused to sell Texas. Soon the Mexicans also began to have second thoughts about inviting in so many Americans.

1. Why did Mexico encourage American settlement in Texas?

_____

_____

Texas Fights for Independence
(pages 290–292)

What happened at the Alamo?

Tensions soon erupted between Texas's Anglo population and Mexico. First, the Anglo settlers spoke English instead of Spanish. Second, the Anglos tended to be Protestant instead of Catholic. Third, many of the settlers were Southerners who had brought their slaves with them. Mexico had outlawed slavery in 1829.

In 1830, Mexico banned more American settlers from coming to Texas. In 1834, Stephen Austin convinced Mexican leaders to drop the ban. Once again, large numbers of Americans began streaming into Texas.

As the American colony grew, Austin went to Mexico City to visit the Mexican president, **Antonio López de Santa Anna.** Austin asked Santa Anna for greater self-government for Texas. Santa Anna responded by throwing Austin in jail.

Austin eventually was freed. He returned to Texas and called for Texans to arm themselves. Soon afterward, Santa Anna led an army to San Antonio to force the Texans to obey Mexican law. As a result, war broke out between the two sides in 1835. The war became known as the **Texas Revolution.**

One of the most famous battles of war occurred at the **Alamo,** a mission in San Antonio. In February of 1836, a small group of American forces tried to defend the Alamo from Mexcian troops. For 12 days, Santa Anna and his troops attacked the rebels in the Alamo. The Mexicans finally captured the mission after killing all 187 of the Americans.

Even as the battle for the Alamo raged, Texans met and declared independence from Mexico. "Remember the Alamo!" became a rallying cry for Texas rebels to defeat the Mexicans. Under their commander, **Sam Houston,** the Texans captured Santa Anna and won their independence. Houston was elected president of the new **Republic of Texas** in 1836.

The Mexican government refused to acknowledge Texas's independence. However, France and Great Britain recognized Texas's new status. Texas certainly acted like a new nation. It established an army and a navy. It also created its own flag.

Many Texans hoped that the United States would **annex,** or incorporate, Texas as part of the country. The nation was divided on the issue. Southerners welcomed another slave state to the Union. Northerners, however, did not want another slave state.

In 1838, Sam Houston invited the United States to annex Texas. Antislavery Northerners, however, blocked any action on the matter. In 1844, James Polk was elected president. Polk, a slaveholder, favored the annexation of Texas. In 1845, Texas finally was admitted into the union. This angered the Mexican government.

2. Why were some Northerners opposed to Texas joining the United States?

_____

_____

Name _____ Date _____

The War with Mexico

BEFORE YOU READ

In the last section, you learned about the conflict between the United States and Mexico over Texas.

In this section, you will learn how these conflicts led to war and how the United States expanded across the continent.

AS YOU READ

Use this chart to take notes about how each event added territory to the United States.

TERMS AND NAMES

James K. Polk 11th president

Zachary Taylor American general in war with Mexico and 12th president

Stephen Kearny American general in war with Mexico

Republic of California Nation declared by American settlers after defeating Mexicans

Winfield Scott American general in war with Mexico

Treaty of Guadalupe Hidalgo Treaty ending the War with Mexico

Gadsden Purchase Purchase of land from Mexico in 1853 that established the present U.S.-Mexico boundary

forty-niners People who came to California in 1849 in search of gold

gold rush Movement of people to a place in which gold has been discovered

EVENT	CAUSES	EFFECT
War with Mexico	Mexican soldiers kill eleven American soldiers near the Rio Grande.	Treaty of Guadalupe Hidalgo gives much Mexican land to the United States.
Gadsden Purchase		
Gold Rush		

Polk Urges War (pages 293–294)

Why did President Polk want war?

The United States's annexation of Texas increased tensions with Mexico. U.S. President **James K. Polk** wanted a war with Mexico. He believed that a war would bring the United States even more Mexican lands—such as California and New Mexico.

Polk decided to *provoke* a war. He ordered General **Zachary Taylor** to lead the U.S. army to blockade the Rio Grande River. Mexico viewed this action as a violation of its territorial rights.

The two countries moved closer to war. Americans were divided about going to war with Mexico. At first, Southerners were opposed to war. Once they learned that slavery might be extended to any new lands acquired from Mexico, they supported war. Northerners did not want to see slavery extended. As a result, they opposed going to war to acquire new lands.

1. How did President Polk try to provoke a war with Mexico?

_____

_____

The War Begins (pages 294–297)

What sparked the war?

In 1845, Americans sent an exploration party into California. Mexicans were angered by this invasion into their territory. As a result, Mexico sent troops across the Rio Grande into Texas. A *skirmish* broke out. The Mexicans killed 11 American soldiers. Polk asked Congress to declare war. Congress did.

The United States army was led by Colonel **Stephen Kearny.** He marched his troops into Santa Fe, New Mexico. U.S. forces took the area without firing a shot. New Mexico immediately asked to join the United States.

Kearny's troops then moved into California. American settlers there had already declared their independence. They set up the **Republic of California.** American troops easily took control of California.

American troops also pushed into Mexico. One military victory followed another. Mexican soldiers gallantly defended their home soil. However, their army labored under poor leadership, while U.S. soldiers served under capable leaders. They included General Zachary Taylor and General **Winfield Scott.**

Taylor captured Monterrey and won against Santa Anna at Buena Vista. Scott captured the port of Veracruz and then took Mexico City, the capital.

2. What event started the war with Mexico?

_____

_____

America Claims the Spoils of War; The California Gold Rush
(pages 297–299)

What lands did the United States get from Mexico?

In 1848, Mexico and the United States signed the **Treaty of Guadalupe Hidalgo** ending the war. Under the treaty, a defeated Mexico handed much of its northern land to the United States. This land included present-day California, Nevada, New Mexico, Utah, most of Arizona, and parts of Colorado and Wyoming. As a result of its war with Mexico, the United States grew by one-third.

Five years later, in 1853, the United States bought more land from Mexico. This deal was known as the **Gadsden Purchase.** This set the current borders of the lower 48 states.

Due to poor health, Polk declined to run for reelection in 1848. The Democrats nominated Lewis Cass. They remained silent on the issue of extending slavery to the nation's vast new holdings. A group of antislavery Democrats nominated Martin Van Buren. Van Buren captured 10 percent of the popular vote—but no electoral votes. The winner was the Whig nominee, war hero Zachary Taylor.

In 1848, American settlers discovered gold in California. Thousands of people streamed into California in search of gold. These settlers were known as **forty-niners.** This mass migration became known as the great gold rush. As a result of the **gold rush,** California's population exploded. San Francisco became a boom town.

By 1849, California's population exceeded 100,000. California had a *diverse* population including Chinese, Mexicans, and freed blacks. California applied for statehood as a state that outlawed slavery. California's application for statehood provoked much debate in Congress. It became just one more sore point between Northerners and Southerners—each intent on winning the argument over slavery.

3. Which lands did the United States get as a result of the Treaty of Guadalupe Hidalgo?

_____

_____

Name _____ Date _____

diverse Different
frontier A region at the edge of a settled area
harvest Act of gathering a crop

interdependent Relying upon each other
persecuted Treated badly because of beliefs or background
provoke To bring on

restriction Something that limits
skirmish Minor fight between troops

AFTER YOU READ

Terms and Names

A. Write the name or term that best completes each sentence.

Stephen F. Austin

John Deere

annex

Gadsden Purchase

manifest destiny

Mormons

James K. Polk

market revolution

1. In the _____, people began to buy and sell goods rather than to make them for themselves.

2. The invention of the steel plow by _____ helped farmers farm their land more efficiently.

3. _____ was the belief that the United States would control the West.

4. The _____ traveled westward on the Oregon Trail to escape persecution in the East.

5. _____ was a leader of the American colony in Texas.

6. After winning the Texas Revolution, many Texans wanted the United States to _____ Texas.

7. _____ was the U.S. president during the War with Mexico.

8. The _____ set the current borders of the lower 48 states.

B. Circle the name or term that best completes each sentence.

1. The invention of the telegraph by _____ improved communication in the United States.

    John Deere   Cyrus McCormick   Samuel F. B. Morse

2. The Mormon leader _____ led the Mormons along the Oregon Trail to Utah.

    Brigham Young   Stephen Kearny   Stephen F. Austin

3. _____ was the commander-in-chief of the Texas rebels in the Texas Revolution.

    Stephen F. Austin   Zachary Taylor   Sam Houston

4. Colonel _____ led American soldiers to Santa Fe and accepted the surrender of New Mexico.

    Stephen Kearny   Sam Houston   Zachary Taylor

5. In 1849 many people came to California as part of the _____.

    gold rush   manifest destiny   land grants

AFTER YOU READ (continued) *CHAPTER 9* Expanding Markets and Moving West

Main Ideas

1. Why were the steel plow and the mechanical reaper important inventions?

_____

_____

2. What were two reasons Americans moved west?

_____

_____

3. What three cultural issues created conflicts between Texas Anglos and Mexico?

_____

_____

4. What happened at the Alamo?

_____

_____

5. Why was the gold rush important?

_____

_____

Think Critically

Answer the following questions on a separate sheet of paper.

1. How did the market revolution change the way people worked and lived?

2. Do you think President James K. Polk was right in going to war with Mexico? Explain.

The Divisive Politics of Slavery

BEFORE YOU READ

In the last section, you read about American expansion to the West.

In this section, you will see how the issue of slavery in the western territories caused conflict in the nation.

AS YOU READ

Use this chart to find out how the events listed were viewed by the North and by the South.

> ### TERMS AND NAMES
>
> **Wilmot Proviso** Bill that would ban slavery in the territories acquired after the War with Mexico
>
> **secession** Decision by a state to leave the Union
>
> **Compromise of 1850** Series of measures that were intended to settle the disagreements between free states and slave states
>
> **popular sovereignty** Idea that people living in a territory should make their own decisions, especially the decision to admit slavery
>
> **Stephen A. Douglas** Senator from Illinois who worked to pass the Compromise of 1850
>
> **Millard Fillmore** 13th president

EVENT	NORTH'S REACTION	SOUTH'S REACTION
The Wilmot Proviso	favored the bill;	
California asks to be admitted as a state.		

Differences Between North and South; Slavery in the Territories
(pages 304–306)

How did the North and South differ?

By the early 1850s, the North and South had grown further apart. The North was industrial. It had 20,000 miles of railroad track, factories, and large cities. Many immigrants came to the North to find jobs in the factories. These immigrants opposed slavery. The South remained rural and agricultural. It had very little industry and few immigrants.

In 1846, Congress *debated* the **Wilmot Proviso.** This was a bill that would ban slavery in the new territories acquired from Mexico. Northerners favored the bill. They felt that more slave states would give the South too much power in Congress. Southerners opposed the Proviso. They argued that they had a right to slaves in the new territories, because slaves were property—and property was protected by the Constitution. The Wilmot Proviso never passed.

In 1849, California asked to enter the Union as a free state. Southerners thought it should be a slave state since most of it lay south of the Missouri Compromise line. (This imaginary line running through the western territories was created in 1820. South of the line, slavery was legal; north of the line it was outlawed.)

President Zachary Taylor supported California's admission as a free state. Taylor believed that its climate and terrain were not suited to slavery. More importantly, Taylor felt that the South would be better off leaving the slavery issue up to individual territories rather than Congress—and its many abolitionist members.

However, Taylor soon found that feelings in the South were more passionate than he expected. Southerners saw the move to block slavery in the territories as an attack on the southern way of life. They began to question whether the South should remain in the Union.

1. Why was the issue of slavery in the territories so important to the North and South?

_____

_____

_____

The Senate Debates (pages 307–309)

What was the Compromise of 1850?

The 31st Congress opened in December 1849 in an atmosphere of distrust and bitterness. The question of statehood for California topped the agenda. So too did other disputes. Northerners demanded the abolition of slavery in the District of Columbia. Southerners accussed the North of failing to enforce the Fugitive Slave Act of 1793. As the tension mounted, some southern states threatened **secession,** or formal withdrawal from the union.

In Congress, Henry Clay of Kentucky presented the **Compromise of 1850.** To please the North, the compromise called for California to be admitted as a free state. To satisfy the South, the compromise called for a stricter *fugitive* slave law. This law required Northerners to return escaped slaves to their masters.

Other provisions of the compromise had elements that appealed to the North and South. For example, Northerners were happy with a *provision* that gave **popular sovereignty** to the territories of New Mexico and Utah. This allowed the territories to decide for themselves whether to be a slave or free state. That provision appealed to Southerners as well.

Also, as part of the compromise, the federal government would pay Texas $10 million to surrender its claim on New Mexico. This provision satisfied Northerners because, in effect, it limited slavery in Texas to its current borders. For Southerners, the money would help to offset Texas's expenses and debts from the war with Mexico.

Congress debated the Compromise of 1850 for months. The North, represented by Daniel Webster of Massachusetts, supported the plan. The South, represented by John C. Calhoun of South Carolina, opposed the compromise.

The compromise failed to pass. Senator **Stephen A. Douglas** of Illinois then took action. He was able to pass the compromise by submitting each part of the plan as a separate bill. The unexpected death of President Taylor aided Douglas's efforts. On July 9, 1850, Taylor fell ill and died. **Millard Fillmore** became president. Unlike Taylor, he supported the compromise. Finally, the Compromise of 1850 became law. However, it did not settle the issue of slavery for long.

2. What were the features of the Compromise of 1850?

_____

_____

_____

CHAPTER 10 Section 2 (pages 310–317)

Resistance and Violence

BEFORE YOU READ

In the last section, you read about the issue of slavery in the territories.

In this section, you will learn how the controversy became violent.

AS YOU READ

Use this diagram to take notes on how people opposed slavery.

TERMS AND NAMES

Fugitive Slave Act Law that provided for harsh treatment for escaped slaves and for those who helped them

personal liberty laws Laws passed by Northern states forbidding the imprisonment of escaped slaves

Underground Railroad Secret network of people who hid fugitive slaves who went north to freedom

Harriet Tubman Famous "conductor" on the Underground Railroad

Harriet Beecher Stowe Author of the antislavery novel *Uncle Tom's Cabin*

Uncle Tom's Cabin Antislavery novel

Kansas-Nebraska Act Law that split Nebraska into the territories of Nebraska and Kansas and allowed for popular sovereignty there

John Brown Fierce opponent of slavery who led a raid that killed five proslavery people

Bleeding Kansas Nickname given to the Kansas Territory because of the bloody violence there

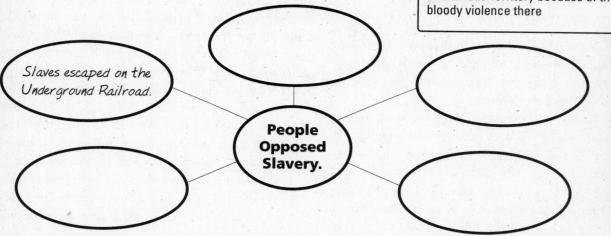

Slaves escaped on the Underground Railroad.

People Opposed Slavery.

Fugitive Slaves and the Underground Railroad (pages 310–312)

How did the North react to the Fugitive Slave Act?

The Compromise of 1850 made the **Fugitive Slave Act** much stricter. It required harsh punishment for escaped slaves—and for anyone who helped them. This made many Northerners angry.

As a result, nine Northern states passed **personal liberty laws.** These laws banned the imprisonment of escaped slaves. The laws also guaranteed that escaped slaves would have jury trials.

In addition, free African Americans and white abolitionists organized the **Underground Railroad.** This was a secret network of volunteers who hid fugitive slaves on their dangerous journey north to freedom. **Harriet Tubman,** an escaped slave, was a famous leader of the Underground Railroad.

Meanwhile, a popular book helped many in the North see the fight to ban slavery as a moral struggle. In 1852, **Harriet Beecher Stowe** published *Uncle Tom's Cabin.* This novel showed the horrors of slavery.

The book prompted Northern abolitionists to increase their protests against the Fugitive Slave Act. Southerners criticized the book as an attack on their way of life. Several Southern writers wrote novels that attempted to show that *Uncle Tom's Cabin* was based on lies. However, they were unable to *dispel* the growing belief that slavery was evil and that it damaged families, both white and black.

1. **What was the Underground Railroad?**

_____

_____

_____

Tension in Kansas and Nebraska
(pages 312–315)

What conflict arose over the Nebraska Territory?

In 1854, the issue of slavery in the territories again erupted. That year, Stephen Douglas proposed splitting the Nebraska Territory into two territories—Nebraska and Kansas.

He had several motives. Douglas was anxious to organize these territories because he believed that most of the nation's people wished to see the western lands become part of the Union. Douglas also believed that continued expansion would help unify the nation. He assumed that one state would enter as a free state, the other a slave state. This would keep a balance between the North and South.

However, Douglas did not realize was how strongly the North had come to oppose slavery. The entire Nebraska territory was north of the Missouri Compromise line. Because of this, the North argued that both Nebraska and Kansas

should be free states. Northerners opposed Douglas's proposal. They saw it as an attempt to increase slavery.

Douglas's bill caused bitter debates in Congress. **The Kansas-Nebraska Act** became law in 1854. It split Nebraska into the territories of Nebraska and Kansas. Each state would decide whether or not to allow slavery.

2. **What did the Kansas-Nebraska Act do?**

_____

_____

_____

Violence Erupts in "Bleeding Kansas" (pages 315–317)

Why did violence erupt in Kansas?

Proslavery and antislavery people rushed into Kansas. Each side wanted to have enough people to decide the vote on slavery its way. Violence soon erupted in Kansas. **John Brown,** a fierce opponent of slavery, killed five proslavery people in a raid. This killing triggered dozens of violent actions throughout the territory. About 200 people were killed. Because of the violence on both sides, the territory was nicknamed **Bleeding Kansas.**

The violence over the issue of slavery also spread to the Senate. As senators debated the situation in Kansas, a relative of an antislavery senator attacked a proslavery senator on the Senate floor.

The widening gulf between North and South affected the nation's political parties, as well. As the debate over slavery grew more intense, national parties broke apart—and groups started new parties.

3. **Why was Kansas referred to as Bleeding Kansas?**

_____

_____

_____

The Birth of the Republican Party

BEFORE YOU READ

In the last section, you read about the violence that erupted over the slavery issue.

In this section, you will learn why new political parties formed in the mid-1800s.

AS YOU READ

Use this chart to take notes about the new political parties that formed and what they stood for.

TERMS AND NAMES

Franklin Pierce 14th president

nativism Favoring native-born people over immigrants

Know-Nothing Party Political party formed to stop the influence of immigrants

Free-Soil Party Political party formed to oppose extending slavery in the territories

Republican Party Political party formed to oppose extending slavery in the territories

Horace Greeley Newspaper editor who strongly supported the newly-formed Republican Party

John C. Frémont Republican candidate in the 1856 presidential election

James Buchanan 15th president

POLITICAL PARTY	WHAT IT STOOD FOR
Know-Nothing Party	Nativism,
Liberty Party	
Free-Soil Party	
Republican Party	

New Political Parties Emerge
(pages 318–319)

How did the slavery issue affect the Whig Party?

The issue of slavery caused the nation's Whig Party to split. The party became divided into Northern antislavery Whigs and Southern proslavery Whigs. Because it was *disunified*, the Whig Party lost much of its political power. As a result, Democratic candidate **Franklin Pierce** won the presidential election in 1852.

The Whig party soon split even further. Some Whig members joined the American Party. This party was concerned about the growing number of immigrants in the United States. They believed in **nativism,** the favoring of native-born Americans over immigrants.

Nativists were primarily middle-class Protestants. They were dismayed not only by the growing immigrant population, but also by the increasing number of Catholics. Anti-Catholic bias often resulted from a fear that Catholics would be influenced by the Pope on issues involving the United States. Nativists felt that the Catholic immigrants who had flooded into the country during the 1830s and 1840s could form a conspiracy to overthrow democracy.

Nativists soon formed the **Know–Nothing Party.** Members wanted to extend the time needed before immigrants could become citizens. The party did well in the elections of 1854. But the party soon split over the issue of slavery and disappeared.

1. What did the Know-Nothing Party favor?

_____

_____

Antislavery Parties Form

(pages 319–321)

What antislavery parties formed in the 1800s?

Other new parties arose during the mid-1800s. The **Free-Soil Party** was against extending slavery in the western territories. In the presidential election of 1848, the party chose former Democrat Martin Van Buren as its candidate. The Free-Soil Party did not receive any electoral votes. However, it did get 10 percent of the popular vote.

Northern opposition to slavery in the territories was not necessarily based on positive feelings toward African Americans. Many Northerners were free-soilers, but not abolitionists. They supported racist laws prohibiting settlement by blacks in their communities and denying them the right to vote.

What free-soilers primarily objected to was slavery's competition with free white workers. The extension of slavery, they believed, directly threatened the free labor system.

The new **Republican Party** formed in 1854. This party took in people of many viewpoints. People frustrated by the split in the Whig Party, such as newspaper editor **Horace Greeley,** supported the Republicans. Like the Free-Soil Party, the Republicans wanted to keep slavery out of the territories.

The Republican Party's main competition was the well-organized Know-Nothing Party. Both parties targeted the same groups of voters. By 1855, the Republicans had set up party organizations in about half the Northern states. However, they lacked a national organization. What they needed was a national slavery issue. Then came several national incidents, including Bleeding Kansas. As a result, the Republican Party gained greater prominence.

In 1856, the Republicans ran their first candidate for president—**John C. Frémont.** Democrat James Buchanan won the election. However, he received less than half the popular vote.

The Democrats nominated **James Buchanan** of Pennsylvania. Buchanan was the only truly national candidate in the election. He won the election, but only with 45 percent of the popular vote. The election showed that the democrats could win the presidency with a national candidate who could compete in the North without *alienating* Southerners. It also showed that the Know-Nothings were in decline and the Republican Party was a political force in the North.

2. What view did the new Republican Party and Free-Soil Party share?

_____

_____

CHAPTER 10 Section 4 (pages 324–331)

Slavery and Secession

BEFORE YOU READ

In the last section, you read about the formation of new political parties.

In this section, you will learn how slavery divided the nation.

AS YOU READ

Use this chart to take notes about how the events listed contributed to the split between North and South.

EVENT	RESULT
Dred Scott decision	The North thought slavery would expand everywhere.
Lincoln-Douglas debates	
Harpers Ferry raid	
Hanging of John Brown	
Election of 1860	

Slavery Dominates Politics
(pages 324–325)

What was the Dred Scott decision?

As new political parties formed, the North and South grew further apart. Several events led to the final split between the North and the South. The first was an 1857 Supreme Court decision involving a slave, **Dred Scott.** Scott claimed that residing in the free states made him a free man. In *Dred Scott v. Sandford,* Chief Justice **Roger B. Taney** wrote that being in a free state did not make a slave free. The Court also ruled that slaves were considered property according to the Constitution. As a result,

territories could not exclude slavery—for it would be denying a person their property. Southerners cheered the decision. They felt that it allowed slavery to be extended into all the western territories.

That year, proslavery forces in Kansas applied for statehood with a constitution allowing slavery. Congress quickly passed a law that required a vote on the new sate constitution. Voters in Kansas rejected it. Northerners cheered the outcome, while Southerners criticized it.

1. What did the Supreme Court rule in the Dred Scott decision?

_____

Lincoln-Douglas Debates (pages 325–327)

How did Lincoln and Douglas view slavery?

In 1858, Stephen Douglas ran for re-election to the Senate in Illinois. Republican **Abraham Lincoln** ran against him. They held a series of debates about slavery in the territories. Douglas opposed slavery but favored popular sovereignty—each territory's right to chose. Lincoln also opposed slavery. However, he did not support popular sovereignty. He called slavery "a vast moral evil" and insisted on federal legislation to outlaw slavery.

Their second debate took place in Freeport, Illinois. There, Senator Douglas issued what became known as the **Freeport Doctrine.** It was a call for people in the western territories to get around the Dred Scott decision by electing representatives who would not enforce slave property laws.

2. What was the Freeport Doctrine?

Passions Ignite (pages 327–328)

What happened at Harpers Ferry?

In 1859, another act of violence over slavery grabbed the nation's attention. John Brown, a Northern white abolitionist, tried to start a slave rebellion. Brown and a few followers attacked a federal *arsenal* in **Harpers Ferry,** Virginia. They hoped to steal guns and arm slaves.

Federal soldiers captured Brown. He was convicted of *treason* and hanged. Many Northerners praised Brown. Southerners attacked his actions and began calling again for secession.

3. Why did John Brown stage a raid on Harpers Ferry?

Lincoln Is Elected President; Southern Secession (pages 328–331)

What were the results of the 1860 presidential election?

The Republican candidate, Abraham Lincoln, won the presidential election of 1860. He received no electoral votes in the South. Lincoln's victory convinced Southerners that they had lost their political power in the United States. They feared an end to their whole way of life.

As a result, Southern states began to leave the Union. South Carolina seceded on December 20, 1860. By February 1861, six other states followed. They formed the **Confederacy,** or Confederate States of America. They elected **Jefferson Davis** president. What many people had feared—a divided country—had finally happened.

4. What major event led to the secession of Southern states from the Union?

ELECTION OF 1860 Electoral and Popular Votes

Party	Candidate	Electoral votes	Popular vote
Republican	Abraham Lincoln	180	1,865,593
Southern Democratic	J. C. Breckinridge	72	848,356
Constitutional Union	John Bell	39	592,906
Northern Democratic	Stephen Douglas	12	1,382,713

Skillbuilder

Use the map to answer the questions.

1. Which candidate won the most electoral votes?

2. In general, how did the North and the South vote in this presidential election?

Glossary   **CHAPTER 10** The Union in Peril

alienate To push away

arsenal Place where weapons are stored

debated Engaged in an argument by taking opposite points of view on the issue

dispel To rid one's mind of something

disunified Not together, split apart

fugitive A person who is running away

provision A clause in a document or agreement

treason Crime of plotting against one's country

AFTER YOU READ

Terms and Names

A. If the statement is true, write "true" on the line. If it is false, change the underlined word or words to make it true.

1. _____ The <u>Wilmot Proviso</u> was a bill that would ban slavery in territories gotten after the War with Mexico.

2. _____ The <u>Compromise of 1850</u> contained a law that provided for harsh treatment for escaped slaves.

3. _____ <u>Harriet Tubman</u> wrote *Uncle Tom's Cabin*, which told about the horrors of slavery.

4. _____ The <u>Underground Railroad</u> was a secret network of volunteers who hid escaped slaves.

5. _____ The <u>Republican Party</u> supported the idea of nativism.

6. _____ The Southern states that seceded from the Union formed the <u>Confederacy</u>.

B. Write the letter of the name or term next to the statement that describes it best.

a. Abraham Lincoln

b. Harriet Tubman

c. Dred Scott

d. James Buchanan

e. John Brown

f. Stephen A. Douglas

_____ **1.** I am the senator who succeeded in passing the Compromise of 1850.

_____ **2.** I am an escaped slave and a leader of the Underground Railroad.

_____ **3.** I am the Democratic candidate and the winner of the election of 1856.

_____ **4.** I am the person whose case brought a Supreme Court decision that said slaves were property protected by the Constitution.

_____ **5.** I am the Republican candidate and the winner of the election of 1860.

_____ **6.** I am the Northern abolitionist who tried to start a slave rebellion by leading a raid on Harpers Ferry.

AFTER YOU READ (continued)   *CHAPTER 10* The Union in Peril

Main Ideas

1. Why did California's request to be admitted into the Union cause a problem?

_____

_____

_____

2. What were two ways that people resisted the Fugitive Slave Act?

_____

_____

_____

3. What led to the end of the Whig Party?

_____

_____

_____

4. How did Lincoln and Douglas differ in their views on slavery?

_____

_____

_____

5. Why did Southern states secede after Lincoln's election in 1860?

_____

_____

_____

Think Critically

Answer the following questions on a separate sheet of paper.

1. How did economic differences between the North and the South contribute to their different views toward slavery?

2. Suppose your state wanted to secede. What arguments would you make against it?

CHAPTER 11 Section 1 (pages 338–345)

The Civil War Begins

BEFORE YOU READ

In the last section, you learned how conflicts between the North and the South led to Southern secession.

In this section, you will learn about the early battles in the Civil War.

AS YOU READ

Use this chart to take notes. List the important military battles in the first two years of the Civil War and their effect on the North or South.

TERMS AND NAMES

Fort Sumter Union fort in Charleston, South Carolina

Anaconda plan Three-part Union strategy to win the Civil War

Bull Run Battle won by the Confederates

Stonewall Jackson Confederate general

George McClellan Union general

Ulysses S. Grant Union general

Shiloh Union victory

David G. Farragut Commander of the Union navy

Monitor Union ironclad ship

Merrimack Confederate ironclad ship

Robert E. Lee Confederate general

Antietam Union victory

BATTLE	EFFECT
Fort Sumter, 1861	Confederates take fort and begin Civil War.

Confederates Fire on Fort Sumter (pages 338–339)

How did the Civil War begin?

The Confederate states took over federal property in the South, especially forts. In April of 1861, the Confederacy demanded that the Union surrender **Fort Sumter,** in Charleston Harbor. President Lincoln refused to abandon the fort. However, he sent only food for the people there.

In March of 1861, the Confederacy attacked the fort and seized it. In response, Lincoln decided to go to war. The Civil War had begun. The remaining slave states quickly took sides. Virginia and three other states joined the Confederacy. Only four slave states remained in the Union. They were Maryland, Kentucky, Delaware, and Missouri.

1. **What event started the Civil War?**

_____

_____

Americans Expect a Short War
(pages 340–342)

What was the first battle of the Civil War?

Northerners and Confederates alike expected a short glorious war. Both sides felt that right was on their side and were convinced that their opponents would go down easily to defeat.

In reality, the North had many advantages over the South. It had more people, more factories, more food production, and better railroads. It also had a skilled leader—Lincoln.

The South's advantages included better generals and soldiers eager to defend their way of life. Also, the North would have to conquer Southern territory to win.

The North had a three-part plan for victory: 1) to *blockade* Southern ports in order to keep out supplies; 2) to split the Confederacy in two at the Mississippi; 3) to capture the Confederate capital of Richmond, Virginia. This plan was called the **Anaconda plan,** after a snake that suffocates its victims by squeezing them.

The Confederates won the first battle of the war, **Bull Run,** just 25 miles from Washington, D.C. The winning Southern general was **Stonewall Jackson.** He earned his nickname because he stood as firm as a stone wall in battle.

2. Who won the battle at Bull Run?

_____

_____

Union Armies in the West; A Revolution in Warfare
(pages 342–344)

Who led Union forces in the West?

Lincoln appointed General **George McClellan** to lead the Union army in the East. In the meantime, Union forces in the West began their fight to control the Mississippi.

In 1862, a Union army led by General **Ulysses S. Grant** captured two Confederate forts in Tennessee. Both sides suffered terrible losses in the Union victory at **Shiloh.**

Grant pushed on toward the Mississippi River. Meanwhile, a Union fleet approached the river's mouth in Louisiana. The navy, under the command of **David C. Farragut,** captured the port of New Orleans.

New weapons changed warfare. The ironclad ships **Monitor** and **Merrimack** made all wooden warships *obsolete.* New rifles made military *trenches* necessary in battle.

3. Which side won most of the battles for control of the Mississippi River region?

_____

_____

The War for the Capitals
(pages 344–345)

Who won the battle of Antietam?

In 1862, the Union army in the East marched toward Richmond, Virginia—the Confederate capital. Confederate General **Robert E. Lee** successfully defended the capital. He forced the Union army to retreat. Lee then began marching his troops toward Washington, D.C.

In August, Lee's troops won a resounding victory at the second Battle of Bull Run. A few days later, they crossed the Potomac River into the Union State of Maryland. At this point McClellan had a tremendous stroke of luck. His troops found a plan that revealed that Lee's and Stonewall Jackson's armies were temporarily separated. McClellan decided to go after Lee.

Union forces met Lee's army at **Antietam,** Maryland. It was the bloodiest clash of the war. This time, Lee was forced to retreat. Union troops did not chase Lee back into Virginia. If they had, they might have won the war then and there. Lincoln fired McClellan in November 1862.

4. How did General Lee have mixed success in the East?

_____

_____

The Politics of War

BEFORE YOU READ

In the last section, you read about the early battles of the Civil War.

In this section, you will learn about the political issues that arose during the Civil War.

AS YOU READ

Use this chart to take notes on the steps that Lincoln took to solve several problems during the Civil War.

TERMS AND NAMES

Emancipation Proclamation Order issued by Lincoln freeing slaves behind Confederate lines

habeas corpus Court order that says that a person who is jailed has to appear before the court to determine why he or she is being jailed.

Copperhead Northern Democrat who advocated making peace with the Confederacy during the Civil War

conscription Drafting of civilians to serve in the army

PROBLEMS	LINCOLN'S RESPONSE
Slavery	Issued the Emancipation Proclamation
Dissent	
Shortage of soldiers	

Britain Remains Neutral
(pages 346–347)

Why did Britain remain neutral?

For many years, the South had supplied Britain with much of its cotton. When the Civil War broke out, the South hoped that Britain would lend its support. But by the time the war broke out, Britain had a large supply of cotton—and thus no longer depended on the South for the material. Britain decided to remain neutral, which meant that it did not support either side.

In 1861, an incident, better known as the Trent Affair, tested that neutrality. A Union warship stopped the British merchant ship *Trent*, on the high seas. The captain removed two Confederate diplomats traveling to Great Britain. The British threatened war against the Union and sent troops to Canada. Lincoln freed the prisoners and had the Union captain apologize.

1. Why did Britain remain neutral?

_____

_____

Proclaiming Emancipation

(pages 347–348)

What led Lincoln to issue the Emancipation Proclamation?

As the war dragged on, a growing number of people in the North felt that slavery should be abolished. At first, Lincoln hesitated to act on this issue. He did not feel he had the constitutional right to end slavery where it already existed.

But pressure to free the slaves steadily increased. As a result, Lincoln issued the **Emancipation Proclamation** on January 1, 1863. The Proclamation freed all slaves behind Confederate lines. Lincoln considered the Proclamation a military policy. He reasoned that the slaves were enemy resources that contributed to the war effort. By declaring them free, they would no longer have to work for the Southern cause. The Proclamation did not apply to slave states still in the Union.

In the North, the Emancipation Proclamation gave the war a high moral purpose. Free blacks cheered the fact that they could now enlist in the Union army. However, the Proclamation did not please everyone in the North. The Democrats claimed it would only prolong the war by antagonizing the South. Many Union soldiers accepted the Proclamation grudgingly. They said they had no love for abolitionists or African Americans. However, they insisted they would support emancipation if that was what it took to reunify the nation.

Confederates reacted to the Proclamation with fury. As Northern Democrats had predicted, the Proclamation made the Confederacy more determined than ever to fight to preserve its way of life.

After the Emancipation Proclamation, compromise was no longer possible. The Confederacy knew that if it lost, its slave-holding society would perish. The Union knew that it now could win only by completely defeating the Confederacy. From January 1863 on, it was a war to the death.

2. **Name two reactions to the Emancipation Proclamation.**

_____

_____

Both Sides Face Political Problems

(pages 349–350)

What political problems did both leaders face?

Neither side in the Civil War was completely unified. Some Northerners sided with the Confederates. Some Southerners sympathized with the Union.

Both governments had to figure out what to do about *dissent*. Both presidents Davis and Lincoln expanded their presidential power to keep order and to put down opposition. Both presidents *suspended* the right of **habeas corpus.** This is a court order that says that a person who is jailed has to appear before the court to determine why he or she is being jailed. Suspending this right allowed police to arrest and hold *dissenters* without trial. Among those arrested were **Copperhead** politicians. These were Northern Democrats who urged peace with the South.

As the war continued, it claimed the lives of many soldiers. Soldiers on both sides *deserted.* Both the North and South turned to **conscription,** or the drafting of civilians to serve in the army. The Union law allowed drafted white men to hire substitutes or pay $300 to avoid being drafted. In the end, only 4,600 men were drafted. Ninety-two percent of the 2 million soldiers who served in the Union Army were volunteers.

In parts of the North, workers who opposed conscription started several riots. The worst riot, in New York, lasted four days.

Much of the rioting in New York was aimed against African Americans. Poor white workers resented having to fight a war to free slaves, who— the whites believed—would swarm north and take their jobs. By the time Federal troops ended the riot, more than 100 persons lay dead.

3. **How did Presidents Davis and Lincoln deal with political opposition to the war?**

_____

_____

CHAPTER 11 Section 3 (pages 351–356)

Life During Wartime

TERMS AND NAMES

Fort Pillow Site of Confederate massacre of more than 200 African American war prisoners

income tax Tax that takes a percentage of an individual's income

Clara Barton Union nurse

Andersonville Confederate war camp

BEFORE YOU READ

In the last section, you read about the political issues that existed during the Civil War.

In this section, you will learn about how the war affected American society.

AS YOU READ

Use this chart to take notes on the effects of the war on African Americans, the economy, and soldiers in the North and South.

NORTH	SOUTH
African Americans	Made up about 10 percent of the Union army; suffered discrimination in army
Economy	
Soldiers	

African Americans Fight for Freedom (pages 351–352)

What discrimination did African Americans face?

In 1862, Congress allowed African Americans to serve in the Union army. After the Emancipation Proclamation of 1863, many African Americans *enlisted.* By the end of the war, they made up 10 percent of the Union army. African-American soldiers served in separate regiments. They were usually paid less than whites and suffered other kinds of *discrimination.*

African-American soldiers who were captured by the Confederacy were returned to slavery or executed on the spot. At **Fort Pillow,** Tennessee, Confederate troops murdered more than 200 captured African Americans.

Ironically, the Confederacy considered drafting slaves and free blacks to fight in 1863 and again in 1864. One planter argued that since slaves "*caused* the fight," they should have to help fight it. The South ended up arming some slaves in the spring of 1865 as the war drew to a close and the Confederate army was desperate for men.

Meanwhile, as the war dragged on, slaves in the South resisted their condition. Some refused to work or destroyed property. Others ran away to

Union armies. By 1864, the plantation system and the institution of slavery were crumbling.

1. What kind of discrimination did African-American soldiers in the Union army face?

_____

_____

The War Affects Regional Economies (pages 353–354)

How did the war affect the Northern and Southern economies?

As Union forces pushed deeper into the South, many slaves ran away. This led to a decline in the South's workforce. As a result, the South's economy suffered. Food became scarce. Prices rose. In 1863, food riots broke out in some Southern cities.

The Union blockade of Southern ports created shortages of other items. They included salt, sugar, coffee, nails, needles, and medicines. As a result, many Confederates smuggled cotton into the North in exchange for gold, food, and other goods.

In the North, the war caused the economy to grow rapidly. Factories produced supplies needed by the army. But wages for factory workers did not keep up with prices. Some workers went on strike for higher wages.

The economies of both sides changed in another significant way: a greater involvement by women. In both the North and the South, women replaced men in the factories and on the farms. In the North, women also obtained government jobs for the first time. They worked mostly as clerks.

Due to the booming economy and rising prices, many businesses in the North made immense profits. This led to corrupt practices—especially by businesses with government contracts. For example, they made uniforms and blankets made of poor material that came apart in the rain. Others passed off spoiled meat as fresh and demanded twice the usual price for guns.

To help pay for the war, Congress decided to collect the nation's first **income tax.** This tax took a part of an individual's earned income.

2. How did the economies of the North and South differ during the war?

_____

_____

Soldiers Suffer on Both Sides
(pages 354–356)

What conditions did soldiers face?

Life for soldiers on both sides was difficult. Many soldiers suffered and died from wounds they received in battles. They also suffered from poor army food, filthy conditions, and disease.

Early in the war, some Northern women and doctors founded the United States Sanitary Commission to improve sanitary conditions for soldiers. They set up hospital trains and ships to move wounded soldiers from the battlefield.

More than 3,000 Northern women served as nurses during the war. Some, like **Clara Barton,** worked on the front lines. The Confederacy had many volunteer nurses, too.

Conditions for soldiers in war prisons were even worse. The worst Confederate camp was at **Andersonville,** Georgia. The camp was terribly overcrowded. Prisoners were not provided with any shelter.

Prison camps in the North were not much better. Northern prisons provided about five times as much space per man. However, they provided little or no heat to the Confederate prisoners unaccustomed to the cold winters. As a result, thousands of Southern prisoners contracted pneumonia and died.

3. What was the purpose of the U.S. Sanitary Commission?

_____

_____

CHAPTER 11   Section 4 (pages 357–365)

The North Takes Charge

TERMS AND NAMES

Gettysburg Most decisive battle of the war

Chancellorsville Confederate victory in Virginia

Vicksburg Union victory in Mississippi

Gettysburg Address Important speech by President Lincoln

William Tecumseh Sherman Commander of Union troops in Georgia and South Carolina

Appomattox Court House Site of the Confederate surrender

BEFORE YOU READ

In the last section, you read how the Civil War affected society and the economy in the North and South

In this section, you will learn about the battles in the final years of the Civil War.

AS YOU READ

Use the time line to take notes on the battles of the last years of the Civil War.

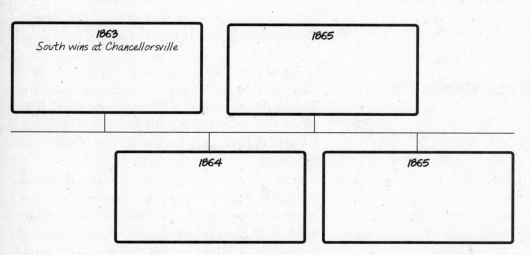

1863
South wins at Chancellorsville

1865

1864

1865

Armies Clash at Gettysburg

(pages 357–360)

What battle turned the tide of the war?

In 1863 General Robert E. Lee decided again to invade the North. Lee's forces clashed with the Union army at **Gettysburg,** Pennsylvania. The Union army defeated Lee's troops after three days of fierce fighting. Each side lost more than 50,000 soldiers.

The South, however, won several battles in 1863. Confederate forces defeated the Union army in **Chancellorsville,** Virginia. During the battle, the South's famous general, Stonewall Jackson, died when he was shot accidentally by his own troops.

The Battle of Gettysburg was considered a turning point in the war. Northerners became rejuvenated due to the fact that they had finally broken through and defeated Lee's army.

Lee would continue to lead his men brilliantly in the next two years of the war. But the Confederacy would never recover from the loss and never again hope to invade the North.

1. Why was the Battle of Gettysburg so important?

_____

_____

_____

Grant Wins at Vicksburg; The Gettysburg Address (pages 360–361)

How did the battle at Vicksburg affect the Confederacy?

The day after Gettysburg, General Grant captured **Vicksburg,** Mississippi, for the Union. It was another significant defeat for the Confederacy. As a result of the battle, the Union controlled the Mississippi River. The Confederacy was split in two.

In November 1863, a cemetery was dedicated at Gettysburg. President Lincoln delivered a short speech. The **Gettysburg Address** honored the dead and asked Americans to rededicate themselves to preserving the Union. Lincoln promised that "this government of the people, by the people, for the people" would survive.

2. What was the result of the battle at Vicksburg?

_____

_____

The Confederacy Wears Down (page 362–365)

How did Union forces wear down the South?

The losses at Gettysburg and Vicksburg caused Southern *morale* to drop. Many men had been lost in battle. The Confederate army was low on food, ammunition, and supplies. Soldiers began to desert. Some even joined the Union Army.

The South was exhausted and had few resources left. Southern leaders started to fight among each other. The Confederate Congress accused President Davis of ineffective leadership. Some Southerners began calling for peace.

Meanwhile, Lincoln made Ulysses S. Grant commander of all Union armies. Grant gave **William Tecumseh Sherman** command of the military division of the Mississippi. Both generals sought a total victory over the South. This meant conquering not only the South's army and government but also its civilian population.

In 1864, Grant fought Lee's army in Virginia. Grant's basic tactic was to attack and then attack again. Even if his casualties ran twice as high as those of Lee, the North could afford it. The South could not.

Grant threw his troops into battle after battle. During a six-week period, Grant lost nearly 60,000 men to Lee's 32,000. Democrats and Northern newspapers called Grant a butcher. However, Grant kept fighting. He had promised Lincoln, "whatever happens, there will be no turning back."

Meanwhile, Sherman's troops invaded Georgia. His forces marched across the state to the sea. They destroyed cities and farms as they went. They did the same in South Carolina. The South was quickly becoming a wasteland.

Despite the Union's military success, Lincoln feared he would not be re-elected in 1864. Many Northerners felt the war had gone on too long and had caused too much destruction. But news of Sherman's victories helped Lincoln win a second term.

By March 1865, it was clear that the end of the Confederacy was near. President Davis fled Richmond. On April 9, 1965, Generals Lee and Grant met in a Virginia village called **Appomatox Court House** and arranged the Confederate surrender.

The terms were generous. Lincoln did not want to impose harsh terms on the Confederates. As a result, Grant paroled Lee's soldiers. He sent them home with their personal possessions, horses, and three days' worth of rations. Officers were permitted to keep their sidearms. Within a month, all Confederate resistance collapsed. After four long years, The Civil War was over.

3. Why were Sherman's victories important to Lincoln?

_____

_____

Name _____ Date _____

The Legacy of the War

BEFORE YOU READ

In the last section, you learned how the South lost important battles and surrendered at Appomattox.

In this section, you will learn how the Civil War changed the nation in many ways.

AS YOU READ

Use this diagram to take notes on the effects of the Civil War on the nation. List the political, economic, social, and technological changes.

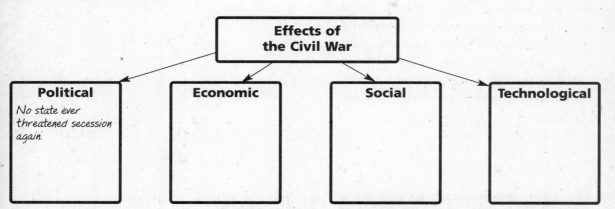

Effects of the Civil War

Political — *No state ever threatened secession again.*

Economic

Social

Technological

The War Changes the Nation
(pages 366–368)

How did the Civil War change the nation?

The Civil War changed the nation in many ways. The nation experienced significant political changes. After the war, no state ever threatened secession again. The federal government became much more powerful and a part of people's everyday lives. During the war, the federal government had passed conscription and an income tax for the first time.

The Civil War also affected the nation's economy. During the war, the federal government did much to help businesses in the nation. The government helped fund a national railroad system. The government also passed the **National Bank Act** of 1863, which created a new national banking system.

The war widened the economic gap between North and South. The Northern economy boomed, as the region produced many different kinds of goods. The Southern economy, however, had collapsed. The labor system of slavery was gone. Southern industry and railroads were destroyed. Many farms also lay in ruins. As a result, the South would remain poor for many decades.

The human cost of the war was huge. More than 600,000 soldiers died. More than 500,000 were wounded. Nearly 10 percent of the nation's population had served in the military, leaving their jobs, farms, and families.

1. What happened to the economies of the North and the South as a result of the Civil War?

_____

_____

_____

The War Changes Lives (pages 368–371)

How did African Americans' lives change?

The war also led to great changes in individual lives. After the war, African Americans' lives began to slowly improve—at least on paper. In 1865, the nation added the **Thirteenth Amendment** to the Constitution. It abolished slavery everywhere in the United States.

After the war, military leaders in both the North and South had to find a new direction for their lives. Many *veterans* returned to their small towns or farms. Some moved to large cities in search of work or to the West to build the railroads or to mine gold. Some turned their wartime experience to good. Clara Barton, for example, helped to start the American **Red Cross**. This organization provided help to civilians as well as soldiers in times of natural disaster or war.

Only five days after General Lee surrendered at Appomattox, President Lincoln was shot by a Southern *sympathizer*. Lincoln was at a play in Ford's Theater in Washington, D.C., when **John Wilkes Booth** shot him. The president died the next day. Lincoln's body was carried by train from Washington to his hometown of Springfield, Illinois. Seven million people, or almost one-third of the Union population, turned out to pay their respects.

2. What did the Thirteenth Amendment do?

_____

_____

_____

The Costs of the Civil War

CASUALTIES

Casualties (in thousands)

800
700
600
500
400
300
200
100
0

Civil War   All Other U.S. Wars

▉ Union
▉ Confederacy

Sources: *The World Book Encyclopedia; Historical Statistics of the United States: Colonial times to 1970; The United States Civil War Center*

Skillbuilder

Use the graph to answer the questions.

1. Which side in the Civil War suffered more casualties?

_____

_____

_____

2. How did the Union and Confederate Casualties compare with those of other wars?

_____

_____

_____

Glossary

blockade Close off a port or harbor and keep traffic from coming in or out

desert To run away from or abandon the army illegally

discrimination Unfair treatment of a person because of that person's racial, religious, ethnic, or other characteristics

dissent Difference of opinion; disagreement

dissenter Person who has a difference of opinion

enlist To join the armed forces

morale Mood or spirits of a person or group of people

obsolete Out of date

suspend Stop for a time

sympathizer One who supports a particular cause

trenches Long, narrow ditches used to protect soldiers in battle

veteran Person who has served in the armed forces

AFTER YOU READ

Terms and Names

A. Fill in each blank with the name or term that best completes the paragraph.

Ulysses S. Grant   Robert E. Lee   Fort Sumter   Appomattox Court House   Gettysburg   Bull Run

The Civil War began in 1861 when Confederate forces fired on **1** _____ in Charleston, South Carolina. Then, in the Battle of **2** _____, the South won an early victory only 25 miles from Washington, D.C. However, the tide turned at **3** _____, Pennsylvania. There, Confederate General **4** _____ was turned back from his attempt to invade the North. He finally surrendered to the Union commander **5** _____ at **6** _____, Virginia, in 1865.

B. Write the letter of the name or term next to the description that explains it best.

a. Thirteenth Amendment

b. Clara Barton

c. John Wilkes Booth

d. William Tecumseh Sherman

e. Emancipation Proclamation

f. conscription

g. Copperhead

h. *Monitor*

i. income tax

j. Vicksburg

k. *Merrimack*

_____ **1.** Lincoln's freeing of all slaves behind Confederate lines

_____ **2.** The name given to a Northern Democrat who advocated making peace

_____ **3.** The drafting of civilians to serve in the army

_____ **4.** A tax that takes a percentage of an individual's income

_____ **5.** A Union nurse who helped establish the American Red Cross

_____ **6.** Union victory in Mississippi that led to the Union control of the Mississippi River

_____ **7.** Union general who destroyed Georgia in his march to the sea

_____ **8.** A Northern ironclad warship

_____ **9.** Abolished slavery in the entire United States

_____ **10.** The assassin of President Lincoln

Main Ideas

1. What advantages did the North have over the South?

_____

_____

2. What was the North's plan for winning the Civil War?

_____

_____

3. How did the Civil War affect women?

_____

_____

4. What were some signs that the South was exhausted after major battlefield losses in 1863?

_____

_____

5. What was the significance of the *Monitor* and the *Merrimack*?

_____

_____

Think Critically

Answer the following questions on a separate sheet of paper.

1. Generals Grant and Sherman believed that total war was the way to defeat the South. Explain total war. Do you think that it should be a way to fight wars? Why do you think so?

2. What were three ways in which the Civil War changed the nation? Which change do you think was most significant? Why do you think so?

The Politics of Reconstruction

BEFORE YOU READ

In the last section, you read how the Union won the Civil War.

In this section, you will learn how political leaders set out to rebuild the nation after the war.

AS YOU READ

Use this chart to take notes about the Reconstruction plans of President Lincoln, President Andrew Johnson, and Congress.

RECONSTRUCTION PLANS	
Lincoln's Plan	
Johnson's Plan	
Congressional Plan	

TERMS AND NAMES

Reconstruction Period of rebuilding the nation after the Civil War

Radical Republican One of the Congressional Republicans who wanted to destroy the political power of slaveholders and to give African Americans citizenship and the right to vote

Thaddeus Stevens One of the leaders of the Radical Republicans

Wade-Davis Bill Bill passed by Congress, and vetoed by President Lincoln, that would have given Congress control of Reconstruction

Andrew Johnson President after Lincoln's assassination

Freedmen's Bureau Government agency that helped former slaves and poor whites by giving out food and clothing and by setting up schools and hospitals

black codes Laws enacted in many Southern states that discriminated against African Americans

Fourteenth Amendment Gave African Americans citizenship

impeach Legal process to formally charge the president with misconduct in office

Fifteenth Amendment Banned states from denying African Americans the right to vote

Lincoln's Plan for Reconstruction (pages 376–377)

What was Reconstruction?

Reconstruction was the period of rebuilding after the Civil War. It also refers to the process of bringing the Southern states back into the nation. Reconstruction lasted from 1865 to 1877.

During the war, President Lincoln made a plan for Reconstruction that was easy on the South. It included pardoning Confederates if they would swear *allegiance* to the Union. It also called for a state to be readmitted in the Union as soon as 10 percent of the state's voters swore allegiance to the nation. Thus it was known as the Ten Percent Plan.

Four states applied for readmission under Lincoln's plan. But a small group of Republicans, called **Radical Republicans,** blocked them. The Radicals thought Lincoln's plan was too easy on the South. They wanted to punish the South for the war. They also wanted to give African Americans the right to vote. The Radical Republicans were led by Representative **Thaddeus Stevens** of Pennsylvania and Senator Charles Sumner of Massachusetts.

In July 1864, the Radicals passed the **Wade-Davis Bill.** This bill called for Congress, not the president, to be in charge of Reconstruction. The bill also declared that a state could be readmitted to the Union when a majority—not just 10 percent—of its voters swore allegiance to the Constitution. Lincoln vetoed the bill.

1. **What was Lincoln's plan for readmitting Confederate states to the Union?**

_____

_____

_____

Johnson's Plan (pages 377–379)

What was Johnson's plan for Reconstruction?

After Lincoln was killed, his vice-president, **Andrew Johnson,** became president. Johnson's Reconstruction plan was similar to Lincoln's. Many states met the plan's terms. As a result, these states were readmitted to the Union. In December 1865, Southern members of Congress began arriving once again in Washington.

The Radical Republicans, however, refused to seat the new members. In addition, they passed a law creating the **Freedmen's Bureau.** It gave food and clothing to former slaves and set up hospitals and schools.

Congress also passed the Civil Rights Act of 1866. The act declared that states could not enact **black codes**—laws that discriminated against African Americans.

Johnson felt that the two bills made the federal government too powerful. So he vetoed both.

2. **Why did President Johnson veto the bill extending the Freedmen's Bureau and the Civil Rights Act of 1866?**

_____

_____

_____

Congressional Reconstruction
(pages 379–382)

What was the congressional plan for Reconstruction?

Congress voted to *override* Johnson's vetoes. It also passed the **Fourteenth Amendment.** This amendment gave African Americans full citizenship. Johnson urged Southern states to oppose the amendment. He argued that the amendment was too hard on the South. He added that states should not have to ratify an amendment that their legislators had little to do with. The amendment was not ratified until 1868.

The Radical Republicans won numerous seats in the 1866 Congressional elections. They now had enough votes in Congress to take control of Reconstruction

In 1867, the new Congress passed the Reconstruction Act. The act declared that state governments created under Lincoln and Johnson's plan were *invalid.* In addition, the act put the Southern states under military control and called for new state constitutions. The law also said that no state could re-enter the Union until it approved the Fourteenth Amendment and gave the vote to African-American men. Johnson vetoed the bill. Congress overrode his vetoes.

The fight between Congress and Johnson intensified. Congress began looking for a way to **impeach** the president in order to remove him from office. They soon found a way. Johnson had removed a cabinet member in 1867. Congress said he did it illegally. As a result, Congress voted to impeach Johnson. The President's impeachment trial went to the Senate in 1868. The Senate found him not guilty. Johnson remained in office.

In 1868, Civil War hero Ulysses S. Grant was elected president. African-American votes in the South helped him win. Then, in 1870, the **Fifteenth Amendment** was ratified. It banned states from denying the vote to African Americans.

3. **How did the Fourteenth and Fifteenth Amendments improve the lives of African Americans?**

_____

_____

_____

CHAPTER 12 Section 2 (pages 383–392)

Reconstructing Society

BEFORE YOU READ

In the last section, you learned about presidential and congressional Reconstruction plans.

In this section, you will read how Reconstruction affected Southern society.

AS YOU READ

Use the chart below to take notes on the problems facing the South after the Civil War and the way people tried to solve these problems.

<table>
<tr><td>TERMS AND NAMES</td></tr>
</table>

TERMS AND NAMES

scalawag White Southerner who joined the Republican Party

carpetbagger Northerner who moved to the South after the war

Hiram Revels First African-American senator

sharecropping System in which landowners leased a few acres of land to farmworkers in return for a portion of their crops

tenant farming Renting land from landowners for cash

PROBLEM	SOLUTION
The South was in ruins	Public works programs were started

Conditions in the Postwar South; Politics in the Postwar South (pages 383–387)

What political groups existed in the postwar South?

By 1870, all former Confederate states had been readmitted to the Union. Republicans—the party that had long opposed slavery—ran their governments.

The South faced terrible economic conditions throughout Reconstruction. Many plantations and small farms remained destroyed. The population of the South also was devastated. More than one-fifth

of the adult white men of the Confederacy died in the war. Tens of thousands of Southern African-American men also died. The women and children who stayed home often suffered *malnutrition* and illness.

The Southern state governments began *public works* programs to repair the region's physical damage. They also provided *social services*. State governments raised taxes to pay for these programs.

Three different groups made up the Republican party in the South. **Scalawags** were white Southerners. They were small farmers who did not want wealthy planters to regain power. **Carpetbaggers** were Northerners who had moved South. Some moved there to reform Southern society. Others moved there to make money. The third group was African Americans eager to vote and take part in politics.

The differences between the three Republican groups led to a lack of unity in the party. Meanwhile, the issue of African American rights divided Southern society as a whole. Some whites thought that the end of slavery would help the South. But most Southern whites refused to accept equal rights for African Americans.

1. **What three groups made up the Republican Party after the war?**

_____

_____

Former Slaves Face Many Challenges (pages 387–389)

How did former slaves improve their situation?

African Americans worked hard to improve their lives during Reconstruction. Many African Americans moved to find family members who had been sold elsewhere in the South. The Freedmen's Bureau worked to reunite African-American families. Once reunited, African Americans married and raised their families.

Thousands of African Americans of all ages sought an education. African-American groups organized schools, colleges, and universities. They raised money to buy land and to pay teachers' salaries.

After the war, many African Americans founded their own churches. African-American ministers often became important community leaders. African Americans also formed thousands of volunteer organizations. These organizations provided financial and emotional support for their members.

After the war, many African Americans participated in government. Not only did they vote, but they organized conventions to demand equal rights and protection under the law. Some joined the new state governments. More than a dozen African

Americans served in the U.S. Congress. Among these was **Hiram Revels,** the first African-American senator.

2. **In what ways did African Americans participate in government after the war?**

_____

_____

Changes in the Southern Economy (pages 389–392)

How did the Southern economy change after the war?

African Americans wanted to own and farm their own land. They had been promised "forty acres and a mule" by General Sherman. Congress, though, did not honor this promise.

Meanwhile, Southern planters wanted to return to the plantation system. To regain their control of land and labor, Southern planters turned to two systems that kept African Americans under their control.

One system was known as **sharecropping.** To survive, many former slaves became sharecroppers. Sharecropping is a system in which landowners give a few acres of land to their farmworkers. The farmers keep a small portion of their crops and give the rest to the landowner.

Another system in which whites controlled the labor of African Americans was **tenant farming.** Tenant farmers rented land from the landowners for cash.

Another change in the Southern economy was the fact that cotton was no longer in great demand. The world demand for Southern cotton began to drop as other countries increased their cotton production. As a result, the price of Southern cotton fell dramatically.

3. **How did planters regain control of the land and labor in the South?**

_____

_____

CHAPTER 12 Section 3 (pages 393–401)

The Collapse of Reconstruction

TERMS AND NAMES

Ku Klux Klan (KKK) Terrorist group of white Southerners who used violence to keep blacks from voting

panic of 1873 Financial crisis that started an economic depression

redemption Southern Democrats' term for their return to power in the South in the 1870s

Rutherford B. Hayes President who ended Reconstruction in 1877

Samuel J. Tilden Democratic presidential candidate in 1876

Compromise of 1877 The political deal that gave the presidency to Hayes and ended Reconstruction

home rule Ability to run state governments without the interference of the federal government

BEFORE YOU READ

In the last section, you read about the effects of Reconstruction on the South.

In this section, you will learn how Reconstruction ended.

AS YOU READ

Use this time line to take notes on the events that led to the end of Reconstruction.

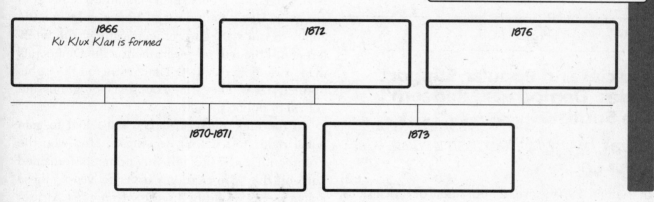

1866
Ku Klux Klan is formed

1872

1876

1870-1871

1873

Opposition to Reconstruction
(pages 393–395)

What was the Ku Klux Klan?

Many Southerners did not like the notion of greater rights for African Americans—especially the right to vote. Some Southern citizens formed terrorist groups that opposed rights for African Americans. One such group was known as the **Ku Klux Klan.** This group used violence to keep blacks from voting.

The Klan and other groups also tried to prevent African Americans from making economic progress. They killed livestock that belonged to African Americans. They attacked African Americans who owned their own land and forced them to work for white landowners.

In 1872, Congress weakened the power of the Republican Party in the South. Many white Southerners had complained about Republican abuses of power during Reconstruction. They claimed that Republicans kept many white Southerners from reaching public office. As a result, Congress passed the Amnesty Act in 1872. The act gave many former Confederates the right to vote. Southern Democrats began to regain power in the South.

1. What did the Ku Klux Klan attempt to do?

_____

_____

Scandals and Money Crises Hurt Republicans; Economic Turmoil (pages 395–397)

What weakened the Republican Party in the early 1870s?

Meanwhile, corruption and scandals hurt the Republican Party nationwide. General Ulysses S. Grant had been elected president in 1869. Though Grant was not corrupt, many people in his administration were.

The **Panic of 1873** further upset the nation. Many investors had taken advantage of the expanding economy after the Civil War. Some took on more debt than they could afford. Many could not pay their debts and went bankrupt. As a result, many banks closed. A nation-wide *depression* soon followed.

2. What caused the Panic of 1873?

_____

_____

Judicial and Popular Support Fades; Democrats "Redeem" the South (pages 397–401)

What brought Reconstruction to an end?

In the mid-1870s, several Supreme Court decisions weakened the power of the Fourteenth and Fifteenth Amendments. At the same time, more and more people in the North wanted to *reconcile* with the South. As time passed, the nation focused on the scandals and the economic problems of the nation. The country began to lose interest in the problems of the South.

As Republican power in the South weakened, Southern Democrats began to recapture many state governments. Democrats referred to their return to power as **redemption.**

In 1876, Republicans decided not to run Grant for a third term. Instead, they chose **Rutherford B. Hayes.** The Democrats ran **Samuel H. Tilden.** Tilden won the popular vote. However, he fell one vote short of the number of electoral votes needed to win.

Congress appointed a commission to settle the election. Democrats and Republicans made a political deal called the **Compromise of 1877.** Democrats allowed Hayes to become president and Republicans agreed to withdraw federal troops from the South, ending Reconstruction.

The 1876 elections also brought an end to Republican influence in Southern state governments. After the elections, Democrats, called Redeemers, controlled every Southern state government. Using the power of **home rule**—or the ability to run state governments without the interference of the federal government—the Democrats made sweeping changes. They restricted the rights of freed slaves. They wiped out social programs and got rid of public schools.

In the end, Reconstruction had failed to gain equal rights for African Americans. However, the Fourteenth and Fifteenth Amendments remained part of the Constitution. In later years, these amendments would be used to strengthen African Americans' rights.

3. In what two ways did the 1876 elections signal the end of Reconstruction?

_____

_____

U. S. GRANT: "I HOPE I SHALL GET TO THE BOTTOM SOON."

IN FOR IT.

Skillbuilder

Use the cartoon to answer the questions.

1. How is President Grant shown in the cartoon?

_____

2. What is Grant trying to do?

_____

Name _____ Date _____

allegiance Loyalty

depression Period when economic activity declines

invalid Not acceptable according to the law or rules

malnutrition Condition caused by having too little food to eat or by eating the wrong kinds of food

override Reverse

public works Construction projects, such as highways, paid for by the government for the benefit of the general public

reconcile Settle differences

social services Services that help people improve their lives, such as schools

AFTER YOU READ

Terms and Names

A. Fill in the blanks with the letter of the term that best completes the sentence.

a. Reconstruction

b. black codes

c. scalawags

d. carpetbaggers

e. Hiram Revels

f. Ku Klux Klan

g. Rutherford B. Hayes

_____ **1.** Congress outlawed _____, which were laws that discriminated against African Americans.

_____ **2.** The _____ was a terrorist organization that used violence to prevent African Americans from voting.

_____ **3.** The election of _____ as president in 1876 helped to bring Reconstruction to an end.

_____ **4.** _____ was the first African-American senator.

_____ **5.** _____ was the period of rebuilding the nation after the Civil War, which lasted from 1865 to 1877.

_____ **6.** The _____ were white Southern Republicans who did not want wealthy planters to regain power.

B. Write the letter of the name or term that matches the description.

a. sharecropping

b. Samuel J. Tilden

c. Fourteenth Amendment

d. home rule

e. tenant farming

f. redemption

g. Fifteenth Amendment

h. Rutherford B. Hayes

_____ **1.** It gave African Americans citizenship.

_____ **2.** It banned states from denying the vote to African Americans.

_____ **3.** A system in which landowners give a few acres of land to their farmworkers and the farmworkers keep a small portion of their crops and give the rest to the landowners

_____ **4.** A system in which farmers rented land from the landowners for cash

_____ **5.** The Democrat candidate in the 1876 presidential election

_____ **6.** The Southern Democrats' term for their return to power in the South

_____ **7.** The ability to run state governments without federal intervention

Main Ideas

1. What did the Congressional plan for Reconstruction include?

_____

_____

2. How did African Americans try to rebuild their lives after the Civil War?

_____

_____

3. What systems replaced the plantation system in the South?

_____

_____

4. What did the Ku Klux Klan do to prevent African Americans from making political and economic progress?

_____

_____

5. How did Southern Democrats regain political power during Reconstruction?

_____

_____

Thinking Critically

Answer the following questions on a separate sheet of paper.

1. How was Reconstruction undone?

2. Did African Americans come through Reconstruction better or worse off? Explain.

CHAPTER 13 Section 1 (pages 408–417)

Cultures Clash on the Prairie

BEFORE YOU READ

In the last section, you read about Reconstruction and its effects on the nation.

In this section, you will read how Americans began settling the West in the years following Reconstruction. This spelled disaster for Native Americans.

AS YOU READ

Use this diagram to take notes about the battles between Native Americans and settlers.

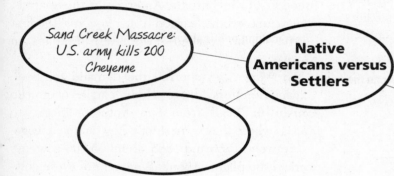

Sand Creek Massacre: U.S. army kills 200 Cheyenne

Native Americans versus Settlers

TERMS AND NAMES

Great Plains The grassland region of the United States

Treaty of Fort Laramie 1868 treaty in which the Sioux agreed to live on a reservation

Sitting Bull Leader of Hunkpapa Sioux

George A. Custer Colonel in U.S. Cavalry

assimilation Name of plan to make Native Americans part of white culture

Dawes Act Law that broke up Native American reservations

Battle of Wounded Knee U.S. massacre of Sioux at Wounded Knee Creek, South Dakota

longhorn Sturdy cattle accustomed to dry grasslands

Chisholm Trail Major cattle route from San Antonio, Texas, through Oklahoma to Kansas

long drive Three-month long overland transport of cattle

The Culture of the Plains Indians; Settlers Push Westward (pages 408–410)

How did the Plains Indians live?

Native Americans lived on the **Great Plains,** the grasslands in the west-central portion of the United States. They followed a way of life that centered on the horse and buffalo. The horse allowed them to hunt more easily and to travel farther. The buffalo provided food, clothing, shelter, and other important items.

The Indians of the Great Plains lived in small extended family groups. The men hunted for food. The women helped butcher the *game* and prepare the buffalo hides that the men brought back to

camp. Children learned the skills they would need as adults.

After the Civil War, thousands of white settlers moved to the Great Plains. Some travelled there searching for gold. Others wanted to own land. They argued that because Native Americans had not settled down to "improve" the land, white settlers could *stake* their claim.

1. **What were the responsibilities of the different members of Indian families?**

_____

_____

_____

_____

The Government Restricts Native Americans; Bloody Battles Continue (pages 410–412)

Why did Indians and settlers fight each other?

Along the Great Plains, Native Americans and white settlers often clashed—mainly over land and resources. One of the more tragic clashes occurred in 1864. The army was on the side of the settlers. The Cheyenne, living in an area of the Colorado Territory known as Sand Creek, had attacked settlers. In response, the army attacked and killed about 200 Cheyenne in an incident known as the Sand Creek Massacre.

In the **Treaty of Fort Laramie,** most Sioux agreed to live on a *reservation.* But **Sitting Bull,** an important Sioux leader, never signed the treaty. In 1876, he defeated army troops led by **George A. Custer,** at the Little Bighorn River. The Sioux won decisively, killing Custer and all his soldiers. The army recovered, however. Within months it defeated the Sioux.

2. What were the reasons for the clashes between the U.S. government and the Sioux?

_____

_____

The Government Supports Assimilation; The Battle of Wounded Knee (pages 412–414)

Why did assimilation fail?

To deal with the Native American problem, the U.S. government adopted a plan of **assimilation.** In this plan, Native Americans would give up their beliefs and culture and become part of white culture.

To push assimilation, Congress passed the **Dawes Act** in 1887. The act broke up reservations and gave some of the land to each Native American family for farming. The plan, however, failed. Native Americans were cheated out of the best land. As a result, they had little success farming. Worse yet, by 1900, whites had killed nearly all the buffalo. Native Americans depended on the buffalo for their food, clothing, and shelter.

The Sioux adopted a *ritual* called the Ghost Dance which they hoped would bring the buffalo back. This made the Army nervous. In 1890 they rounded up a group of Sioux including Sitting Bull. When they tried to take the Sioux's weapons a fight broke out. Army troops killed 300 unarmed Sioux in the **Battle of Wounded Knee.**

3. What were two reasons why assimilation failed?

_____

Cattle Becomes Big Business; A Day in the Life of a Cowboy; The End of the Open Range (pages 414–417)

What caused the cattle business to grow?

Cattle ranching became a big business after the Civil War. Ranchers raised **longhorns,** a sturdy breed first brought to the Americas by the Spanish. American cowboys learned from *vaqueros,* the first cowboys who worked on Spanish ranches in Mexico.

Growing cities spurred the demand for beef. Cattle ranchers drove their cattle over the **Chisholm Trail** from San Antonio, Texas, to Kansas where they were shipped by rail to Chicago.

Between 1866 and 1885, about 55,000 cowboys worked the plains. About 12 percent of these cowboys were Mexican. About 25 percent were African American.

A cowboy's life was difficult. Cowboys worked between 10 and 14 hours a day in all kinds of weather. They worked hard all spring and summer. In the winter, they lived off their savings or went from ranch to ranch and looked for odd jobs. In the spring, cowboys rounded up their cattle and headed them out on the **long drive.** This was the journey from the plains to the shipping yards in Abilene, Kansas. The days of the open range and cattle drive did not last long. Bad weather in the 1880s wiped out many ranchers. Others started using barbed wire to fence in their ranches.

4. What two factors helped the cattle business to grow?

_____

_____

CHAPTER 13 **Section 2** (pages 420–424)

Settling on the Great Plains

TERMS AND NAMES

Homestead Act Act that offered free land to western settlers

exodusters African-American settlers in the West

soddy A frontier home, usually dug into a hill or made from sod

Morrill Act Act that helped establish agricultural colleges

bonanza farm Large, single-crop farms

BEFORE YOU READ

In the last section you read about how Native Americans and white settlers clashed over the land in the American West, and the growth of the cattle industry and the life of cowboys.

In this section, you will read about life on the Great Plains for the men and women who settled there in search of land and prosperity.

AS YOU READ

Use this time line to make notes of the important events that shaped the settling of the Great Plains.

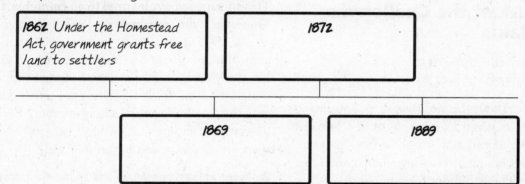

1862 Under the Homestead Act, government grants free land to settlers

1872

1869

1889

Settlers Move Westward to Farm (pages 420–422)

How did the U.S. get people to go west?

More and more people migrated to the Great Plains with the building of the *transcontinental* railroads. From 1850 to 1871, the federal government gave huge tracts of land to companies ready to lay tracks through the West.

In 1867, the Central Pacific company began laying tracks east from Sacramento, California. Another railroad company, the Union Pacific, began laying tracks west from Omaha, Nebraska. Much of the work was done by Irish and Chinese immigrants. African Americans and Mexican Americans

also did the back-breaking work. In 1869, the two routes met at Promontory, Utah. America's first transcontinental railroad was finished.

The railroad companies sold some of their land at low prices to settlers willing to farm it. Some companies even recruited people from Europe to settle on the land.

In addition, a growing number of people were responding to the **Homestead Act** of 1862. Under this law, the government offered 160 acres of free land to anyone who would farm it for five years. By 1900, the Great Plains was filled with more than 400,000 homesteaders, or settlers on this free land.

Several thousand settlers were **exodusters**— African Americans who moved from the post-Reconstruction South to Kansas.

But the law did not always work as the government had planned. Only about 10 percent of the land was settled by the families for whom it was intended. Cattlemen and miners claimed much of the rest.

The government continued to pass other laws to encourage people to settle the West. In 1889, Oklahoma offered a major land giveaway. This led thousands of settlers to claim 2 million acres in less than 24 hours.

As more and more settlers gobbled up land in the West, the government took action to preserve some wilderness. In 1872, the government set aside land in Wyoming to create Yellowstone National Park. Millions of acres more were set aside later.

1. How did the government and the railroads encourage settlement of the West?

_____

_____

Settlers Meet the Challenges of the Plains (pages 422–424)

What was life like for settlers of the West?

From 1850 to 1900, the number of people living west of the Mississippi River grew from 1 percent of the nation's population to almost 30 percent. These new settlers had to endure many hardships.

The Great Plains did not have many trees. As a result, people built what became known as **soddys**. These homes were dug into the side of hills or made from sod. A soddy was warm in winter and cool in summer. However, it offered little light or air.

Homesteaders were largely isolated from one another. They had to make nearly everything they needed. Women worked in the fields alongside men. They also took care of the children, ran the house, and did the cooking and laundry.

Farming the Great Plains was difficult work. But several inventions helped make the task easier. The steel plow helped break up the prairie's tough soil. A new reaper cut wheat even faster.

The government also helped in the effort to improve farming techniques. The **Morrill Act** of 1862 and 1890 helped establish agricultural colleges. The government also established experiment stations on the Great Plains. Researchers there developed new types of crops as well as new growing techniques.

To buy much of the new farming machinery, farmers often went into *debt*. When crop prices fell, farmers ended up losing money. As a result, they had trouble repaying their loans. To make more money, they often had to raise more crops. This in turn led to the growth of **bonanza farms**. These were huge single-crop farms.

By 1900, the average farmer had nearly 150 acres under *cultivation*. However, when a drought hit the Plains between 1885 and 1890, many bonanza farms folded. They could not compete with the smaller farmers, who were more flexible in the crops they grew. The high price of shipping their crops also added to farmers' debt.

2. Name at least one social and economic hardship settlers faced.

_____

_____

A frontier family stands outside its home on the plains of Nebraska in 1889.
Credit: Nebraska State Historical Society, The Solomon D. Butcher Collection

Skillbuilder

Use the photograph to answer the questions.

1. What type of home does the family appear to live in?

_____

2. How does this photograph reinforce the geographical description of the Great Plains?

_____

CHAPTER 13 Section 3 (pages 425–429)

Farmers and the Populist Movement

TERMS AND NAMES

Oliver Hudson Kelley Farmer who founded the Grange

Grange Organization that fought for farmers' rights

Farmers' Alliances Groups of farm organizations

Populism Political movement that sought advancement for farmers and laborers

bimetallism backing money with silver and gold

gold standard Backing dollars solely with gold

William McKinley 1896 Republican presidential nominee

William Jennings Bryan 1896 Populist/Democratic presidential nominee

BEFORE YOU READ

In the last section, you read about life for thousands of farmers trying to make a living on the Great Plains

In this section, you will read how these farmers organized and fought to improve their conditions.

AS YOU READ

Use this chart to take notes about the causes of the rise of the Populist Party and the effects the party had.

CAUSES	EFFECTS
farmers felt cheated	strong showing in the presidential election

Farmers Unite to Address Common Problems (pages 425–427)

How did farmers fight back?

Farmers faced serious problems after the Civil War. The prices they could sell their crops for kept going down. This was because the United States was withdrawing greenbacks—money printed for the Civil War—from circulation. The decline in prices also meant that farmers had to pay back their loans in money that was worth more than when they borrowed it. Farmers urged the government to increase the the money supply. But the government refused.

Meanwhile, farmers continued to pay high prices to transport grain. Often they paid as much

to ship their crops as they received for them. Many farmers were on the brink of ruin. The time, it seemed, had come for *reform.*

Many farmers joined together to push for reform. In 1867, a farmer named **Oliver Hudson Kelley** started an organization that became known as the **Grange**. Its original purpose was to provide a place for farm families to discuss social and educational issues. By the 1870s, however, Grange members spent most of their time and energy fighting the railroads.

The Grange gave rise to other organizations. They included the **Farmers' Alliances.** These organizations included teachers, preachers, and newspaper editors who sympathized with farmers.

Alliance members traveled throughout the Great Plains. They educated farmers about a variety of issues, including how to obtain lower interest rates and ways to protest the railroads.

1. What steps did farmers take to address their concerns?

_____

_____

The Rise and Fall of Populism
(pages 427–429)

What did the Populist movement hope to achieve?

Alliance leaders realized that to make far-reaching changes, they needed political power. So in 1892, they created the Populist Party, or People's Party. This party was the beginning of **Populism.** This was a movement to gain more political and economic power for common people.

The Populist Party pushed for reforms to help farmers. It also called for reforms to make government more democratic. These reforms included direct election of senators and a secret ballot to stop cheating in voting.

Most Americans thought the populists' beliefs too radical. However, the party appealed to many struggling farmers and laborers. In 1892, the Populist presidential candidate won more than a million votes. That was almost 10 percent of the total vote. In the West, Populist candidates won numerous local elections. While not as strong as the two major parties, the Populist Party had become a political force.

Then, in 1893, the nation faced an economic crisis called the Panic of 1893. The causes of the panic started in the 1880s. During that decade, many companies and individuals had borrowed too much money. But starting in 1893, many of these companies went *bankrupt* because they were not making enough money to pay back their loans. Many people lost their jobs.

The panic continued into 1895. Then political parties began to choose candidates for the 1896 presidential election. One important issue was whether the country's paper money should be backed with both gold and silver.

The central issue of the campaign was which metal would be the basis of the nation's monetary system. On one side were the "silverites" who favored **bimetallism,** a monetary system in which the government would give people either gold or silver in exchange for paper currency or checks. On the other side were the "gold bugs" who favored the **gold standard**—backing dollars solely with gold.

"Gold bugs" favored gold because using the gold standard would keep prices from rising. Silverites favored bimetallism because it would make more dollars available and therefore prices and wages would rise.

Republicans were "gold bugs." They elected **William McKinley** for president. The Democrats and the Populists both favored bimetallism. Both parties nominated **William Jennings Bryan.** At the Democratic convention, Bryan delivered an emotional speech, known as the "Cross of Gold" speech, in support of bimetallism.

But on election day McKinley won. McKinley's election brought an end to Populism. The movement left two powerful legacies: a message that poor people and less powerful groups in society could organize and have a political impact, and an agenda of reforms many of which would be enacted in the 20th century.

2. Which groups did the Populists appeal to most?

_____

_____

Name _____ Date _____

bankrupt A condition in which a person or company cannot pay back debts

cultivate To prepare land for raising crops

debt The condition of owing something, such as money

game A wild animal hunted for food or sport

reform A change for the better; a correction of abuses

reservation An area of land set aside for Native Americans

ritual A ceremonial act

stake To claim as one's own

transcontinental Spanning or crossing a continent

AFTER YOU READ

Terms and Names

A. Write the letter of the term or name that matches the description.

a. exodusters
b. Populism
c. Homestead Act
d. longhorn
e. soddy
f. gold standard

_____ **1.** A law that offered 160 acres of land free to anyone who would live on and farm it for five years

_____ **2.** The name given to African Americans who moved from the Reconstruction South to the Great Plains in the mid-1800s

_____ **3.** A type of cattle brought to the Americas by the Spanish

_____ **4.** A type of home made from prairie turf

_____ **5.** The political movement that sought advancement for farmers and laborers during the late 1800s

B. Write the name or term that best completes each sentence.

Populism
Grange
assimilation
bonanza farms
homesteaders
long drive

1. Under the policy of _____, Native Americans would give up their beliefs and culture and become part of white culture.

2. The _____ consisted of rounding up the cattle and leading them to the shipping yards in Abilene, Kansas.

3. Forced to grow more and more crops, many settlers built _____, huge, single-crop farms.

4. The _____ began as a social organization for farmers, but soon began to concentrate on battling the railroads.

5. _____, also known as the movement of the people, gave rise to the Populist Party.

AFTER YOU READ (cont.) *CHAPTER 13* Changes on the Western Frontier

Main Ideas

1. How effective was the Dawes Act in helping Native Americans become part of white culture?

_____

_____

2. What led to cattle becoming big business by the late 1800s?

_____

_____

3. How did the government support settlement of the West?

_____

_____

4. What economic problems confronted American farmers in the 1890s?

_____

_____

5. How would bimetallism help the economy, according to its supporters?

_____

_____

Thinking Critically

Answer the following questions on a separate sheet of paper.

1. Do you think that trying to assimilate Native Americans into white society was a good idea? Why or why not?

2. Explain why by the late 1800s there seemed to be two Americas—East and West.

CHAPTER 14 Section 1 (pages 436–439)

The Expansion of Industry

TERMS AND NAMES

Edwin L. Drake First person to use steam engine to drill for oil

Bessemer process Technique used to make steel from iron

Thomas Alva Edison Inventor of the light bulb

Christopher Sholes Inventor of the typewriter

Alexander Graham Bell Inventor of the telephone

BEFORE YOU READ

In the last section, you read about the growth of the Populist movement.

In this section, you will read how Americans used their natural resources and technological breakthroughs to begin building an industrialized society.

AS YOU READ

Use this diagram to take notes on the technological breakthroughs during the late 1800s and their impact on society.

TECHNOLOGICAL BREAKTHROUGH	IMPACT
electrical power	revolutionized business and daily life

Natural Resources Fuel Industrialization (pages 436–438)

What were America's important natural resources?

In the years after the Civil War, advances in technology began to change the nation. There were three causes of these advances: a large supply of natural resources, an explosion of inventions, and a growing city population that wanted the new products.

One of the more important natural resources was oil. In 1840 a Canadian *geologist* discovered that *kerosene* could be used to light lamps. Kerosene was produced from oil. This increased Americans' demand for oil.

In 1859, **Edwin L. Drake** used a steam engine to drill for oil. This technological breakthrough

helped start an oil boom. Oil-refining industries started in Cleveland and Pittsburgh. There, workers turned oil into kerosene.

Oil produced yet another product—gasoline. At first, gasoline was thrown away. However, when the automobile became popular, gasoline was in great demand.

In addition to oil, Americans discovered that their nation was rich in coal and iron. In 1887, explorers found large amounts of iron in Minnesota. At the same time, coal production increased from 33 million tons in 1870 to more than 250 million tons in 1900.

Iron is a strong metal. However, it is heavy and tends to break and rust. Researchers eventually removed the element carbon from iron. This produced a lighter, more flexible metal that does not rust. It became known as steel. The **Bessemer**

process, named after British manufacturer Henry Bessemer, provided a useful way to turn iron into steel.

Americans quickly found many uses for steel. The railroads, with their thousands of miles of track, bought large amounts of the new metal. Steel was also used to improve farm tools such as the plow and reaper. It also was used to make cans for *preserving* food. Engineers used steel to build bridges. One of the most remarkable bridges was the Brooklyn Bridge. It connected New York City and Brooklyn. Steel also was used to build skyscrapers, such as the Home Insurance Building in Chicago.

1. **Name two ways Americans used steel.**

_____

_____

Inventions Promote Change
(pages 438–439)

How did the new inventions change Americans' way of life?

Beginning in the late 1800s, inventors produced items that changed the way people lived and worked. In 1876, **Thomas Alva Edison** established the world's first research laboratory in Menlo Park, New Jersey. He used the lab to develop new inventions. Edison perfected an early light bulb there. He then worked to establish power plants to generate electricity.

Another inventor, George Westinghouse, developed ways to make electricity safer and less expensive.

The use of electricity changed America. By 1890, electricity ran machines such as fans and printing presses. Electricity soon became available in homes. This led to the invention of many appliances. Cities built electric streetcars. They made travel cheaper and easier.

In 1867, **Christopher Sholes** invented the typewriter. This led to dramatic changes in the workplace. Almost ten years later, in 1876, **Alexander Graham Bell** and Thomas Watson invented the telephone.

The wave of inventions during the late 1800s helped change Americans' daily life. More women began to work in offices. By 1910, women made up about 40 percent of the nation's office work force. In addition, work that had been done at home—such as sewing clothes—was now done in factories. Unfortunately, many factory employees worked long hours in unhealthy conditions.

Inventions had several positive effects. Machines allowed employees to work faster. This led to a shorter work week. As a result, people had more *leisure* time. In addition, citizens enjoyed new products such as phonographs, bicycles, and cameras.

2. **Name two ways in which electricity changed people's life.**

_____

_____

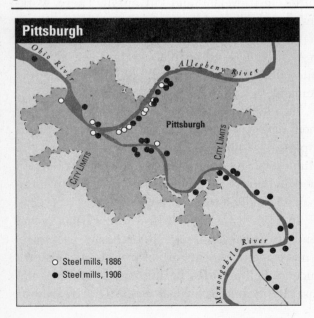

Pittsburgh

Ohio River

Allegheny River

Pittsburgh

CITY LIMITS

CITY LIMITS

Monongahela River

○ Steel mills, 1886
● Steel mills, 1906

Geography Skillbuilder
Use the map to answer the questions.

1. **Along what feature are all the mills located?**

_____

2. **What does this map say about the steel industry during the late 1800s and early 1900s?**

_____

The Age of the Railroads

BEFORE YOU READ

In the last section you read about how Americans used their natural resources and numerous inventions to begin transforming society.

In this section you will read about the growth of the nation's railroad industry and its effect on the nation.

TERMS AND NAMES

transcontinental railroad A railroad that crosses the entire country

George M. Pullman Inventor of the sleeping car

Crédit Mobilier Name of company involved in stealing of railroad money

Munn v. Illinois Court case that gave government right to regulate private industry

Interstate Commerce Act Law granting Congress authority to regulate railroad activities

AS YOU READ

Use this diagram to take notes on the effects of the rapid growth of railroads.

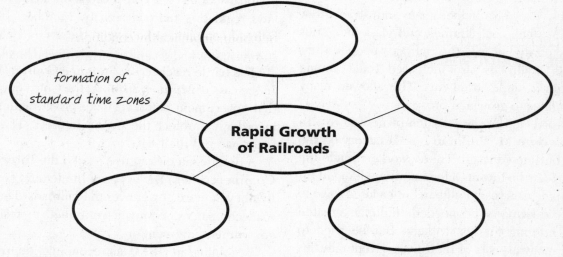

Railroads Span Time and Space
(pages 442–443)

How did the railroads change the way Americans told time?

Before and after the Civil War, railroads were built to span the entire United States. In 1869, the nation completed work on its first **transcontinental railroad**—a railroad that crossed the entire continent. In the years that followed, railroad tracks spread throughout the country. By 1890, more than 200,000 miles of rail lines zigzagged across the United States.

Railroads made long-distance travel a possibility for many Americans. However, building and running the railroads was difficult and dangerous work. Those who did most of the work were Chinese and Irish immigrants and desperate out-of-work Civil War veterans. Accidents and diseases affected thousands of railroad builders each year. By 1888, more than 2,000 workers had died. Another 20,000 workers had been injured.

Railroads eventually linked the many different regions of the United States. However, railroad schedules proved hard to keep. This was because each community set its own times—based mainly on the movement of the sun. The time in Boston, for example, was almost 12 minutes later than the time in New York.

To fix this problem, officials devised a plan in 1870 to divide the earth into 24 time zones, one for each hour of the day. Under this plan, the United States would contain four time zones: Eastern, Central, Mountain, and Pacific. Everyone living in a particular zone would follow the same time. The railroad companies supported this plan. Many communities also supported it.

1. How did times zones first come about?

_____

_____

Opportunities and Opportunists
(pages 443–444)

How did the growth of the railroads affect the nation?

Railroads made it easier for people to travel long distances. They also helped many industries grow. The iron, steel, coal, lumber, and glass industries all grew partly because the railroads needed their products. Railroads also increased trade among cities, towns, and settlements. This allowed many communities to grow and prosper.

Railroads led to the creation of new towns. In 1880, **George M. Pullman** built a factory on the prairie outside Chicago. There, workers made the sleeping cars he invented for trains. As demand for his sleeping cars rose, Pullman built a large town to house the workers he needed. Pullman created quality housing for his workers. But he tried to control many aspects of their lives. Eventually, his workers rebelled.

The railroad industry offered people the chance to become rich. The industry attracted many *corrupt* individuals. One of the most well-known cases of corruption was the Crédit Mobilier scandal. In 1868, some officers of the Union Pacific railroad formed a construction company called **Crédit Mobilier.** They gave their company contracts to lay railroad track at two to three times the actual cost. They kept all profits. To prevent the government from interfering, they paid off members of Congress. Eventually, authorities uncovered the *scheme.*

2. What was one positive and negative effect of the growth of railroads?

_____

_____

The Grange and the Railroads
(pages 444–446)

Why did the farmers fight the railroads?

One group angered by corruption in the railroad industry were farmers. Farmers were upset for a number of reasons. First, they claimed that railroads sold government land grants to businesses rather than to families. They also accused the railroad industry of setting high shipping prices to keep farmers in debt.

In response to these abuses, the Grangers took political action. They convinced some states to pass laws regulating railroad activity. Members of the railroad companies challenged the states' rights to regulate them.

The battle reached the Supreme Court in 1877. In the case of ***Munn v. Illinois,*** the Court declared that government could regulate private industries in order to protect the public interest. The railroads had lost their fight.

A decade later, Congress passed the **Interstate Commerce Act.** The act gave the federal government even more power over the railroads. The railroad companies, however, continued to resist all government intervention.

Beginning in 1893, an economic depression struck the country. It affected numerous institutions—including the railroads. Many railroad companies failed. As a result, they were taken over by financial firms. By 1900, seven companies owned most of the nation's railways.

3. Give two reasons why farmers were upset with the railroad companies.

_____

_____

Big Business and Labor

BEFORE YOU READ

In the last section, you read about the growth of the railroad industry in the United States.

In this section you will read about the growth and power of big business in America and how workers united to improve conditions in the nation's growing industries.

AS YOU READ

Use the diagram below to take notes on the growth of big business and labor.

PERSON	BUSINESS OR LABOR ACHIEVEMENT
Carnegie	vertical and horizontal integration

Carnegie's Innovations; Social Darwinism and Business
(pages 447–449)

How did Carnegie take control of the steel industry?

Andrew Carnegie attempted to control the entire steel industry. Through **vertical integration** he bought companies that supplied his *raw materials* such as iron and coal, and railroads needed to transport the steel. He used **horizontal integration** by buying out or *merging* with other steel companies.

Carnegie's success helped popularize the theory of **Social Darwinism**. This theory, based on the ideas of biologist Charles Darwin, said that "*natural selection*" enabled the best-suited people to survive and succeed. Social Darwinism supported the ideas of competition, hard work, and responsibility.

1. **Describe two ways in which Carnegie tried to control the steel industry.**

_____

_____

Fewer Control More; Labor Unions Emerge (pages 449–451)

How did entrepreneurs try to control competition?

Most entrepreneurs tried to control competition. Their goal was to form a *monopoly* by buying out competitors or driving them out of business. **John D. Rockefeller** used the Standard Oil trust to almost completely control the oil industry. Rockefeller's ruthless business practices earned him huge profits, but caused people to label him a *robber baron*. In 1890, the **Sherman Antitrust Act** made it illegal to form a trust, but many companies were able to avoid prosecution under the law. The business boom in the United States bypassed the South which continued to suffer economic stagnation.

Workers responded to business consolidation by forming labor unions. Many workers worked long hours under dangerous conditions for low wages. Women, children, and workers in *sweatshops* worked under especially harsh conditions. The National Labor Union (NLU) was an early labor union that persuaded Congress to legalize an eight-hour day for government workers in 1868. The NLU excluded African-American workers who formed the Colored National Labor Union (CNLU). The Knights of Labor also enjoyed success but declined after the failure of a series of strikes.

2. Why did entrepreneurs form trusts?

_____

_____

Union Movements Diverge; Strikes Turn Violent

(pages 451–455)

What were the two major types of unions?

Two major types of unions made great gains. One was craft unions. **Samuel Gompers** formed the **American Federation of Labor (AFL)** in 1886. Gompers used strikes and *collective bargaining*—negotiations between labor and management to

win higher wages and shorter workweeks. **Eugene V. Debs** believed in industrial unionism—a union of all workers, both skilled and unskilled in a single industry. He formed the American Railway Union (ARU). Debs and other workers turned to socialism. In 1905, a union of radicals and socialists was formed called the **Industrial Workers of the World (IWW)** or the Wobblies. In the West, Japanese and Mexican farm workers formed a union to improve conditions.

Unions used strikes to improve conditions. In 1877, workers for the Baltimore and Ohio railroad went out on strike. The strike was broken up when the railroad president persuaded President Rutherford B. Hayes to bring in federal troops to end the strike.

Later strikes turned violent. The Haymarket Affair took place in 1886. A bomb exploded at a demonstration in Chicago's Haymarket Square in support of striking workers. Several people were killed. Labor leaders were charged with inciting a riot and four were hanged although no one knows who actually set off the bomb. In 1892, steel workers and Pinkerton Guards fought a battle at Homestead, Pennsylvania, near Pittsburgh, that left dead on both sides. Two years later a strike against the Pullman Company led by Eugene Debs and his American Railway Union turned violent when federal troops were called out to break the strike.

Mary Harris Jones, known as Mother Jones, gained fame as an organizer for the United Mine Workers. The unions' struggle for better conditions was hurt by government intervening on the side of management. Courts used the Sherman Antitrust Act against the workers. Despite the pressures of government action, unions continued to grow.

3. What were the two types of unions?

_____

_____

Glossary

collective bargaining Negotiations between labor and management

corrupt Immoral or dishonest

geologist Someone who studies the origin, history, and structure of the earth

kerosene A thin oil used as a fuel

leisure Freedom from duties or responsibilities

merge To join together

monopoly Complete control over an industry

preserve To protect from injury

raw materials Unprocessed natural products

robber baron Industrial leader of great wealth

scheme A plan, usually secret

sweatshop A small factory with poor working conditions

AFTER YOU READ

Terms and Names

A. If the statement is true, write "true" on the line. If it is false, change the underlined word or words to make it true.

1. _____ The <u>Bessemer process</u> was a useful way of turning iron into steel.

2. _____ <u>Edwin L. Drake</u> invented the telephone.

3. _____ The <u>Interstate Commerce Act</u> increased the federal government's power over the railroads.

4. _____ A business firm that controls all the competition in an industry holds a <u>trust</u> over the industry.

5. _____ In the late 1800s some unions looked to <u>collective bargaining</u> to reach agreements between workers and employers.

B. Write the letter of the name or term that matches the description.

a. Andrew Carnegie
b. Knights of Labor
c. *Munn* v. *Illinois*
d. Industrial Workers of the World
e. Thomas Alva Edison
f. Mary Harris Jones

_____ **1.** Developed the light bulb and a research laboratory in Menlo Park, New Jersey

_____ **2.** The court ruling that won states the right to regulate the railroads

_____ **3.** Millionaire businessman who gained control of the steel industry

_____ **4.** Union organized by a group of radical union members and socialists.

_____ **5.** Activist who helped lead the United Mine Workers of America

AFTER YOU READ (continued)   CHAPTER 14   A New Industrial Age

Main Ideas

1. In what ways did natural resources and inventions help change the nation in the years after the Civil War?

_____

_____

2. How did the growth of the railroad industry affect the development of other industries?

_____

_____

3. Who benefited more from the ideas of Social Darwinism, business leaders or workers?

_____

_____

4. How successful was the Sherman Anti-Trust Act in accomplishing its goals?

_____

_____

5. What role did the government take in the conflict between unions and management?

_____

_____

Think Critically

Answer the following questions on a separate sheet of paper.

1. Which invention do you consider more important, the telephone or electricity? Explain.

2. Do you think workers today can benefit from unions? Why or why not?

CHAPTER 15 **Section 1** (pages 460–465)

The New Immigrants

TERMS AND NAMES

Ellis Island Inspection station for immigrants arriving on the East Coast

Angel Island Inspection station for immigrants arriving on the West Coast

melting pot A mixture of different cultures living together

nativism Overt favoritism toward native-born Americans

Chinese Exclusion Act Act that limited Chinese immigration

Gentlemen's Agreement Agreement that limited Japanese emigration to U.S.

BEFORE YOU READ

In the last section, you read about the nation's labor union movement.

In this section, you will read how millions of immigrants entered the United States, where they faced culture shock, prejudice, and opportunity.

AS YOU READ

Use this diagram to take notes on the anti-immigration measures that the United States took.

MEASURE	DESCRIPTION
Chinese Exclusion Act	
Gentlemen's Agreement	

Through the "Golden Door"
(pages 460–462)

Where did the immigrants come from?

Between 1870 and 1920, about 20 million Europeans *immigrated* to the United States. Many of them came from eastern and southern Europe.

Some immigrants came to escape religious *persecution*. Many others were poor and looking to improve their economic situation. Still others came to experience greater freedom in the United States. Most European immigrants arrived on the East Coast.

A smaller number of immigrants came from Asia. They arrived on the West Coast. About 200,000 Chinese immigrants came between 1851 to 1883. Many Chinese immigrants helped build the nation's first transcontinental railroad. When the United States *annexed* Hawaii in 1898, several thousand Japanese immigrants came to the United States.

From 1880 to 1920, about 260,000 immigrants arrived from various islands in the Caribbean Sea. They came from Jamaica, Cuba, Puerto Rico, and other islands. Many left their homelands because jobs were *scarce*.

Many Mexicans came to the United States as well. Some became U.S. citizens when the nation acquired Mexican territory in 1848 as a result of the Mexican War. About a million Mexicans arrived between 1910 to 1930 to escape *turmoil* in their country.

1. Name two regions of the world where immigrants to the U.S. came from.

_____

_____

Life in the New Land (pages 462–464)

How did immigrants cope in America?

Many immigrants traveled to the United States by steamship. On board the ship they shared a cramped, unsanitary space. Under these harsh conditions, disease spread quickly. As a result, some immigrants died before they reached America.

Most European immigrants to the United States arrived in New York. There, they had to pass through an immigration station located on **Ellis Island** in New York Harbor. Officials at the station decided whether the immigrants could enter the country or had to return. Any immigrant with serious health problems or a *contagious* disease was sent home. Inspectors also made sure that immigrants met the legal requirements for entering the United States.

Asian immigrants arriving on the West Coast went through **Angel Island** in San Francisco. The inspection process on Angel Island was more difficult than on Ellis Island.

Getting along in a new country with a different language and culture was a great challenge for new immigrants. Many immigrants settled in communities with other immigrants from the same country. This made them feel more at home. They also formed organizations to help each other.

2. Name two ways immigrants dealt with adjusting to life in the United States.

_____

_____

Immigration Restrictions
(pages 464–465)

How did some Americans react to immigration?

By the turn of the century, some observers called America a **melting pot.** This term referred to the fact that many different cultures and races had blended in the United States.

However, this was not always the case. Many new immigrants refused to give up their culture to become part of American society.

Some Americans also preferred not to live in a melting pot. They did not like the idea of so many immigrants living in their country. The arrival of so many immigrants led to the growth of **nativism.** Nativism is an obvious preference for native-born Americans. Nativism gave rise to anti-immigrant groups. It also led to a demand for immigration restrictions.

On the West Coast, *prejudice* against Asians was first directed at the Chinese. During the depression of the 1870s, many Chinese immigrants agreed to work for low wages. Many American workers feared they would lose their jobs to the Chinese. As a result, labor groups pressured politicians to restrict Asian immigration. In 1882, Congress passed the **Chinese Exclusion Act.** This law banned all but a few Chinese immigrants. The ban was not lifted until 1943.

Americans showed prejudice against Japanese immigrants as well. In San Francisco, the local school board put all Chinese, Japanese, and Korean children in special Asian schools. This led to anti-American riots in Japan. President Theodore Roosevelt persuaded San Francisco officials to stop their separation policy. In exchange, Japan agreed to limit *emigration* to the United States under the **Gentlemen's Agreement** of 1907–1908.

3. Give two examples of anti-immigration measures in the U.S.

_____

_____

Name _____   Date _____

The Challenges of Urbanization

BEFORE YOU READ

In the last section, you read about the arrival of millions of immigrants to America's shores.

In this section, you will read how the arrival of so many immigrants caused cities' populations to swell—and their problems to increase.

AS YOU READ

Use this diagram to take notes on the problems that residents faced in America's rapidly growing cities.

TERMS AND NAMES

urbanization The growth of cities

Americanization movement Program to teach American culture to immigrants

tenement Multifamily urban dwellings

mass transit Transportation system designed to move large numbers of people along fixed routes

Social Gospel movement Movement that urged people to help the poor

settlement house Community center that addressed problems in slum neighborhoods

Jane Addams Social reformer who helped the poor

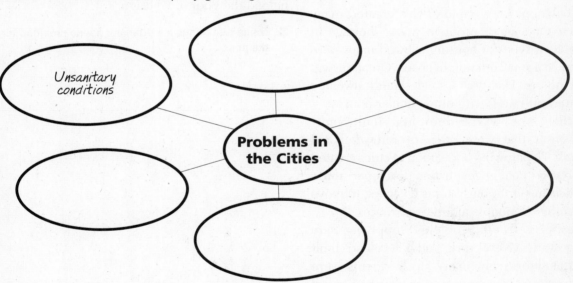

Unsanitary conditions

Problems in the Cities

Urban Opportunities (pages 468–469)

Why did people move to the cities?

Many of the nation's new immigrants settled in the cities in the early 1900s. They came there to find jobs in the cities' growing factories and businesses. Immigrants settled mainly in cities in the Northeast and Midwest. The result was rapid **urbanization,** or growth of cities, in those regions.

By 1910, immigrants made up more than half of the populations of 18 major American cities. Many immigrants settled in neighborhoods with others from the same country or even from the same village.

Newcomers to the United States learned about their new country through an education program known as the **Americanization movement.** Under this program, schools taught immigrants English, and American history and government. These subjects helped immigrants become citizens.

Immigrants were not the only people who settled in the cities around the turn of the century. On the nation's farms, new machines replaced workers. As a result, many workers in the rural areas lost their jobs. Unemployed farm workers soon moved to cities to find jobs.

Many of the Southern farmers who lost their jobs were African Americans. Between 1890 and 1910 about 200,000 African Americans moved from the South to cities in the North. They hoped to escape economic hardship and racial violence. However, many found prejudice and low wages in the North.

1. Name two groups that settled in the cities.

_____

_____

Urban Problems (pages 470–472)

What problems did city dwellers face?

City populations grew rapidly. This created many problems. One major problem was a shortage in housing. New types of housing allowed many people to live in a small amount of space. One type was the row house. This was a single-family dwelling that shared side walls with other similar houses.

Another type was **tenements,** multifamily urban houses that were often overcrowded and unsanitary. The growing population of cities created transportation challenges. Cities developed **mass transit**—transportation systems designed to move large number of people along fixed routes.

Cities also faced problems supplying safe drinking water. New York and Cleveland built public waterworks but many city residents were still left without convenient water and had to get their water from taps on the street. Sanitation was also a problem. People threw garbage out their windows. Sewage flowed in the streets. By 1900, many cities had built sewers and created sanitation departments.

Crime and fire were also ongoing problems. Overcrowded and poorly built tenements and lack of water made fire especially dangerous.

2. Name two problems that city residents faced.

_____

_____

Reformers Mobilize (page 472)

How did reformers help the poor?

A number of social reformers worked to improve life in the cities. One early reform program was the **Social Gospel movement.** Leaders of this movement preached that people reached *salvation* by helping the poor. Many reformers responded to the movement's call. They established **settlement houses.** These were community centers located in slum neighborhoods. Workers there provided help and friendship to immigrants and the poor.

Many of these houses were run by middle-class, college-educated women. The settlement houses also offered schooling, nursing, and other kinds of help to those in need.

One of the more well-known social reformers of this time was **Jane Addams**. She helped establish Hull House. This was a settlement house that helped the poor of Chicago.

3. Name two things a settlement house provided for the poor.

_____

_____

CHAPTER 15 Section 3 (pages 473–477)

Politics in the Gilded Age

BEFORE YOU READ

In the last section, you read about the problems that residents faced in America's growing cities.

In this section, you will read about the people and organizations that controlled the nation's major cities and how reformers tried to end corruption.

AS YOU READ

Use this diagram to take notes on the achievements of these presidents regarding patronage and tariffs.

PRESIDENT	ACHIEVEMENTS
Chester Arthur	Pendleton Act—reformed civil service
Grover Cleveland	
Benjamin Harrison	

TERMS AND NAMES

political machine A group that controlled a political party

graft Illegal use of political influence for personal gain

Boss Tweed Head of New York City's powerful Democratic political machine

patronage The giving of government jobs to people who had helped a candidate get elected

civil service Government administration

Rutherford B. Hayes 19th president of the United States

James A. Garfield 20th president of the United States

Chester A. Arthur 21st president of the United States

Pendleton Civil Service Act That implemented merit system in civil service hiring

Grover Cleveland 22nd and 24th president of the United States

Benjamin Harrison 23rd president of the United States

The Emergence of Political Machines (pages 473–474)

How did political machines control the cities?

During the late 1800s, many cities were run by a **political machine.** This was an organized group, headed by a city boss, that controlled the activities of a political party in a city. The machine offered services to voters and businesses in exchange for political or financial support.

The boss controlled city government, as well as jobs in the police, fire, and sanitation departments.

Bosses also controlled city agencies that granted licenses to businesses, and funded construction projects. By controlling the cities' finances, and by solving problems for voters, bosses won loyalty and influence. Furthermore, many bosses were immigrants who had worked their way up in politics. They could speak to the immigrants in their own language, helping them to find jobs and housing. In return, the immigrants pledged their votes.

1. Name two ways in which political machines held power.

_____

_____

Municipal Graft and Scandal
(pages 475)

How were political bosses corrupt?

Political machines provided city dwellers with vital services. But as they gained power, many bosses became corrupt. They became rich through **graft,** or the illegal use of political influence for personal gain. To win elections, some bosses filled the list of *eligible* voters with the names of dogs, children, and people who had died. They then used those names to cast votes for themselves.

Another illegal practice was the *kickback*. Workers on city construction projects would charge a higher price for their service and then "kick back" part of the fee to the bosses, who were also taking *bribes* from businesses in return for allowing illegal or unsafe activities.

One of the most powerful political bosses was William Marcy Tweed, known as **Boss Tweed.** He became the head of Tammany Hall, New York City's most powerful Democratic political machine. The Tweed Ring was a group of corrupt politicians led by Boss Tweed.

Thomas Nast, a political cartoonist, made fun of Tweed in newspapers. Eventually, the public grew outraged by Tweed's corrupt practices. Authorities broke up the Tweed Ring in 1871. Tweed and many of his followers were sentenced to prison.

2. Describe two forms of corruption practiced by political bosses.

Civil Service Replaces Patronage
(pages 476–477)

How was civil service reformed?

For many decades, presidents had complained about the problem of **patronage.** This is the giving of government jobs to people of the same party who had helped a candidate get elected. As a result, many unqualified and corrupt workers were hired.

Reformers wanted to end the patronage system. They called for a merit system, in which jobs in **civil service**—government administration—would go to the most qualified people, regardless of their political views.

President **Rutherford B. Hayes** attempted to reform civil service, but when some members of the Republican party objected, Hayes decided not to run for reelection in 1880.

The party quickly divided over the issue of patronage hiring. The Stalwarts opposed changes in the patronage system. The reformers supported changing the system. The party eventually settled on an independent candidate, **James A. Garfield,** who won the presidential election but turned out to have ties to the reformers. Shortly after being elected he was assassinated by a Stalwart.

Garfield's vice-president, **Chester A. Arthur,** succeeded him. Despite being a Stalwart, Arthur turned reformer when he became president. He pushed through a civil service reform bill known as the **Pendleton Civil Service Act** of 1883. This act created a civil service commission to give government jobs based on merit, not politics. It helped reform the civil service.

However, the Pendleton Act had mixed results. More qualified workers did fill government positions. But because politicians had no jobs to offer, they had trouble seeking money from supporters. As a result, some politicians turned to wealthy leaders for financial support. This strengthened the ties between government and business.

3. Describe two effects of the Pendleton Act.

Business Buys Influence (page 477)

What happened to tariffs?

Political reformers in the late 1800s also addressed the issue of tariffs. A tariff is a tax placed on goods coming into or going out of a country. Most Americans believed that tariffs were necessary to protect U.S. industries from foreign competition. But tariffs did cause prices to rise.

For 12 years tariffs were a key issue in presidential elections. President **Grover Cleveland,** a Democrat, tried, but failed to reduce tariffs. In 1890, Republican President **Benjamin Harrison,** who was supported by big business, signed the McKinley Tariff Act into law, raising tariffs to their highest level ever. Cleveland defeated Harrison in 1892 but was unsuccessful in reducing tariffs.

4. Which two presidents raised tariffs?

Glossary   CHAPTER 15   Immigration and Urbanization

annexed Incorporated territory into an existing country

bribe An illegal payment given for a favor

contagious Spreading or tending to spread from one person to another

eligible Qualified to do something

emigration The act of leaving a country to settle in another

immigrate To enter and settle in a new country

kickback An illegal payment

persecution The act of oppressing or treating badly

prejudice A judgment formed without knowledge of the facts

salvation Deliverance from evil, the act of being saved

scarce Not often seen or found

turmoil Extreme unrest and commotion

unsanitary Dirty, unhealthy

AFTER YOU READ

Terms and Names

A. Write the letter of the name or term that best answers the question.

a. Social Gospel movement

b. Jane Addams

c. "Boss" Tweed

d. melting pot

e. political machine

f. patronage

_____ **1.** Which term refers to a mixture of different cultures living together?

_____ **2.** Which term refers to a reform program that urged Christians to help improve the lives of the poor?

_____ **3.** Who was the founder of Chicago's Hull House?

_____ **4.** Who was one of the most powerful political bosses and the head of a New York City political machine?

_____ **5.** Which term refers to the giving of government jobs to people who had helped a candidate get elected?

B. Write the name or term that best completes each sentence.

mass transit

Ellis Island

tenement

Angel Island

civil service

nativism

1. Immigrants arriving on the East Coast in the late 1800s gained entry into the United States through _____.

2. A _____ was a new type of multifamily urban dwelling.

3. A _____ job is one in government administration.

4. Many growing cities developed _____ systems to alleviate transportation challenges.

5. Favoritism toward native-born Americans is called _____.

AFTER YOU READ (cont.)   *CHAPTER 15* Immigrants and Urbanization

Main Ideas

1. What difficulties did immigrants face in the United States?

_____

_____

_____

2. What problems did rapid growth pose for cities?

_____

_____

_____

3. Why were immigrants such strong supporters of political machines?

_____

_____

_____

4. What problems did the patronage system create?

_____

_____

_____

5. Why did big business support high tariffs?

_____

_____

_____

Thinking Critically

Answer the following questions on a separate sheet of paper.

1. Do you think America should be a melting pot? Why or why not?

2. Consider modern cities. What problems that existed at the turn of the 20th century have been fixed? Which do you think still exist?

CHAPTER 16 Section 1 (pages 482–487)

Science and Urban Life

TERMS AND NAMES

Louis Sullivan Early leader of architecture

Daniel Burnham Chicago architect

Frederick Law Olmsted Developer of Central Park

Orville and Wilbur Wright Brothers who flew the first airplane

George Eastman Inventor of the camera

BEFORE YOU READ

In the last section, you read about the people and organizations that controlled the nation's major cities and how reformers tried to end corruption.

In this section, you will read about how technology improved life in the cities and dramatically changed the world of communications.

AS YOU READ

Use this diagram to take notes on the new technology that helped transform communications.

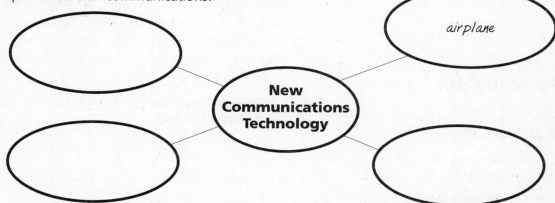

Technology and City Life
(pages 482–485)

How did cities cope with their growing populations?

By 1900, millions of Americans had settled in the nation's cities. To *accommodate* their growing populations, cities had to rely on technology. One example of this was the development of the skyscraper. Skyscrapers are tall buildings that allow people to live many floors above ground. As a result, skyscrapers save space.

Two factors allowed architects to design taller buildings: the invention of elevators, and the development of steel. One of the early skyscraper architects was **Louis Sullivan.** In 1890, he designed the

ten-story Wainwright building in St. Louis. In 1902, **Daniel Burnham** designed the Flatiron Building, a skyscraper at one of New York's busiest intersections.

Skyscrapers allowed cities to grow upward. Changes in transportation helped cities spread outward. In 1888, Richmond, Virginia, became the first American city to use electric-powered streetcars. Soon other cities installed electric streetcars. By the turn of the century, electric streetcars carried people from their homes in outlying neighborhoods to downtown stores, offices, and factories. People could now live in one part of a city and work in another.

To avoid overcrowding on streets, a few large cities moved their streetcars above street level. This created elevated or "el" trains. Other cities built subways by moving rail lines underground. Steel bridges joined sections of cities across rivers.

City planners also tried to make cities more livable by creating parks and *recreational* areas. Journalist and farmer **Frederick Law Olmsted** led the movement for planned city parks. In 1858, he and an architect drew up plans for Central Park in New York. The finished park included boating and tennis facilities, a zoo, and bicycle paths. All of these were placed in a natural setting.

In Chicago, Daniel Burnham designed a plan that would change a swampy region near Lake Michigan into a recreational area. His plan resulted in *elegant* parks and sandy beaches along Chicago's Lake Michigan shores.

1. Name two technological advances that helped make cities more livable.

_____

_____

New Technologies (pages 485–487)

How did technology transform communications?

Technology also improved the field of communications. There were several technological advances in printing. American mills began to produce huge amounts of cheap paper from wood *pulp*. A new kind of high-speed printing press was able to print on both sides of the paper, making magazines and newspapers more affordable. Two brothers, **Orville and Wilbur Wright,** built the first airplane. Their first successful flight occurred in 1903 at Kitty Hawk, North Carolina. It covered 120 feet and lasted 12 seconds.

People paid little attention to the Wright brothers' achievement. Many newspapers didn't even bother to print the story. Within two years, though, the Wright brothers were making distant flights of 24 miles. By 1908, however, the government took an interest in the new technology and by 1920, the United States had established the first transcontinental airmail service.

In 1888, **George Eastman** invented his Kodak camera. This provided millions of Americans with an easy way to take pictures. The camera also changed news reporting. Reporters could now photograph events as they occurred, and this helped create the field of photojournalism. When the Wright brothers made their first successful flight at Kitty Hawk, an amateur photographer caught the event on film.

2. Name two inventions that helped change the world of communications.

_____

_____

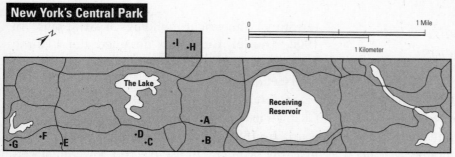

New York's Central Park

The Lake

Receiving Reservoir

0   1 Mile

0   1 Kilometer

A Cleopatra's Needle
B Metropolitan Museum of Art
C Alice in Wonderland Status
D Hans Christian Andersen Statue
E Children's Zoo
F Zoo
G General Sherman Statue
H Hayden Planetarium
I American Museum of Natural History

Skillbuilder

Use the map to answer the questions.

1. Roughly how long is Central Park? How wide? (Do not include the small section with locations H and I.)

_____

2. Categorize the types of attractions found in the park.

_____

_____

CHAPTER 16 Section 2 (pages 488–491)

Expanding Public Education

TERMS AND NAMES

Booker T. Washington Prominent African-American educator

Tuskegee Normal and Industrial Institute School headed by Booker T. Washington

W.E.B. Du Bois First African American to receive Ph.D from Harvard

Niagara Movement Insisted that blacks should seek a liberal arts education

BEFORE YOU READ

In the last section, you read about how technology transformed cities and the world of communications.

In this section, you will read about the growth of public education in America.

AS YOU READ

Use this diagram to take notes on the changes made to America's educational institutions during the late 19th and early 20th centuries.

INSTITUTION	CHANGES
elementary school	mandatory school attendance
high school	
college	

Expanding Public Education
(pages 488–489)

How did education change in the late 1800s?

During the late 1800s, reformers tried to improve public education. At that time, most children in the United States received little education. Many children did not even attend school. Those who did left after only four years.

Eventually, the situation began to improve. Between 1865 and 1895, 31 states passed laws requiring children from 8 to 14 years-old to attend school for at least three months out of every year. By 1900, almost three-quarters of American children between those ages attended school. Schools taught reading, writing, and arithmetic.

By the turn of the century, the number of schools had increased greatly. The number of kindergartens grew from 200 in 1880 to 3,000 in 1900. The number of high schools increased even more. In 1878 there were 800 high schools in the United States. By 1898, that number had grown to 5,500.

The high-school *curriculum* also expanded. It included courses in science, civics, home economics, history, and literature. Many people realized that the new industrial age needed people who had technical and managerial skills. As a result, high schools also included courses such as drafting and bookkeeping. This prepared students for industrial and office jobs.

The growth of public education mainly affected the nation's white communities. During the late

1880s, only 34 percent of African-American children attended elementary school. Fewer than one percent attended high school.

Unlike African Americans, immigrants attended schools in large numbers. Some immigrant parents hoped that school would "Americanize" their children.

Many adult immigrants also went to school. They attended night classes to learn American culture and English. Some employers offered daytime programs to Americanize their workers.

1. Provide two examples of how public education changed in the late 1800s.

_____

_____

_____

Expanding Higher Education
(pages 490–491)

What changes did colleges make?

At the turn of the century, only about 2 percent of Americans attended college. Most college students came from middle-class or wealthy families. Colleges prepared well-to-do young men for successful careers in business.

Between 1880 and 1900, more than 150 new colleges were founded in the United States. From 1880 to 1920, the number of students enrolled in college *quadrupled.*

During this time, colleges added more subjects. Before, many universities had taught only classical subjects such as Greek and Latin. Now they began teaching more modern subjects. In response to the needs of expanding big business, the research university emerged offering courses in modern languages, physical sciences, and the new disciplines of psychology and sociology. Professional schools in law and medicine were established. Many private colleges and universities began requiring entrance exams, while some state universities required only a high school diploma for admission.

Thousands of freed African Americans began attending college in greater numbers after the Civil War. With the help of the Freedmen's Bureau and other groups, blacks founded Howard, Atlanta, and Fisk Universities between 1865 and 1868. Still, blacks were excluded from many private institutions. Financially, it was difficult for private donors to support or educate enough black college graduates to meet the needs of their communities. In 1900, only about 4 percent of all African Americans were in attendance at colleges or professional schools.

Booker T. Washington founded the **Tuskegee Normal and Industrial Institute.** Washington believed that racism would end when blacks acquired useful labor skills and were valuable to society. Washington taught those skills at Tuskegee. **W. E. B. Du Bois** was a black educator who disagreed with Washington. Du Bois had been the first black to get a doctorate from Harvard. Du Bois founded the **Niagara Movement** which insisted that blacks should seek a liberal arts education.

2. Name two ways in which colleges changed during the late 1800s.

_____

_____

_____

CHAPTER 16 **Section 3** (pages 492–495)

Segregation and Discrimination

BEFORE YOU READ

In the last section, you read about improvements made to public education around the turn of the century.

In this section, you will read about how life for African Americans and other nonwhites remained one of hardship and discrimination.

AS YOU READ

Use this diagram to take notes on the discrimination against African Americans at the turn of the century.

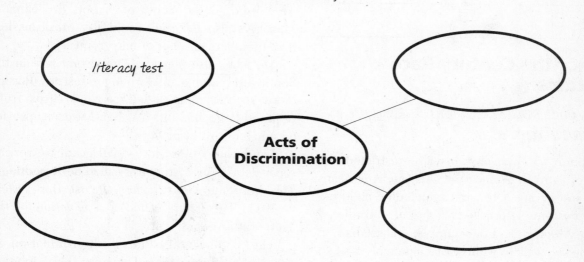

literacy test

Acts of Discrimination

African Americans Fight Legal Discrimination (pages 492–493)

How were African Americans kept from voting?

Ida B. Wells was a leader in the fight against discrimination. Wells crusaded against racial violence. After Reconstruction, African Americans were kept from voting in the South. By 1900, however, all Southern states had set up new voting restrictions meant to keep blacks from voting.

For example, some states required voters to be able to read. To determine this, officials gave each voter a literacy test. They often gave African

Americans more difficult tests. The officials giving the test could pass or fail people as they wished.

Another voting requirement was the **poll tax.** This was a tax that one had to be pay to enter a voting booth. African Americans and poor whites often did not have the money to pay the tax. So they were unable to vote.

Several Southern states wanted to make sure that whites who could not read or pay a poll tax still could vote. So they added a **grandfather clause** to their constitutions. This clause stated that any person could vote if their father or grandfather was qualified to vote before January 1, 1867. This date was important because before that time, freed slaves did not have the right to vote. Therefore, the grandfather clause did not allow African Americans to vote. Some Americans challenged the literacy test and poll tax laws. But the Supreme Court allowed the laws to stand.

Separating people on the basis of race became known as **segregation.** Racial segregation developed in such places as schools, hospitals, and transportation systems throughout the South. The Southern states also passed **Jim Crow laws.** These laws separated whites and blacks in private and public places.

Eventually a legal challenge to segregation reached the U.S. Supreme Court. However, in the case *Plessy v. Ferguson,* the Supreme Court ruled that separating the races in public places was legal.

1. Name two ways that Southern states restricted the voting rights of African Americans.

_____

_____

Turn-of-the-Century Race Relations (pages 493–494)

How did social customs restrict African Americans?

In addition to laws, customs also restricted the rights of African Americans. African Americans had to show respect to whites, including children. These customs often *belittled* and humiliated African Americans. For example, blacks had to yield the sidewalk to whites. Black men always had to remove their hats for whites.

African-American reformers debated over how to address racial discrimination. Booker T. Washington argued that blacks should not insist on full legal equality—which whites would never allow. Instead, he argued, blacks should concentrate on gaining economic power. Other African Americans, like W. E. B. Du Bois and Ida B. Wells, demanded legal equality right away.

African Americans who did not follow the customs could face severe punishment. Often, African Americans accused of failing to perform the customs were lynched—hanged without trial.

African Americans in the North also faced *discrimination.* They lived in segregated neighbor-

hoods. They faced discrimination in the workplace, some of which turned violent.

2. Name two ways blacks had to show respect to whites.

_____

_____

Discrimination in the West (pages 494–495)

What other groups faced discrimination in America?

African Americans were not the only ones who faced discrimination at the turn of the century. Mexican Americans faced similar treatment. In the 1880s and 1890s, railroad companies hired many Mexicans to build new rail lines in the Southwest. Railroad managers hired Mexicans because they were used to the Southwest's hot, dry climate. Managers also felt they could pay Mexicans less than members of other ethnic groups.

Mexicans also played an important role in the Southwest's mining and farming industries. Raising crops such as grapes, lettuce, and citrus fruits required large amounts of labor. Mexicans provided much of this farm work.

Landowners often forced Mexicans to work to repay debts. This system was called **debt peonage.** The Supreme Court ruled against this system in 1911. The Court called it a *violation* of the Thirteenth Amendment.

The Chinese also faced discrimination in America. Whites feared losing their jobs to Chinese workers. Chinese workers lived in segregated neighborhoods and their children attended segregated schools.

3. Name two groups that faced discrimination in the West.

_____

_____

CHAPTER 16 Section 4 (pages 498–503)

The Dawn of Mass Culture

TERMS AND NAMES

Joseph Pulitzer Owner of the *New York World* newspaper

William Randolph Hearst Owner of the New York *Morning Journal San Francisco Examiner*

Ashcan school A school of painting that featured urban life and working people with gritty realism

Mark Twain Pen name of the novelist and humorist Samuel Langhorne Clemens

rural free delivery (RFD) System that brought packages directly to homes

BEFORE YOU READ

In the last section, you read about how African Americans and other nonwhites continued to suffer racial discrimination at the turn of the century.

In this section, you will read about how Americans developed new forms of entertainment and ways to spend their money.

AS YOU READ

Use this diagram to take notes on how these people helped transform American culture.

PEOPLE	ACHIEVEMENTS
Pulitzer/Hearst	Created sensational newspapers
Marshall Field	
F.W. Woolworth	

American Leisure (pages 498–500)

How did Americans spend their free time?

The use of machines allowed workers at the turn of the century to do their jobs faster. This led to a shorter workweek. As a result, Americans had more leisure time.

Americans found new ways to use that time. Many city dwellers enjoyed trips to amusement parks. There, rides such as the roller coaster and the Ferris wheel thrilled people.

Another recreational activity that became popular at the turn of the century was bicycling. This activity entertained both men and women. Many Americans also grew fond of playing tennis.

Several kinds of snack foods also became popular. Americans turned to brand-name snacks such as a Hershey chocolate bar and drinks such as a Coca-Cola.

Those Americans who did not wish to exercise watched professional sports. Boxing became popular in the late 1800s. Baseball also became a well-loved spectator sport. The National League was formed in 1876 and the American League in 1901. African-American baseball players were not allowed to play in either league. As a result, they formed their own clubs—the Negro National League and the Negro American League.

1. Name two activities that were popular in the United States at the turn of the century.

_____

_____

The Spread of Mass Culture
(pages 500–502)

How did newspapers attract more readers?

Newspapers also entertained Americans. Many publishers changed their newspapers in order to attract more readers. They filled their pages with *sensational* headlines. They also devised promotional stunts. In 1889, for example, one newspaper introduced its story about the horrors of a flood in Johnstown, Pennsylvania with the headline "THE VALLEY OF DEATH."

Some publishers used other techniques. **Joseph Pulitzer,** the owner of the *New York World,* introduced a large Sunday edition. It included comics, sports coverage, and women's news. Pulitzer presented news in a sensational way to beat his main competitor, **William Randolph Hearst.** Hearst owned the New York *Morning Journal* and the San Francisco *Examiner.* Hearst tried to outdo Pulitzer by publishing *exaggerated* and even made-up stories. By 1898, both publishers were selling more than one million copies each day.

By 1900, at least one art gallery could be found in every large city. American artists like Thomas Eakins of Philadelphia used realism to portray life as it was really lived. Eakins was a leader of the **Ashcan School** which painted urban life and working people with gritty realism and no frills.

Light fiction such as "dime novels" was popular as more people read books. **Mark Twain,** the pen name of the humorist and novelist Samuel Langhorne Clemens, wrote realistic portrayals of American life that became popular. His novel *The Adventures of Huckleberry Finn* became a classic of American literature. The efforts of American libraries and art galleries to raise public taste were not always successful. Many Americans had no interest in high culture. African Americans and others were denied access to most white-controlled cultural institutions.

2. **Name two ways in which publishers tried to sell more newspapers.**

_____

_____

_____

New Ways to Sell Goods (pages 502–503)

How did Americans shop?

Americans at the turn of the century also began to change the way they shopped. As cities grew, shopping centers emerged. These structures made many kinds of stores available in one area.

Another new development was the department store. This type of store offered consumers a wide range of goods to buy. Marshall Field of Chicago was the first department store in America. Chain stores—groups of stores owned by the same person—also started in the late 1800s. F. W. Woolworth's "five-and-dime store" and other chain grocery stores became popular. These types of stores offered consumers brand names and low-cost sales.

As shopping became more popular, so too did advertising. Companies filled magazines and newspapers with ads for their products. Advertisers also placed their products on barns, houses, and billboards.

In the late 1800s, Montgomery Ward and Sears Roebuck introduced mail-order catalogs. These books brought department store items to those who lived outside of the cities. Each company's catalog contained a description of its goods. The company mailed its catalog to farmers and small town residents. These people then could order goods from the catalog. By 1910, about 10 million Americans shopped by mail.

The United States Post Office increased mail-order business by starting a **rural free delivery (RFD)** system. This brought packages directly to every home.

3. **Name two developments in the ways goods were sold.**

_____

_____

Glossary · CHAPTER 16   Life at the Turn of the 20th Century

accommodate To provide for

belittle To make someone feel small and unimportant

curriculum All of the courses of studies offered by a school

discrimination To judge someone differently based on certain factors, including race

elegant Refined and graceful; tasteful

exaggerated That which goes beyond the truth or reality

pulp The soft inner contents of the stem of a plant

quadrupled Increased by four times

recreational Having to do with activities away from work, play

sensational Intended to stir curiosity or interest

violation The act of breaking a law or regulation

AFTER YOU READ

Terms and Names

A. Write the letter of the term that best answers the question.

a. Booker T. Washington

b. George Eastman

c. Joseph Pulitzer

d. segregation

e. Louis Sullivan

f. W. E. B. Du Bois

_____ **1.** Who invented the Kodak camera?

_____ **2.** Who is the architect who built an early skyscraper in St. Louis?

_____ **3.** Who is the African American who founded Tuskegee Normal and Industrial Institute in an effort to enable African Americans to teach and to do agricultural or mechanical work?

_____ **4.** Which term refers to the system of separating people on the basis of race?

_____ **5.** Who is the newspaper owner who introduced a large Sunday edition featuring comics, sports coverage, and women's news?

B. If the statement is true, write "true" on the line. If it is false, make it true by changing the underlined word or words and placing the new word on the line.

_____ **1.** Elevator and steel supports helped to make <u>skyscrapers</u> possible.

_____ **2.** <u>Booker T. Washington</u> became the first African American to earn a Ph.D.

_____ **3.** <u>Jim Crow laws</u> were added to the constitutions of several Southern states to allow white people who could not pass a literacy test or pay a poll tax to vote anyway.

_____ **4.** In <u>*Plessy v. Ferguson,*</u> the Supreme Court ruled in favor of the separation of the races in public facilities.

_____ **5.** Montgomery Ward and Sears Roebuck created what became known as <u>"five-and-dime stores."</u>

AFTER YOU READ (cont.)   *CHAPTER 16*   Life at the Turn of the 20th Century

Main Ideas

1. How did the methods of communications improve around the turn of the 20th century?

_____

_____

2. How did college and high school change around the turn of the century?

_____

_____

3. How were the works of Thomas Eakins and Mark Twain similar?

_____

_____

4. How did Southern states restrict African Americans politically? Socially?

_____

_____

5. What leisure activities flourished in the late 19th and early 20th centuries?

_____

_____

Thinking Critically

Answer the following questions on a separate sheet of paper.

1. Why might someone argue that the federal government played a key role in making African Americans second-class citizens?

2. Consider how you spend your leisure time. Explain how it is similar as well as different from how people spent it at the turn of the 20th century.

CHAPTER 17 Section 1 (pages 512–518)

The Origins of Progressivism

BEFORE YOU READ

In the last section, you read about popular culture at the turn of the century.

In this section, you will learn about the social reforms that made up the progressive movement.

AS YOU READ

Use this web diagram to take notes. Fill it in with names of the organizations and people who campaigned for the four types of reform. The notes will help you remember what you learned about the progressive movement.

TERMS AND NAMES

progressive movement Social reform movement in the early 20th century

Florence Kelley Social reformer

prohibition Making the sale or use of alcohol illegal

muckraker Writer who exposes wrongdoing

scientific management Using scientific ideas to make work more efficient

Robert M. LaFollette Progressive Wisconsin governor and senator

initiative A way for people to propose laws directly

referendum A way for people to approve changes in laws by a vote

recall A vote on whether to remove a public official from office

Seventeenth Amendment Amendment providing for senators to be elected directly

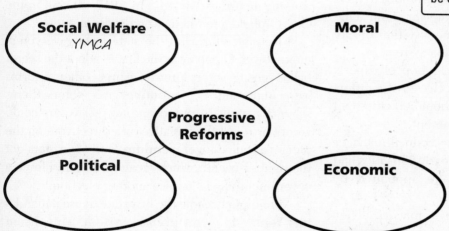

Four Goals of Progressivism
(pages 512–515)

What did reformers want?

As the 1900s opened, reformers pushed for a number of changes. Together their efforts built the **progressive movement.** The progressive movement had four major goals: (1) to protect social welfare, (2) to promote moral improvement, (3) to create economic reform, and (4) to foster efficiency.

Reformers tried to promote social welfare by easing the problems of city life. The YMCA built libraries and exercise rooms. The Salvation Army fed poor people in the cities and cared for children in nurseries. *Settlement houses* helped families. One reformer, **Florence Kelley,** helped to win the passage of the Illinois Factory Act in 1893. The law prohibited child labor and limited women's working hours. The law became a model for other states.

Reformers promoted moral reform by working for **prohibition**—the banning of alcoholic drinks. Many of these reformers, called prohibitionists, were members of the Woman's Christian Temperance Union (WCTU). The well-organized union became the largest women's group the country had ever seen.

Reformers tried to make economic changes by pointing out the great *inequality* between the rich and the poor. They pushed for better treatment of workers. *Journalists* called **muckrakers** wrote stories about corruption and unfair practices in business.

To help make businesses more *efficient* and *profitable*, some reformers promoted the idea of **scientific management.** The idea was to apply scientific ideas to make each task simpler. One outcome was the *assembly line.*

1. How did reformers try to make businesses more efficient and profitable?

Cleaning Up Local Government
(pages 515–516)

How did progressives change city governments?

Progressives also reformed politics. City governments were sometimes corrupt. For instance, they might be run by *party bosses* who gave jobs to their friends and bribed people to vote for them. One answer to this problem was a new system of city government called the commission system.

In the commission system a group of experts runs the city. Each expert takes charge of a different city department. By 1917, about 500 cities had commission forms of city government.

Another reform idea was the council-manager form of government. By 1925, nearly 250 cities had managers. These managers were appointed by councils elected by the people.

Some cities had progressive mayors. They improved cities without changing their system of government. They put in such reforms as fairer tax systems and lower public transportation fares.

2. How did the commission system help clean up city government?

Reform at the State Level
(pages 516–518)

How did state laws change?

Reformers also worked at the state level. Many states had progressive governors. These states passed laws to *regulate* railroads, mines, telephone companies, and other large businesses.

Robert M. La Follette, as governor of Wisconsin, led the way in regulating big business. His reforms of the railway industry taxed railroad property at the same rate as other business property. He set up a commission to regulate rates and forbade railroads to issue free passes to state officials.

Progressives also worked to improve conditions in the workplace and to end the employment of children. Factories hired children because children could do the same unskilled work as adults for less money. Often wages were so low that every member of the family needed to work.

Progressive reformers did not get a federal law to ban child labor. They did, however, get state legislatures to ban child labor. States also set maximum hours for all workers.

Progressives also won some reforms from the Supreme Court. In the case of *Muller* v. *Oregon,* the Court decided that a state could legally limit the working hours of women. In 1917, the Supreme Court upheld a ten-hour workday for men.

Electoral reforms at the state level gave voters more power. Oregon was the first to adopt the secret ballot, giving voters privacy. Three other reforms were important: (1) **initiative** gives voters themselves the right to propose a law, (2) voters could accept or reject the initiative by a direct vote on the initiative, called a **referendum,** and (3), voters got the right of **recall,** which meant they could force a government official to face another election.

Minnesota became the first state to use a mandatory statewide direct primary system. This meant that voters, instead of political machines, would choose candidates for public office through a special popular election. The direct primary led to the passage of the **Seventeenth Amendment** to the Constitution. This amendment called for senators to be elected directly by the people instead of by state lawmakers.

3. What are three ways progressive reforms helped ordinary people?

CHAPTER 17 Section 2 (pages 519–522)

Women in Public Life

TERMS AND NAMES

NACW National Association of Colored Women; founded in 1896 to improve living and working conditions for African-American women

suffrage The right to vote; a major goal of women reformers

Susan B. Anthony Leader of the woman suffrage movement, who helped to define the movement's goals and beliefs and to lead its actions

NAWSA National American Woman Suffrage Association; founded in 1890 to help women win the right to vote

BEFORE YOU READ

In the last section, you read about the progressive movement.

In this section, you will learn about the new, active roles women were taking in the workplace and in politics.

AS YOU READ

Use this diagram to take notes. Fill it in with details about women and their work in the four settings shown. The notes will help you remember what you learned about women's work in the late 1800s.

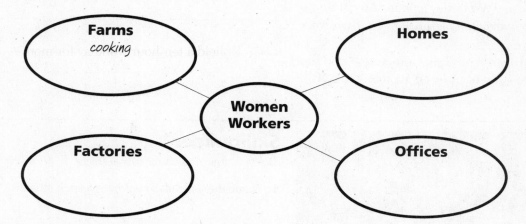

Women in the Work Force
(pages 519–520)

What jobs did women do?

Before the Civil War, most married women worked at home. They cared for their families and did not have paid jobs. By the end of the 19th century, however, many women had to work outside the home in order to earn money.

Farm women continued to work as they always had. They did the cooking, cleaning, sewing, and child rearing. They helped with the crops and animals.

As better-paying opportunities in towns and cities became available, more women began work-ing outside the home. By 1900, one in five American women held jobs; 25 percent of them worked in manufacturing. About half of the women working in manufacturing were employed in the garment trades. They typically held the least skilled positions and were paid only half as much as men. Women also began filling new jobs in offices, stores, and classrooms. Women went to new business schools to learn to become *stenographers* and typists. These jobs required a high school education. Women without a formal education took jobs as domestic workers, cleaning, and taking care of children of other families. Almost two million African-American workers—forced by economic necessity—worked on farms and in cities as domestic workers, laundresses, scrubwomen, and maids. Unmarried immigrant women did domestic labor, took in *piecework*, or cared for *boarders* at home.

1. What are three jobs that women without a formal education often held?

_____

_____

Women Lead Reform

(pages 520–522)

What reforms did women want?

Dangerous conditions, long hours, and low wages caused working women to fight for reforms. The Triangle Shirtwaist fire in New York City in 1911 killed 146 young workers, mostly women, and spurred the cause for reform.

Women who became active in public life attended college. New women's colleges such as Vassar, Smith, and Wellesley opened. By the late 19th century, marriage was no longer a woman's only alternative.

In 1896, African-American women founded the National Association of Colored Women (**NACW**).

This organization created nurseries, reading rooms, and kindergartens.

Women's crusade for **suffrage,** or the right to vote, began at the Seneca Falls Convention in 1848. The women's movement split over whether or not to support the Fourteenth and Fifteenth Amendments which granted the vote to African-American men, but not to women of any race. **Susan B. Anthony** led the opposition. By 1890, suffragists had united in the National American Woman Suffrage Association (**NAWSA**).

Women tried three approaches to win the vote: (1) they tried to convince state legislatures; (2) they went to court to clarify whether the provisions of the Fourteenth Amendment meant women should be allowed to vote, and (3) they pushed for a national constitutional amendment. This was voted down several times.

2. What are three ways in which women tried to win the vote?

_____

_____

_____

Angry crowds confront the militia at the Lawrence mill workers' strike in 1912. Credit: Corbis-Bettmann

Skillbuilder

Use the photograph to answer these questions.

1. Name the two sides confronting each other.

_____

_____

2. Cite one example of what you think workers might strike over.

_____

_____

CHAPTER 17 Section 3 (pages 523–531)

Teddy Roosevelt's Square Deal

TERMS AND NAMES

Theodore Roosevelt President from 1901 to 1909

Square Deal President Roosevelt's program of progressive reforms

Upton Sinclair Novelist who exposed social problems

The Jungle Novel by Upton Sinclair describing meatpacking

Meat Inspection Act Law reforming meatpacking conditions, 1906

Pure Food and Drug Act Law to stop the sale of unclean food and drugs, 1906

conservation The planned management of natural resources

NAACP National Association for the Advancement of Colored People, founded in 1909 to work for racial equality

BEFORE YOU READ

In the last section, you read about women who worked for reforms in their communities and for the right to vote.

In this section, you will learn about President Theodore Roosevelt's success in promoting reforms at the national level.

AS YOU READ

Use this diagram to take notes. Read the list of problem areas on the left and fill in the columns to give examples of how these problems were solved.

PROBLEM AREAS	EXAMPLES	SOLUTIONS
Strikes	1902, Pennsylvania coal miners	
Trusts		
Meat processing		
The environment		

A Rough-Riding President
(pages 523–525)

What was Roosevelt like?

Theodore Roosevelt became president in 1901. He was bold, ambitious, and full of energy. He had been active in sports and politics. In the Spanish–American War he led a fighting unit called the Rough Riders. His personality made him a popular president.

Roosevelt used his popularity to get his programs passed. He wanted to see that the common people received what he called a **Square Deal**. This term referred to a program of progressive reforms sponsored by his administration.

1. How did Roosevelt's personality shape his presidency?

_____

_____

Using Federal Power (pages 525–526)

How did Roosevelt handle big business?

President Roosevelt used the power of the government to help solve the nation's problems.

Roosevelt also used the power of his government to deal with the problem of trusts. Trusts were large companies that had control over their markets. Trusts, or monopolies, first drove smaller companies out by lowering their own prices. Then when the smaller companies were gone, the trusts could raise their prices. They no longer had any competition.

By 1900, trusts controlled about 80 percent of U.S. industries. Roosevelt supported big business, but he also wanted to stop trusts that harmed people. He had the government sue harmful trusts under the Sherman Antitrust Act of 1890. In all, Roosevelt filed 44 *antitrust* suits. He was called a trustbuster.

In 1902, about 140,000 coal miners in Pennsylvania went on strike. The mine owners refused to *negotiate* with them. President Roosevelt called both sides to the White House to talk. He threatened to have the government take over the mines. The two sides agreed to have an *arbitration* commission help settle their differences. The commission succeeded in reaching a compromise. From then on, the federal government would often step in to help settle a strike.

In 1887, the Interstate Commerce Commission (ICC) had been set up to regulate the railroad industry. It had not been effective. Roosevelt pushed through laws such as the Hepburn Act of 1906, which strictly limited the distribution of free railroad passes, a common form of bribery. Roosevelt's efforts resulted in fairer shipping rates and less corruption in the railroad industry.

2. How did Roosevelt use the power of the federal government to change business practices?

Health and the Environment (pages 526–530)

What did Roosevelt do for public health and the environment?

After reading **The Jungle** by **Upton Sinclair** which described filthy conditions in the meatpack-ing industry, Roosevelt pushed for passage of the **Meat Inspection Act.** This law, passed in 1906, called for strict cleanliness requirements for meat-packers. It created a program of federal meat inspection.

Also in 1906, Congress passed the **Pure Food and Drug Act** which halted the sale of contaminated foods and medicines and called for truth in labeling.

Before Roosevelt became president, the federal government had paid little attention to the nation's natural resources. John Muir, a naturalist and writer, persuaded Roosevelt to set aside 148 million acres of forest reserves and other land for waterpower sites and mineral and water resources. Roosevelt appointed Gifford Pinchot as head of the U.S. Forest Service. Roosevelt and Pinchot believed in the **conservation** of land, meaning some land should be preserved as wilderness while other areas would be developed for the common good. Roosevelt and Pinchot were opposed by Muir, who believed in complete preservation of the wilderness. Indeed, Roosevelt signed the Newlands Act which funded irrigation projects that transformed dry wilderness into land suitable for agriculture.

3. What are two ways that Roosevelt helped to make people's lives safer and healthier?

Roosevelt and Civil Rights
(pages 530–531)

What did Roosevelt do for African Americans?

Roosevelt supported individual African Americans like Booker T. Washington. But he did not help African Americans in general. In 1909, black leaders, including W. E. B. Du Bois, founded the National Association for the Advancement of Colored People (**NAACP**). The organization pushed for civil rights and racial equality. The progressive movement, however, continued to focus on the needs of middle-class whites.

4. What action did the NAACP take?

CHAPTER 17 Section 4 (pages 534–537)

Progressivism Under Taft

BEFORE YOU READ

In the last section, you read about the reforms of Teddy Roosevelt's presidency.

In this section, you will learn about the reforms and political problems of the next president, William Howard Taft.

AS YOU READ

Use this diagram to take notes. Fill in the boxes with causes of Taft's problems in office. The notes will help you remember what you learned about Taft's presidency.

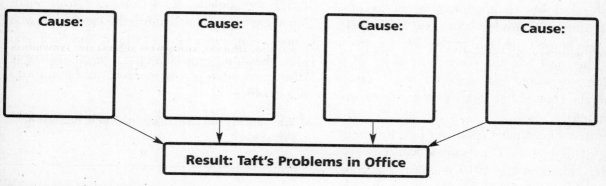

| Cause: | Cause: | Cause: | Cause: |

Result: Taft's Problems in Office

Taft Becomes President (pages 534–535)

Why *did Taft have problems?*

President Roosevelt promised not to run for another *term*. Instead, he wanted **William Howard Taft** to become president. Taft had been Roosevelt's secretary of war, and Roosevelt felt Taft would carry out his policies. Taft was elected in 1909, and he did continue many of the progressive programs. In fact, he busted more than twice as many trusts as Roosevelt had. However, Taft was not as effective as Roosevelt had been. He had many problems in office.

His first problem came over *tariffs*. Taft wanted to lower tariffs. He supported the Payne bill, which was passed in the House. However, the Senate passed a weakened version of the bill, the **Payne-Aldrich Tariff.** The revised bill did not

lower tariffs much at all. The progressives in Taft's own Republican Party were annoyed.

Another problem for Taft arose over conservation. *Conservationists* like **Gifford Pinchot,** the head of the U.S. Forest Service, believed that wilderness areas could be managed for public enjoyment as well as private development. This meant, for instance, that someone could make a profit by logging land that belonged to the federal government. This was called a multi-use land program.

Taft appointed Richard A. Ballinger as secretary of the interior. Ballinger did not want to keep so much federal land in reserve. He wanted to free up land for forestry and mining. He wanted to sell some land for private uses. When he did these things, Pinchot complained. Pinchot accused him of misusing the natural resources for *commercial*

TERMS AND NAMES

William Howard Taft President from 1909 to 1913, successor to Roosevelt

Payne-Aldrich Tariff Bill meant to lower tariffs on imported goods

Gifford Pinchot Head of the U.S. Forest Service under Roosevelt, who believed that it was possible to make use of natural resources while conserving them

Bull Moose Party Nickname for the new Progressive Party, which was formed to support Roosevelt in the election of 1912

Woodrow Wilson Winner of the 1912 presidential election

interests. As a result of Pinchot's criticism, Taft felt he had to fire him from the U.S. Forest Service.

1. In what two areas did Taft have problems?

_____

_____

The Republican Party Splits

(pages 535–536)

Why did the Republican Party split?

The Republican Party had two wings: (1) the progressives, who wanted change and (2) the conservatives, who did not want reform. Taft was not able to hold the two wings of his party together.

The two groups disagreed over Taft's support of political boss Joseph Cannon. Cannon was Speaker of the House of Representatives, and he ran the House his own way. He appointed people to committee positions who weren't the next in line. He even made himself the head of the Committee on Rules. This gave him the power to control what bills Congress would take up. As a result, under Cannon, the House often did not even vote on progressive bills.

The Republican party split over how to handle Cannon. This gave the Democrats a chance to take over the House in the 1910 *midterm* elections. Democrats had control of the House for the first time in almost 20 years.

By 1912, Teddy Roosevelt had decided to run for a third term as president, after all. Taft had an advantage because he was already in office. The Republican Party nominated Taft, but Roosevelt's supporters broke off and formed the Progressive Party. This third party was also called the **Bull Moose Party**. It ran on a *platform* of reform. The Democrats were in a stronger position now that the Republicans were split. They nominated the reform governor of New Jersey, **Woodrow Wilson**.

2. Who formed the Bull Moose Party?

_____

_____

Democrats Win in 1912

(pages 536–537)

Who won the election of 1912?

The 1912 election offered Americans four main choices: Wilson, Taft, Roosevelt, and the socialist Eugene V. Debs.

Wilson campaigned on a progressive platform, called the New Freedom. He wanted stronger antitrust legislation, banking reform, and lower tariffs.

Both Roosevelt and Wilson wanted to give the government a stronger role in the economy. But they differed over strategies, that is, how to do that. Roosevelt supported government supervision of big business. Wilson opposed all business monopolies, or trusts. Debs went even further. He wanted the government to distribute national wealth more equally among the people.

Wilson won the 1912 election. He also brought in a Democratic majority in Congress. In all, about 75 percent of the vote went to the candidates who favored economic reform—Wilson, Roosevelt, and Debs. Because so many people supported reform, Wilson had more power to carry out his reforms once in office.

3. What did Wilson have in common with Roosevelt? With Debs?

_____

_____

CHAPTER 17 Section 5 (pages 538–543)

Wilson's New Freedom

TERMS AND NAMES

Clayton Antitrust Act Law that weakened monopolies and upheld the rights of unions and farm organizations

Federal Trade Commission (FTC) A federal agency set up in 1914 to investigate businesses to help enforce the laws

Federal Reserve System National banking system begun in 1913

Carrie Chapman Catt President of NAWSA, who led the campaign for woman suffrage during Wilson's administration

Nineteenth Amendment Amendment to the Constitution giving women the right to vote

BEFORE YOU READ

In the last section, you read about the problems Taft faced as president.

In this section, you will learn how Woodrow Wilson managed to get some parts of his progressive platform passed but had to give up others.

AS YOU READ

Use this time line to take notes. Fill in the boxes with key events during Wilson's first term.

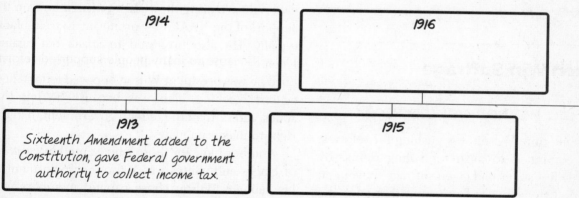

| 1914 | 1916 |

| 1913 | 1915 |
Sixteenth Amendment added to the Constitution, gave Federal government authority to collect income tax.

Wilson Wins Financial Reforms
(pages 538–540)

What reforms did Wilson support?

Woodrow Wilson grew up in a religious family in the South. He began his career as a lawyer and then became a college professor, university president, and finally state governor. As governor of New Jersey, he worked for many progressive causes. When he was elected president, he pushed for a reform program called the New Freedom.

Under Wilson, Congress passed two antitrust measures. The first was the **Clayton Antitrust Act** of 1914. This law had several important effects. The law (1) made it more difficult for monopolies to form, (2) said that the people who ran a company could be held personally responsible if the company violated the law, and (3) ruled that labor unions and farm organizations were not themselves to be considered trusts. This made strikes, peaceful picketing, and *boycotts* legal.

The second antitrust measure was the Federal Trade Act of 1914, which set up the **Federal Trade Commission (FTC).** This agency had the power to investigate businesses for the government. The FTC became very active during Wilson's administration. It issued nearly 400 orders telling companies to stop breaking the law.

Wilson also worked to lower tariffs. He believed that high tariffs encouraged monopolies. By raising the cost of imported goods, they cut competition against American goods. He supported the Underwood Tariff of 1913, which lowered tariffs for the first time since the Civil War.

With less money coming in from tariffs, however, the government needed another source of money. It turned to an income tax. This tax on people's earnings was created by the Sixteenth Amendment to the Constitution, which was ratified by the states in 1913. The tax gave to the federal government a small percentage of all workers' income and business profits.

After reforming tariffs, Wilson turned his attention to the banking system. It was difficult for people far from banking centers to obtain credit. The new **Federal Reserve System** solved this problem by dividing the country into 12 districts, each with a federal reserve bank. This system controlled the money supply and made credit more easily available. Setting up the federal reserve was one of Wilson's most important reforms.

1. **What were three areas that Wilson reformed?**

_____

_____

Women Win Suffrage
(pages 540–541)

How did women get the vote?

At the same time Wilson was pushing for reforms, women continued to push for voting rights. By 1912, only five states had given suffrage to women. But several things were happening that gave the suffrage movement hope.

Local suffrage organizations used door-to-door campaigns to win support. College-educated women joined in reaching out to working-class women. Women who had visited Europe adopted the more bold tactics of British suffragists such as heckling government officials.

Carrie Chapman Catt succeeded Susan B. Anthony as president of NAWSA. Catt believed in continuing the cautious tactics of the past. Lucy Burns and Alice Paul formed the National Woman's Party and adopted more radical tactics such as around-the-clock picketing of the White House.

Some of the picketers went to jail and even started a hunger strike. But it took World War I to bring women the vote. A great number of women became active in supporting the war effort.

Women ran committees, rolled bandages, and sold liberty bonds in order to raise funds for the war. Once they were active in public life, women felt more strongly than ever that they should have the right to vote. At last, in 1919 Congress passed the **Nineteenth Amendment.** This amendment giving women the vote was ratified by the states the next year.

2. **How did World War I help women get the right to vote?**

_____

_____

The Limits of Progressivism
(pages 541–543)

Did Wilson support civil rights?

Like Roosevelt and Taft, Wilson backed away from civil rights. During the 1912 campaign he won the support of the NAACP by promising to treat blacks equally. He also promised to speak out against lynching, that is, mob killings of blacks. However, once he was president Wilson opposed federal laws against lynching. This was because he felt that states, rather than the federal government, had the right to make such laws.

Another blow for those who wanted *integration* of blacks and whites was Wilson's appointment of his cabinet. Wilson chose cabinet members who extended segregation, or separate facilities for blacks and whites. Wilson's angry meeting with an African-American delegation led by a Boston newspaper editor brought African Americans' feeling of betrayal to a head.

Even before the U.S. entered World War I, the war became a factor in dimming the reform spirit as legislators had less interest in reform.

3. **Why did African Americans feel betrayed by President Wilson?**

_____

_____

Glossary

antitrust Against monopolies

arbitration Process of having a third party make a decision when two sides can't settle an argument

assembly line An efficient way of putting together a product in which each worker does a different specific task

boarders People who pay to live and eat at another person's house

boycott Protest in which people refuse to buy a certain product

commercial Aimed at making a profit

conservationist Person who favors using natural resources carefully

efficient Done with the least possible effort and expense

inequality Unfair difference in the way people are treated

integration Mixing racial groups

journalist News writer

midterm The election halfway between two presidential elections

negotiate To try to reach an agreement by talking

party boss Person who controls a political party

piecework Work, such as sewing, that is paid for by the piece rather than by the hour

platform Official statement of political beliefs

profitable Earning a profit, for instance, selling something for more than it costs to make

regulate To set rules for

settlement house A center where poor people can get help

stenographer Office worker who takes notes in shorthand

tariff Tax charged on goods coming into the country

term Length of time an official is elected to serve

AFTER YOU READ

Terms and Names

A. Write the letter of the choice that best completes the sentence.

_____ **1.** Recall is

    a. a bill initiated by citizens.

    b. a vote on an initiative.

    c. a vote to remove a public official.

    d. a law making alcohol illegal.

_____ **2.** Suffrage means the

    a. separation of races.

    b. denial of the right to vote.

    c. illegal sale of alcohol.

    d. right to vote.

_____ **3.** The Clayton Antitrust Law

    a. stopped the sale of spoiled foods.

    b. created federal meat inspection.

    c. weakened monopolies.

    d. preserved wilderness areas.

_____ **4.** The Nineteenth Amendment

    a. established the FTC.

    b. recognized woman's suffrage.

    c. made monopolies illegal.

    d. decentralized private banking.

B. Write the letter of the name or term that matches the description.

a. NAACP

b. Bull Moose Party

c. Payne-Aldrich Tariff

d. prohibition

e. NACW

_____ **1.** A cause taken up by the Women's Christian Temperance Union

_____ **2.** An organization of African American women

_____ **3.** An organization started by prominent African-American and white reformers to promote civil rights for African Americans

_____ **4.** Weakened bill that got Taft in trouble with the progressives

_____ **5.** Supporters of Roosevelt who broke away from the Republican Party

Name _____   Date _____

AFTER YOU READ (continued)   *CHAPTER 17* The Progressive Era

Main Ideas

1. What were the four major goals of the progressive movement?

_____

_____

2. Name two women's organizations and describe their mission.

_____

_____

3. How did the novel *The Jungle* lead to changes in American laws governing meatpacking?

_____

_____

4. Why was Roosevelt's handling of the 1902 coal strike important?

_____

_____

5. How did the Clayton Antitrust Act benefit labor?

_____

_____

Thinking Critically

Answer the following questions on a separate sheet of paper.

1. How did Theodore Roosevelt expand the role of the Federal government?

2. How might you characterize most African Americans' view of the progressive era? Why?

180 CHAPTER 17 AFTER YOU READ

CHAPTER 18 Section 1 (pages 548–551)

Imperialism and America

BEFORE YOU READ

In the last section, you read about Woodrow Wilson.

In this section, you will learn how economic activity led to political and military involvement overseas.

AS YOU READ

Use this web diagram to take notes. Fill it in with details about the causes of U.S. imperialism.

TERMS AND NAMES

Queen Liliuokalani The Hawaiian queen who was forced out of power by a revolution started by American business interests

imperialism The practice of strong countries taking economic, political, and military power over weaker countries

Alfred T. Mahan American imperialist and admiral who urged the United States to build up its navy and take colonies overseas

William Seward Secretary of state under Presidents Lincoln and Johnson

Pearl Harbor Naval port in Hawaii

Sanford B. Dole American businessman who became president of the new government of Hawaii after the queen was pushed out

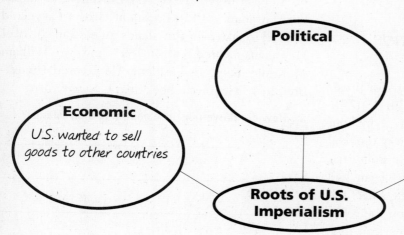

Political

Economic
U.S. wanted to sell goods to other countries

Cultural

Roots of U.S. Imperialism

American Expansionism
(pages 548–550)

Why did Americans support imperialism?

In 1893, **Queen Liliuokalani** of Hawaii gave up her throne. Hawaii was about to be taken over by the United States.

By the 1880s, many American leaders thought the United States should establish colonies overseas. This idea was called **imperialism**—the policy in which stronger nations extend economic, political or military control over weaker territories. European countries had competed for territory all over the world. Most Americans gradually accepted the idea of overseas expansion.

Three factors fueled American imperialism: desire for military strength, thirst for new markets, and a belief in the superiority of American culture.

Admiral **Alfred T. Mahan** of the U.S. Navy supported growing American naval power so the U.S. could compete with other nations. The U.S. built such modern battleships as the *Maine* and the *Oregon*. The new ships made the U.S. the world's largest naval power.

By the late 1800s, *technology* had changed American farms and factories. They produced more than Americans could consume. So the U.S. needed foreign trade. American businesses needed markets for their products and raw materials for their factories.

The third root of American imperialism was a belief that the people of the United States were better than the people of other countries. This *racist* belief came from people's pride in their Anglo-Saxon (Northern European) heritage. People sometimes felt they had a duty to spread their culture and Christian religion among other people.

1. What were three reasons Americans supported imperialism?

_____

_____

_____

The United States Acquires Alaska; The United States Takes Hawaii (pages 550–551)

How did the Hawaiian Islands become a U.S. territory?

William Seward was Secretary of State for presidents Lincoln and Andrew Johnson. In 1867 he purchased Alaska from Russia for $7.2 million. Some opponents in Congress made fun of the deal calling it "Seward's Icebox" or "Seward's Folly."

The Hawaiian Islands, in the Pacific Ocean, had been important to the United States since the 1790s. Merchants had stopped there on their way to China and India. In the 1820s, American missionaries founded Christian schools and churches on the islands.

A number of Americans had established sugar plantations in Hawaii. In the mid-1800s, these large farms accounted for about three-quarters of the wealth in the islands. Plantation owners brought thousands of laborers to Hawaii from Japan, Portugal, and China. This weakened the influence of the native Hawaiians. By 1900, the foreign laborers outnumbered the Hawaiians three to one.

In 1875, the United States agreed to import Hawaiian sugar *duty-free*. Over the next 15 years, Hawaiian sugar production increased nine times. Then the McKinley Tariff caused a crisis for Hawaiian sugar growers. With the duty on their sugar, Hawaiian growers faced stiff competition from other growers. The powerful Hawaiian sugar growers called for the U.S. to *annex* Hawaii. The U.S. military had already understood the value of Hawaii. In 1887, the U.S. forced Hawaii to let it build a naval base at **Pearl Harbor,** Hawaii's best port.

When the Hawaiian king died in 1891, his sister became queen. Queen Liliuokalani wanted a new constitution that would give voting power back to ordinary Hawaiians. American business interests did not want this to happen.

American business groups organized a revolt against the queen. The U.S. ambassador John L. Stevens helped them. The planters took control of the island. They established a temporary government and made American businessman **Sanford B. Dole** the president.

Stevens urged the U.S. government to annex the Hawaiian Islands. President Grover Cleveland refused to take over the islands unless a majority of Hawaiians favored that. In 1897, however, William McKinley became president. He favored annexation. In 1898, Hawaii became a U.S. *territory*.

2. How did Hawaiians lose control of their islands?

_____

_____

_____

CHAPTER 18 Section 2 (pages 552–557)

The Spanish–American War

BEFORE YOU READ

In the last section, you learned how the United States became an imperialist power and took over the Hawaiian Islands.

In this section, you will learn how the United States became involved in Cuba and fought a war with Spain.

AS YOU READ

Use this time line to take notes. In each box, write what happened on that date.

TERMS AND NAMES

José Martí Political activist who worked for Cuban independence

Valeriano Weyler General sent from Spain to Cuba to restore order in 1896

yellow journalism Reporting in newspapers and magazines that exaggerates the news in order to make it more exciting

U.S.S. *Maine* U.S. warship that exploded in a Cuban harbor in 1898

George Dewey U.S. naval commander who led the American attack on the Philippines

Rough Riders Fighting unit led by Theodore Roosevelt in Cuba

San Juan Hill Location of an important American land victory in Cuba

Treaty of Paris The treaty that ended the Spanish-American War

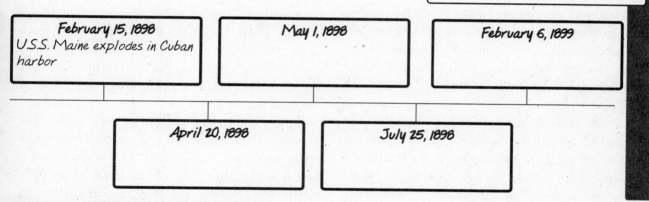

| February 15, 1898 U.S.S. Maine explodes in Cuban harbor | May 1, 1898 | February 6, 1899 |
| April 20, 1898 | July 25, 1898 | |

Cubans Rebel Against Spain
(pages 552–553)

What happened when Cuba rebelled against Spain?

Between 1868 and 1878, Cubans fought their first war for independence from Spain. The rebels did not win, but they did force Spain to *abolish* slavery in 1886. After that, United States *capitalists* invested heavily in sugar cane plantations in Cuba.

Sugar was the most important product of Cuba. The United States was the main market for the sugar. As long the United States did not charge a tariff on Cuban sugar, the Cuban economy thrived. But the Cuban economy collapsed in 1894 when a tariff on sugar was imposed.

In 1895, Cubans began a second war for independence. The rebellion was led by **José Martí**. He was a Cuban poet and journalist who had been living *in exile* in New York. The rebels wanted the United States to join their cause.

American opinion was mixed. Some wanted to support Spain in order to keep their investments safe. Others wanted to help the Cuban people win their freedom from Spain just as the United States had won its independence from England.

1. How did Cuba's two wars for independence affect American business interests?

_____

_____

War Fever Escalates
(pages 553–554)

Why did Americans become angry with Spain?

In 1896, Spain sent an army to Cuba to restore order. The army was led by General **Valeriano Weyler.** Weyler rounded up the entire rural population of central and western Cuba. He kept 300,000 people as prisoners in concentration camps. That way they could not help the rebels. Many of them died of hunger and disease.

This story was widely reported in the United States. Rival newspapers in New York made the terrible events sound even worse. They exaggerated the *brutality* of the story in order to attract readers. These sensational stories became known as **yellow journalism**—reporting that exaggerates the news in order to make it more exciting.

William McKinley became president in 1897. At that time, many Americans wanted the United States to help the rebels against Spain. McKinley tried to find a peaceful solution to the crisis. His efforts had several positive results. Spain sent General Weyler home, changed the concentration camp policy, and gave Cuba limited self-government.

Then two events made Americans very angry at Spain. The first was the publication of a letter that insulted the American president. The de Lôme letter was written by a Spanish *diplomat*. It criticized McKinley for being weak. Although some Americans agreed that the president was weak, they did not want to hear this criticism from a Spanish official.

Only a few days after the letter was published, something worse happened. The battleship **U.S.S. Maine** was stationed in Cuba to protect American lives and property. On February 15, 1898, the ship exploded. The ship sank, and 260 officers and crew on board died. The cause of the explosion was not known. However, newspapers blamed Spain. Americans cried for war.

2. **What two events led Americans to call for war against Spain?**

_____

_____

War with Spain Erupts (pages 554–557)

Where and when did the fighting take place?

On April 20, 1898, the United States went to war with Spain. The first battle took place in the Philippines. The Philippines had been a Spanish colony for 300 years. They had rebelled many times. In 1896, they began another rebellion.

On May 1, 1898, the American naval commander **George Dewey** sailed into Manila Bay in the Philippines. His ships destroyed the Spanish fleet there. In the next two months, U.S. soldiers fought on the side of the *Filipino* rebels. The Spanish surrendered to the United States in August.

In Cuba, the American navy blocked off the harbor of Santiago de Cuba. Spanish ships could not leave. Then American troops landed on the island in June 1898.

One unit of volunteer soldiers was called the **Rough Riders.** Theodore Roosevelt was one of their leaders. They helped win the important battle of **San Juan Hill.** American newspapers made Roosevelt a hero.

When the Spanish ships tried to leave the harbor, their fleet was destroyed. This led the Spanish to surrender on July 25.

Spain quickly agreed to a peace treaty. The **Treaty of Paris** granted Cuba its independence. Spain gave Puerto Rico and the Pacific island of Guam to the United States. The United States paid Spain $20 million for the annexation of the Philippine Islands. The Treaty of Paris touched off a great debate in the United States about imperialism. President McKinley was in favor of it. But some Americans said annexing territories violated the spirit of the Declaration of Independence by denying self-government to the new territories. Booker T. Washington and Samuel Gompers also opposed the treaty. The Senate approved the treaty on February 6, 1899.

3. **What three territories did the United States get from the war with Spain?**

_____

_____

CHAPTER 18 Section 3 (pages 558–564)

Acquiring New Lands

TERMS AND NAMES

Foraker Act Law which ended military rule in Puerto Rico

Platt Amendment Provisions in the Cuban constitution that gave the United States broad rights in that country

protectorate A country that is partly controlled by another, stronger country

Emilio Aguinaldo Filipino rebel leader

John Hay U.S. secretary of state

Open Door notes Message sent by John Hay to other countries to protect U.S. trading rights in China

Boxer Rebellion Chinese rebellion against Western influence, 1900

BEFORE YOU READ

In the last section, you learned how the United States and Spain fought over Cuba and the Philippines.

In this section, you will read how the United States continued its imperialism.

AS YOU READ

Use this diagram to take notes. Fill in the boxes to describe the relationships between the United States and Puerto Rico, Cuba, the Philippines, and China.

COUNTRY	AMERICAN ACTIONS	RESPONSES TO ACTIONS
Puerto Rico	sent military forces to Puerto Rico in 1898	
Cuba		
The Philippines		
China		

Ruling Puerto Rico (pages 558–559)

How did Puerto Ricans feel about U.S. control?

Puerto Rico had become an American territory as a result of the Spanish–American War. American forces landed in Puerto Rico in July 1898. The commanding officer declared that the Americans were there to protect the Puerto Ricans. But other U.S. military officials insulted the Puerto Ricans. They spoke of them as children and set limits on their personal freedom. Many Puerto Ricans began to resent the military government. In 1900, Congress passed the **Foraker Act** which ended military rule and set up a civil government.

The United States kept strict control over the people and their government. In 1917, however, Congress made Puerto Ricans U.S. citizens.

1. Why did some Puerto Ricans resent U.S. control of their government?

_____

Cuba and the United States
(pages 559–561)

How did the United States keep control over Cuba?

Cuba was officially independent after the war. The U.S. army, however, remained in Cuba for four years. It punished Cubans who did not like this American *occupation*.

In 1900, the new Cuban government wrote a constitution. The United States insisted they add the **Platt Amendment.** The amendment limited Cuba's rights in dealing with other countries. It gave the United States special privileges, including the right to intervene to preserve order.

Cuba became a U.S. **protectorate**—a country whose affairs are partially controlled by a stronger power. The United States insisted on these rights because of its economic interests in Cuba.

2. What did the United States do to protect business interests in Cuba?

Filipinos Rebel (page 561)

Why did the Filipinos rebel against the United States?

Filipinos had been fighting for independence for years. They were angry that the United States had annexed their islands. Rebel leader **Emilio Aguinaldo** believed that the United States had promised independence. He felt that the United States had betrayed the Filipinos after helping them win independence.

In 1899, Aguinaldo started a rebellion, which lasted three years. After winning that war, the United States set up a government similar to the one it had set up in Cuba.

3. Why did Aguinaldo feel betrayed by the United States?

Foreign Influence in China
(pages 562–563)

What were U.S. interests in China?

By 1899, many countries had economic interests in China. The United States wanted to be able to

trade with China. The Secretary of State **John Hay** sent a statement of this policy to the other countries. His policy statements were called the **Open Door notes.** They called for China's ports to remain open and for China to remain independent. No country would have special trading rights. The other countries agreed.

In 1900, a secret society in China started a rebellion. They were protesting the influence of Western countries in China. Troops from many countries including the United States fought against the rebels, or Boxers. After the **Boxer Rebellion** was defeated, the United States issued more Open Door notes to make sure other countries did not make colonies out of China.

4. Why did Secretary of State John Hay issue the Open Door notes?

The Impact of U.S. Territorial Gains (page 564)

How did Americans feel about U.S. imperialism?

President William McKinley was reelected in 1900. His opponent had been an anti-imperialist, William Jennings Bryan. The outcome of the election suggests that most Americans disagreed with Bryan. Imperialism was popular.

An Anti-Imperialist League formed including some prominent Americans. Among its members were former president Grover Cleveland, Andrew Carnegie, Jane Addams, and Mark Twain. Each had their own reasons for being against imperialism. But all agreed it was wrong for the United States to rule other people without their consent.

5. What did McKinley's reelection show about American attitudes toward imperialism?

CHAPTER 18 Section 4 (pages 565–571)

America as a World Power

BEFORE YOU READ

In the last section, you learned about the growth of American imperialism.

In this section, you will learn how Roosevelt and Wilson used American military and economic power.

AS YOU READ

Use this diagram to take notes. Fill in the boxes as you read about Roosevelt's and Wilson's use of American power.

TERMS AND NAMES

Panama Canal A channel across Central America, between the Atlantic and Pacific Oceans, opened in 1914

Roosevelt Corollary Roosevelt's 1904 extension of the Monroe Doctrine, stating that the United States has the right to protect its economic interests in South and Central America by using military force

dollar diplomacy The policy of intervening in other countries to protect U.S. business interests

Francisco "Pancho" Villa Mexican revolutionary

Emiliano Zapata Mexican rebel

John J. Pershing U.S. general who led troops to capture Villa

USING AMERICAN POWER	
Roosevelt	**Wilson**
Mediated settlement in Russo-Japanese War	

Teddy Roosevelt and the World
(pages 565–569)

How did Roosevelt use American power?

In 1901, President McKinley was assassinated, and Theodore Roosevelt became president. Roosevelt continued the policies of imperialism. He first used U.S. influence to help settle the Russo-Japanese War.

The war began in 1904. Both Russia and Japan wanted to control Korea. Japan captured Korea and also invaded Manchuria, which was controlled by Russia.

Then Japan wanted to stop the fighting. The Japanese asked President Roosevelt to *mediate* the conflict. In 1905, representatives of Russia and Japan met. Roosevelt used his personal charm to help them *negotiate* a compromise. They signed a

treaty, and Roosevelt received the 1906 Nobel Peace Prize for his efforts.

Roosevelt also used his influence to help build the **Panama Canal.** The idea of a canal connecting the Atlantic and Pacific Oceans had been discussed for some time. Such a canal would cut travel time for military and commercial ships. Ships would no longer have to go all the way around South America in order to get from one ocean to the other.

The narrow *Isthmus* of Panama was a logical place to cut a canal. Political problems stood in the way, however. Panama was a province of Colombia. When Colombia did not agree to the canal, the United States helped Panama to rebel against Colombia. Panama became independent. Then the United States got Panama's permission to build the canal.

Construction of the Panama Canal was one of the world's greatest *engineering* accomplishments. Work began in 1904 and took 10 years. In 1913, there were 43,400 workers on the project. The work was hard and dangerous.

On August 15, 1914, the canal opened for business. It was a success from the start. More than 1,000 ships passed through during its first year. However, relations between the United States and Latin America had been damaged by the takeover of Panama.

President Roosevelt wanted the United States to be the major power in the Caribbean and Central America. He declared his policy in a message to Congress in 1904. His statement was called the **Roosevelt Corollary.** A corollary is a logical result of another statement, in this case the Monroe Doctrine of 1823. That doctrine had said the United States would not allow European influence in the Western Hemisphere. Roosevelt now said that the United States had the right to intervene in Latin American countries to protect U.S. business interests.

In 1911, President Taft used this policy in Nicaragua. A rebellion had left the country in debt. Taft arranged for U.S. bankers to loan Nicaragua money. In exchange, American business took control of the railroads and banks in the country. They also collected Nicaragua's custom duties.

Nicaraguans did not like this arrangement. They rebelled. The United States then sent troops to Nicaragua to preserve the peace. Those who did not like this kind of *intervention* called it **dollar diplomacy.**

1. What are two ways Roosevelt used U.S. power in other countries?

_____

_____

Woodrow Wilson's Missionary Diplomacy (pages 569–571)

Why did President Wilson send troops to Mexico?

President Woodrow Wilson took a step beyond Presidents Monroe and Roosevelt by adding a *moral* tone to Latin American policy. He said that the United States must act in certain circumstances.

This so-called "missionary diplomacy" meant that the United States could not officially *recognize* governments that were *oppressive,* undemocratic, or opposed to U.S. business interests. The new doctrine put pressure on countries to have democratic governments. A revolution in Mexico tested this policy.

In 1910, Mexican peasants and workers rebelled against their military dictator. Two new governments followed, the second headed by General Victoriano Huerta.

Wilson refused to support the Huerta government because it came to power through violence.

Wilson sent in troops. When a new leader, Venustiano Carranza, took power in Mexico, Wilson withdrew the troops.

Mexico remained in *turmoil.* Under the leadership of **Francisco "Pancho" Villa** and **Emiliano Zapata,** rebels revolted against Carranza. Some of Villa's followers killed Americans. The United States wanted to capture Villa.

Finally the Mexican government gave permission to send in troops. Wilson sent General **John J. Pershing** with 15,000 soldiers. A year later, Villa was still free. Wilson then stationed 150,000 National Guardsmen along the border.

Mexicans were angered by the U.S. invasion. In 1916, U.S. troops fought with Carranza's army. In 1917, Wilson withdrew U.S. troops. At that time, he was facing possible war in Europe.

Finally, Mexico adopted a constitution. The Mexicans regained control of their own resources and put limits on foreign investment. American intervention in Mexico showed how far the United States was willing to go to protect its economic interests.

In the early 20th century, the U.S pursued several foreign policy goals. It expanded its access to foreign markets. It built a modern navy to protect its interest abroad. It used its international police power to get its way in Latin America.

2. What were two reasons Wilson sent troops to Mexico?

_____

_____

Glossary   CHAPTER 18   America Claims an Empire

abolish Put an end to

annex Add to a country as a territory or protectorate

brutality Cruelty

capitalist A person who invests money in business

diplomat A person sent to another country as a representative

duty-free Free from government tax

engineering Applying science and mathematics to practical problems

Filipino A native or inhabitant of the Philippines

in exile Not allowed to live in one's own country

intervention To interfere in the affairs of another country

isthmus A narrow strip of land

mediate To help two sides negotiate, as a peacemaker

moral Based on a judgment of right and wrong

negotiate To try to reach an agreement by talking

occupation The act of taking over and holding a place

oppressive Cruel, harsh

racist Based on the prejudice that one race is better than another

recognize To accept officially that a government has the right to be in power

technology Practical devices and machines invented by science

territory Area under the control of a country as a colonial possession

turmoil Confusion and upset

AFTER YOU READ

Terms and Names

A. Write the letter of the name that best matches each description.

a. Francisco "Pancho" Villa
b. Alfred T. Mahan
c. Theodore Roosevelt
d. Woodrow Wilson
e. John Hay
f. José Martí

_____ **1.** U.S. naval officer who supported imperialism

_____ **2.** Cuban poet and journalist who launched a revolution

_____ **3.** Secretary of state who issued the Open Door notes

_____ **4.** President who used missionary diplomacy

_____ **5.** Mexican revolutionary leader American troops tried to capture

B. Fill in the blank with the letter of the name or term that best completes each sentence.

a. Rough Riders
b. the Philippines
c. Sanford B. Dole
d. Roosevelt Corollary
e. Platt Amendment
f. U.S.S. *Maine*
g. San Juan Hill
h. Boxer Rebellion
i. Panama
j. Emilio Aguinaldo

1. American business groups created a government in Hawaii with _____ as president.

2. The United States declared war on Spain, soon after the _____ exploded in a Cuban harbor.

3. After the Spanish–American War, the United States paid Spain $20 million to annex _____.

4. The _____ gave the United States broad rights in the affairs of Cuba.

5. The Filipino rebel leader _____ believed that the United States had betrayed his people.

6. The United States helped to start a revolution in _____ in order to get land for a canal.

7. The battle of _____ in Cuba helped the United States defeat Spain.

8. A Chinese secret society led the _____ to protest Western influence in their country.

9. The _____ stated that the United States could intervene in Latin American countries.

10. _____ was the nickname of Theodore Roosevelt's cavalry unit.

Main Ideas

1. What benefits did countries get from practicing imperialism?

_____

_____

2. How were Americans divided about Cuban independence?

_____

_____

3. What sparked the Boxer Rebellion in 1900 and how was it crushed?

_____

_____

4. How did the Roosevelt Corollary lead to dollar diplomacy?

_____

_____

5. How did President Wilson justify his invasion of Mexico?

_____

_____

Thinking Critically

Answer the following questions on a separate sheet of paper.

1. Which of Admiral Mahan's goals for becoming a world power do you consider most important? Why?

2. Do you think it was right for the United States to get involved in the affairs of Columbia, Nicaragua, and Mexico? Why or why not?

Name _____ Date _____

World War I Begins

BEFORE YOU READ

In the last section, you learned how Presidents Roosevelt and Wilson used American power around the world.

In this section, you will read how war broke out in Europe while the United States tried to remain neutral.

AS YOU READ

Use this diagram to take notes. Fill it in with events that speeded up or slowed down the entrance of the United States into the war. The notes will help you remember the beginnings of World War I.

TERMS AND NAMES

nationalism A devotion to the interests and culture of one's nation

militarism Building up armed forces to prepare for war

Allies One side in World War I: Great Britain, France, and Russia, later joined by the U.S.

Central Powers One side in World War I: Germany, Austria-Hungary, and the Ottoman Empire

Archduke Franz Ferdinand Young heir whose assassination triggered the war

no man's land The space between armies fighting each other

trench warfare Fighting between fortified ditches

Lusitania British passenger ship attacked and sunk by Germans

Zimmermann note Message proposing an alliance between Germany and Mexico

THE U.S. ENTRANCE INTO WORLD WAR I	
What Speeded It Up?	**What Slowed It Down?**
Many Americans sympathized with the Allies	

Causes of World War I
(pages 578–580)

What conditions led to war?

Four main factors led to the outbreak of World War I in Europe. The first was **nationalism**—the belief that the interests of a single country were more important than cooperation among countries. This led to competition.

The second cause was imperialism. Countries tried to increase the power and influence around the world. This led to conflicts among them.

The third main cause was **militarism.** Militarism meant building up armies, navies, and other armed forces. It also meant using them as a tool for negotiating with other countries.

The fourth cause was the alliance system. Some countries in Europe had made treaties promising to defend each other. These mutual-defense treaties placed European countries in two main groups. The **Allies** were made up of France, Great Britain, and Russia. The **Central Powers** were made up of Germany, Austria-Hungary, and the Ottoman Empire.

1. Name two causes of World War I.

_____

_____

An Assassination Leads to War

(page 580)

What sparked the war?

In 1914, **Archduke Franz Ferdinand** was assassinated. He had been the *heir* to the throne of Austria-Hungary. His killer was a Serb who wanted to unite all Serbs (including those in Austria-Hungary) under one government. This touched off an action to punish Serbia.

The alliance system pulled one nation after another into the conflict. If a nation had sworn to protect another, it had to declare war on that nation's enemies. Germany and Austria-Hungary were facing France, Great Britain, and Russia.

2. Why did the assassination lead to fighting?

The Fighting Starts (pages 580–582)

Where did the fighting begin?

Germany began by invading Belgium. It planned to overrun France and then to attack Russia. The British and French could not save Belgium. They did, however, manage to stop Germany's advance.

By the spring of 1915, two lines of deep trenches had developed in France. Germans occupied one line. The Allies occupied the other line. Between the two lines lay **"no man's land."** The soldiers would climb out of their trenches and try to overrun enemy lines. They did this while facing machine-gun fire and poison gas.

This bloody **trench warfare** continued for more than three years. Neither side gained territory, but more than one million soldiers died.

3. Why did the fighting take place in France?

Americans Question Neutrality
(page 583)

How did Americans feel?

In the United States, public opinion about the war was strong but divided. Socialists saw the war as an imperialist struggle between German and English businessmen. *Pacifists* believed that all wars were bad. They urged the United States to set an example

for peace. Many other Americans simply did not want to send their sons to war.

Many *naturalized* U.S. citizens still had ties to the countries they came from. Many immigrants from Germany, for example, sympathized with Germany.

Americans tended to sympathize with Great Britain and France. They shared a common language and heritage with Britain. They were horrified at Germany's brutal attack on Belgium. And they had strong economic ties with the Allies.

4. What were three things that influenced Americans' feelings about the war?

The War Hits Home (pages 584–585)

How did the war affect Americans?

The war affected American shipping. Great Britain set up a *blockade* along the German coast to keep goods from getting through. American ships would not challenge Britain's blockade. German U-boats attacked ships from all nations. A U-boat sank the British ship **Lusitania,** killing more than a thousand people, including 128 Americans.

5. In what ways did the war affect American citizens?

The United States Declares War
(pages 585–586)

Why did the U.S. join the war?

Three incidents brought the United States into the war. First, in January 1917, Germany announced it would sink all ships in British waters on sight whether they were hostile or neutral. Second, British agents *intercepted* the **Zimmermann note,** a telegram that proposed an alliance between Germany and Mexico against the United States. Third, the replacement of the Russian monarchy with a representative government allowed American to characterize the war as a struggle of democracies against brutal monarchies. On April 6, 1917, at President Wilson's request, Congress declared war on Germany.

6. What are the three incidents that led the United States to declare war?

Name _____   Date _____

American Power Tips the Balance

BEFORE YOU READ

In the last section, you learned how the United States was drawn into the war.

In this section, you will read how Americans prepared to fight and how they helped the Allies win.

AS YOU READ

Use this web diagram to take notes. Fill it in with problems the United States faced as it entered the war.

TERMS AND NAMES

Selective Service Act Law requiring men to register for military service

convoy system Having merchant ships travel in groups protected by warships

American Expeditionary Force The name given to the American military force that fought in World War I

General John J. Pershing The commander of the American Expeditionary force

Eddie Rickenbacker Famous American fighter pilot

Alvin York American war hero

conscientious objector A person who believes fighting is wrong and therefore does not want to serve in the military

armistice Truce agreement

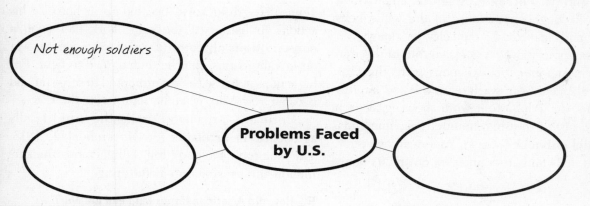

Not enough soldiers

Problems Faced by U.S.

America Mobilizes (pages 587–589)

How did the U.S. prepare for war?

The United States first needed to build up its armed forces. When war was declared, only about 200,000 men were in service. To solve this problem, Congress passed the **Selective Service Act.** It required men to register with the government so that some of them could be selected for military service. This process—called the draft—put about 3 million men in uniform.

Many African Americans served in the military. They were placed in separate units, but some blacks were trained as officers. Blacks were among the first to receive the French honor of the Croix de Guerre.

Women were not drafted. The army would not let them join. But the navy accepted women in *noncombat* positions. Woman served as nurses, secretaries, and telephone operators.

The U.S. built ships to transport men and supplies to Europe. Shipyard workers were *exempted* from the draft and the importance of their work was publicized. *Prefabrication* techniques were used to speed the production of ships.

1. How did the United States build up its armed forces?

_____

_____

America Turns the Tide (page 589)

How did the United States help?

To reduce the loss of ships to German submarine attacks, the United States and Britain began to use the **convoy system.** In this system, merchant ships traveled in a large group guarded by naval vessels.

American soldiers helped turn the tide of battle in Europe. The Allies had absorbed many casualties and were running out of men. Thousands of fresh American soldiers were eager for battle.

2. How did the United States help the Allies?

_____

_____

Fighting "Over There" (pages 590–591)

What new weapons were used?

The **American Expeditionary Force** was led by **General John J. Pershing.** American infantrymen were called doughboys because of the white belts they wore and cleaned with pipe clay, or "dough."

New weapons played a decisive role in the war. The two most *innovative* weapons were the tank and the airplane. Air warfare developed rapidly during the war. Pilots went from shooting at each other with pistols to using mounted machine guns. **Eddie Rickenbacker** was an American ace pilot. He fought in 34 air battles and shot down 26 enemy planes.

3. Name two new weapons used in the war.

The War Introduces New Hazards
(page 591)

What made World War I hard for soldiers?

New weapons and tactics made World War I very destructive. Soldiers faced miserable conditions, including filth, trench foot, trench mouth, "shell shock" from constant bombardment, vermin, poison gas, and disease.

4. What hardships did soldiers face in World War I?

_____

American Troops Go on the Offensive (pages 592–593)

How did American troops help end the war?

American soldiers arrived in Europe just in time to stop a German advance on Paris. One soldier from Tennessee, **Alvin York,** became a war hero for his actions in battle. At the start, York had been a **conscientious objector** (a person who opposes war on moral grounds), but he then agreed to fight. For his actions in battle he was promoted to sergeant and became a *celebrity* when he returned to the U.S.

Germany, exhausted from the war, finally agreed to an **armistice** on November 11, 1918. The war took a bloody toll, killing more than 22 million and causing untold suffering.

5. How did American troops help end the war?

_____

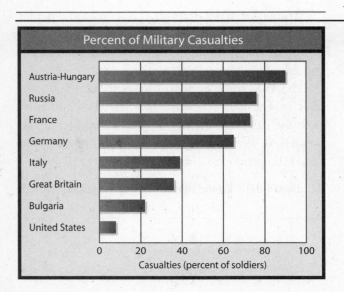

Percent of Military Casualties

Casualties (percent of soldiers)

Austria-Hungary
Russia
France
Germany
Italy
Great Britain
Bulgaria
United States

0   20   40   60   80   100

Skillbuilder
Use the chart to answer these questions.

1. Which nation suffered the most casualties?

_____

2. How does the chart reflect America's late entry into the war?

_____

CHAPTER 19 Section 3 (pages 594–601)

The War at Home

TERMS AND NAMES

War Industries Board Agency to improve efficiency in war-related industries

Bernard M. Baruch Leader of the War Industries Board

propaganda A kind of biased communication designed to influence people's thoughts and actions

George Creel Head of the Committee on Public Information (CPI), the government's propaganda agency

Espionage and Sedition Acts Laws that enacted harsh penalties against anyone opposing U.S. participation in World War I

Great Migration Movement of many African Americans to northern cities from the South in the early 1900s

BEFORE YOU READ

In the last section, you learned how the United States fought in World War I.

In this section, you will read about how the war changed American society at home.

AS YOU READ

Use this diagram to take notes. Fill it in with ways in which Americans at home supported the war effort.

GROUP OR INDIVIDUAL	CONTRIBUTIONS TO THE WAR EFFORT
War Industries Board	

Congress Gives Power to Wilson
(pages 594–596)

How did business and government work together?

To fight the war, the United States needed the help of industry. The economy had to change from making *consumer goods* to making weapons and war supplies. Congress gave President Wilson direct control over much of the economy. He had the power to fix prices and to regulate war-related industries.

Wilson created the **War Industries Board (WIB)** and named **Bernard M. Baruch** to run it. This agency helped boost industrial production by 20 percent. Other federal agencies also regulated the economy for the war effort. The Railroad Administration controlled the nation's railroads.

The Fuel Administration watched over the use of coal, gasoline, and heating oil.

Wages in some industries went up. But workers in other jobs lost money because of *inflation*. As a result, many workers joined unions. Wilson established the National War Labor Board. This agency worked to settle disputes between management and labor. It also helped to improve working conditions.

Another new agency, the Food Administration, was established to help produce and conserve food supplies. It encouraged people to grow their own food. It taught them to eat differently. Americans were able to send more food to the Allies.

1. How did Wilson control the economy?

_____

_____

Selling the War (pages 596–597)

How did the government win over public opinion?

The government needed to raise money for the war. They did this by increasing several kinds of taxes and by selling war bonds. Thousands of volunteers sold the bonds. Famous people spoke at rallies to promote the sales. Newspapers and billboards carried advertisements free of charge.

To popularize the war, the government created the Committee on Public Information (CPI). It was the nation's first **propaganda** agency. The agency was headed by **George Creel.** He had been a muckraking journalist. He used artists and advertising people to create thousands of posters, paintings, and cartoons to promote the war. He distributed pamphlets in many languages.

2. How did the U.S. government pay for the war?

_____

_____

Attacks on Civil Liberties Increase (pages 597–598)

How did the war affect civil liberties?

The war brought out anti-immigrant feelings. Immigrants from Germany were often targeted for attack. Americans with German-sounding names lost their jobs. Orchestras refused to play German music. Some towns with German names changed them.

Congress passed the **Espionage and Sedition Acts** to punish people who did not support the war effort. People could not interfere with the draft or *obstruct* the sale of war bonds. They could not even speak against the war effort.

These laws violated the spirit of the First Amendment, which guarantees freedom of speech. The law led to 6,000 arrests and 1,500 convictions for antiwar activities.

The chief targets of the Espionage and Sedition Acts were socialists and union leaders. Labor leader Eugene V. Debs was jailed for making a speech about the economic causes of the war. The Industrial Workers of the World urged workers to strike. This was considered an antiwar activity, and they received jail sentences.

3. How did the Espionage and Sedition Acts contradict the First Amendment?

_____

_____

The War Encourages Social Change (pages 598–601)

How did the war affect women and African Americans?

The war brought many social changes for African Americans and women.

African-American leaders were divided over the war. W. E. B. Du Bois believed that helping the war effort would help the fight for equality. Others believed that blacks should not help a government that did not support equality for everyone.

The war sped up the **Great Migration.** This was the movement of thousands of African Americans from the South to cities of the North. They wanted to escape racial discrimination. They also wanted to find jobs in Northern industries.

American women played new roles during the war. They did jobs that had previously been done only by men. They worked as truck drivers, cooks, dockworkers, and builders. Women volunteered in the Red Cross and sold war bonds.

Women's activities made them more visible. They were not paid the same as men. But, soon after the war, Congress finally passed an amendment giving them the right to vote.

Also during the war, a worldwide flu *epidemic*, probably spread by American soldiers, killed 500,000 Americans and caused disruptions in the American economy.

4. How did women's roles change during the war?

_____

_____

CHAPTER 19 Section 4 (pages 604–609)

Wilson Fights for Peace

TERMS AND NAMES

Fourteen Points Wilson's plan for world peace following World War I

League of Nations An international peace-keeping organization proposed by Wilson and founded in 1920

Georges Clemenceau French premier

David Lloyd George British prime minister

Treaty of Versailles The 1919 treaty that ended World War I

reparations Payments made by defeated countries after a war

war-guilt clause Part of the Treaty of Versailles in which Germany took responsibility for the war

Henry Cabot Lodge Conservative senator who wanted to keep the United States out of the League of Nations

BEFORE YOU READ

In the last section, you learned how the war in Europe changed life at home.

In this section, you will read about the treaty that ended the war and Wilson's proposal for a League of Nations.

AS YOU READ

Use this diagram to take notes. Fill it in with details about the Treaty of Versailles. The notes will help you remember the consequences of World War I.

TREATY OF VERSAILLES	
Provisions	**Weaknesses**
Established 9 new nations	

Wilson Presents His Plan (pages 604–605)

What were Wilson's peace plans?

President Wilson presented his plan for world peace to Congress in January 1918. The plan was called his **Fourteen Points.**

The first five points suggested ways that wars could be avoided. They stated that (1) countries should not make secret treaties with one another, (2) freedom of the seas should be maintained, (3) tariffs should be lowered to promote free trade, (4) countries should reduce their arms, and (5) the interests of the colonial people should be considered.

The next eight points suggested new national boundaries. Wilson believed in self-determination: different ethnic groups should be able to decide for themselves what nation they would belong to.

The fourteenth point called for a **League of Nations.** This international organization would address problems between countries before they led to war.

Wilson met with leaders of France and Great Britain, **George Clemenceau** and **David Lloyd George,** to discuss the terms of peace. These leaders had won the war, and they wanted to punish Germany. Wilson had to give up most of his Fourteen Points. The one he insisted on was the League of Nations.

1. What did Wilson's first first five points address?

_____

_____

_____

Debating the Treaty of Versailles (pages 606–608)

What did the treaty say?

On June 28, 1919, the leaders of the Allies and the Central Powers met at the Palace of Versailles in France. They were to sign the **Treaty of Versailles.**

The treaty created new national boundaries by (1) establishing nine new nations, including Poland, Czechoslovakia, and Yugoslavia; (2) shifting the boundaries of other nations; and (3) carving out parts of the Ottoman Empire to create colonies in the Middle East for Great Britain and France.

The treaty took away Germany's army and navy. It forced Germany to pay **reparations,** or war damages, to the winners. In addition, the treaty contained a **war-guilt clause.** Germany had to admit that it was responsible for causing the war.

The Treaty of Versailles had three basic weaknesses. The first was its harsh treatment of Germany. Germany was humiliated. Germany was not the only country that had also been militaristic, yet Germany alone was punished. And, Germany would not be able to pay the huge reparations.

The second weakness was that the Soviet Union (formerly Russia) lost more territory than Germany did. Russia had been one of the Allies, and had suffered more *casualties* than any other country. The Soviet Union was determined to get its territories back.

The third weakness concerned colonies. The treaty did not recognize the claims of colonies for self-determination, in Southeast Asia, for instance.

Wilson brought the treaty back to the United States for approval. He found several groups opposed it. Some thought the treaty too harsh. Others thought it favored the imperialists. Some ethnic groups objected to the treaty because of the way it treated their homelands.

The main opposition to the treaty was over the League of Nations. The League was the only one of Wilson's Fourteen Points that was included in the treaty. Conservative senators, headed by **Henry Cabot Lodge,** opposed joining the League. They did not like the idea of working with other countries to take economic and military action against aggression. They wanted the treaty to include the constitutional right of Congress to declare war.

Wilson refused to compromise on the League. He would not accept amendments proposed by Republican leaders. As a result, the Senate failed to ratify the treaty. The United States never entered the League of Nations. It finally signed a separate treaty with Germany in 1921, when Wilson was no longer president.

2. Name the three weaknesses of the treaty.

_____

_____

_____

The Legacy of the War (page 609)

What was the legacy of the war?

The end of the war made Americans yearn for what Warren G. Harding called "normalcy." But the war had transformed the United States and the world. World War I had strengthened both U.S military power and the power of government. It accelerated change for African Americans and women. However, the propaganda campaign left a legacy of mistrust and fear.

In Europe, the war left a legacy of massive destruction, loss of life, political instability, and violence. Communists ruled in Russia and soon after the war fascist organizations seized power in Italy.

Americans hoped that the war had convinced the world to never fight again. But in Europe the war settled nothing. In Germany, Adolf Hitler exploited Germans' discontent with the Treaty of Versailles and threatened to fight again. Hitler was true to his predictions; America did have to fight again years later in a second world war.

3. What were the long-term results of the war?

_____

_____

_____

Glossary

blockade The blocking of a harbor or shipping lanes by hostile ships

casualties People killed or wounded

celebrity Famous person

consumer goods Things made for household use

epidemic A widespread outbreak of an infectious disease

exempted Allowed to avoid serving in the armed forces

heir Person who is next in line to receive a title

inflation A sustained rise in the average level of prices

innovative Introducing something new and different

intercepted Stopped before it was delivered

naturalized Naturalized citizens are those who come to a country from somewhere else and become

citizens—as compared with people who are citizens of a country because they are born there

noncombat Not fighting

obstruct Get in the way of

pacifist Someone who opposes war and violence

prefabrication Some assembly in advance, making for easier final assembly

AFTER YOU READ

Terms and Names

A. Write the letter of the name or term that matches the description.

a. **Allies**
b. **George Creel**
c. **conscientious objector**
d. **Henry Cabot Lodge**
e. **Central Powers**

_____ **1.** The alliance, in 1914, that was made up of Germany, Austria-Hungary, and the Ottoman Empire

_____ **2.** The alliance, in 1914, that was made up of France, Great Britain, and Russia

_____ **3.** A person who opposes warfare on moral grounds

_____ **4.** The muckraking journalist who led the Committee on Public Information

_____ **5.** A conservative United States senator who strongly opposed the Treaty of Versailles

B. If the statement is true, write "true" on the line. If it is false, write the word or words that would replace the underlined words to make it true.

_____ **1.** The assassination of <u>Archduke Franz Ferdinand</u> sparked the beginning of World War I.

_____ **2.** <u>Alvin York</u> shot down at least 26 enemy planes and was America's leading ace pilot in the war.

_____ **3.** The war damages the Treaty of Versailles required Germany to pay to the Allies were called <u>reparations</u>.

_____ **4.** Under the <u>National War Labor Board</u>, the nation's main wartime regulatory body, industrial production in the United States increased by about 20 percent.

_____ **5.** The <u>first</u> point in Wilson's Fourteen Points called for the establishment of a League of Nations.

AFTER YOU READ (continued)   The First World War

Main Ideas

1. What were the long-term causes of World War I?

_____

_____

2. What acts brought the United States into the war?

_____

_____

3. How did the U.S. government sell the war to the nation?

_____

_____

4. What events during the war undermined Americans' civil liberties?

_____

_____

5. Why did the U.S. Senate reject the Treaty of Versailles?

_____

_____

Thinking Critically

Answer the following questions on a separate sheet of paper.

1. What do you think would have happened if the United States had not entered the war on the side of the Allies?

2. How did the Treaty of Versailles make conditions ripe for the rise of Hitler in Germany?

Americans Struggle with Postwar Issues

TERMS AND NAMES

nativism Suspicion of foreign-born people

isolationism Pulling away from world affairs

communism An economic system that supports government control over property to create equality

anarchists People who opposed any form of government

Sacco and Vanzetti Immigrant anarchists accused of murder

quota system A system that established the maximum number of people who could enter the United States from each country

John L. Lewis President of the United Mine Workers

BEFORE YOU READ

In the last section, you read about the end of the First World War.

In this section, you will see how Americans adjusted to the end of the war.

AS YOU READ

Use the chart below to take notes on the results of the Red Scare and labor strikes.

RED SCARE	LABOR STRIKES
Civil rights violated	Coolidge used force to put down Boston police strike

Postwar Trends (page 618)

How did World War I affect America?

World War I left much of the American public divided about the League of Nations. The end of the war hurt the economy. Returning soldiers took jobs away from many women and minorities, or faced unemployment themselves. A wave of **nativism** and **isolationism** swept over America as people became suspicious of foreigners and wanted to pull away from world affairs.

1. What attitudes became prevalent in America after WWI?

_____

_____

Fear of Communism (pages 619–620)

Why did Americans fear communism?

Americans saw **communism** as a threat to their way of life. Communism is an economic and political system that supports government control over property to create equality. Some communists said there should be only one political party: the Communist Party. Communists came to power in Russia through violent revolution.

World War I created economic and political problems in Russia. In 1917, the Russian *czar*, or emperor, stepped down. Later, a group of revolutionaries called Bolsheviks took power. Their leader was Vladimir I. Lenin. They established the world's first communist state. This new government called for worldwide revolution. Communist leaders wanted workers to seize political and economic power. They wanted to overthrow *capitalism*.

In the United States, about 70,000 people joined the Communist Party. Still, the ideas of the communists, or "Reds," frightened many people. A fear of communism, known as the "Red Scare," swept the nation.

Attorney General A. Mitchell Palmer set up an agency in the Justice Department to arrest communists, *socialists*, and **anarchists,** who opposed all forms of government. (The agency later became the Federal Bureau of Investigation, or FBI.)

Palmer's agents trampled on people's civil rights. Many *radicals* were sent out of the country without trial. But Palmer found no evidence of a plot to overthrow the government. Many suffered because of *abuses of power* during the Red Scare. One case involved two Italian immigrants, Nicola Sacco and Bartolomeo Vanzetti. **Sacco and Vanzetti** were arrested for robbery and murder in Massachusetts. They admitted they were anarchists. But they denied committing any crime. The case against them was weak. But they were convicted anyway. Many people protested the conviction. They believed it was based on a fear of foreigners. Sacco and Vanzetti were executed in 1927.

2. How did Americans show their fear of communism?

Limiting Immigration (pages 620–623)

How did Americans show their Nativist feelings?

Some Americans used the Red Scare as an excuse to act against any people who were different. For example, the Ku Klux Klan, which had threatened African Americans during Reconstruction, revived.

Now the Klan turned against blacks, Jews, Roman Catholics, immigrants, and union leaders. They used violence to keep these groups "in their place." The Klan briefly gained political power in several states.

As a result of nativism, or anti-immigrant feelings, Congress passed the Emergency Quota Act of 1921. It established a **quota system.** This set a limit on how many immigrants from each country could enter the

United States every year. In 1924, a new quota limited immigration from Eastern and Southern Europe, mostly Jews and Roman Catholics.

The 1924 law also banned immigration from Japan. People from the Western Hemisphere still entered the United States in large numbers.

3. What was the quota system?

A Time of Labor Unrest (pages 623–624)

What were the three major strikes of 1919?

Strikes were not allowed during World War I because they might have hurt the war effort. But in 1919, three important strikes occurred.

Boston police officers went on strike for a *living wage*. The *cost of living* had doubled since their last raise. Massachusetts governor Calvin Coolidge used force to put down the strike.

A strike by steelworkers began at U.S. Steel Corporation. Workers demanded the right to join unions, which employers prohibited. In 1923, a report revealed the harsh conditions in steel mills. Public opinion turned against the steel companies, and workers were given an eight-hour day. But they still had no union.

A more successful strike was led by **John L. Lewis,** the president of the United Mine Workers. When Lewis's workers closed the coal mines, President Wilson tried to help to settle the dispute between the miners and mine owners. The miners got higher wages, but they did not get shorter hours.

In 1925, A. Philip Randolph founded the Brotherhood of Sleeping Car Porters, an African-American union of railroad workers. But few blacks belonged to other unions. Overall, the 1920s was a bad time for unions. Union membership declined from 5 million to 3.5 million for the following reasons: (1) immigrants were willing to work in poor conditions, (2) language barriers made organizing people difficult; (3) farmers who had migrated to cities were used to relying on themselves, and (4) most unions excluded African Americans.

4. Why did union membership decline?

The Harding Presidency

TERMS AND NAMES

Warren G. Harding 29th president of the United States

Charles Evans Hughes Secretary of state under Harding

Fordney-McCumber Tariff High tax on imports adopted in 1922

Ohio gang Harding's friends and advisors

Teapot Dome scandal Scandal surrounding Albert Fall

Albert B. Fall Secretary of the interior under Harding

BEFORE YOU READ

In the last section, you learned about some of the issues Americans faced following World War I.

In this section, you will read about President Harding and the issues his administration faced at home and abroad.

AS YOU READ

Make a chart like the one below and fill it in with the major events of Harding's presidency. Take notes on the effects of each event.

EVENT	NOTES
Washington conference	reduced arms

Harding Struggles for Peace
(pages 625–626)

How did Harding handle foreign affairs?

In 1921, **Warren G. Harding** invited several major world powers to the Washington Naval Conference. Once there, Secretary of State **Charles Evans Hughes** urged that no more warships should be built for ten years and that the five major naval powers—the U.S., Great Britain, Japan, France and Italy—would scrap many of their existing warships. For the first time, nations agreed to *disarm* or reduce their weapons. In 1928, long after Harding left office, 64 nations signed the Kellogg-Briand Pact. By signing the Pact, these nations said they would give up war as national policy.

Americans wanted to stay out of world affairs. But the United States still wanted France and Britain to repay the money they had borrowed during World War I.

Those two nations had suffered during the war. Their economies were too weak for them to repay the loans. To make matters worse, Congress passed the **Fordney-McCumber Tariff** in 1922. This tariff protected American business from foreign competition. But the tariff made it impossible for Britain and France to sell their goods in the United States.

As a result, France and Britain put pressure on Germany to pay its promised *reparations*. But Germany's economy had been destroyed. When Germany failed to make payments to France, French troops marched into Germany. To avoid another war, American banker Charles Dawes negotiated a settlement to end the loan crisis. Under the Dawes Plan, as the solution was called, the U.S. loaned money to Germany to pay back Britain and France which then repaid their American loan. Thus, the U.S. ended up getting paid with its own money. The solution left bitter feelings. Britain and France saw the U.S. as a miser for not paying its fair share of the costs of war; the U.S. felt Britain and France were financially irresponsible.

1. How did the Fordney-McCumber Tariff affect other countries?

_____

_____

Scandal Hits Harding's Administration (pages 626–627)

How did scandal hurt Harding's administration?

Some of Harding's cabinet appointments were excellent. But others caused problems. Three honest members of his cabinet were Charles Evans Hughes, Herbert Hoover, and Andrew Mellon. Hughes was secretary of state. He later became chief justice of the Supreme Court. The talented Herbert Hoover became secretary of commerce. Secretary of the Treasury Andrew Mellon reduced the *national debt* by about a third.

Other cabinet appointments caused problems. Some were part of the so-called **Ohio gang.** These were the president's poker-playing buddies from back home. They caused the president a great deal of embarrassment. It became apparent to some that the president's main problem was that he didn't understand many of the country's financial issues. This left him in the dark about practices going on in his own cabinet. He had to comply with whatever his advisers told him. Many of these people took advantage of the situation.

Charles R. Forbes, the head of the Veterans Bureau, was caught selling government and hospital supplies to private companies, and pocketing the money. Colonel Thomas W. Miller, the head of the Office of Alien Property, was caught taking a bribe.

One of the worst cases of corruption was known as the **Teapot Dome scandal.** It involved pieces of land called Teapot Dome and Elk Hills. This land was owned by the government and held large reserves of oil. **Albert B. Fall,** Harding's secretary of the interior, secretly leased the land to two oil companies. He received money and property in return.

Harding was not charged with corruption himself. He suddenly died in 1923, and Calvin Coolidge became president. Coolidge was then elected president in 1924.

2. What does the Teapot Dome scandal tell about President Harding?

_____

_____

The Business of America

TERMS AND NAMES

Calvin Coolidge President of the U.S. (1923–1929) succeeded to presidency on death of Harding, elected in 1924

urban sprawl The outward expansion of cities

installment plan An easy way to borrow money to buy goods

BEFORE YOU READ

In the last section, you read about Harding's presidency.

In this section, you will read about the economy of the 1920s.

AS YOU READ

In the chart below, use the boxes on the left to take notes on the changes in business and technology in the 1920s. Use the boxes on the right to show some of the effects of these changes.

CHANGES	EFFECT
Standard of living goes up	Pro-business attitude

America's Industries Flourish
(pages 628–631)

How did the success of certain industries affect American life?

The new president, **Calvin Coolidge** said, "The chief business of the American people is business." Both Coolidge and his Republican successor, Herbert Hoover, favored government policies that promoted business and limited government interference.

The automobile changed the American landscape. New roads were built, and new businesses sprang up such as gas stations, repair shops, public garages, motels, tourist camps and shopping centers. Automobiles ended the isolation of rural families and gave young people and women more independence. Cars also made it possible for people to live farther from their jobs. This led to **urban sprawl,** as cities spread out in all directions.

Cities in Ohio and Michigan grew as major centers of automobile manufacturing. States that produced oil such as California and Texas also prospered.

The automobile also became a *status symbol.* Everyone wanted to have one. By the late 1920s, about 80 percent of all the cars in the world were in the United States.

The airline industry also grew. Planes carried the nation's mail. Passenger service began.

1. Name three ways the automobile changed American life.

_____

America's Standard of Living Soars (pages 631–632)

How did the American household change?

Another major change was the spread of electricity. In the 1920s, electric power stretched beyond big cities to the *suburbs*. Still, farms lacked electricity.

Americans began to use all kinds of electrical appliances. Radios, washing machines, and vacuum cleaners became popular. These appliances made housework easier. One result was more leisure time for families. Another effect was to increase the number of women working outside the home.

More consumer goods appeared on the market. Businesses used advertising to sell these goods. Ads didn't just give information about the product. Now, they used *psychology*. They tried to use people's desire for youth, beauty, and popularity to sell products. Things that once were luxuries became necessities. Some brand names became known nationwide.

Businesspeople formed organizations to do charity work. They also formed organizations to promote business.

2. How did advertising change American life?

_____

_____

A Superficial Prosperity (pages 632–633)

What hidden problems did the economy have?

Most Americans had confidence in the prosperity of the 1920s. The *national income* rose from $64 billion in 1921 to $87 billion in 1929. Most businesses seemed to make fortunes. The stock market reached new heights. But this prosperity hid two big problems.

First, business was not as healthy as it seemed. As workers produced more goods, businesses grew. Large businesses bought up, or merged with, smaller ones. But as businesses grew, business managers made much more money than workers did. Also, mining companies, railroads, and farms were not doing well.

Second, *consumer debt* rose to high levels. Businesses needed to sell all the goods they were now producing. So they encouraged customers to buy on the **installment plan.** This was a form of borrowing. Customers could make low payments over a period of time. That way people could afford to buy more. Banks provided money at low *interest rates*. Advertising also pushed the idea of buying on credit. Average Americans were spending more money than they actually had.

3. Describe two economic problems hidden by the business boom of the 1920s.

_____

_____

_____

Distribución de ingresos: 1929

$10,000+ 1%
$6,000–$9,999 3%
$5,000–$5,999 2%
$4,000–$4,999 4%
$3,000–$3,999 8%

$2,000–$2,999 17%

Menos de $1,999 65%

Fuente: *Historical Statistics of the United States: Colonial Times to 1970.*

Skillbuilder

Use the chart to answer these questions.

1. What percentage of Americans earned more than $5000 in 1929?

_____

_____

2. How much money did most Americans earn in 1929?

_____

_____

Glossary

abuses of power Efforts by officials to use their offices in corrupt ways

capitalism An economic system based on private ownership of property

consumer debt Money people owe to banks or stores for goods they have purchased

cost of living The average cost of the basic necessities of life

czar Emperor of Russia

disarm To reduce weapons

interest rate The charge for a loan

living wage Wage needed to keep a person or family out of poverty

national debt The money the government owes from borrowing or issuing bonds

national income The total amount of money earned by individuals and businesses in one nation

psychology Study of the way people think

radicals People in favor of revolutionary change

reparations Payments to make up for damages

socialists People who believe in an economic system based on government control over the economy and on equal distribution of wealth

status symbol Something that shows that its owner is a person of high rank

suburbs The residential area around a major city

AFTER YOU READ

Terms and Names

A. Write the letter of the name or term next to the description that explains it best.

a. **Charles Evans Hughes**
b. **Calvin Coolidge**
c. **John L. Lewis**
d. **Sacco and Vanzetti**
e. **Warren G. Harding**

_____ **1.** This president of the United Mine Workers led a successful strike.

_____ **2.** These radicals were executed for murder, probably as a result of the Red Scare.

_____ **3.** This president of the United States suffered from scandal.

_____ **4.** This secretary of state was a leader at the Washington Naval Conference in 1921.

_____ **5.** This American president said, "The chief business of the American people is business."

B. Write the name or term that best completes each sentence.

Fordney-McCumber Tariff   quota system   urban sprawl   communism   installment plan

1. Congress passed the _____ to protect American business, but it prevented Britain and France from selling their products in the United States.

2. During the 1920s, many Americans feared _____, an economic and political system based on state ownership of property.

3. People who couldn't afford to pay the whole price of a car could buy it on the _____ and make small payments over time.

4. Fear of foreign influences and racism led to a _____ that limited immigration from Eastern and Southern Europe.

5. The spreading out of cities is called _____.

AFTER YOU READ (cont.) *CHAPTER 20* Politics of the Roaring Twenties

Main Ideas

1. How did the Sacco and Vanzetti case reflect the fears of many Americans?

_____

_____

2. Why were strikes risky for workers in the 1920s?

_____

_____

3. What was the main goal of the quota system?

_____

_____

4. Who was most closely linked to the Teapot Dome scandal?

_____

_____

5. What new methods did advertisers use in the 1920s?

_____

_____

Thinking Critically

Answer the following questions on a separate sheet of paper.

1. How are isolationism and nativism related? In the 1920s, what actions did Americans take that reveal their distrust of others?

2. What were signs of American business success in the 1920s? What were some signs that the economic situation might not be as good as it seemed?

Name _____ Date _____

Changing Ways of Life

TERMS AND NAMES

Prohibition The era that prohibited the manufacture and sale of alcoholic beverages

speakeasy Hidden saloons and nightclubs that illegally sold liquor

bootlegger Smugglers who brought alcohol in from Canada and the Caribbean

fundamentalism Religious movement based on the belief that everything written in the Bible was literally true

Clarence Darrow Famous trial lawyer

Scopes trial Trial of John Scopes for teaching evolution

BEFORE YOU READ

In the last section, you learned about American business in the 1920s.

In this section, you will read about new lifestyles and values that emerged in the 1920s.

AS YOU READ

Make a chart like the one below and fill it in. Take notes on the effects of Americans moving from rural areas to the cities.

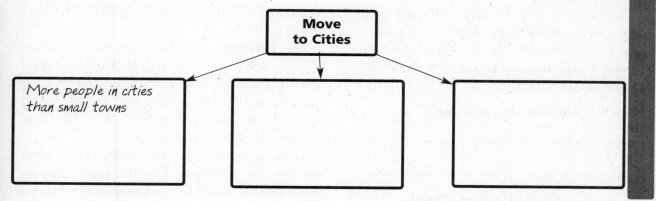

Move to Cities

More people in cities than small towns

Rural and Urban Differences
(pages 640–643)

What was Prohibition?

The 1920 *census* showed a change in America. For the first time, more Americans lived in large towns and cities than in small towns and on farms.

The values that most Americans had grown up with were small-town values. They included conservative social standards, hard work, *thriftiness*, and close families. People knew their neighbors and followed the teachings of their churches.

By the 1920s, *urbanization*, or the movement of Americans from rural areas to the cities, had increased. New York, Chicago, and Philadelphia had become huge cities. There were over 65 cities

with more than 100,000 people. Two million people a year left their farms and small towns for the cities.

Urban values began to dominate the nation. Life in big cities was different from in small towns. People with different backgrounds came into contact with one another.

City people were more open to new ideas in art, science, and politics. They went out at night. They were more tolerant of drinking and gambling. Life was fast-paced. Sometimes it was impersonal and lonely. Many people who were new to city life found it hard to adjust.

One clash between small-town and city values led to an era known as **Prohibition.** Prohibition was the ban on alcoholic beverages set forth in the Eighteenth Amendment. It took effect in 1920.

Most support for prohibition came from religious rural white Protestants.

Even though it was the law, the effort to stop drinking was doomed. The government did not have enough officers to enforce it. People made their own alcohol illegally.

In cities, even respectable middle-class people flocked to **speakeasies.** These were hidden saloons and nightclubs that served liquor illegally.

People also bought liquor from **bootleggers,** or smugglers who brought it in from Canada and the Caribbean. Bootleggers created a chain of corruption by bribing police officers and judges.

Prohibition caused a general disrespect for the law. It also caused a great deal of money to flow out of lawful businesses and into organized crime. Underworld gangs took control of the illegal liquor business. The most famous gang was headed by Chicago's Al Capone. Chicago became known for bloody gang killings.

This rise in crime and violence led many people to demand the repeal of prohibition. By the middle of the decade, only 19 percent of Americans supported it. Prohibition was repealed by the Twenty-first Amendment in 1933.

1. How did prohibition affect the nation?

_____

_____

Science and Religion Clash
(pages 644–645)

What was the Scopes Trial?

During the 1920s, the nation saw the rise of Christian **fundamentalism.** This religious movement was based on the belief that everything written in the Bible was literally true. Fundamentalists rejected the growing trust in science that most Americans had. They were also against the religious faiths of other people, especially immigrants.

These beliefs led fundamentalists to reject Charles Darwin's *theory of evolution.* According to that theory, plant and animal species had developed over millions of years.

Fundamentalists believed that the Bible was correct in stating that the world and all its plants and animals were created by God in six days. They did not want evolution taught in schools.

Fundamentalist preachers drew large crowds to religious revivals, especially in the South and West. Fundamentalists also gained political power. In 1925, Tennessee passed a law making it a crime to teach evolution.

Many people opposed this law. The American Civil Liberties Union (ACLU) promised to defend in court any teacher who would challenge the law.

John Scopes, a young biology teacher from Dayton, Tennessee, challenged the law. He openly taught about evolution. He was arrested, and his case went to trial. The ACLU hired **Clarence Darrow,** the most famous trial lawyer in the nation, to defend Scopes. William Jennings Bryan was the prosecutor.

Scopes was guilty because he broke the law. But the trial was really about evolution. It was also about religion in schools. Reporters came from all over the world to cover the **Scopes trial.** Huge crowds gathered.

The highlight of the trial was when William Jennings Bryan took the stand. Darrow questioned Bryan until Bryan said that while the earth was made in six days, they were "not six days of 24 hours." Bryan was admitting that the Bible could be interpreted in different ways.

Even so, Scopes was found guilty. His conviction was later overturned by the state Supreme Court. But the ban on teaching evolution remained a law in Tennessee.

2. How did fundamentalist beliefs lead to the Scopes trial?

_____

_____

The Twenties Woman

TERMS AND NAMES

flapper Young woman who embraced the new fashions and values of the 1920s

double standard Set of principles granting one group more freedom than another group

BEFORE YOU READ

In the last section, you read about some lifestyle changes in the 1920s.

In this section, you will learn how women's lives changed during the 1920s.

AS YOU READ

Use the web below to take notes on the changes women experienced in the 1920s.

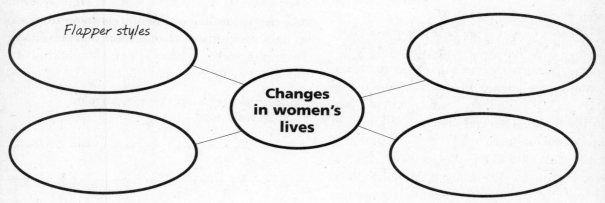

Flapper styles

Changes in women's lives

Young Women Change the Rules (pages 646–647)

What was a flapper?

In some ways, the spirit of the twenties was a reaction to World War I. Many young soldiers had witnessed horrible events in Europe. This led them to rebel against traditional values. They wanted to enjoy life while they could.

Young women also wanted to take part in the rebellious, pleasure-loving life of the twenties. Many of them demanded the same freedom as men.

The new urban culture also influenced many women. Their symbol was the **flapper.** She was an *emancipated* young woman. She held new independent attitudes and liked the sophisticated new fashions of the day.

She wore make-up, short skirts, short hair, and more jewelry than would have been proper only a few years before. She often smoked cigarettes and drank alcohol in public. She went dancing to new, exciting music.

Other attitudes changed, too. Many young men and women began to see marriage as more of an equal partnership.

At the same time, churches and schools protested the new values. The majority of women were not flappers. Many people felt torn between the old values and the new ones.

One result of this clash between old values and the image of the flapper was the **double standard.** This was a set of principles or values generally accepted by society. One American double standard allowed men to have greater sexual freedom than women. Women still had to observe stricter standards of behavior than men did.

1. How did the flapper represent the spirit of the twenties?

_____

_____

Women Shed Old Roles at Home and at Work (pages 647–649)

How did women's roles change?

Many women had gone to work outside the home during World War I. This trend continued in the twenties. But their opportunities had changed after the war. Men returned from the war and took back traditional "men's jobs." Women moved back into the "women's professions" of teaching, nursing, and social work.

Big business provided another role for women: clerical work. Millions of women became secretaries. Many others became salesclerks in stores. Many women also worked on *assembly lines* in factories. By 1930, 10 million women had paid jobs outside the home. This was almost one-fourth of the American work force.

Women did not find equality in the workplace. Few women rose to jobs in management. Women earned less than men. Men regarded women as

temporary workers whose real job was at home keeping house and raising children. In the twenties, patterns of discrimination against women in the business world continued.

Family life changed, too. Families had fewer children. Electrical appliances made housework easier. Many items that had been made at home—from clothing to bread—could now be bought ready-made in stores.

Public agencies took over some family responsibilities, too. They provided services for the elderly and the sick. Nevertheless, most women remained homemakers. Some women had to work and also run their homes. It was hard for them to combine these roles.

In the 1920s, marriages were more often based on romantic love than arranged by families. Children were no longer part of the work force. They spent their days in school and other activities with people of their own age. *Peer pressure* began to be an important influence on teens' behavior. This reflected the conflict between traditional attitudes and modern ways of thinking.

2. Describe two changes in women's roles in the workplace.

_____

_____

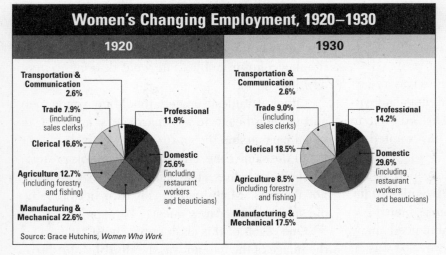

Women's Changing Employment, 1920–1930

1920

1930

Transportation & Communication 2.6%
Trade 7.9% (including sales clerks)
Professional 11.9%
Clerical 16.6%
Agriculture 12.7% (including forestry and fishing)
Domestic 25.6% (including restaurant workers and beauticians)
Manufacturing & Mechanical 22.6%

Transportation & Communication 2.6%
Trade 9.0% (including sales clerks)
Professional 14.2%
Clerical 18.5%
Agriculture 8.5% (including forestry and fishing)
Domestic 29.6% (including restaurant workers and beauticians)
Manufacturing & Mechanical 17.5%

Source: Grace Hutchins, *Women Who Work*

Skillbuilder

Use the chart to answer these questions.

1. How were the greatest number of working women employed in 1920?

_____

2. Did the percentage of women with clerical jobs increase or decrease between 1920 and 1930?

_____

_____

Name _____ Date _____

Education and Popular Culture

TERMS AND NAMES

Charles A. Lindbergh First person to fly solo across the Atlantic

George Gershwin Composer

Georgia O'Keeffe Artist

Sinclair Lewis Novelist

F. Scott Fitzgerald Novelist

Edna St. Vincent Millay Poet

Ernest Hemingway Novelist

BEFORE YOU READ

In the last section, you learned about women in the 1920s.

In this section, you will read about education and popular culture during the 1920s.

AS YOU READ

Use the web below to take notes on the factors that helped create American popular culture in the 1920s.

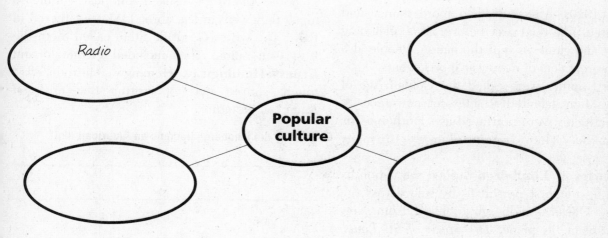

Schools and the Mass Media Shape Culture (pages 652–654)

How did popular culture change in America?

America was becoming more prosperous. Business and industry required a more educated work force. These two factors caused a huge increase in the number of students going to high school. In 1914, only 1 million American students went to high school after elementary school. In 1926, the number was nearly 4 million.

Schools changed as they grew. Before the 1920s, high schools were mostly for students who were going on to college. In the twenties, high schools had a wide range of students. Schools offered vocational, or work-related, training for industrial jobs. They offered home economics courses for future homemakers.

High schools also saw an increase in the number of children of immigrants. Many of these students did not speak English. Even so, the nation's schools were successful in teaching large numbers of Americans to read.

As a result of increased *literacy*, more people read newspapers than before. Newspaper circulation rose. Big city papers and newspaper chains swallowed up small town newspapers.

National magazines were also popular. Some of them delivered the news. Other magazines published fiction and articles.

The most powerful of the *mass media* was radio. Radio networks with stations in many cities were formed in the twenties. The networks did research to find out what people wanted to hear—and gave it to them. Radio networks created something new in America: the shared national experience of hearing things as they happened. By 1930, 40 percent of American households had radios.

1. What was an effect of increased literacy in the United States?

_____

_____

America Chases New Heroes and Old Dreams (pages 654–657)

Who was Charles Lindbergh?

In the 1920s, Americans had more money and more free time than ever before. *Fads,* including puzzles and games, swept the nation. People also spent a great deal of money at sports events.

The twenties were called the Golden Age of Sports. Many talented athletes set new records. These athletes were portrayed as superheroes by the media. They became heroes to many Americans.

Charles A. Lindbergh thrilled the nation by becoming the first person to fly solo across the Atlantic Ocean. Lindbergh took off from New York City in his plane, *The Spirit of St. Louis.* After 33 hours, Lindbergh landed outside of Paris, France. On his return to the United States, Lindbergh became the idol of America. In an age of sensationalism and excess, Lindbergh stood for the honesty and bravery the nation seemed to have lost.

Even before the introduction of sound, movies became a national pastime. *The Jazz Singer,* the first movie with sound, was released in 1927. Walt Disney's *Steamboat Willie,* the first animated film with sound was made the next year. By 1930, the "talkies" had caused movie attendance to double.

In the 1920s, American artists broke away from European traditions. Eugene O'Neill wrote plays about the confusion of modern American life. Composer **George Gershwin** merged jazz with traditional elements creating music with a new American sound.

American painters recorded the America they saw and felt. Edward Hopper painted the loneliness of American life. **Georgia O'Keeffe** showed the grandeur of New York City. She later became famous for her paintings of the Southwest.

Many gifted American writers criticized American society. **Sinclair Lewis** was the first American to win a Nobel Prize for Literature. His novels *Main Street* and *Babbitt* made fun of middle-class America's *conformity* and *materialism.*

Novelist **F. Scott Fitzgerald** coined the term "Jazz Age" to describe the twenties. His books, such as *This Side of Paradise* and *The Great Gatsby,* showed the negative side of the age. But the poems of **Edna Vincent Millay** celebrated youth and freedom from traditional restrictions.

Some Americans disliked American culture so much they went to live abroad. Many gathered in Paris. The writer Gertrude Stein called them the Lost Generation. They included Fitzgerald and **Ernest Hemingway.** Hemingway introduced a tough, simple style of writing that changed American literature.

2. Why did Lindbergh become an American idol?

_____

_____

CHAPTER 21 Section 4 (pages 658–663)

The Harlem Renaissance

BEFORE YOU READ

In the last section, you read about education and popular culture in the 1920s.

In this section, you will learn about the Harlem Renaissance.

AS YOU READ

Use the chart below to take notes on how African-American artists expressed themselves in the 1920s.

James Weldon Johnson	Author, lawyer, led antilynching effort

African-American Voices in the 1920s (pages 658–660)

How did African Americans approach civil rights in the 1920s?

Between 1910 and 1920, hundreds of thousands of African Americans had moved from the South to the big cities of the North. This was called the *Great Migration.* It was a response to racial violence and economic discrimination against blacks in the South. By 1929, 40 percent of African Americans lived in cities. As a result, racial tensions increased in Northern cities. There were race riots.

The National Association for the Advancement of Colored People (NAACP) worked to end violence against African Americans. W. E. B. Du Bois led a peaceful protest against racial violence.

The NAACP also fought to get laws against *lynching* passed by Congress. **James Weldon Johnson,** a poet and lawyer, led that fight. While no law against lynching was passed in the twenties, the number of lynchings gradually dropped.

Marcus Garvey voiced a message of black pride that appealed to many African Americans. Garvey thought that African Americans should build a separate society. He formed a black nationalist group called the Universal Negro Improvement Association (UNIA).

Garvey promoted black-owned businesses. He also urged African Americans to return to Africa to set up an independent nation.

1. How did the NAACP and Marcus Garvey's followers respond to racial discrimination?

The Harlem Renaissance Flowers in New York (pages 660–663)

What was the Harlem Renaissance?

In the 1920s, many African Americans moved to Harlem, a section of New York City. So did blacks from the West Indies, Cuba, Puerto Rico, and Haiti. Harlem became the world's largest black urban community.

This neighborhood was also the birthplace of the **Harlem Renaissance.** This literary and artistic movement celebrated African-American culture.

Above all, the Harlem Renaissance was a literary movement. It was led by well-educated middle-class blacks. They took pride in their African heritage and their people's *folklore.* They also wrote about the problems of being black in a white culture. An important collection of works by Harlem Renaissance writers, *The New Negro,* was published by Alain Locke in 1925.

The Harlem Renaissance produced many outstanding poets. **Claude McKay** wrote about the pain of prejudice. He urged African Americans to resist discrimination.

One of the most famous Harlem Renaissance poets was **Langston Hughes.** In the 1920s, he wrote about the daily lives of working-class blacks. He wove the tempos of jazz and the blues into his poems.

Zora Neale Hurston was the most famous female writer of the Harlem Renaissance. She collected the folklore of poor Southern blacks. Hurston also wrote novels, short stories, and poems.

Music and drama were important parts of the Harlem Renaissance, too. Some African-American performers became popular with white audiences. **Paul Robeson** became an important actor and singer. He starred in Eugene O'Neill's play *The Emperor Jones* and in Shakespeare's *Othello.*

Jazz became more popular in the twenties. Early in the 20th century, musicians in New Orleans blended ragtime and blues into the new sound of jazz. Musicians from New Orleans traveled North, and they brought jazz with them. The most important and influential jazz musician was **Louis Armstrong.**

Many whites came to Harlem to hear jazz in night clubs. Edward Kennedy **"Duke" Ellington** led an orchestra there. He was a jazz pianist and one of the nation's greatest composers.

The outstanding singer of the time was **Bessie Smith.** Some black musicians chose to live and perform in Europe. Josephine Baker became a famous dancer, singer, and comedy star in Paris.

2. Describe the contributions of one artist of the Harlem Renaissance.

_____

This photo shows Louis Armstrong with King Oliver's Creole Jazz Band in the 1920s. Credit: Culver Pictures

Skillbuilder

1. What does this photograph tell you about the 1920s?

_____

_____

2. How do pictures of popular bands today compare with this picture?

_____

_____

Glossary · CHAPTER 21 The Roaring Life of the 1920s

assembly line An arrangement of workers and machines in which a product is put together as it passes from one worker to another

census An official, government count of citizens, including where they live

conformity Being like everyone else

emancipated Freed from restraint or from limits on thought and behavior

fad A fashion that is very popular for a short period of time

folklore The traditional myths and tales of a people

Great Migration Movement of African Americans from the South to the North in the early 20th century

literacy The ability to read and write

lynching An execution without due process of law, especially a hanging by a mob

mass media Means of communication that reach a large audience

materialism Placing great value on money and possessions

peer pressure The influence of a person's friends to be like everyone else

urbanization The movement of Americans from rural areas to cities

theory of evolution The theory that modern plant and animal life developed slowly over millions of years

thriftiness Careful spending of money

AFTER YOU READ

A. Write the name or term in each blank that best completes the meaning of the paragraph.

Paul Robeson
Duke Ellington
speakeasy
flapper
bootlegger

What was life like in the twenties? On a Saturday night in a big city, a young woman might stand in front of her mirror admiring her new short hairstyle and new short dress. This **1**_____ might then go out on a date with a young man. They might go to a **2**_____ where they could drink illegal liquor. (The liquor was probably bought from a **3**_____ who smuggled it into the country.) And they might go to the Cotton Club in Harlem to listen to the jazz orchestra of **4**_____. Perhaps on a second date they might plan to go to a performance of Shakespeare's *Othello* starring **5**_____. Or they might decide to listen to a program on the radio.

B. Write the letter of the name or term next to the description that explains it best.

a. Harlem Renaissance
b. fundamentalism
c. Scopes trial
d. Marcus Garvey
e. James Weldon Johnson

_____ **1.** A Tennessee court case about teaching evolution in the public schools

_____ **2.** An African-American literary and artistic movement of the 1920s

_____ **3.** A religious movement based on the belief that everything in the Bible is literally true

_____ **4.** An African-American leader who promoted black pride and black nationalism

_____ **5.** A leader of the NAACP who worked for anti-lynching laws

AFTER YOU READ (continued)   *CHAPTER 21*   The Roaring Life of the 1920s

Main Ideas

1. Name two consequences of the Scopes trial.

_____

_____

2. What did the typical flapper look like?

_____

_____

3. Describe how American writers, composers, and artists broke away from European traditions in the 1920s.

_____

_____

4. What caused the Great Migration?

_____

_____

5. What was the Harlem Renaissance?

_____

_____

Thinking Critically

Answer the following questions on a separate piece of paper.

1. How did the 1920s change the lives and expectations of women and African Americans?

2. The 1920s included changes in values, lifestyles, and popular culture. How did some people try to hold onto older, more conservative values?

CHAPTER 22 Section 1 (pages 670–677)

The Nation's Sick Economy

BEFORE YOU READ

In the last section, you learned about the Harlem Renaissance in the 1920s.

In this section, you will read about the economic problems that led to the Great Depression.

AS YOU READ

Use the chart below to take notes about the economic situation each group faced in the late 1920s.

Farmers	Income declined
Industry	
Consumers	

TERMS AND NAMES

price support Law that keeps prices above a set level

credit Short-term loans to buy goods with promises to pay later

Alfred E. Smith Democratic presidential candidate in 1928

Dow Jones Industrial Average Index of stock prices of select companies

speculation Investments in high-risk ventures

buying on margin Buying stock by paying only a portion of the full cost up-front with promises to pay the rest later

Black Tuesday October 29, 1929, the day the stock market crashed

Great Depression Period of bad economic times in the United States that lasted from 1929 to 1941

Hawley-Smoot Tariff Act Law that raised taxes on imports and worsened the Depression

Economic Troubles on the Horizon (pages 670–672)

Why was the nation's economy sick in the late 1920s?

During the 1920s, the economy boomed. But there were economic problems under the surface. Industries, such as clothing, steel-making, and mining, were hardly making a profit.

Many industries had been successful in the early 1920s. But by the late 1920s, they were losing money. These industries included auto manufacturing, construction, and consumer goods.

The biggest problems were in farming. After the war, the demand for food dropped and farmers suffered. Farmers' incomes went down. Many could not make the *mortgage* payments on their farms. As a result, many farmers lost their land.

Congress tried to help farmers by passing **price supports.** With price supports, the government would not allow food prices to fall below a certain level. But Calvin Coolidge vetoed the bill. Farmers' incomes continued to drop.

Farmers were not the only problem with the economy. Americans were buying less. Many found that prices were rising faster than their salaries. Many people bought goods on **credit**—an arrangement in which consumers agreed to make monthly payments with interest. But too many Americans were accumulating debt they could not afford to pay off.

In the late 1920s, much of America seemed prosperous, but there was an uneven distribution of income. A small number of rich people were getting richer. But a large number of people were not doing well and falling further behind.

1. What problems did farmers face in the 1920s?

Hoover Takes the Nation
(pages 672–673)

How healthy was the stock market?

Few people recognized the problems with the economy in 1928. The Republican Herbert Hoover easily defeated the Democratic challenger, **Alfred E. Smith.** People believed Hoover when he said the American economy was healthy. The **Dow Jones Industrial Average,** a measure of 30 popular stocks, was way up. People rushed to buy stocks. Many people were engaging in **speculation,** buying risky stocks in hopes of a quick profit. To do so, they were **buying on margin**—paying just a small down payment and borrowing the rest. The problem of buying on margin was that there was no way to pay off the loan if the stock price declined sharply.

2. What was dangerous about how Americans bought stock?

The Stock Market Crashes
(pages 673–675)

What was Black Tuesday?

Stock prices did begin to fall in September 1929. On Tuesday, October 29, 1929, called **Black Tuesday,** prices fell so sharply that people said the market had "crashed." People frantically tried to sell their shares which drove prices down further. There were no buyers. Many people lost all their savings. By mid-November, $30 billion—more than America had spent in World War I—had been lost.

3. What happened on Black Tuesday?

Financial Collapse (pages 675–677)

How did the stock market crash affect businesses?

The stock market crash signaled the **Great Depression.** This period of bad economic times when many people were out of work lasted from 1929 to 1940. Although the crash did not cause the Depression, it did make it worse. After the crash, many people panicked and took their money out of banks. Many banks were forced to close. When the banks failed, other depositors lost the savings they had in the banks.

Businesses also began to close. Millions of Americans lost their jobs. Workers who kept their jobs experienced pay cuts or reduced hours.

The Depression spread around the world. Germany was still paying war reparations. Other European countries were struggling with debts from the war. With Americans unable to buy their goods now, European economies suffered even more.

The situation became worse when Congress passed the **Hawley-Smoot Tariff Act.** Congress hoped that higher tariffs would push Americans to buy goods made in the United States. The result would be to help American industry. Instead, when the United States charged more to bring goods in, imports from Europe declined. Then Europeans had even less money to spend on U.S. goods, and American industry suffered.

The Great Depression had several causes:

- Tariffs and war debt policies that cut down the foreign market for American goods
- A crisis in the farm sector
- The availability of easy credit
- An unequal distribution of income

These factors led to a falling demand for consumer goods. The federal government hurt the economy with its policy of low interest rates causing businesses and consumers to borrow easily and build up too much debt.

4. Why did many banks fail after the stock market crashed?

Hardship and Suffering During the Depression

BEFORE YOU READ

In the last section, you learned about the start of the Great Depression.

In this section, you will read about the hardships caused by the Depression.

AS YOU READ

Use the web below to take notes about the problems people faced during the Depression.

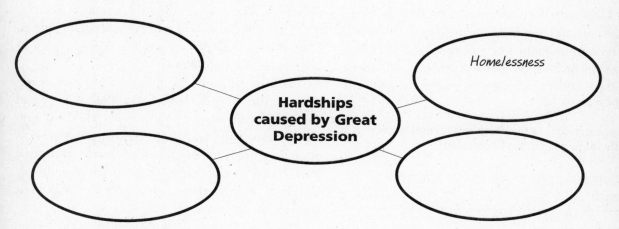

Hardships caused by Great Depression

Homelessness

The Depression Devastates People's Lives (pages 678–680)

How did the Depression affect people in cities and on farms?

The Depression brought suffering and hardship to many Americans. The hard economic times ruined many lives. Millions of people lost their jobs. Some went hungry or became homeless. Those who could not meet their housing payments were thrown out of their homes.

Cities across the country were full of these homeless people. Some slept in parks and wrapped themselves up in newspapers to keep warm. Others built **shantytowns,** where they lived in little shacks they made out of scrap material. Some ate in **soup**

kitchens, where charities served meals to the needy. Those who could not afford to buy food stood in **bread lines** to receive free food.

African Americans and *Latino Americans* who lived in the cities had a very hard time. They had a higher unemployment rate than whites. If they did have work, they were paid less than white workers.

There was even violence directed against African Americans and Latinos. Angry whites who had lost their jobs did not want to compete against these minority groups for the few jobs that were left. They sometimes attacked African Americans. They demanded that Latino Americans be sent back to the countries they came from.

The Depression hurt people in rural areas, too. Food prices continued to go down as the

Depression deepened. Farmers earned less and less. Many farm families could not meet their mortgage payments. More and more of them lost their farms. From 1929 to 1932, about 400,000 farmers lost their land.

To make matters worse, a long *drought* hit *the Great Plains*. There was little rain from Texas to North Dakota. Much of this area had been grassland that farmers broke up with their plows in order to grow crops.

The soil was now *exhausted* from over-farming. The grass that had once held the soil in place was gone. When powerful winds swept across the Great Plains, the soil simply blew away. This dry area of blowing soil was called the **Dust Bowl.** Huge dust storms covered the plains and blew dust as far away as the East Coast.

The hardest hit region included parts of Kansas, Oklahoma, Texas, New Mexico, and Colorado. Many Oklahoma farmers packed up their belongings and started for California to look for work. They became migrant workers, moving from place to place to pick crops. Because so many of them came from Oklahoma, migrant workers were often called Okies.

1. How did people in the cities and in rural areas suffer during the Great Depression?

_____

_____

Effects on the American Family
(pages 680–683)

How did the Depression affect families?

The Depression put a heavy strain on family life. Many families pulled together during the hard times. They shared what they earned. Instead of going out for entertainment, parents and children often stayed home. They played board games or listened to the radio.

But some families broke apart under the strain of poverty and unemployment. Many men felt ashamed because they had lost their jobs. Some of them simply left their families and wandered the country looking for work.

Women tried to find work, too. But they were usually paid less than men. Many people complained that employers should not hire women. They thought that men should have the jobs instead. These people argued that men were the ones who supported families, so it was more important for them to have jobs.

Children suffered terribly from poverty and the break-up of families. Many children had poor *diets* and no health care. Their parents could not afford to buy healthy food or to pay doctor bills. Many children suffered from malnutrition and diet-related illnesses like rickets. Many children ran away from home, hopping rides aboard freight trains. It was exciting, but also dangerous. Many were robbed or killed by criminals or beaten by railroad guards.

During the early years of the Great Depression, the federal government did not give **direct relief**—cash or food directly to poor people. Charities and some city governments struggled to help. But they could not provide enough relief to keep people out of poverty.

Because so many people were out of work, cities and states collected less tax money. They had to cut their budgets for programs like child welfare. Some cities could not afford to keep their schools open for a full term. Many school boards shortened the school year. Other schools simply closed. Children often went to work to try to help their families survive.

The Great Depression caused great suffering. Rates of suicide and mental illness increased dramatically. Hardship forced young people to give up dreams of college.

While the Great Depression caused much suffering, it sometimes brought out the best in individuals, families, and communities. Many people shared resources with their neighbors or gave food and clothing to the needy.

2. Describe two ways the Great Depression affected families.

_____

_____

CHAPTER 22 Section 3 (pages 684–687)

Hoover Struggles with the Depression

BEFORE YOU READ

In the last section, you read about how the Depression affected common people.

In this section, you will learn how President Hoover tried to stop the Depression.

AS YOU READ

Use the chart below to take notes about the actions President Hoover took to end the Depression.

ACTIONS	
Boulder Dam	Public works project to put people to work

Hoover Tries to Reassure the Nation (pages 684–687)

How could the nation recover?

Economic slowdowns occur regularly. Over time, economies go through cycles. There are times of economic growth and prosperity. They are followed by slumps when the economy slows down. In the 1930s, many experts believed that it was best not to interfere with these *economic cycles*. They argued that slumps would end on their own and good times would return.

At first, President **Herbert Hoover** believed that the Great Depression was just another slowdown that would end on its own. His advisors thought that it was best to do nothing. The economy would heal itself. Hoover believed the government should take some action. But he also believed that government should not take too much power or give direct aid to poor people.

Hoover believed government should help different groups work together to improve the economy. For example, Hoover thought government should help managers and workers find solutions to their problems. But he did not think government should decide on the solution.

Hoover also believed in "rugged individualism"—the idea that people should succeed through their own efforts. He believed people should take care of themselves and each other, and that the government should encourage private groups to help the needy. He thought that charities—not government—should give food and shelter to people who were poor or out of work. Hoover felt that government could guide these private relief efforts. None of these steps made a difference. The economy shrank and unemployment continued to go up.

One project that did help was the **Boulder Dam**, a huge dam on the Colorado River. Still, economic difficulties increased, the country turned against Hoover. In the 1930 elections, the Democrats gained more seats in Congress. Farmers burned crops and dumped milk rather than sell it for less than it cost them to produce it. People called the shantytowns that sprang up "Hoovervilles." Despite public criticism, Hoover stuck to his principles.

Hoover met with bankers, businessmen, and labor leaders. He urged them to work together to help improve the economy. He asked employers not to fire workers or to lower their pay. He asked labor leaders not to ask for higher pay or to strike.

1. What did Hoover think government should do in bad economic times?

_____

Hoover Takes Action (page 687)

What did Hoover do?

Hoover did not offer direct aid to the poor. But he did worry about the suffering of the American people. He took some steps to use the government to improve the economy.

Hoover used the Boulder Dam project as a model of how the federal government could encourage cooperation between private groups. He tried to help farmers with the Federal Farm Board, and banks by creating the National Credit Corporation. Another program tried to raise the prices farmers received for their crops. Hoover also urged bankers to join a credit organization. It gave loans to banks that were in danger of failing.

By 1931, the economy had not improved. Congress passed the **Federal Home Loan Bank Act.** This law lowered mortgage rates. Congress hoped that low mortgage rates would help farmers change the terms of their mortgages. This would help protect their farms from *foreclosure*.

Hoover also created the **Reconstruction Finance Corporation.** The RFC provided money for projects to create jobs.

Hoover became less popular with the public. His popularity fell even more in 1932 when World War I veterans came to the *capital*. These veterans had been promised bonuses to make up for their poor wartime pay. Congress was about to vote on a bill to give the veterans their bonuses so they wouldn't have to wait for their money.

Thousands of veterans and their families came to Washington. This so-called **Bonus Army** set up tents to live in near the *Capitol* building. Hoover first sent the veterans food. But after the bonus was voted down in Congress, Hoover told the veterans to leave. About 2,000 stayed. Hoover ordered the army to remove them. The sight of U.S. Army troops using tear gas on citizens outraged many people.

2. What actions did Hoover take to improve the economy?

_____

Skillbuilder

Use the cartoon to answer these questions.

1. What does this cartoon suggest most Americans felt about Hoover and the Depression?

_____

_____

2. Do you think that view of Hoover is justified?

_____

_____

In this cartoon, a circle of Americans all point their fingers at President Hoover. Credit: Reprinted from the Albany *Evening News*, June 7, 1931, with permission of the *Times Union*, Albany, New York

Glossary	**CHAPTER 22** The Great Depression Begins

capital The city of Washington, D.C., is the capital of the United States

Capitol The building in Washington, D.C., where Congress meets

diet The food people eat

drought A long period of unusually low rainfall

economic cycles Periods of good times, or prosperity, alternating with periods of economic hard times

exhausted Used up, worn out

foreclosure The taking of mortgaged property by the lender because the borrower cannot make the payments on the loan

the Great Plains A large flat area of the west-central United States originally covered by a type of grass that does not need much rain and that has strong roots which hold the soil in place

Latino Americans Americans whose families originally came from Spanish-speaking areas in South America, Central America, or the Caribbean

mortgage The payments made to pay back the loan used to buy a house or land

AFTER YOU READ

Terms and Names

A. Fill in each blank with the letter of the name or term that best completes the paragraph.

a. bread lines

b. Bonus Army

c. Great Depression

d. shantytowns

e. soup kitchens

The **1**_____ was the worst economic crisis in U.S. history. People suffered terribly during it. Groups of homeless people built **2**_____ where they lived in shacks made of scrap metal. People who could not afford to buy food stood in **3**_____ to receive free meals in **4**_____ where charities provided meals for the needy. A group of World War I veterans called the **5**_____ marched to Washington to try to get their war bonuses immediately. But they were forced to leave the Capitol.

B. Write the letter of the term that best completes the sentence.

a. Black Tuesday

b. Dust Bowl

c. Hawley–Smoot Tariff Act

d. Herbert Hoover

e. price supports

1. On _____ stock prices fell so sharply that people said the stock market "crashed."

2. Congress passed the _____ that raised taxes on imports to help industry. Instead, it hurt American industry.

3. Farmers on the Great Plains faced a terrible drought that created the _____.

4. _____ believed that the government should do something to stop the Depression. But he did not want the government to take too much power.

5. Congress passed _____ to help protect farmers from falling prices.

AFTER YOU READ (continued) **CHAPTER 22** The Great Depression Begins

Main Ideas

1. Describe two weaknesses in the economy in the 1920s.

_____

_____

2. How did the Hawley-Smoot Tariff affect the economy?

_____

_____

3. How did the Depression create shantytowns, soup kitchens, and bread lines?

_____

_____

4. What did Hoover do about the Bonus Army?

_____

_____

5. How did Hoover try to use the government to end the Depression?

_____

_____

Thinking Critically

Answer the following questions on a separate piece of paper.

1. Describe two causes and two effects of the Great Depression.

2. What did President Hoover do to end the Depression?

CHAPTER 23 Section 1 (pages 694–700)

A New Deal Fights the Depression

BEFORE YOU READ

In the last section, you read about Herbert Hoover's reaction to the Great Depression.

In this section, you will learn about Franklin Delano Roosevelt's programs to fight the Depression.

AS YOU READ

Use the chart below to take notes on the problems Roosevelt faced at the beginning of his presidency and how he tried to solve them.

TERMS AND NAMES

Franklin Delano Roosevelt
32nd president

New Deal Franklin Roosevelt's programs to end the Depression

Glass-Steagall Act Law that created insurance for bank deposits

Federal Securities Act Law to regulate stock information

Agricultural Adjustment Act (AAA) Programs to help farmers

Civilian Conservation Corps (CCC) Program to employ young men in work projects

National Industrial Recovery Act (NIRA) Programs to help industry

deficit spending Spending more than the government receives in revenue

Huey Long Political leader from Louisiana who criticized the New Deal

PROBLEM	SOLUTION
Bank failures	bank holiday Emergency Banking Relief Act

Americans Get a New Deal

(pages 694–696)

What were the goals of the New Deal?

By the end of 1932, Americans were ready for a change. Democratic candidate **Franklin Delano Roosevelt**—often called FDR—beat Hoover in the presidential election of 1932 by a landslide. Democrats also won large majorities in the House and Senate.

Roosevelt and his advisors planned programs to end the Depression. These programs became known as the **New Deal.** It had three goals: relief for the needy, economic recovery, and financial reform.

In the first Hundred Days, Congress quickly passed many important laws. These laws expanded the federal government's role in the nation's economy.

Roosevelt declared a "bank holiday." He closed the banks to prevent more bank failures. Then Congress passed the Emergency Banking Relief Act, which allowed healthy banks to reopen. This restored public confidence in banks. So did the **Glass-Steagall Act.** It established the Federal Deposit Insurance Corporation (FDIC), which protects the savings people put in banks. Congress also passed the **Federal Securities Act.** This law made companies give accurate information in its stock offerings. Later, Congress created the

Securities and Exchange Commission (SEC) to *regulate* stock markets.

FDR spoke directly to the American people in radio talks called "fireside chats." He explained the New Deal measures and asked for public support. These chats did a lot to restore the nation's confidence.

1. Describe the three goals of the New Deal.

_____

_____

Helping the American People
(pages 697–698)

Who did the New Deal help?

Roosevelt worked to help farmers and other workers. The **Agricultural Adjustment Act (AAA)** helped to raise crop prices by lowering production.

The New Deal included programs that gave relief through work projects and cash payments. The **Civilian Conservation Corps (CCC)** put young men to work building roads and planting trees. The Federal Emergency Relief Administration (FERA) provided direct relief of food, clothing, and cash to the needy.

The **National Industrial Recovery Act (NIRA)** set codes of fair practice for industries. It also guaranteed the workers' right to organize unions. The NIRA set up the National Recovery Administration (NRA) to stop the trend of wage cuts, falling prices, and *layoffs*.

The Home Owners Loan Corporation (HOLC) was set up to provide government loans to homeowners who faced foreclosure because they could not make their loan payments. The Federal Emergency Relief Administration (FERA) provided direct relief to the needy.

2. How did the New Deal provide help to different groups of Americans?

_____

_____

The New Deal Comes Under Attack (pages 698–700)

Who criticized the New Deal?

Roosevelt reluctantly financed the New Deal through **deficit spending**—spending more money than the government receives in revenue. Although the New Deal programs benefited many people and helped restore public confidence, some people criticized it. Some liberals said it did not do enough to help the poor. Conservative critics said it gave the federal government too much control over agriculture and business.

The Supreme Court found two important parts of the New Deal unconstitutional. The Court struck down the NIRA and the AAA. This upset Roosevelt. He proposed a bill to allow him to appoint more new Supreme Court justices.

Critics claimed that Roosevelt was trying to "pack the Court" with justices who supported him. Protest over this proposal cost Roosevelt support. But as justices resigned from the Court, Roosevelt was able to appoint seven new justices. Court decisions began to favor the New Deal.

Three critics of Roosevelt were particularly important. Father Charles Coughlin was a Roman Catholic priest. He used his popular radio sermons to criticize Roosevelt. His anti-Jewish views eventually cost him support.

Dr. Francis Townsend proposed a *pension plan* to give monthly payments to the elderly. Many elderly voters liked Townsend's plan.

The most serious challenge to the New Deal came from Senator **Huey Long** of Louisiana. He was an early supporter of the New Deal. But he wanted to become president himself. Long proposed a program called Share Our Wealth. In 1935, at the height of his popularity, Long was assassinated.

3. List two critics of the New Deal and describe their arguments.

_____

_____

The Second New Deal Takes Hold

TERMS AND NAMES

Eleanor Roosevelt First lady, social reformer, political adviser

Works Progress Administration (WPA) New Deal jobs program

National Youth Administration Program to provide aid and jobs to young people

Wagner Act Law to protect workers' rights

Social Security Act Program that provided aid to people with disabilities and pensions for retired workers

BEFORE YOU READ

In the last section, you read about the early days of the New Deal.

In this section, you will learn about the Second New Deal.

AS YOU READ

Use the web below to take notes on the major programs of the Second New Deal.

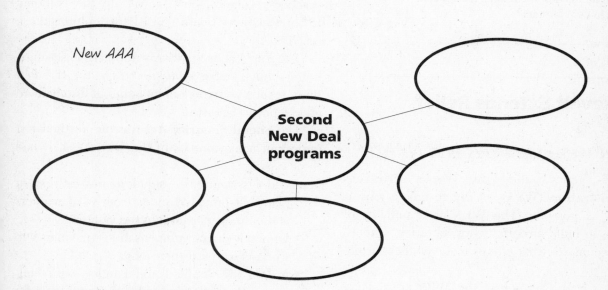

New AAA

Second New Deal programs

The Second Hundred Days
(pages 701–702)

What did voters think about the New Deal?

The economy improved in the first two years of Roosevelt's presidency. But it did not improve much. Still, the New Deal was very popular. Democrats increased their majority in Congress in the *midterm elections* of 1934.

FDR launched a second wave of reforms—sometimes called the Second New Deal. These were programs designed to help poor people. The president's wife, **Eleanor Roosevelt,** traveled around the country. She reported to the president on the suffering of the poor. She spoke up for women and minorities.

The 1936 election was an overwhelming victory for Roosevelt, the Democrats, and the New Deal. It also marked the first time most African Americans voted Democratic. And it was the first time that labor unions supported a single candidate. They supported Roosevelt.

1. What did the elections of 1934 and 1936 tell about the New Deal?

_____

_____

_____

Helping Farmers (pages 702–704)

How did the Second New Deal help farmers?

Things were still tough for farmers in the mid 1930s. The first AAA had helped some farmers before it was struck down by the Supreme Court.

Now Congress passed new laws to replace the first AAA. One program paid farmers to use *soil conservation* measures in managing their land. The second AAA was passed without the tax that had made the first one unconstitutional.

Other laws helped sharecroppers and tenant farmers. They provided loans to help farmers buy land. New laws also helped migrant workers by providing better housing for them.

2. What action did the Second New Deal take to help farmers?

_____

_____

Roosevelt Extends Relief

(pages 704–705)

What were the WPA and NYA?

A new agency called the **Works Progress Administration (WPA)** set out to create jobs as quickly as possible. The WPA used millions of workers to build airports, roads, libraries, schools, and hospitals. Sewing groups made clothes for the needy.

Some people criticized the WPA as a *make-work program* that created useless jobs just to give people a paycheck. But the WPA created works of lasting value. And it gave working people a sense of hope and dignity along with their paychecks.

The WPA also employed teachers, writers, artists, actors, and musicians. And it made special efforts to help women, minorities, and the young.

The **National Youth Administration** (NYA) provided aid and part-time jobs to many high school and college students. This allowed them to get an education even in tough economic times.

3. How did the WPA and NYA help people?

_____

_____

Improving Labor and Other Reforms (pages 705–707)

How did the Second New Deal help workers?

The Second New Deal created important reforms for labor. Congress passed the National Labor Relations Act to replace the NIRA, which the Supreme Court struck down. This law is often called the **Wagner Act.**

The Wagner Act supported workers' right to *collective bargaining*. It also banned unfair labor practices. The Wagner Act set up the National Labor Relations Board (NLRB) to enforce these reforms.

The Fair Labor Standards Act of 1938 set maximum hours and a *minimum wage* for the first time. It set a workweek of 44 hours. It also banned child labor in factories.

The **Social Security Act** was one of the most important achievements of the New Deal. It had three parts:

- Old-age insurance—supplemental retirement plan that provided funds from what workers and employers paid into the system
- Unemployment compensation—payments to workers who lost their jobs
- Aid to the disabled and families with children—this helped people who could not be expected to work

The Second New Deal also extended electricity to rural areas through the Rural Electrification Administration (REA).

4. How did the Second New Deal try to protect workers?

_____

_____

CHAPTER 23 Section 3 (pages 710–715)

The New Deal Affects Many Groups

TERMS AND NAMES

Frances Perkins Secretary of labor

Mary McLeod Bethune Head of the Office of Minority Affairs in the NYA

John Collier Commissioner on Indian Affairs

New Deal coalition Voters from different groups that supported the Democratic party because of the New Deal

Congress of Industrial Organizations (CIO) Labor union

BEFORE YOU READ

In the last section, you read about the Second New Deal.

In this section, you will learn about some of the effects of the New Deal.

AS YOU READ

Use the chart below to take notes on how the New Deal affected the groups listed in the chart.

GROUP	EFFECT OF NEW DEAL
Women	First women in cabinet
African Americans	
Mexican Americans	
Native Americans	

The New Deal Brings New Opportunities (pages 710–711)

How did the New Deal affect women?

Women made some important gains during the New Deal. More women were appointed to important federal jobs.

Frances Perkins became the first female cabinet member as secretary of labor. Perkins helped create the Social Security system. Roosevelt also appointed women as federal judges. Roosevelt hoped that these appointments would make him more popular among women voters.

Many New Deal agencies did not discriminate in hiring. This gave women more opportunities. But some government agencies and many businesses did not hire as many women as men. For example, the Civilian Conservation Corps hired men only. And women were almost always paid less than men. For instance, the National Recovery Administration set lower wage levels for women than for men.

1. Describe two ways that the New Deal expanded and limited opportunities for women.

_____

_____

African-American Activism

(pages 711–712)

How did the New Deal affect African Americans?

President Roosevelt gave a number of African Americans a voice in government. **Mary McLeod Bethune** was an educator who became head of the Minority Affairs Office of the National Youth Administration.

She worked to ensure that the NYA hired some African Americans. Bethune also helped organize the "Black Cabinet." This was a group of influential African Americans that advised Roosevelt on racial issues.

However, President Roosevelt did not push for full civil rights for African Americans. He was afraid of losing the support of white Southerners.

2. What gains did African Americans make during the New Deal?

_____

_____

Mexican-American Fortunes; Native American Gains (pages 712–713)

What gains did Mexican Americans and Native Americans make?

Mexican Americans tended to support the New Deal. But they received few benefits from New Deal programs. Many were farm workers who were not covered by federal laws. Some New Deal agencies discriminated against them.

Native Americans got support from the New Deal. In 1933, Roosevelt made **John Collier** commissioner on Indian affairs. He was a strong supporter of Native American rights. Collier helped pass the Indian Reorganization Act. This law strengthened Native American land claims.

3. How did Mexican Americans and Native Americans fare under the New Deal?

_____

_____

FDR Creates the New Deal Coalition (pages 713–715)

Who supported the New Deal?

Roosevelt got votes from Southern whites, city people, African Americans, and workers who belonged to unions. Together these groups of voters formed a *coalition* that supported FDR. It became known as the **New Deal coalition.**

Labor unions made gains in the 1930s. New Deal laws made it easier for workers to form unions and to bargain with employers. Union membership soared from 3 million to more than 10 million.

Divisions emerged between labor unions. The American Federation of Labor (AFL) was made up of mostly *crafts unions*, such as plumbers or carpenters. Other unions wanted to represent workers in a whole industry, such as the automobile industry. These unions broke away to form the **Congress of Industrial Organizations (CIO).**

Labor employed a new kind of strike in the 1930s—a sit-down strike. In a sit-down strike, workers did not leave their workplace. They remained inside but refused to work. That prevented factory owners from using strikebreakers or scabs to get the work done.

Some strikes led to violence. On Memorial Day, 1937, police killed ten people during a steel strike in Chicago. The National Labor Relations Board stepped in. It forced the steel company to negotiate with the union. This helped labor gain strength.

The Democratic Party got a great deal of support from people living in cities. Powerful city political organizations helped build this support. So did New Deal programs that helped the urban poor. Roosevelt also appealed to people of many ethnic groups. He appointed people of urban-immigrant backgrounds to important government jobs.

4. What was the New Deal coalition?

_____

_____

CHAPTER 23   Section 4 (pages 716–720)

Culture of the 1930s

TERMS AND NAMES
Gone With the Wind Popular movie
Orson Welles Actor, director, and filmmaker
Grant Wood Artist
Richard Wright Author
The Grapes of Wrath Novel by John Steinbeck

BEFORE YOU READ

In the last section, you learned about the New Deal coalition.

In this section, you will learn about American culture during the Depression.

AS YOU READ

Use the chart below to take notes on radio, the movies, literature, and the arts during the Depression.

Movies	Popular escape inexpensive
Radio	
Literature	
Arts	

The Lure of Motion Pictures and Radio (pages 716–718)

What did Americans do for fun during the Depression?

The 1930s were a golden age for the radio and film industries in spite of the hard economic times. Movie tickets were not expensive, and films provided an escape from the problems of Depression life. About two-thirds of Americans went to a movie once a week.

Hollywood studios made a wide variety of movies and created many new movie stars. One of the most popular films of all time was ***Gone With***

the Wind (1939). Fred Astaire and Ginger Rogers were dancing partners who made many movies together. Other popular movies in the 1930s included *The Wizard of Oz* and the Disney animated film, *Snow White and the Seven Dwarfs*. Audiences flocked to see comedies starring the Marx Brothers and also to see dark, gritty gangster movies.

Frank Capra made a different type of movie. In his movies, honest, kind-hearted people won out over greedy people.

Radio showed the democratic spirit of the times. There were radios in nearly 90 percent of American homes. Most American families listened to their favorite radio shows together. The radio offered inexpensive entertainment. There were comedy and variety shows, news programs, soap operas, and children's shows. There were also excellent dramas and mysteries.

Radio made people like Bob Hope, Jack Benny, and George Burns and Gracie Allen stars long before they had success on television. In order to reach the greatest number of people, President Roosevelt went on the radio during his famous fireside chats.

The most famous radio broadcast was by **Orson Welles.** He was an actor, director, and filmmaker. His fictional radio show "The War of the Worlds" was so realistic that it convinced many Americans that Martians had landed in New Jersey. It showed the power of radio at a time when many Americans got their news that way.

1. **What was the appeal of movies and radio during the Depression?**

_____

_____

The Arts in Depression America

(pages 718–720)

How did the New Deal help artists?

The art and literature of the Depression was more serious and sober than radio and movies. Many artists used realism to show the hardships of Depression life. Some criticized American society. Others praised the strength of character and the democratic values of the American people.

Some people believed that the government should not play any role in funding arts projects. But New Deal officials believed the arts were important for the nation. They created several programs to put artists to work.

The Federal Arts Project was part of the WPA. It paid artists to create posters, murals, and other works of art for public places. Artists such as Thomas Hart Benton and **Grant Wood** painted rural midwestern subjects. Wood's *American Gothic*, a portrait of a serious-looking man and woman standing in front of their farmhouse, remains symbolic of life during the Depression.

The Federal Theater Project was another part of the WPA. It helped support American playwrights. It also brought live drama to many communities around the country.

Woody Guthrie was a folksinger who used music to capture the hardships of the Depression. Guthrie traveled the country and met thousands of people struggling to get by and wrote songs about what he saw. The Federal Writers' Project funded writers. Saul Bellow was one of these writers. He later won a Pulitzer Prize. **Richard Wright** was an African-American writer. He received financial help while writing *Native Son*. This novel shows the problems racism caused for a young African-American man.

John Steinbeck also got help from the FWP. His novel ***The Grapes of Wrath*** is one of the most famous books about the Depression. It shows the problems faced by Oklahoma farmers who were forced from their homes during the Dust Bowl. They became migrant workers. They made it to California, but their hardships continued.

Another notable book of the Depression was by the writer James Agee and the photographer Walker Evans. *Let Us Now Praise Famous Men* showed the dignity of Alabama sharecroppers in the face of hardship. The play *Our Town* by Thornton Wilder captured the warmth and beauty of small-town life.

2. **Describe two New Deal programs that supported the arts.**

_____

_____

The Impact of the New Deal

BEFORE YOU READ

In the last section, you learned about American culture during the Depression.

In this section, you will read about the legacy of the New Deal.

AS YOU READ

Use the chart below to take notes on the lasting effects of the New Deal.

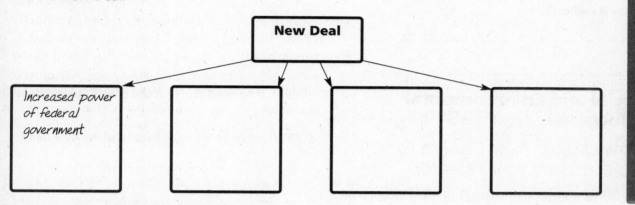

> **TERMS AND NAMES**
>
> **Federal Deposit Insurance Corporation (FDIC)** Insurance for savings
>
> **Securities and Exchange Commission (SEC)** Agency to regulate stock markets
>
> **National Labor Relations Board (NLRB)** Agency to regulate business
>
> **parity** An equal or fair amount
>
> **Tennessee Valley Authority (TVA)** Regional work project of lasting value

New Deal Reforms Endure
(pages 721–724)

What do critics say about the New Deal?

By the end of the 1930s, the economy had improved somewhat. Industrial production had reached 1929 levels. Unemployment was still high. But it was much lower than during the worst days of the Depression. Congress urged Roosevelt to cut back on New Deal programs. Roosevelt did, and the economy slid back a bit. Still, Roosevelt did not start another phase of the New Deal.

One reason FDR did not launch another New Deal was that he did not want any more deficit spending. Roosevelt was also more and more worried about events in Europe, particularly the rise of Hitler.

People still disagree over whether the New Deal was good or bad for the country. Conservative critics say that the New Deal made the government too big and too powerful. They say that it got in the way of free enterprise. They feel that government should not be so involved in the economy.

Liberal critics say that the New Deal did not go far enough. They think it should have done more to change the economy. They think that Roosevelt should have done more to end the differences in wealth between the rich and the poor.

Supporters of the New Deal say that it was well balanced between saving capitalism and reforming it. They point to many lasting benefits of the New Deal.

The New Deal expanded the power of the federal government. It gave the federal government and particularly the president, a greater role in shaping the economy. It did this by putting millions of dollars into the economy, creating federal jobs, regulating supply and demand, and participating in settling labor disputes. The government also created agencies such as the **Federal Deposit Insurance Corporation (FDIC)** and the **Securities and Exchange Commission (SEC)** to regulate banking and investment activities. To do all this, the government went deeply into debt. In the end, what really ended the depression was the massive spending for World War II.

The New Deal left a lasting impact on workers' rights, banking, and investment. Today the **National Labor Relations Board (NLRB)** still *mediates* labor disputes. And the FDIC and SEC help regulate the banking and securities industries.

1. How did some liberals and conservatives criticize the New Deal?

_____

_____

Social and Environmental Effects (pages 724–725)

How did the New Deal make the economy more stable?

New Deal reforms had lasting effects. They helped make the economy more stable. The nation has had economic downturns. But none have been as bad as the Great Depression. And people's savings are insured.

One of the most important and lasting benefits of the New Deal is the Social Security system. It provides old-age insurance and unemployment benefits. It also helps families with dependent children and those who are disabled. For the first time, the federal government took responsibility for the welfare of its citizens.

The Second Agricultural Adjustment Act made loans to farmers. The loans were based on the **parity** value—a price based on 1910–1914 levels—of farmers' surplus crops. Projects that spread electric power to rural areas also helped farmers.

The New Deal also helped the environment. Roosevelt was very interested in protecting the nation's natural resources. New Deal policies promoted soil conservation to prevent a repeat of the Dust Bowl. The **Tennessee Valley Authority (TVA)** helped prevent floods and provided electricity. And New Deal programs also added to the national park system. They set up areas to protect wildlife. However, the TVA did contribute to pollution through *strip mining*.

2. What are two continuing benefits of the New Deal?

_____

_____

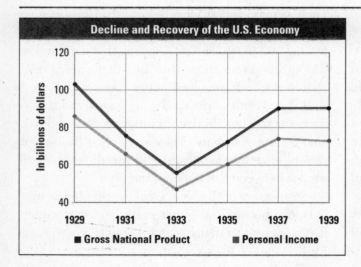

Decline and Recovery of the U.S. Economy

In billions of dollars

120
100
80
60
40

1929 1931 1933 1935 1937 1939

■ Gross National Product   ■ Personal Income

Skillbuilder

Use the chart to answer these questions.

1. Which year according to the chart was the worst year of the Depression?

_____

2. In which year in the 1930s was the economy the strongest?

_____

Glossary

coalition An alliance of groups supporting a political party or cause

collective bargaining Negotiations between organized workers and their employer to decide wages and work rules

crafts unions Labor organizations made up of skilled workers who do a particular kind of job, no matter what industry they work in

layoffs The firing or temporary suspension of employees, especially because of lack of work

make-work program A program that creates useless jobs just to give workers a paycheck

mediate To resolve or settle differences by working with all the conflicting parties

midterm elections Congressional elections held in years when there is no presidential election

minimum wage The lowest wage that law will allow a worker to be paid

pension plan A plan that provides for money to be paid as a retirement benefit

regulate To set rules for an industry

soil conservation Ways to keep the soil fertile and prevent it from blowing away

strip mining Mining that removes the topsoil of large areas of land

AFTER YOU READ

A. Write the name or term that best completes each sentence on the blank.

Civilian Conservation Corps

New Deal

Franklin Delano Roosevelt

The Grapes of Wrath

Tennessee Valley Authority

Social Security Act

Works Progress
  Administration

Wagner Act

Federal Deposit Insurance
  Corporation

Richard Wright

1. _____ became president in 1933.

2. FDR's programs to end the Depression were called the _____ .

3. The president and Congress created the _____ to insure people's bank accounts.

4. A program supported by FDR to put people to work, the _____ hired young men to plant trees and build roads.

5. The _____ hired people to build schools and hospitals, and it employed artists, writers, and actors.

6. The _____ protected workers' rights to collective bargaining and banned unfair labor practices.

7. One of the most important laws was the _____. It set up a system of old-age insurance, unemployment insurance, and aid to people unable to work.

8. Another part of the New Deal was the _____, which prevented flooding and brought electricity to a large area.

9. John Steinbeck's novel _____ tells the story of Oklahoma farmers during the Depression.

10. The novel *Native Son* by _____ describes the difficulties faced by a young African-American man.

B Write the name or term after the description that explains it best.

Eleanor Roosevelt

New Deal coalition

Orson Welles

deficit spending

Congress of Industrial
  Organizations

1. Groups of voters including Southern whites, urban voters, African Americans, and labor who supported FDR

2. The creator of a radio broadcast that convinced many Americans that Martians had landed in New Jersey

3. The act of a government paying out more money than it is taking in

4. An organization of industrial labor unions started in the 1930s

5. The wife of the president, who fought for equality for women and minorities

Main Ideas

1. What were the three goals of the New Deal?

_____

_____

2. Describe two reasons that people opposed the New Deal.

_____

_____

3. What did the Wagner Act do to help workers?

_____

_____

4. Why were movies popular during the Depression?

_____

_____

5. List three New Deal programs that still exist today.

_____

_____

Thinking Critically

Answer the following questions on a separate sheet of paper.

1. How did the New Deal help people during the Depression?

2. How did the New Deal make lasting changes in American government?

Dictators Threaten World Peace

TERMS AND NAMES

Joseph Stalin Communist dictator of the Soviet Union

totalitarian Government that has complete control over its citizens and puts down all opposition

Benito Mussolini Fascist dictator of Italy

fascism Political system based on a strong, centralized government headed by a dictator

Adolf Hitler Nazi dictator of Germany

Nazism Fascist political philosophy of Germany under Nazi dictator Hitler

Francisco Franco Fascist dictator of Spain

Neutrality Acts Laws passed by Congress to ban the sale of arms or loans to nations at war

BEFORE YOU READ

In the last section, you saw the effects of the New Deal reforms in the United States during the Great Depression.

In this section, you will see how economic and political conditions in Europe and Asia in the 1930s gave rise to expansionist totalitarian states.

AS YOU READ

Take notes on the chart below. Fill it in with the beliefs and goals of these dictators and on what they did to reach their goals.

DICTATOR / NATION	BELIEFS AND GOALS	ACTIONS
Stalin/Soviet Union	communism, stamp out free enterprise	

Nationalism Grips Europe and Asia (pages 734–740)

How did dictators take power in Europe and Asia?

Woodrow Wilson had hoped that the Treaty of Versailles would provide a "just and lasting peace," among the world's most powerful nations. However, the Treaty mostly caused anger and resentment. The German government was angry about losing territory it considered Germany's, as well as being blamed for starting the war. The Soviet Union resented losing its own territories.

The peace settlement failed to make the world "safe for democracy" as Woodrow Wilson had hoped. New democratic governments, hurt by economic and social problems, floundered and turned to dictatorships.

In the Soviet Union, **Joseph Stalin** came to power in 1924. He was a ruthless leader who let nothing stand in his way. Stalin focused on creating a model communist state. He wanted to stamp out private enterprise. He did away with private farms and created collectives, or huge state-owned farms. The state also took over industry. Stalin made the Soviet Union into a leading industrial power.

But he also made it into a police state. Anyone who criticized him or his policies was arrested by the secret police. Many were executed. Millions of others died in famines caused by Stalin's restructuring of Soviet society. It is believed that Stalin was responsible for between 8 and 13 million deaths in the Soviet Union. Stalin created a **totalitarian** government—a government with complete control over its citizens. Individuals had no rights, and the government put down all opposition.

At the same time, **Benito Mussolini** was creating a totalitarian state in Italy. His political movement was called **fascism.** It was based on a strong, centralized government headed by a dictator. Fascism grew out of extreme nationalism. Mussolini, called *Il Duce,* or the leader, was known for his efficiency in running all aspects of Italian life. But he did not want the government to own farms and factories. Fascism was actually anti-communist.

In Germany, another fascist party came to power under the leadership of **Adolf Hitler.** Hitler's political philosophy was called **Nazism.** He hoped to unite all German-speaking people into a new German empire, or Reich. He believed that Germans—especially blond, blue-eyed "Aryans"—were the master race. According to Hitler, Aryans were meant to have power over all "inferior races," such as Jews and nonwhites. Hitler believed Germany needed to expand—to gain territory—so that the German people could thrive.

Nazism combined extreme nationalism, racism, and expansionism. It appealed to unemployed, desperate, and resentful Germans during the Great Depression. In the 1932 elections, the Nazi Party gained power. Hitler became *chancellor* in January 1933. He did away with the *Weimar Republic* and set up the Third Reich, or third German empire.

Meanwhile, in Asia, military leaders had taken over Japan. They believed that Japan needed more land and resources. Japan attacked Manchuria, a province of China, in 1931. The League of Nations protested, but Japan left the League and kept Manchuria.

The League's failure to stop Japan made Hitler and Mussolini bolder. Hitler sent troops into the Rhineland and rebuilt the German army. These acts broke the Versailles Treaty. Mussolini captured the African nation of Ethiopia. Haile Selassie, the leader of Ethiopia, asked the League for help. When the League did nothing, he said, "It is us today. It will be you tomorrow."

In Spain, the fascist general **Francisco Franco** led a rebellion to overthrow the elected government. Many American volunteers went to Spain to fight the fascists. These volunteers felt that Spain was the place to stop fascism and defend democracy. The governments of the Western democracies sent only food and clothing to democratic forces in Spain. Hitler and Mussolini supported Franco with troops and weapons. When Franco won in 1939, Europe had another totalitarian government.

1. What five major countries were ruled by dictatorships in the 1930s?

_____

_____

The United States Responds Cautiously (pages 740–741)

How did the United States respond to the rise of dictators?

Most Americans wanted the United States to stay out of foreign conflicts. Many people thought that the United States had made a mistake in getting involved in World War I. Anti-war rallies were held. *Isolationism* became more popular.

Congress passed the **Neutrality Acts.** These laws banned loans or arms sale to nations at war. Because of the Spanish Civil War, the Neutrality Acts included those involved in civil wars.

In 1937, Roosevelt found a way around the Neutrality Acts. Since Japan had not declared war on China, Roosevelt felt free to send military aid to China. He gave a speech in which he talked of "quarantining the aggressors," but growing criticism from isolationists forced FDR to back down.

2. How did the United States react to the rise of expansionist dictatorships in Europe and Asia?

_____

_____

CHAPTER 24 Section 2 (pages 742–747)

War in Europe

BEFORE YOU READ

In the last section, you saw how dictatorships rose in Europe and Asia in the 1930s.

In this section, you will see how the expansionist policies of Hitler led to World War II in Europe.

AS YOU READ

Fill in the time line below with the major events in Hitler's and Stalin's attempts to expand their territory.

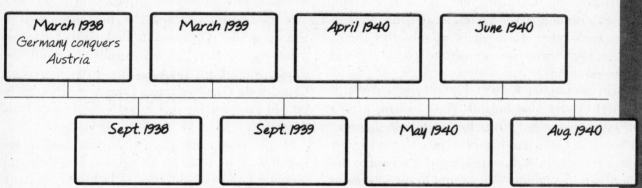

March 1938
Germany conquers Austria

March 1939

April 1940

June 1940

Sept. 1938

Sept. 1939

May 1940

Aug. 1940

Austria and Czechoslovakia Fall
(pages 742–744)

How did Britain and France react to Hitler's aggression?

Hitler decided that the new living space the German people needed would come from nearby nations. He would annex, or add, Austria and Czechoslovakia. And he was willing to use force to do it.

A majority of Austria's six million people were German-speaking and favored unification with Germany. In March 1938, German troops marched into Austria. They met no opposition. Germany announced an Anschluss, or "union" with Austria.

Then Hitler claimed that the Czechs were mistreating German-speaking people in an area called the Sudetenland. He massed troops on the border. France and Britain promised to defend Czechoslovakia. Their leaders met with Hitler in Munich, Germany. Hitler promised that the Sudetenland would be his "last territorial demand." France, Britain, and Germany signed the Munich Pact in September 1938. It gave the Sudetenland to Germany.

Neville Chamberlain was the British prime minister who signed the Munich Pact. He called it "peace with honor." Another British leader, **Winston Churchill,** disagreed. He called the Pact dishonorable **appeasement.** That means giving up your principles in order to *pacify* an *aggressor*. Churchill predicted that appeasement would eventually lead to war.

The German Offensive Begins
(pages 744–746)

What did Britain and France do about Nazi and Soviet aggression?

Hitler did not keep the promise he made at Munich. In March of 1939, he conquered the rest of Czechoslovakia.

Then Hitler began to claim that Germans living in Poland were being persecuted. Many people thought Hitler would never attack Poland. They thought he would be afraid that the Soviet Union, on Poland's eastern border, would then fight Germany. But Germany and the Soviet Union signed a **nonaggression pact,** an agreement not to fight each other. In a secret part of this treaty, Hitler and Stalin also agreed to divide Poland between them.

On September 1, 1939, Hitler launched World War II by attacking Poland. The Germans used a new strategy called a *blitzkrieg*, or lightning war. They used tanks and planes to take the enemy by surprise and crush them quickly. Poland fell to the Germans in a month. Britain and France declared war on Germany. Meanwhile, the Soviets attacked Poland from the east, and grabbed some of its territory.

For the next few months, not much happened. This was called the "phony war." French and British troops gathered on the French border. German troops also waited.

Meanwhile, Stalin seized regions that the Soviet Union had lost in World War I. He took the Baltic states in September and October of 1939. Finland resisted, and was conquered only after fierce fighting in March 1940.

In April, Hitler launched surprise invasions of Denmark and Norway. Then in May, he quickly took the Netherlands, Belgium, and Luxembourg. This war was very real indeed.

France and Britain Fight On
(pages 746–747)

How did Hitler's attacks on France and on Britain turn out?

Germany attacked France in May 1940—but not where the Allies expected. It cut off Allied forces in the north. The British sent all kinds of boats—from fishing vessels to yachts—to bring nearly 340,000 British, French, and other Allied troops safely across the English Channel.

Meanwhile, Italy joined the war on the side of Germany. The Italians attacked France from the south. France surrendered quickly, in June 1940. The Germans *occupied* the northern part of France while a Nazi-controlled *puppet government,* called the Vichy government, ruled the southern part of France. The French general **Charles de Gaulle** set up a French *government in exile* in England. He promised to free France from the Nazis.

Hitler now made plans to invade Britain. He began with air raids over England. The Germans bombed London night after night in August 1940. The British air force (RAF) defended Britain against these attacks. They used a new technology called radar, and shot down hundreds of German planes. This air war was called the Battle of Britain. The new prime minister, Winston Churchill, rallied the spirits of the British people and declared that Britain would never surrender. Hitler gave up the idea of invading Britain.

3. What happened to Hitler's plans for conquering France and Britain?

The Holocaust

BEFORE YOU READ

In the last section, you saw how Hitler began World War II.

In this section, you will see how Hitler put his plan of Aryan domination into place by killing Jews and other groups he considered inferior.

AS YOU READ

Take notes on the chart below. Fill it in with the attitudes and actions that led to the Holocaust.

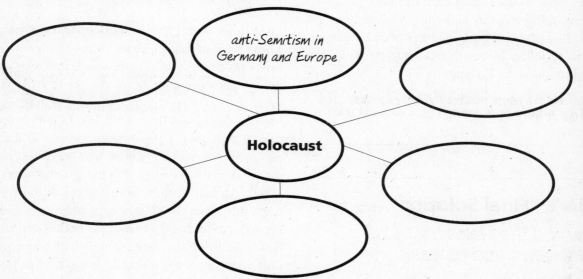

anti-Semitism in Germany and Europe

Holocaust

The Persecution Begins (pages 748–750)

How did the persecution of the Jews begin in Germany?

Part of Hitler's plan for Germany was to make the country racially pure. In 1933, just three months after taking power, Hitler ordered all non-Aryans out of government jobs. Then Hitler began an organized persecution of non-Aryans, particularly of Jews. This resulted in the **Holocaust**—the systematic murder of over 11 million people across Europe. Over half of the murdered people were Jews.

Anti-Semitism, or hatred of Jews, had a long history in Germany and in other parts of Europe.

For a long time, Germans had used Jews as a scapegoat, someone to blame for their own failures and frustrations. Therefore, when Hitler blamed Jews for Germany's defeat in World War I, many Germans agreed. When Hitler blamed the Jews for Germany's economic problems, many Germans supported him.

Persecution of Jews increased under Hitler. In 1935, new laws took away Jews' civil rights and their property. Jews were forced to wear yellow stars of David on their clothing.

On November 9, 1938, organized, violent persecution began with **Kristallnacht.** (*Kristallnacht* is a German word meaning "crystal night," or night of broken glass.) Gangs of Nazi *storm troopers* attacked Jewish homes, businesses, and *synagogues* across Germany. The streets were littered with broken glass. Then the Nazis blamed Jews for the destruction. Many Jews were arrested; others were fined.

Many Jews started to flee Germany. Nazis were in favor of this, but other nations did not want to accept the Jewish refugees. Some refugees, including Albert Einstein and Thomas Mann, were allowed into the United States. But the United States would not change its immigration quotas. This was partly American anti-Semitism. It was also because many Americans feared competition for the few jobs during the Depression.

Once war broke out in Europe, Americans said they feared that refugees would be "enemy agents." The Coast Guard even turned away a ship carrying refugees who had *emigration papers* for the United States. Three-quarters of those passengers were killed by the Nazis after the ship was forced to return to Europe.

1. How did the world react to Germany's persecution of the Jews?

_____

_____

Hitler's "Final Solution" (pages 750–752)

How did the Nazis try to kill off the Jews and others?

In 1939, there were only about a quarter of a million Jews left in Germany. But other countries that Hitler occupied had millions more Jews. Hitler's ultimate goal was to get rid of all of Europe's Jews. He began implementing the "final solution." This plan amounted to **genocide,** the deliberate and systematic killing of an entire population.

The "final solution" was based on the Nazi belief that "Aryans" were a superior people and that their strength and racial purity must be preserved. To accomplish this, the Nazis arrested people they identified as "enemies of the state," condemning these people to slavery and death. In addition to Jews, the Nazis rounded up political opponents—Communists, Socialists, liberals—and other groups including Gypsies, Freemasons, Jehovah's Witnesses, homosexuals, the disabled, and the terminally ill.

Some Jews were forced into **ghettos**—segregated Jewish areas where they were made to work in factories or left to starve. Despite brutal conditions, Jews hung on, resisting the Germans and setting up schools and underground newspapers.

2. Who were the targets of the "final solution"?

_____

_____

The Final Stage (pages 753–755)

How did the Nazis kill so many people?

Most Jews were sent to **concentration camps,** where they suffered hunger, illness, overwork, torture, and death. The early concentration camps did not kill Jews fast enough for the Nazis. In 1941, six death camps were built in Poland. These camps had gas chambers that could kill 12,000 people a day. Prisoners were separated upon arrival at death camps by SS doctors. Those who were too old or too weak to work were led to the gas chambers and killed. At first bodies were buried or burned in huge pits. Then the Nazis built huge ovens called crematoriums that destroyed the bodies and all evidence of the mass murder that had taken place. Other prisoners were shot or hanged or subjected to horrible medical experiments by camp doctors.

Six million Jews died in death camps and Nazi *massacres.* Some Jews, however, were saved. Ordinary people sometimes risked their own lives to hide Jews or to help them escape.

Some Jews even survived the concentration camps. Elie Wiesel, who won the Nobel Peace Prize in 1986, is a survivor of Auschwitz. He has written memorably about his concentration camp experiences and the need to prevent such genocide from ever happening again.

3. Why were certain people separated from the others and led to the gas chambers?

_____

_____

CHAPTER 24 Section 4 (pages 756–763)

America Moves Toward War

BEFORE YOU READ

In the last section, you saw how Hitler's plan to make Germany racially pure killed millions of people.

In this section, you will see how the United States moved closer to entering the war against the Nazis.

AS YOU READ

Take notes on the time line below. Fill it in with the events in each year that brought the United States to war.

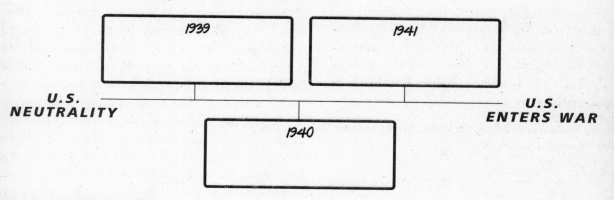

U.S. NEUTRALITY — 1939 — 1940 — 1941 — U.S. ENTERS WAR

The United States Musters Its Forces (pages 756–757)

How did the United States try to stay out of war but be prepared?

According to the Neutrality Acts, the United States could not enter the war in Europe. However, President Roosevelt asked for a change in the Acts. He suggested a cash-and-carry provision. Such a provision would allow Britain and France to buy and transport American arms. Congress passed this new Neutrality Act in November 1939.

In 1940, Germany, Italy, and Japan signed a mutual defense treaty. They became the **Axis powers.** The treaty meant that if the United States went to war against any one of them, all three would fight. That would put America at war on two *fronts*: in Europe and in Asia. Nevertheless,

Roosevelt gave the British "all aid short of war" to help them fight Hitler.

Roosevelt assured the nation that the United States would stay out of war. But he prepared for war. Congress increased spending for national defense. It passed the nation's first *peacetime draft* in September 1940.

FDR broke the tradition of a two-term presidency and ran for re-election in 1940. His opponent, Wendell Willkie, shared Roosevelt's beliefs that the United States should help Britain, but that it should not get involved in war. Voters chose the candidate they knew. FDR won a third term.

1. How did the United States slowly move toward war?

_____

_____

_____

"The Great Arsenal of Democracy" (pages 758–760)

Why did the United States change its policy of neutrality?

After the election, Roosevelt spoke to the American people. He said that the United States could not stand by and let Hitler conquer the world. America would become "the great *arsenal* of democracy." At that time, Britain could no longer pay for arms and supplies. Roosevelt suggested lending or leasing arms to any nation "whose defense was vital to the United States." Isolationists bitterly opposed his policy. But Congress passed the **Lend-Lease Act** in March 1941.

Meanwhile, Germany invaded its former ally, the Soviet Union. The United States gave lend-lease support to the Soviets as well as to Britain.

Nazi submarines called U-boats attacked and sank ships carrying arms across the Atlantic to Germany's enemies. In June 1941, Roosevelt ordered the U.S. Navy to protect lend-lease ships. He also gave American warships permission to attack German U-boats in self-defense.

2. Name two ways in which the United States became the "arsenal of democracy."

FDR Plans for War (pages 760)

How did the United States move toward war?

In August 1941, Roosevelt met secretly with British Prime Minister Winston Churchill. Roosevelt did not actually commit the United States to war. But he and Churchill did sign the **Atlantic Charter.** That was a statement of the goals for fighting World War II. These goals included protecting peoples' rights to choose their own form of government and building a secure peace.

Later, 26 nations signed a similar agreement. These nations, called the **Allies,** were united in fighting Germany, Italy, and Japan.

On September 4, 1941, a German U-boat fired on an American *merchant ship*. President Roosevelt ordered the U.S. Navy to fire on German ships on sight. U-boats responded by sinking several American ships, and American seamen were killed. The Senate finally allowed the arming of merchant ships. Full scale war seemed inevitable.

3. What events moved the United States closer to war?

Japan Attacks the United States
(pages 760–763)

What brought the United States into conflict with Japan?

In Japan, expansionists had long dreamed of creating a huge empire. Japan was now acting on this dream. It began seizing Asian territory held as colonies by European nations. The United States also owned islands in the Pacific.

When Japan invaded Indochina, the United States cut off trade with Japan. Japan needed American oil to run its *war machine*. The new prime minister of Japan was a *militant* general named **Hideki Tojo.** He started peace talks with the United States, but he also prepared for war.

The United States broke Japan's secret communications code. The Americans knew Japan was preparing for a military strike. But they did not know when or where the strike would be.

On December 7, 1941—during the peace talks—Japan attacked the main U.S. naval base at Pearl Harbor in Hawaii. The Japanese crippled the U.S. Pacific fleet in one blow. Planes and ships were destroyed. Over 2,400 people were killed.

Roosevelt was grim. He did not want to fight a war on two fronts. He had expected to enter the war in Europe, not to fight in Asia, too. On December 8, 1941, Roosevelt addressed Congress asking for a declaration of war against Japan. He said: "Yesterday, December 7, 1941, a date which will live in infamy . . . [the Japanese launched] an unprovoked and dastardly attack." Congress quickly agreed to declare war. Germany and Italy then declared war on the United States.

4. What event caused the American declaration of war against Japan?

Glossary

aggressor One who starts violence, a war, or an invasion

arsenal Supply of ammunition, arms, and other war materials

chancellor Prime minister; leader of the government

emigration papers Official documents giving permission to enter a nation

front Area of contact between combating forces; battlefront

government in exile Government that has had to flee to a foreign country because its own territory has been conquered and occupied

isolationism Policy of opposing political and economic involvement with other countries

massacre Savage killing of many victims

merchant ship Ship used for trade

militant Aggressive; fighting or warring

occupy Seize and maintain control over by force

pacify Ease the anger of; soothe

peacetime draft Forced enrollment of certain persons into the armed forces when there is not a war

puppet government Government with no real power of its own that is controlled by another nation

storm troopers Special German soldiers trained to carry out sudden attacks or assaults

synagogues Jewish houses of worship

war machine Machinery necessary to wage war, including production of weapons, transport, and military vehicles

Weimar Republic Democratic government of Germany set up after World War I

AFTER YOU READ

Terms and Names

A. Write the letter of the name next to the description that fits it best.

a. Adolf Hitler
b. Joseph Stalin
c. Benito Mussolini
d. Winston Churchill
e. Charles de Gaulle
f. Hideki Tojo

_____ **1.** British prime minister who opposed appeasement

_____ **2.** Italian fascist dictator who formed an alliance with Hitler

_____ **3.** Nazi dictator who believed the Germans were a master race

_____ **4.** French general who set up a government-in-exile when France fell

_____ **5.** Militant general who became prime minister of Japan and planned the attack on Pearl Harbor

_____ **6.** Soviet dictator who signed a nonaggression pact with Hitler and had his own expansionist ideas

B. Circle the name or term that best completes each sentence.

1. _____ is the deliberate and systematic killing of an entire people.
   appeasement   fascism   genocide

2. A _____ is a "lightning war" of quick, crushing surprise attacks.
   Holocaust   blitzkrieg   fascism

3. When Germany, Italy, and Japan formed an alliance, they became known as the _____.
   Allies   Holocaust   Axis powers

4. In the _____, the Nazis systematically murdered over 11 million Jews and others.
   blitzkrieg   Holocaust   appeasement

AFTER YOU READ (continued) CHAPTER 24 World War Looms

5. _____ is a form of very nationalistic totalitarian government with a strong dictator.
  fascism   genocide   blitzkrieg

6. The _____ included Britain, France, the United States, and others fighting the Axis.
  Lend-Lease Act   Allies   Holocaust

7. The policy of _____ at Munich allowed Germany to annex part of Czechoslovakia.
  Lend-Lease Act   appeasement   blitzkrieg

8. The racist, nationalistic, expansionist philosophy of Hitler's Germany was called _____.
  appeasement   Nazism   genocide

9. The Nazis rounded up Jews and other people they felt were inferior and sent them to _____.
  Axis powers   concentration camps   blitzkrieg

Main Ideas

1. What are the characteristics of a totalitarian state?

_____

2. What was the outcome of Britain's and France's policy of appeasement?

_____

3. What groups did the Nazis deem unfit to belong to the Aryan "master race"?

_____

4. How did the United States give aid to nations resisting Hitler?

_____

Thinking Critically

Answer the following questions on a separate sheet of paper.

1. How did the expansionist ideas of Hitler, Stalin, and Tojo lead to World War II?

2. World War II has been called "the good war" because it was fought to rid the world of brutal and dangerous dictatorships. Explain why people think of it this way.

Name _____   Date _____

Mobilizing for Defense

BEFORE YOU READ

In the last section, you learned the reasons why the United States entered World War II.

In this section, you will learn how Americans joined in the war effort.

AS YOU READ

Use the web diagram below to take notes on the changes on the American home front during World War II.

TERMS AND NAMES

George Marshall Army chief of staff during World War II

Women's Auxiliary Army Corps (WAAC) Women volunteers who served in non-combat positions

A. Philip Randolph Important African-American labor leader

Manhattan Project Secret research project that resulted in the Atomic Bomb

Office of Price Administration (OPA) Agency of the federal government that fought inflation

War Production Board (WPB) Government agency that decided which companies would make war materials and how to distribute raw materials

rationing Restricting the amount of food and other goods people may buy during wartime to assure adequate supplies for the military

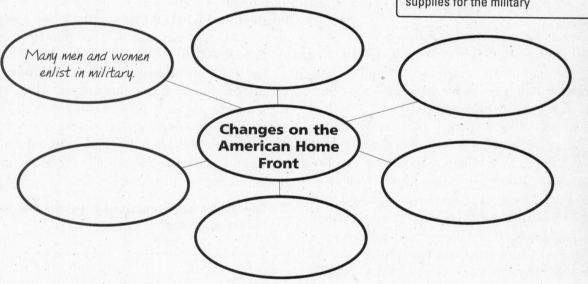

Many men and women enlist in military.

Changes on the American Home Front

Americans Join the War Effort
(page 768–770)

How did Americans react to Pearl Harbor?

The Japanese had expected Americans to react with fear and despair to the attack on Pearl Harbor. Instead, Americans reacted with rage. "Remember Pearl Harbor" became a rallying cry. Five million men volunteered for military service.

But fighting a war on two fronts—in Europe and in the Pacific—required huge numbers of soldiers. Another ten million men were drafted. New soldiers received eight weeks of basic training. Then they were officially "GIs," a nickname coming from the term "Government Issue."

To free more men for combat, Army Chief of Staff General **George Marshall** suggested using women for noncombat military tasks. Congress created the **Women's Auxiliary Army Corps**

(WAAC) in 1942. About 25,000 women served in the military. They did not receive the same pay or benefits as men.

Men and women from minority groups also served in World War II. They included Mexican Americans, Asian Americans, and Native Americans. Some African Americans had mixed feelings about defending a country where they were often segregated and denied the basic rights of citizenship. But they also knew they would be worse off under any of the Axis powers. More than a million African Americans served, but in racially segregated units. These units were not even allowed into combat until the last year of the war.

1. How did women and minorities join in the war effort?

_____

_____

A Production Miracle (pages 770–773)

What changes took place in American life?

The nation's factories quickly switched to war production. Automobile factories made planes and tanks. Pencil-makers turned out bomb parts. Shipyards and defense plants expanded. They produced warships with amazing speed.

About 18 million workers kept these war industries going. Some 6 million new factory workers were women. At first, industry did not want to hire women. Men feared women would not be able to handle the heavy work. Once women proved they could do the work, factories hired them. But they paid women only 60 percent as much as men.

Before the war, most defense contractors had refused to hire African Americans. **A. Philip Randolph,** the president of the Brotherhood of Sleeping Car Porters, was an important African-American labor leader. He threatened to have African Americans march on Washington to demand an end to this discrimination. Roosevelt feared such a march. He issued an *executive order* banning discrimination in defense industries.

Even Hollywood contributed to the war effort with patriotic films. They also made escapist romances and comedies. Public hunger for news of the war made magazines and radio more popular.

The government hired scientists to develop new weapons and medicines. They made improvements in radar and *sonar,* and in "miracle drugs" like penicillin. The government also set up the **Manhattan Project,** which developed the atomic bomb.

2. How did the war change life at home?

_____

_____

The Federal Government Takes Control (pages 773–774)

How did the federal government get involved in the economy?

The federal government was worried about economic issues. Congress wanted to prevent the high inflation that had occurred during World War I. Congress set up the **Office of Price Administration (OPA).** It successfully fought inflation by "freezing," or not increasing, prices on most goods. Congress also raised taxes. The **War Production Board (WPB)** decided which companies would make war materials and how to distribute raw materials.

The OPA also set up a system of **rationing.** Families were issued coupons to be used for buying scarce items, such as meat and gasoline. Most Americans cooperated with the rationing system. They also bought *war bonds* and collected goods, such as tin cans and paper, that could be recycled, or reused, for the war effort.

3. How did the federal government regulate American life during the war?

_____

_____

CHAPTER 25 Section 2 (pages 775–783)

The War for Europe and North Africa

BEFORE YOU READ

In the last section, you saw how the American involvement in World War II affected life on the home front.

In this section, you will see how the United States, Britain, and the Soviet Union combined to defeat Germany and its partners in Europe.

AS YOU READ

Take notes on the time line below. Fill it in with events that led to the defeat of Germany.

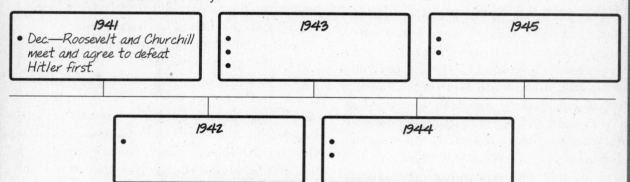

1941
• Dec.—Roosevelt and Churchill meet and agree to defeat Hitler first.

1942
•

1943
•
•
•

1944
•
•

1945
•
•

The United States and Britain Join Forces (pages 775–776)

What were the goals of the American and British alliance?

In late December 1941, a few weeks after Pearl Harbor, President Roosevelt met with British Prime Minister Winston Churchill. They planned their war strategy. They agreed that the first thing to do was to defeat Hitler's Germany. Roosevelt and Churchill began a lasting friendship and a strong alliance between America and Britain.

After war was declared, German U-boats increased attacks on American ships in the Atlantic. Many American ships were sunk. The Allies organized convoys, or groups, for shared protection. Warships and airplanes escorted the convoys. They used sonar and radar to find and destroy many German submarines.

The United States also started building ships at a rapid pace. Soon there were more Allied cargo ships, or Liberty ships, being made than being sunk. By mid-1943, the tide of the Battle of the Atlantic had turned in favor of the Allies.

1. What was the Battle of the Atlantic, and how did the Allies win it?

_____

_____

The Eastern Front and the Mediterranean (pages 777–779)

What happened in the Soviet Union, North Africa, and Italy?

By the summer of 1943, the Allies were winning on land as well as on the sea.

The German invasion of the Soviet Union had begun in 1941. When it stalled early in 1942, Hitler changed his tactics. He moved to capture Soviet oil fields and to take the industrial city of Stalingrad. The Germans bombed Stalingrad until almost the whole city was on fire.

But Stalin refused to give up. In three months of horrible hand-to-hand combat, the Germans took most of Stalingrad. Then the Soviets counter-attacked. They trapped a large German force just as winter came. The Germans froze and starved. In February 1943, the few German soldiers who were still alive surrendered. The Battle of Stalingrad was a turning point. From then on, Soviet forces moved steadily west towards Germany.

Meanwhile, in November 1942, the Allies invaded North Africa. North Africa at the time was controlled by the Axis. American forces led by General **Dwight D. ("Ike") Eisenhower** defeated German troops under General Erwin Rommel. The Germans surrendered in May 1943.

Next, in July 1943, the Allies invaded Italy. They captured Sicily. The war-weary Italian king stripped Prime Minister Mussolini of power and had him arrested. But then Hitler seized Italy. It took 18 long and bloody months of fighting for the Allies to drive the Germans out of Italy. In the Italian campaign, segregated units of African Americans, Mexican Americans, and Japanese Americans all won honors for bravery.

2. How were the Allies victorious in the Soviet Union, North Africa, and Italy?

_____

_____

The Allies Liberate Europe
(pages 780–783)

Why did the Allies invade Normandy?

The Americans and British had been building a huge invasion force for two years. It was designed to *liberate* Europe. June 6, 1944, was **D-Day**—the day the Allies crossed the English Channel and landed in Normandy, France. This invasion was the largest land-sea-air operation in history.

British, American, and Canadian forces landed on the beaches of Normandy. They met fierce German resistance, and many were killed. But they took the beaches. Over 1 million Allied troops landed in France, and began to advance. General **Omar Bradley** opened a huge hole in the German lines. It allowed American General **George Patton** and his Third Army to liberate Paris in August. By September, the Allies had liberated other European nations and had entered Germany itself.

In the United States, Roosevelt won reelection to a fourth term as president.

To the Allies' surprise, Hitler began a counter-attack in December. At first, the Germans cut deeply into Allied lines. After a month of fierce fighting, the Allies pushed the Germans back. The Germans had lost so many men and weapons in this **Battle of the Bulge** that they could only retreat.

Meanwhile, the Soviets pushed through Poland toward Germany. The Soviets were the first to liberate death camps and to describe the unbelievable horrors they saw there. By April 25, the Soviets were in Berlin. Hitler responded to certain defeat by shooting himself.

On May 8, 1945, General Eisenhower accepted the *unconditional surrender* of Nazi Germany. That became known as **V-E Day**—Victory in Europe Day. Roosevelt died on April 12, 1945 before V-E Day. Vice President **Harry S. Truman** became president.

3. How did the Allies liberate Europe and defeat Germany?

_____

_____

The War in the Pacific

BEFORE YOU READ

In the last section, you saw how the Allies won victory in Europe.

In this section, you will see how the Allies defeated Japan in the Pacific.

AS YOU READ

Use the diagram below and list the key military and diplomatic actions of the last years of the war. Tell why they were important.

MILITARY/DIPLOMATIC ACTION	IMPORTANCE
U.S. withdraws from Philippines	Japan begins conquering Pacific islands

The Allies Stem the Japanese Tide (pages 784–786)

What was so important about the Battle of Midway?

In the first six months after Pearl Harbor, the Japanese military had great success. They conquered huge areas of the Asian mainland and many islands in the Pacific. In 1942, Japanese forces threatened the American army in the Philippines. General **Douglas MacArthur** was the commander of the American army. In March 1942, MacArthur left the Philippines but told people left behind, "I shall return."

The United States started to fight back against the Japanese. In the spring of 1942, Lt. Colonel James Doolittle led a bombing raid on Tokyo. The U.S. Navy defeated the Japanese at the Battle of Coral Sea. This ended the Japanese threat to invade Australia.

Then, in June 1942, the Japanese steamed toward Midway, an island northwest of Hawaii. American forces broke the Japanese code and knew of their plans. Admiral **Chester Nimitz** commanded American forces that crushed the Japanese. The **Battle of Midway** was a turning point in the Pacific War. After Midway, the Allies began "island hopping," moving closer to Japan.

1. Why was the Battle of Midway important?

_____

The Allies Go on the Offensive (pages 787–789)

What were the important battles in the Pacific?

American forces, led by General MacArthur, now went island-hopping towards Japan. They avoided islands that were well defended by the Japanese. Airfields were built on captured islands. Planes could then bomb Japanese supply lines.

American marines stormed the island of Guadalcanal in August 1942. This marked Japan's first defeat on land. In October 1944, Americans landed on the island of Leyte in the Philippines. The Japanese launched **kamikaze** raids. In these suicide attacks, Japanese pilots crashed their planes into Allied ships supporting the invasion. Still, Japan lost so many ships in the Battle of Leyte Gulf that the Japanese Navy was essentially knocked out of the war.

The Americans took the island of Iwo Jima in March 1945. This extremely bloody battle gave the United States a base to launch heavy bombers that could reach Japan itself.

A fierce battle raged over the island of Okinawa. The island was Japan's last defensive *outpost*. The Americans finally won on June 22, 1945, but it cost 7,600 American lives. Japan lost 110,000 men. The Allies feared the human cost of invading Japan.

2. Why was the Battle of Leyte Gulf so important?

_____

_____

The Atomic Bomb Ends the War (pages 789–790)

Why did the United States use the atomic bomb?

As American forces neared Japan in March 1945, President Roosevelt died. Vice-President Harry S. Truman became president.

President Truman was told about the Manhattan Project. This was the secret development of the atomic bomb led by **J. Robert Oppenheimer.** On July 16, 1945, the first atomic bomb was tested. It was even more powerful than predicted. Many sci-entists felt it would be immoral to drop the bomb on Japan. Others said it would shorten the war and save lives. It would also give the United States an advantage over the Soviets after the war. Truman decided to use the bomb.

On August 6, 1945, an atomic bomb was dropped on **Hiroshima,** Japan. Almost every building collapsed into dust. But Japan did not surrender. A second bomb was dropped on **Nagasaki,** killing 200,000. Emperor Hirohito was horrified. Japan surrendered September 2, 1945. The war was over.

3. Why did Truman decide to use the atomic bomb?

_____

Rebuilding Begins (pages 791–793)

How did the Allies try to shape the postwar world?

In February 1945, Roosevelt, Churchill, and Stalin met at the Yalta Conference. Stalin and Churchill disagreed on how to treat Germany. Roosevelt made concessions to Stalin. He wanted Stalin to help in the fight to defeat Japan. And he wanted Stalin to support the United Nations. At Yalta, the allies agreed to divide Germany into four zones. Stalin agreed to allow free elections in Poland and other Eastern European countries now occupied by the Soviet Army.

The **Nuremberg Trials,** trials held by an international *tribunal*, was held to try Nazi leaders. For the first time, a nation's leaders were held legally responsible for their wartime acts. They were tried for starting the war; for acts against the customs of war, such as killing prisoners; and for the murder and enslavement of civilians.

American forces, headed by General MacArthur, occupied Japan for six years. First, Japanese officials were put on trial for war crimes. Then, the Americans helped Japan set up a free-market economic system and create a new democratic constitution.

4. How did the Yalta Conference shape the postwar world?

_____

_____

CHAPTER 25 Section 4 (pages 796–801)

The Home Front

TERMS AND NAMES

GI Bill of Rights Law passed by Congress to help servicemen readjust to civilian life

James Farmer Civil rights leader who founded the Congress of Racial Equality

Congress of Racial Equality (CORE) Interracial organization formed to fight discrimination

internment Confinement under guard, especially during wartime

Japanese American Citizens League (JACL) Civil rights group formed by Japanese Americans

BEFORE YOU READ

In the last section, you saw how the Allies prepared for the postwar world.

In this section, you will see how the war changed the United States.

AS YOU READ

Use the chart below to take notes on the advances and problems in the economy and in civil rights during the war.

	ADVANCES	PROBLEMS
Economy	More jobs Better pay	Housing shortage
Civil Rights: • African Americans		
• Mexican Americans		
• Japanese Americans		

Opportunity and Adjustment
(pages 796–798)

How did the war create opportunities at home?

World War II was a time of opportunity for many Americans. The economy boomed. There were plenty of jobs. Wages rose. Farmers also did well.

Women had many job opportunities during the war. The share of women in the work force rose to 35 percent. (They lost some of these jobs when the men returned from military service.) Women also did a wide range of jobs and entered professions that had not been open to them before the war.

Many Americans relocated—picked up and moved. They moved to where there were defense jobs. States with military bases or defense plants saw huge gains in population. Some city populations grew by one third. The result was a housing shortage. Even though workers had the money to pay, there was no housing to rent. There were also food shortages in some areas.

People had to adjust to new family situations. Many fathers were in the armed forces, so women had to work and raise children on their own.

The war also caused a boom in marriages. Many couples married before the men went overseas.

But when the men returned after years of military service, many of these marriages failed. The divorce rate increased.

In 1944, Congress passed the **GI Bill of Rights** which was designed to help servicemen readjust to civilian life. This bill paid for veterans to attend college or technical school. Over half the returning soldiers took advantage of this opportunity. It also gave federal loan guarantees to veterans buying homes or farms or starting businesses. The GI Bill gave many people opportunities they otherwise would never have had.

1. What opportunities did the war create at home?

_____

_____

Discrimination and Reaction
(pages 798–799)

How did the war affect African Americans and Mexican Americans?

On the *home front,* many African Americans left the South and moved to the West Coast. There they found skilled jobs that paid well. But they also found prejudice. In 1942, civil rights leader **James Farmer** formed a new interracial organization to fight discrimination. It was called the **Congress of Racial Equality (CORE).**

African Americans also moved into the crowded cities of the North. Tension among the races grew. In 1943 it led to *race riots.* The worst one was in Detroit, where over 30 people were killed. President Roosevelt had to send federal troops to restore order. In response, many communities formed committees to improve race relations.

Mexican Americans experienced prejudice during the war years as well. In 1942, there were anti-Mexican riots in Los Angeles. In the "zoot-suit" riots, Mexican Americans were beaten by white servicemen and civilians.

2. How did World War II affect African Americans and Mexican Americans?

_____

_____

Internment of Japanese Americans
(pages 800–801)

What happened to Japanese Americans during the war?

Japanese Americans endured terrible treatment during the war. After Pearl Harbor, panic-stricken Americans believed Japanese Americans living in the U.S. were disloyal to the United States. In Hawaii, the commanding general ordered the **internment,** or confinement of about 1 percent of Japanese-American residents.

On February 19, 1942, President Roosevelt ordered the internment of all Japanese Americans living in California, and parts of other western states. More than 100,000 people were rounded up and shipped to *internment camps*.

No charges were ever filed against Japanese Americans. No evidence of subversion was ever found. In 1944, in the case of *Korematsu* v. *United States*, the Supreme Court said the government policy was justified by "military necessity." After the war, the **Japanese American Citizens League (JACL)** pushed the government to compensate, or pay back those sent to the camps.

Over the years, Congress passed bills to repay those who had been interned for the loss of their property. Finally, in 1990, cash payments were sent to all former internees. In a letter that year, President Bush said the nation "recognized the injustice done to Japanese Americans during World War II."

3. What reason was given for the internment of Japanese Americans?

_____

_____

Glossary   CHAPTER 25   The United States in World War II

executive order Order issued by the president to any part of the executive branch of government

home front Civilian population or the civilian activities of a country at war

internment camp Area where people are kept under guard, especially during wartime

liberate Set free from oppression, imprisonment, or foreign control

outpost Fortified area away from a main settlement, used to prevent an attack on the main settlement

race riots Riots caused by racial hatred or dissension

sonar System using underwater sound waves to detect submerged objects

tribunal Court of justice

unconditional surrender Giving up to an enemy without any demands or requests

war bonds Certificates of debt issued by a government—the government uses the money to pay for a war and pays the investor at a certain future date

AFTER YOU READ

Terms and Names

A. Circle the phrase that best completes each sentence.

1. The Battle of the Bulge was _____.

     an Allied campaign in North Africa   a battle against Japan in the Pacific

     the final German counterattack in Europe

2. On D-Day, the Allies _____.

     landed in Normandy to liberate Europe   defeated Japan   defeated Germany

3. The Manhattan Project _____.

     sent Japanese Americans to internment camps   planned the Allies' strategy   developed the atomic bomb

4. In the Nuremberg Trials, the Nazis _____.

     were tried for war crimes and crimes against humanity   starved and froze outside of a Soviet city

     destroyed Jewish businesses

5. The GI Bill of Rights _____.

     desegregated the armed forces   paid for veterans to go to college   allowed women to serve in the military

6. Rationing was _____.

     the scientific process of developing the atomic bomb   a way of allotting scarce products, like meat and gasoline

     the percentage of women allowed to work in defense industries

7. Hiroshima was _____.

     the Japanese city on which the first atomic bomb was dropped   the emperor of Japan

     an internment camp in the United States

AFTER YOU READ (cont.) CHAPTER 25 The United States in World War II

B. Write the letter of the name or term next to the description that explains it best.

a. A. Philip Randolph

b. Harry S. Truman

c. Nagasaki

d. Dwight D. Eisenhower

e. Douglas MacArthur

f. V-E Day

g. Congress of Racial Equality (CORE)

h. kamikaze

_____ **1.** Japanese city that was the site of the first atomic-bomb drop

_____ **2.** The day Nazi Germany surrendered to the Allies

_____ **3.** An important African-American labor leader

_____ **4.** The American general who liberated the Philippines and supervised the occupation of Japan

_____ **5.** The American general who commanded the D-Day invasion and received Germany's surrender

_____ **6.** Japanese suicide-plane air raids

_____ **7.** An organization formed to fight discrimination

_____ **8.** The vice-president who became president when Roosevelt died

Main Ideas

1. How did the federal government's actions affect civilian life during World War II?

_____

_____

_____

2. How did the Battle of the Bulge signal that the end of World War II in Europe was near?

_____

_____

_____

3. What was the result of dropping atomic bombs on Hiroshima and Nagasaki?

_____

_____

_____

4. What events showed racial tension in the United States during World War II?

_____

_____

Thinking Critically

Answer the following questions on a separate sheet of paper.

1. What social and economic changes in American society arose from World War II?

2. Answer one of the following:

   (a) How did the Allies defeat Germany in Europe?

   (b) How did the United States defeat Japan in the Pacific?

CHAPTER 26 Section 1 (pages 808–814)

Origins of the Cold War

BEFORE YOU READ

In the last section, you saw the social and economic changes that would reshape postwar America.

In this section, you will see how the Allied coalition that won the war fell apart and the United States and the Soviet Union came into conflict.

AS YOU READ

Fill in the chart below with notes on U.S. actions and Soviet actions that contributed to the beginning of the Cold War.

SOVIET ACTIONS	U.S. ACTIONS
Stalin sets up satellite nations.	

Former Allies Clash (pages 808–810)

What caused Soviet-American problems?

The United States and the Soviet Union were wartime allies. But there had been trouble between them for some time. A major reason was that they had opposing political and economic systems. In addition, the Soviets were angry that the United States had taken so long to launch an attack against Hitler in Europe. Stalin also did not like that the United States had kept the development of the atomic bomb a secret. Americans were upset that

Stalin had signed a treaty with Hitler before World War II. Still, at the end of the war, people hoped that the **United Nations (UN)** would help bring a time of peace. Instead, the UN became a place where the two *superpowers* competed and tried to influence other nations.

Meanwhile, Roosevelt had died. Harry S. Truman had become president. Truman was a plain, self-educated man. But he had honesty, self-confidence, and a willingness to make tough decisions.

Truman met with the British and Soviet leaders at the Potsdam Conference in July 1945. He reminded Stalin of his promise at Yalta to allow free elections in Eastern Europe. But Stalin would not listen to Truman. Soviet troops occupied Eastern Europe and Stalin was not going to allow free elections.

1. What were three issues that led to hard feelings between the Soviet Union and the United States?

Tension Mounts (pages 810–811)

What did Stalin and Truman want for postwar Europe?

Truman and Stalin disagreed over the future of Europe. Truman wanted strong democratic nations. He wanted the United States to be able to buy raw materials in Eastern Europe. He also wanted Eastern European markets for American products.

Stalin wished to spread communism. He also wanted to control Eastern Europe to prevent another invasion of Soviet territory. He wanted to use the resources of Germany and Eastern Europe to rebuild his war-torn nation. Stalin also felt that war between the Soviet Union and the West could not be avoided.

Stalin set up Communist governments in the European nations occupied by Soviet troops. They became **satellite nations,** countries that depended on and were dominated by the Soviet Union. The United States answered with a policy of **containment.** This was an effort to block Soviet influence by making alliances and supporting weaker nations.

In 1946, Winston Churchill described "an **iron curtain**" coming down across Europe. It separated the nations in the "Soviet sphere" from the capitalist democracies of *the West.*

2. How did Truman's and Stalin's plans differ?

Cold War in Europe (page 812)

What were the Truman Doctrine and the Marshall Plan?

The conflicting aims of the United States and the Soviet Union led to the **Cold War.** This was a state of hostility between these superpowers, but one without military action. Each tried to spread its political and economic influence worldwide.

Truman's first test of containment was when Greece and Turkey needed economic and military aid

in 1947. In the **Truman Doctrine,** the president argued that aid should be sent to any nation trying to stop Communists from taking over. Congress agreed. Aid was sent to Turkey and Greece.

Western Europe was also in terrible economic shape. Factories and fields had been destroyed. A terrible winter in 1946–1947 increased hardship. Secretary of State George Marshall wanted to send aid to nations that cooperated with American economic goals. Then Soviet troops took over Czechoslovakia in 1949. Congress saw the need for strong, stable governments to resist communism. It approved the **Marshall Plan.** The plan was a great success in rebuilding Western Europe and halting the spread of communism.

3. How did the United States begin to send aid to nations fighting communism?

Superpowers Struggle Over Germany (pages 813–814)

How did the Soviets and the West disagree over Germany?

East and West also disagreed over Germany. Stalin wanted to keep it weak and divided. The Western allies thought Europe would be more stable if Germany were united and productive. Britain, France, and the United States combined their occupied zones into the nation of West Germany.

Berlin was also divided into four occupied zones. But it was located in Soviet-controlled East Germany. The Soviets cut off all transportation to West Berlin. West Berlin was the name given the zones occupied by Britain, France, and the United States. The Soviets said they would hold the city *hostage* until the West gave up the idea of German *reunification.* Instead, the United States and Britain started the **Berlin Airlift.** For 327 days, planes brought food and supplies to West Berlin. Finally, the Soviets gave up the blockade.

The blockade made the West worry about Soviet aggression. The United States and Canada joined with ten European nations in a defensive military alliance called the **North Atlantic Treaty Organization (NATO).** Members agreed that an attack on one was an attack on all.

4. What led to the Berlin blockade?

CHAPTER 26   Section 2 (pages 815–821)

The Cold War Heats Up

BEFORE YOU READ

In the last section, you read about postwar Europe.

In this section, you will read about the postwar situation in Asia and about the Korean War.

AS YOU READ

Fill in the time line below with the major events of the Communist takeover in China and the Korean War.

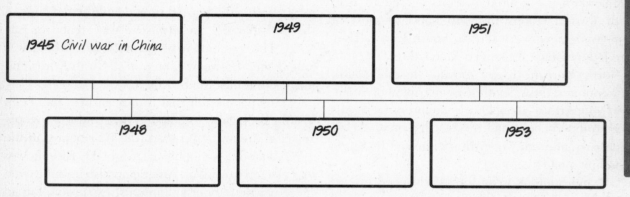

1945 Civil war in China	1949	1951

1948	1950	1953

China becomes a Communist Country (pages 815–817)

How did the Communists gain control of China?

For two decades the Chinese Communists struggled against the Nationalist government led by **Chiang Kai-shek.** The United States supported Chiang because he opposed communism and sent him aid. But U.S. officials knew that Chiang's government was inefficient and corrupt. He overtaxed the Chinese people even during times of *famine*. He did not have the support of the people.

Mao Zedong led the Communist forces in the North. He won the support of many Chinese *peasants*. Mao distributed land to them and reduced rents. He had an experienced army with high morale.

President Truman refused to send American troops to help the Nationalists fight communism. But he did send aid. Even so, in 1949, Chiang and his forces had to flee to **Taiwan,** an island off the coast of China. China was now Communist. Containment in China had failed!

American conservatives said that the United States had "lost" China because not enough had been done to help the Nationalists. Truman's followers said that the Communist success was because Chiang could not win the support of the Chinese people. Conservatives claimed that the U.S. government was filled with Communist agents. American fear of communism began to burn out of control.

1. How did Communists gain control of China?

_____

_____

The Korean War; The United States Fights in Korea (pages 817–821)

What caused the Korean War?

Japan had ruled Korea since 1910. At the end of World War II, Japanese forces in the north surrendered to the Soviets. In the south, the Japanese surrendered to the Americans. Two nations then developed. They were separated by the **38th parallel,** an imaginary line that divides Korea at 38 degrees north *latitude.*

In 1948, South Korea became an independent nation. North Korea became a Communist nation. Each claimed the right to rule all of Korea.

In June 1950, North Korea started the **Korean War** by invading South Korea. Truman was afraid another Asian nation was about to fall to communism. He ordered air and naval support for South Korea. Then the United Nations agreed to help South Korea. Troops from 16 nations—most of them American—were sent to South Korea. They were led by General Douglas MacArthur.

North Korean troops moved steadily south. They conquered the South Korean capital of Seoul. Then MacArthur launched a counterattack. His forces trapped about half the North Korean Army, which surrendered. MacArthur's success in Korea made him a national hero.

UN and South Korean forces advanced toward the 38th parallel. If they crossed it, the war would become an *offensive* rather than a *defensive* one. In October 1950, the UN told MacArthur to cross the 38th parallel and reunite Korea.

The Chinese opposed UN forces moving into North Korea. China said it would not let the Americans near its border. The UN ignored the threat and advanced. Then Chinese troops entered North Korea. They drove UN forces back. In January 1951, the Communists recaptured Seoul.

For two years, fighting continued. But neither side advanced. MacArthur wanted to extend the war into China. He even suggested dropping atomic bombs on China. Truman was against this strategy. The Soviets were allies of the Chinese. Truman felt bombing China would start World War III.

MacArthur continued to argue for his plan. He spoke to the press and to Republican leaders. Truman felt that he could no longer allow MacArthur's *insubordination.* He fired MacArthur as commander. At first, the American public sided with MacArthur. Later, they came to agree with Truman's idea of a *limited war.*

Meanwhile, a cease-fire went into effect in June 1951. Both sides agreed on a *demilitarized zone* at the 38th parallel. An *armistice* was signed in July 1953. The agreement was a *stalemate.* Korea was still divided between Communist North Korea and non-Communist South Korea.

Many people felt that American lives had been lost for little gain. As a result, the American people rejected the party in power, the Democrats, in the 1952 election. Republican Dwight D. Eisenhower was elected president. Americans also became even more worried about Communist expansion abroad and Communist spies at home.

2. **What was gained by the Korean War?**

_____

_____

_____

"Mr. Prima Donna, Brass Hat, Five Star MacArthur" *Harry S. Truman*

Photo Credit: Carl Mydans, *Life* Magazine. Copyright © Time, Inc.

Skillbuilder

Use this picture to answer these questions.

1. **What kind of leader do you think MacArthur was from looking at this photo?**

_____

_____

2. **What does the quote from President Truman tell you about his feelings toward MacArthur?**

_____

_____

CHAPTER 26 Section 3 (pages 822–827)

The Cold War at Home

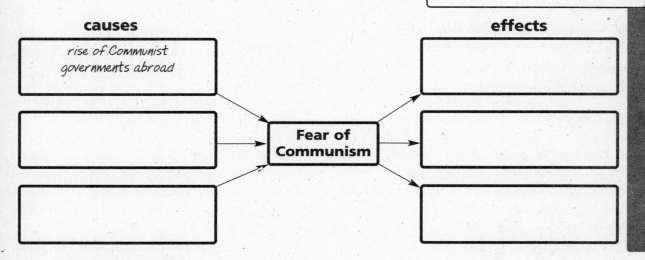

TERMS AND NAMES

HUAC House Committee on Un-American Activities

Hollywood Ten People called before HUAC who did not cooperate

blacklist List of people in the Hollywood film industry who were refused jobs because they did not cooperate with HUAC

Alger Hiss Former State Department official

Ethel and Julius Rosenberg Activists in the American Communist Party who were executed as spies

Joseph McCarthy Republican Senator who claimed Communists were taking over the federal government

McCarthyism Term used to refer to tactic of accusing people of disloyalty without producing evidence

BEFORE YOU READ

In the last section, you read about the Cold War abroad.

In this section, you will read about the effects of the Cold War at home.

AS YOU READ

Fill in the diagram below with the causes of the Fear of Communism in the boxes to the left and the effects in the boxes to the right.

causes

> rise of Communist governments abroad

Fear of Communism

effects

Fear of Communist Influence

(pages 822–824)

How did Americans react to the threat of Communist influence?

Many Americans felt threatened by the rise of Communist governments in Europe and Asia. Some even felt that Communists could threaten the U.S. government from within. These fears increased when people found out about some spies selling U.S. government secrets to the Soviets.

Republicans accused the Truman administration of being "soft on communism." In response to this pressure, Truman set up a Loyalty Review Board. The Board investigated over 3 million people. About 200 were fired. Many people felt that these investigations were unconstitutional. The accused were not allowed to see the evidence against them or to face their accusers.

In 1947, Congress set up the House Committee on Un-American Activities (**HUAC**). Its purpose was to look for Communists both inside and outside government. HUAC concentrated on the movie industry because of suspected Communist influences in Hollywood. Many people were brought before HUAC. Some agreed that there had been Communist *infiltration* of the movie industry. They *informed on* others to save themselves.

Ten people called before HUAC refused to testify. They said the hearings were unconstitutional. The **Hollywood Ten,** as they were called, were sent to prison for their refusal.

In response to the HUAC hearings, Hollywood executives created a list of some 500 people they thought were Communist-influenced. They refused to hire the people on this **blacklist.** Many people's careers were ruined.

In 1950, Congress passed the McCarren Act. It outlawed the planning of any action that might lead to a totalitarian dictatorship in the United States.

1. **What are three ways that the United States reacted to fear of communism at home?**

_____

_____

Spy Cases Stun the Nation
(pages 824–826)

How did spies increase fear of communism?

Two spy cases added to the fear of communism sweeping the nation. One involved an official of the State Department named **Alger Hiss.** A former Soviet spy accused Hiss of spying for the Soviet Union. He had documents that *implicated* Hiss. Hiss claimed the documents were forgeries. Hiss was convicted of *perjury*—for lying about the documents—and went to jail.

In 1949, the Soviet Union tested an atomic bomb. Most people thought that it would take the Soviets much longer to develop their own atomic bomb. A British scientist admitted giving the Soviets secret information about the American bomb. He also implicated two Americans: **Ethel and Julius Rosenberg.**

The Rosenbergs were members of the American Communist Party. They denied the charges of spying. But they were convicted and sentenced to death. People from all over the world appealed for *clemency* for the Rosenbergs. They said the evidence against them was weak. The Supreme Court

refused to overturn the decision, and the Rosenbergs were executed in 1953.

2. **What two spy cases increased fear of communism in the United States?**

_____

_____

McCarthy Launches His "Witch Hunt" (pages 826–827)

Who was Senator McCarthy?

In the early 1950s, Republican Senator **Joseph McCarthy** made headlines. He claimed that Communists were taking over the government. He also said the Democrats were guilty of *treason* for allowing this Communist infiltration.

McCarthy never produced any evidence to support his charges. These unsupported attacks on suspected Communists became known as **McCarthyism.** Later, McCarthyism also came to mean the unfair tactic of accusing people of disloyalty without producing evidence.

Many Republicans encouraged McCarthy. They thought that a strong anti-Communist position would help them win the 1952 elections. But some complained that McCarthy was violating people's constitutional rights.

In 1954, McCarthy made accusations against the U.S. Army. The Senate *hearings* were broadcast on national television. The American people watched McCarthy bully witnesses but produce no evidence. McCarthy lost public favor. The Senate voted to condemn him.

There had been much support for Communist *witch hunts* in the early 1950s. Many people were forced to take *loyalty oaths* in order to get jobs. States passed laws making it a crime to speak of overthrowing the government. These laws violated the constitutional right of free speech. But people became afraid to speak their views. Fear of communism made many Americans willing to give up their constitutional rights.

3. **What was McCarthyism?**

_____

_____

CHAPTER 26 Section 4 (pages 828–833)

Two Nations Live on the Edge

BEFORE YOU READ

In the last section, you saw how the fear of communism affected life in the United States.

In this section, you will see how Cold War tensions increased as both the United States and the Soviet Union tried to spread their influence around the world.

AS YOU READ

Fill in the time line below with events that show how the United States and the Soviet Union competed during the Cold War. Write Soviet actions above the line and U.S. actions below the line. Draw arrows to show how the two nations reacted to each other.

TERMS AND NAMES

H-bomb Hydrogen bomb

Dwight D. Eisenhower President of the United States

John Foster Dulles Secretary of state

brinkmanship Willingness to go to the edge, or brink, of war

CIA Intelligence-gathering, or spy, agency of the United States government

Warsaw Pact Military alliance of the Soviet Union and its satellite nations

Eisenhower Doctrine Policy of the United States that it would defend the Middle East against attack by any Communist country

Nikita Khruschev Soviet leader

Francis Gary Powers Pilot of an American U-2 spy plane

U-2 incident Downing of a U.S. spy plane and the capture of its pilot by the Soviet Union in 1960

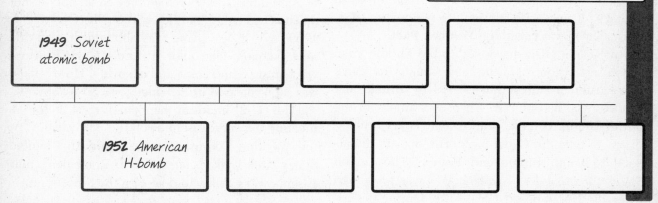

1949 Soviet atomic bomb

1952 American H-bomb

Brinkmanship Rules U.S. Policy

(pages 828–829)

What was the arms race?

The Soviet Union exploded its first atomic bomb in 1949. American leaders wanted to develop a more powerful weapon. In 1952, the United States exploded the first hydrogen bomb, or **H-bomb.**

But the Soviets tested their own H-bomb in 1953. **Dwight D. Eisenhower** was president. His secretary of state, **John Foster Dulles,** was very anti-Communist. He said America must not compromise. The United States must be prepared to

use all of its nuclear weapons against any aggressor. This willingness to go to the edge, or brink, of war was called **brinkmanship.**

The United States began making more nuclear weapons. So did the Soviet Union. This was called the arms race. Many Americans feared a nuclear attack at any time. They had *air-raid drills* and *fallout shelters* to prepare for these attacks.

1. Why did the arms race begin?

_____

_____

_____

The Cold War Spreads Around the World (pages 829–832)

What events increased Cold War tensions?

The United States was in competition with the Soviet Union all over the world. President Eisenhower began to rely on the **Central Intelligence Agency (CIA).** The CIA used spies to get information abroad. It also carried out covert actions, or secret operations, to weaken or overthrow governments unfriendly to the United States.

One CIA action involved Iran. In 1953, the CIA convinced the Shah, or monarch, of Iran to get rid of a prime minister who was not friendly to the West. In 1954, the CIA took action in Guatemala. Eisenhower believed Guatemala was friendly to the Communists. The CIA trained an army that overthrew Guatemala's government.

Soviet dictator Josef Stalin died in 1953. At first, tensions eased between the superpowers. People called it a thaw in the Cold War. But when West Germany joined NATO, the Soviet Union formed a military alliance with its satellite nations in 1955. This alliance was called the **Warsaw Pact.**

In 1956, a crisis developed in the Middle East. Egypt seized control of the Suez Canal. The Canal was located in Egypt but owned by Britain and France, who had built it. Egypt was an ally of the Soviet Union. Britain, France, and Israel invaded Egypt to take the Canal back. The Soviets threatened to bomb Britain and France. The United States threatened to *retaliate.* War was prevented when the UN imposed a cease-fire. During the crisis, Eisenhower issued a warning, known as the **Eisenhower Doctrine.** It said the United States would defend the Middle East against Communist attack.

In 1956, the people of Hungary rose in revolt and called for a democratic government. The new government promised free elections. But when the Hungarians asked to leave the Warsaw pact in 1956, Soviet tanks rolled into Hungary. They crushed the reform movement. Many Hungarian reformers were killed, and others fled the country.

2. How did hostilities increase between the United States and the Soviet Union during the 1950s?

_____

_____

_____

The Cold War Takes to the Skies (pages 832–833)

What was the missile race?

The Soviet leader, **Nikita Khrushchev,** came to power in the years after Stalin's death. Unlike Stalin, he believed communism could triumph through peaceful means.

On October 4, 1957, the Soviets shocked the world by launching *Sputnik I.* It was the first artificial satellite to orbit the earth. American scientists also worked hard to catch up. The first attempt to launch a U.S. satellite was a humiliating failure. On January 31, 1958, the United States successfully launched its first satellite.

Meanwhile, the United States had been flying spy missions over the Soviet Union. The CIA used U-2 aircraft that flew so high they could not be shot down. Or so the Americans thought. On May 1, 1960, a U-2 spy plane was shot down over the Soviet Union. The pilot, **Francis Gary Powers,** was captured and convicted of spying. However, he was soon released in exchange for a Soviet spy.

This **U-2 incident** happened right before a meeting between Eisenhower and Khrushchev. At the meeting, Khrushchev criticized the United States and walked out. The U-2 incident hurt Eisenhower's ability to deal with the Soviets.

3. In what two ways was the Cold War fought in the skies?

_____

_____

Glossary

air-raid drills Practice of what to do during a bombing attack

armistice Temporary stop to fighting by agreement of both sides

clemency Mercy; reduction of a severe sentence given by a court

defensive Intended to withstand or protect against aggression or attack

demilitarized zone An area where military forces are not allowed

fallout shelters Underground living areas that give protection from the explosion and radiation of a nuclear attack

famine Drastic, wide-reaching food shortage, often resulting in the starvation of many people

hearing Session of an investigating committee at which testimony is taken from witnesses

hostage Person or persons held prisoner in order to get a ransom or agreement to certain demands

implicated Suggested the guilt of; incriminated

infiltration Process of entering gradually or secretly, in order to spy or gain control

informed on Implicated; gave incriminating information about others to the authorities

insubordination Act of disobeying authority

latitude Distance north or south of the earth's equator, measured in degrees

limited war War whose objective is less than the enemy's total defeat

loyalty oath Formal pledge of loyalty to the government, sometimes specifically denying membership in the Communist Party

offensive Attacking; starting a war

peasants Small farmers, tenant farmers, sharecroppers, and farm laborers

perjury False testimony under oath, as in a court of law or Congressional hearing; lying

retaliate To strike back in kind; especially to return a military attack

reunification Recombining of the parts of a nation divided by force

Sputnik I First artificial satellite to orbit the Earth

stalemate Situation in which further action is blocked; a deadlock

superpowers Most powerful and influential nations, especially those that lead a power bloc

treason Betrayal of one's country, especially by aiding its enemies

the West Noncommunist countries of Western Europe and the Americas

witch hunt Investigation that says its purpose is to uncover illegal activities but is actually used to harm those whose views differ

AFTER YOU READ

Terms and Names

A. Write the name or term that best completes each sentence.

blacklist

containment

Mao Zedong

McCarthyism

NATO

satellite nations

Taiwan

Warsaw Pact

1. Stalin set up Communist governments in Soviet-dominated countries called _____. The United States tried to block Soviet influence in a policy called _____.

2. The United States, Canada, and ten European nations formed _____ to defend each other against Soviet aggression. Later, the Soviet Union and other Communist nations formed a military alliance called the _____.

3. Fear of Communist influence at home led to _____, a "witch hunt" in which many people were unfairly and unconstitutionally accused of being Communists. These people were sometimes put on a _____, which meant they could no longer find work.

4. _____ and his Communist forces won the civil war in China. They forced Chiang Kai-shek and his Nationalist forces to flee to the island of _____.

B. Write the letter of the name or term next to the description that explains it best.

a. Cold War

b. Korean War

c. John Foster Dulles

d. brinkmanship

e. CIA

f. Nikita Khrushchev

g. U-2 incident

_____ **1.** The willingness to go to the edge of war in order to keep the peace

_____ **2.** The period of competition and hostility between the United States and the Soviet Union

_____ **3.** The shooting down of an American spy plane by the Soviets

_____ **4.** The agency of the U.S. government that used spies to get information and to carry out secret actions abroad

_____ **5.** The fighting between North Korean and Chinese Communist troops and UN forces for control of Korea

_____ **6.** The leader of the Soviet Union who thought Communism could triumph peacefully

_____ **7.** President Eisenhower's secretary of state who developed the policy of brinkmanship

Main Ideas

1. What were the goals of U.S. foreign policy during the Cold War?

_____

_____

2. What goals did the United States achieve by fighting in Korea? What goals did it fail to achieve?

_____

_____

3. What actions of Joseph McCarthy worsened the national hysteria about communism?

_____

_____

_____

4. By what means did the U.S. government, including the CIA, fight the Cold War around the world?

_____

_____

Thinking Critically

Answer the following questions on a separate sheet of paper.

1. What was the Cold War? How did containment and the arms race contribute to the Cold War?

2. What were some effects of the fear of communism that swept the United States in the 1950s?

CHAPTER 27 Section 1 (pages 840–846)

Postwar America

TERMS AND NAMES

GI Bill of Rights Law that provided financial and educational benefits for World War II veterans

suburb Residential town or community near a city

Harry S. Truman President after World War II

Dixiecrat Southern Democrat who left the party

Fair Deal President Truman's economic and social program

BEFORE YOU READ

In the last section, you read about the developments in the Cold War at home and abroad.

In this section, you will read about the economic boom in the United States after World War II.

AS YOU READ

Take notes on the chart below. List the postwar changes in various segments of American society.

SEGMENT OF AMERICAN SOCIETY	POSTWAR CHANGES
veterans	
economy	
labor	
civil rights	

Readjustment and Recovery
(pages 840–842)

How did the end of World War II affect America?

After World War II, millions of returning veterans used the **GI Bill of Rights** to get an education and to buy homes. At first, there was a terrible housing shortage. Then developers such as William Levitt built thousands of inexpensive homes in the **suburbs,** small residential communities near the cities. Many veterans and their families moved in.

The United States changed from a wartime to a peacetime economy. After the war, many defense workers were laid off. Returning veterans added to unemployment. When wartime price controls ended, prices shot up. Congress eventually put back economic controls on wages, prices, and rents.

The economy began to improve on its own. There was a huge pent-up demand for consumer goods. People had been too poor to buy these goods during the Depression. Many items had not been available during the war. Now

Americans bought cars and appliances and houses. The Cold War increased defense spending and employment.

1. What were three effects of the end of World War II on American society?

Meeting Economic Challenges; Social Unrest Persists (pages 842–845)

What were postwar problems?

President **Harry S. Truman** faced a number of problems immediately after the war. One was labor unrest. In 1946, a steel-workers' strike was followed by a coal miners' strike. In addition, the railroad unions threatened to stop all rail traffic in the nation.

Truman was pro-labor. But he would not let strikes cripple the nation. He threatened to draft striking workers into the army and then order them back to work. The unions gave in.

During this time, before the economy turned around, many Americans were disgusted with shortages, rising *inflation,* and strikes. Voters became more conservative. In the 1946 election, conservative Republicans gained control of Congress.

After the war, there was racial violence in the South. African-American veterans demanded their rights as citizens. Truman met with African-American leaders. They asked for a federal *anti-lynching law,* an end to the *poll tax,* and a commission to prevent discrimination in hiring.

Truman put his career on the line for civil rights. But Congress would not pass any of his civil rights measures. Finally, Truman acted on his own. In 1948, he issued an executive order to desegregate the armed forces. He also ordered an end to discrimination in hiring government employees.

Meanwhile, the Supreme Court said that African Americans could not be kept from living in certain neighborhoods. These acts marked the beginning of a federal commitment to deal with racial issues.

Truman was nominated for president in 1948. He insisted on a strong civil rights *plank* in the Democratic Party platform. This split the party. Many Southern Democrats left the Democratic Party. These **Dixiecrats** were against civil rights. They wanted to preserve the "Southern way of life."

They formed the States' Rights Party. Some liberals left the Democratic Party to form the Progressive Party.

It didn't look like Truman could win. But he took his ideas to the people. He criticized the "do-nothing Congress." Truman won a narrow victory. Democrats took control of Congress.

Truman tried to pass economic and social reforms. He called his program the **Fair Deal.** Health insurance and a *crop-subsidy program* for farmers were both defeated by Congress. But an increase in the minimum wage, extension of Social Security, and financial aid for cities passed.

2. What were some issues Truman fought for?

Republicans Take the Middle Road (pages 845–846)

Why did Eisenhower win?

Truman did not run for reelection in 1952. The big issues of that campaign were (1) the stalemate in the Korean War, (2) anti-Communist hysteria and McCarthyism, (3) the growing power of the federal government, (4) strikes, and (5) inflation. Voters wanted a change. The Republicans nominated war hero General Dwight D. Eisenhower. He easily beat Democrat Adlai Stevenson.

Eisenhower was a low-key president with middle-of-the-road policies. He did have to deal with one controversial issue—civil rights. In 1954, the Supreme Court ruled in *Brown* v. *Board of Education* that public schools could not be segregated. Eisenhower believed that the federal government should not be involved in desegregation. But he upheld the law. When the governor of Arkansas tried to keep African-American students out of a white high school, Eisenhower sent federal troops to integrate the school.

The America of the mid-1950s was a place of "peace, progress, and prosperity." Eisenhower won a landslide reelection in 1956.

3. What two important civil rights actions occurred during Eisenhower's presidency?

CHAPTER 27 Section 2 (pages 847–855)

The American Dream in the Fifties

TERMS AND NAMES

conglomerate Major corporation that owns smaller companies in unrelated industries

franchise Company that offers similar products or services in many locations

baby boom Soaring birthrate from 1946 to 1964

Dr. Jonas Salk Developer of a vaccine to prevent polio

consumerism Excessive concern with buying material goods

planned obsolescence Purposely making products to become outdated or wear out quickly

BEFORE YOU READ

In the last section, you read about the postwar boom in the United States.

In this section, you will read how many Americans achieved their dreams of material comfort and prosperity, but some found the cost of conformity too high.

AS YOU READ

Take notes on the chart below. Fill it in with examples of specific goals that characterized the American Dream for suburbanites of the 1950s.

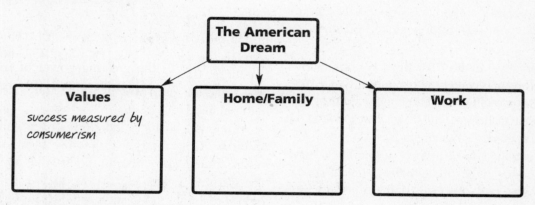

The American Dream

Values — *success measured by consumerism*

Home/Family

Work

The Organization and the Organization Man (pages 847–849)

What changes took place in the American workplace in the 1950s?

The economy grew rapidly in the 1950s. By 1956, more Americans were *white-collar* workers in offices than were in *blue-collar* factory jobs. White-collar workers were paid better. They usually worked in service industries, such as sales and communications.

Businesses also expanded. They formed **conglomerates,** or major corporations that own smaller companies in unrelated industries. Other businesses expanded by franchising. A **franchise** is a company that offers similar products or services in many locations, such as fast-food restaurants.

These large companies offered well-paying, secure jobs to certain kinds of workers. These workers were conformists, or team players. They were "company people" who would fit in and not rock the boat. Businesses rewarded loyalty rather than creativity. They promoted a sameness, or standardization, of people as well as products. Books such as *The Organization Man* and *The Man in the Gray Flannel Suit* criticized this conformity.

1. What changes occurred in the American work force and workplace in the 1950s?

_____

_____

_____

The Suburban Lifestyle (pages 849–851)

What was life like in the 1950s?

Many Americans enjoyed the benefits of the booming economy. Many worked in cities but lived in suburbs. They had the American dream of a single-family home, good schools, and a safe neighborhood with people just like themselves.

There was an increase in births called the **baby boom.** It was caused by the reuniting of families after the war and growing prosperity. Medical advances also wiped out childhood diseases. **Dr. Jonas Salk** developed a vaccine to prevent polio. Polio had killed or crippled 58,000 children a year.

The baby boom created a need for more schools and products for children. Suburban family life revolved around children. Many parents depended on advice from a popular baby-care book by Dr. Benjamin Spock. He said it was important that mothers stay at home with their children. The role of homemaker and mother was also glorified in the media. But many women felt alone and bored at home.

By 1960, 40 percent of mothers worked outside the home. But their career opportunities usually were limited to "women's fields." These included secretarial work, nursing, and teaching. Even if women did the same work as men, they were paid less.

Americans had more *leisure* time. They spent time and money on leisure activities, such as sports. They also watched sports on television and read books and magazines. Youth activities, such as Scouts and Little League, became popular too.

2. What was life like in the suburbs in the 1950s?

The Automobile Culture
(pages 852–853)

Why were cars so important?

Easy credit for buying cars and cheap gasoline led to a boom in automobile ownership. In the 1950s, the number of American cars on the road grew from 40 to 60 million.

A car was a necessity in the suburbs. There was no public transportation. People needed to drive to their jobs in the cities. They also had to drive to shop and do errands. Therefore, more and better roads were also needed. In 1956, the United States began building a nationwide highway network. In turn, these roads allowed long-distance trucking. This led to a decline in the railroads.

Americans loved to drive. They went to drive-in restaurants and movies. They drove long distances on vacation. Motels and shopping malls were built to serve them. These new industries were good for the economy. But the increase in driving also caused problems. These included stressful traffic jams and air pollution. Many white people left the cities. Jobs and industries followed. This left mostly poor people in crowded inner cities.

3. How did cars change American life?

Consumerism Unbound (pages 854–855)

Why did Americans turn to consumerism in the 1950s?

By the mid-1950s, nearly 60 percent of Americans were in the *middle class*. They had the money to buy more and more products. They measured success by their **consumerism,** or the amount of material goods they bought.

American business flooded stores with new products. Consumers had money to spend and leisure time. They bought household appliances like washing machines, dryers, and dishwashers, and recreational items such as television sets, barbecue grills, and swimming pools.

Manufacturers also tried a new marketing strategy called **planned obsolescence.** They purposely made products to become outdated or to wear out quickly. Americans began to throw away items in order to buy "new models." Easy credit, including the introduction of credit cards, encouraged people to buy. Private debt grew.

The 1950s were "the advertising age." Ads were everywhere—even on the new medium of television. They tried to persuade Americans to buy things they didn't need. They appealed to people's desire for status and for a sense of belonging.

4. How was consumerism encouraged in the 1950s?

CHAPTER 27 Section 3 (pages 858–863)

Popular Culture

TERMS AND NAMES

mass media Means of communication that reach large audiences

Federal Communications Commission (FCC) Government agency that regulates the communications industry

beat movement Writers who made fun of the conformity and material-ism of mainstream American society

rock 'n' roll Form of popular music, characterized by heavy rhythms and simple melodies, that developed from rhythm and blues in the 1950s

jazz A style of music characterized by improvisation

BEFORE YOU READ

In the last section, you read about the American dream in the 1950s.

In this section, you will read that popular culture in the 1950s reflected white, middle-class America, and a subcul-ture challenged that conformity.

AS YOU READ

Fill in the chart with notes on what each group con-tributed to popular culture in the 1950s.

GROUP	CONTRIBUTION TO POPULAR CULTURE OF THE 1950s
Families shown on TV	
Beat generation	
Rock 'n' roll	
African Americans	

New Era of Mass Media

(pages 858–861)

What influence did TV have?

Mass media—the means of communication that reach large audiences—include radio, television, newspapers, and magazines. Television became the most important means of communication in the 1950s. It both showed and influenced popular cul-ture of the time.

The number of homes with television jumped. It went from 9 percent of all homes in 1950 to 90 percent in 1960. At first, the number of television stations was limited by the **Federal Communica-tions Commission (FCC).** The FCC is the gov-ernment agency that regulates the communications industry. Soon, however, TV stations spread across the country. Many shows became widely popular all over the nation.

The 1950s were the "golden age of television." Comedy shows starring Milton Berle and Lucille Ball were popular. Edward R. Murrow introduced on-the-scene reporting and interviews. There were also westerns, sports events, and original dramas. At first, all shows were broadcast live.

Advertisers took advantage of this new medium, especially of its children's shows. Young fans wanted to buy everything that was advertised on their favorite shows. TV magazines and TV dinners—frozen meals to heat and eat—became popular.

Television reflected the mainstream values of white suburban America. These values were secure jobs, material success, well-behaved children, and conformity. Critics objected to the *stereotypes* of women and minorities. Women were shown as happy, ideal mothers. African Americans and Latinos hardly appeared at all. In short, TV showed an idealized white America. It ignored poverty, diversity, and problems such as racism.

As dramas and comedies moved to TV, radio changed. It began to focus on news, weather, music, and local issues. The radio industry did well. Advertising increased and so did the number of stations.

The movie industry suffered from competition by television. The number of moviegoers dropped 50 percent. But Hollywood fought back. It responded by using color, stereophonic sound, and the wide screen to create spectacular movies.

1. Was the picture of America portrayed on television accurate?

_____

_____

A Subculture Emerges (page 861)

What *was the beat movement and rock 'n' roll?*

Television showed the suburban way of life. But two *subcultures* presented other points of view. One was the **beat movement** in literature. These writers made fun of the conformity and materialism of *mainstream* American society.

Their followers were called beatniks. They rebelled against consumerism and the suburban lifestyle. They did not hold steady jobs and lived inexpensively. They read their poetry in coffee houses. Their art and poetry had a free, open form. Major works of the beat generation include Allen Ginsberg's long poem *Howl*, Jack Kerouac's novel *On the Road*, and Lawrence Ferlinghetti's *A Coney Island of the Mind*.

2. How did the beat movement criticize mainstream culture?

_____

_____

African Americans and Rock 'n' Roll (pages 861–863)

What *role did African-American artists play in the 1950s?*

Some musicians also took a new direction. They added electronic instruments to the African-American music called rhythm and blues. The result was **rock 'n' roll.** The new music had a strong beat. Its lyrics focused on the interests of teenagers, including *alienation* and unhappiness in love. And teenagers responded. They bought millions of records. The biggest star of all—the King of Rock 'n' Roll—was Elvis Presley. He had 45 songs that sold more than one million copies.

Some adults criticized rock 'n' roll. They said it would lead to teenage crime and immorality. But television and radio helped bring rock 'n' roll into the mainstream.

Many of the great performers of the 1950s were African American. Nat "King" Cole, Lena Horne, Harry Belafonte, and Sidney Poitier were popular with white audiences. They led the way for later African-American stars. **Jazz** musicians like Miles Davis and Dizzy Gillespie also entertained audiences of both races. The most popular black performers were the early rock 'n' roll stars, like Little Richard and Chuck Berry.

Television was slow to integrate. One of the first programs to do so was Dick Clark's popular rock 'n' roll show *American Bandstand*. In 1957, *Bandstand* showed both black couples and white couples on the dance floor.

Before integration reached radio audiences, there were stations that aimed specifically at African-American listeners. They played the popular black artists of the day. They also served advertisers who wanted to reach black audiences.

3. How did African Americans influence the entertainment industry of the 1950s?

_____

_____

CHAPTER 27 Section 4 (pages 866–869)

The Other America

TERMS AND NAMES

urban renewal Plan to tear down decaying neighborhoods and build low-cost housing

bracero Farm workers entering the United States from Mexico

termination policy Federal government decision to end federal responsibility for Native American tribes

BEFORE YOU READ

In the last section, you read about mainstream American society in the 1950s.

In this section, you will read about Americans who were not part of the American mainstream.

AS YOU READ

Fill in the chart below with notes on the problems faced by each of the groups listed. Then circle the problems that all of the groups faced.

GROUP	PROBLEMS
Urban Poor	
Mexican Americans	
Native Americans	

The Urban Poor (pages 866–867)

What was the plight of the inner cities?

Prosperity reached many Americans in the 1950s. But it did not reach all Americans. In 1962, one out of every four Americans was poor. Many of these poor people were members of minority groups.

In the 1950s, millions of middle-class white people left the cities for the suburbs. This was called "white flight." Meanwhile, many poor African Americans moved from the rural South to Northern cities. Businesses—and jobs—followed whites out of the cities. Cities also lost the taxes these people and businesses had paid. City governments could no longer afford to keep up the quali-

ty of schools, public transportation, or other services. The urban poor suffered as their neighborhoods decayed.

Many suburban, middle-class Americans could not believe that a country as rich as the United States had such poverty in its cities. However, Michael Harrington's 1962 book, *The Other America: Poverty in the United States*, made many Americans aware of the problem.

One way the government tried to solve the problem of the *inner cities* was called **urban renewal.** Minorities could not afford the new homes that had been built in the suburbs during the 1950s. Also, minorities were not welcome in the white suburbs. As a result, inner-city neighborhoods became very overcrowded.

Urban renewal was designed to tear down decaying neighborhoods and build low-cost housing. However, sometimes highways and shopping centers were built instead. The people who had lived in the old *slums* ended up moving to other slums—rather than into better housing.

1. What were some reasons for the decay of America's inner cities?

_____

_____

Poverty Leads to Activism

(pages 867–869)

How were Mexican Americans and Native Americans treated?

During World War II, there was a shortage of laborers to harvest crops. The federal government allowed **braceros,** or hired hands, to enter the United States from Mexico. They were supposed to work on American farms during the war, and then go back to Mexico. However, when the war ended, many braceros stayed illegally. Many other Mexicans entered the United States illegally to find jobs.

Mexican Americans suffered prejudice and discrimination, too, even though they were citizens. When Mexican-American veterans came home from the war, they wanted to be treated fairly. They formed an organization to protest injustices. Other groups worked to help Mexican Americans register to vote. Pressure from these groups forced California to stop placing Mexican-American children in segregated classes. Mexican Americans

began to have a nationwide political voice.

Native Americans also struggled for equal rights. This struggle was complicated by federal involvement in Native American affairs. At first, the government had supported assimilation, or absorbing Native Americans into mainstream American culture. That forced Native Americans to give up their own culture. In 1934, the Indian Reorganization Act changed that policy. The government now wanted Native Americans to have more control over their own affairs.

In 1944, Native Americans formed an organization to work for their civil rights and for the right to keep their own customs. After World War II, Native Americans got less financial help from the government. Outsiders grabbed tribal lands for mining and development.

In 1953, the federal government decided to end its responsibility for Native American tribes. This **termination policy** stopped federal economic support. It also ended the reservation system and distributed tribal land among individual Native Americans. One result of this policy was that many acres of tribal lands were sold to developers.

As part of the termination policy, the Bureau of Indian Affairs also moved thousands of Native Americans to the cities. It helped them find jobs and housing. This program was a failure. Native Americans did not have the skills to succeed in the cities. They were cut off from medical care. And they suffered job discrimination. The termination policy was ended in 1963.

2. How did Mexican Americans and Native Americans work for equal rights after World War II?

_____

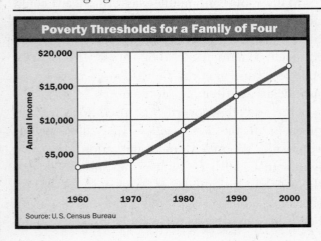

Skillbuilder

Use the chart to answer the questions.

1. What was the poverty threshold in 1960?

_____

2. What was the poverty threshold in 2000?

_____

Glossary

alienation Feeling of being separate from or out of step with the majority or the mainstream

antilynching law Law to protect African Americans from being executed without due process of law, especially being hanged by a mob

blue collar Referring to workers who do manual labor and wear work clothes

crop-subsidy program Grant from the government to farmers to keep crop prices up

inflation Continuing increase in consumer prices

inner cities Older, central parts of cities, with crowded neighborhoods of low-income, minority residents

leisure Freedom from time-consuming duties or activities

mainstream Most common attitudes and values of a society

middle class People whose economic situation places them between the working classes and the wealthy

plank One of the main principles or proposals of a political party

poll tax Tax used to prevent African Americans from voting

slums Poor, overcrowded urban areas with very bad living conditions

stereotype Oversimplified representation of what is typical of a person, group, or situation

subculture Group within a society that has its own set of customs, attitudes, and values

white collar Refers to workers who do not do manual labor and who wear "business dress"

AFTER YOU READ

Terms and Names

A. Write the letter of the phrase that best completes each sentence.

1. Followers of the beat movement were _____.

   a. nonconformist writers who criticized the American emphasis on material goods

   b. musicians who developed a rhythmic new style of popular music

   c. typical families shown on television

2. Manufacturers used the strategy of planned obsolescence to get people to _____.

   a. cater to teenagers

   b. plan carefully for their retirement

   c. throw away "out of date" products and buy new ones

3. The termination policy was _____.

   a. the canceling of credit for consumers

   b. a U.S. government plan to give up responsibility for Native American tribes

   c. the deporting of illegal aliens

4. The mass media include _____.

   a. radio, TV, newspapers, and magazines

   b. business and labor

   c. sports, music, and fashion

5. Urban renewal was _____.

   a. migration of rural African Americans to the cities

   b. white flight to the suburbs

   c. a plan to rebuild the inner cities

B. Write the letter of the name or term next to the description that explains it best.

a. baby boom	_____ **1.** Truman's plan for economic and social reforms
b. Fair Deal	_____ **2.** Mexican farm laborer allowed to enter the United States to work for a period of time
c. conglomerate	
d. consumerism	_____ **3.** Federal agency that regulates the radio and television industries
e. franchise	_____ **4.** Small residential communities near cities
f. bracero	
g. Federal Communications Commission (FCC)	_____ **5.** Corporation that owns smaller companies in unrelated businesses
	_____ **6.** Popular music that developed in the 1950s
	_____ **7.** Business that offers similar products or services in many locations
h. Dixiecrat	_____ **8.** Sharp increase in the birth rate after World War II
i. suburbs	_____ **9.** Southern Democrat who formed a states' rights party
j. rock 'n' roll	_____ **10.** Placing a high value on buying and having material goods

Main Ideas

1. What domestic and foreign issues concerned voters during the 1952 presidential election?

_____

2. What was portrayed as the American Dream in the 1950s?

_____

3. How did the values of the beatniks differ from those of mainstream America?

_____

4. How did many major cities change in the 1950s?

_____

Thinking Critically

Answer the following questions on a separate sheet of paper.

1. What was the American Dream of the 1950s? How did television affect it?

2. How did the postwar boom of the 1950s affect most white Americans? What groups got left out, and why?

CHAPTER 28 **Section 1** (pages 876–884)

Kennedy and the Cold War

TERMS AND NAMES

John F. Kennedy 35th president of the United States

flexible response Policy of using nonnuclear weapons to fight a war

Fidel Castro Ruler of Cuba

Berlin Wall Barrier built to keep East Germans from fleeing to West Berlin

hot line Direct phone line between the White House and the Kremlin

Limited Test Ban Treaty Treaty that barred nuclear testing in the atmosphere

BEFORE YOU READ

In the last section, you read about the poverty that existed in the United States in the 1950s.

In this section, you will read how John F. Kennedy became president and how he handled a period of intense foreign affairs.

AS YOU READ

Use this diagram to take notes on the major foreign crises that the Kennedy administration faced.

CRISIS	KENNEDY'S HANDLING	OUTCOME
Bay of Pigs	okays invasion, promises air support	invaders are captured; Kennedy is embarrassed
Cuban Missile Crisis		
Berlin Crisis		

The Election of 1960; The Camelot Years

(pages 876–878)

How did Kennedy win the election?

In 1960, President Eisenhower's term came to a close. By then, many Americans were worried about the future. The economy was in a *recession*. In addition, the Soviet Union was gaining strength. As a result, some wondered whether the United States was losing the Cold War.

John F. Kennedy and Richard M. Nixon faced off in the 1960 presidential election. Kennedy was a Democratic senator from Massachusetts. Nixon was Eisenhower's vice-president. Kennedy won

the election by a slim margin. Two main factors led him to victory.

During a televised debate, Kennedy impressed viewers with his strong, forceful personality. Nixon appeared nervous and ill at ease.

The second factor was Kennedy's response to the arrest of Dr. Martin Luther King Jr., in October 1960. Kennedy called King's wife to express sympathy and persuaded the judge to release King from jail. His actions won him the support of African-American voters.

President Kennedy and his wife Jacqueline charmed many Americans with their elegance and grace. Jacqueline Kennedy influenced fashion and culture. People talked of the Kennedy Administration as a kind of *Camelot*, the story of King Arthur that was made into a popular Broadway musical. Kennedy surrounded himself with advisers that one journalist called "the best and brightest."

1. What two factors helped Kennedy win the 1960 presidential election?

_____

_____

A New Military Policy; Crises Over Cuba (pages 879–883)

What two crises involving Cuba did Kennedy face?

Upon entering the White House, Kennedy focused on foreign affairs. He urged a tough stand against the Soviet Union. He also supported a policy called **flexible response.** This policy called for the use of *conventional* weapons rather than nuclear weapons in the event of a war. Conventional weapons included jets, tanks, missiles, and guns. In order to build more conventional weapons, Kennedy increased defense spending.

Kennedy's first foreign policy test came from Cuba. Cuba's leader was **Fidel Castro.** Castro had seized power in 1959. Soon after that, he declared himself a Communist. He then formed ties with the Soviet Union.

Kennedy approved a plan to remove Castro from power. The plan called for Cuban exiles to invade Cuba and overthrow Castro. The U.S. government would supply air support for the exiles.

The attack failed. Many exiles were captured. The failed invasion became known as the Bay of Pigs. It left the Kennedy administration greatly embarrassed.

A year later, the United States and Cuba clashed again. Pictures from U.S. spy planes revealed that the Soviets were building nuclear missile bases in Cuba. Some bases already contained missiles ready to launch. These weapons could be aimed at the United States.

President Kennedy demanded that the Soviets remove the missiles. In October 1962, he surrounded Cuba with U.S. Navy ships. These ships forced Soviet vessels trying to reach Cuba to turn around. A tense standoff followed. It appeared that war might break out. However, Soviet leader Nikita

Khrushchev finally agreed to remove the missiles.

The crisis damaged Khrushchev's prestige in the Soviet Union and the world. Kennedy also endured criticism. Some Americans thought Kennedy had acted too boldly and nearly started a nuclear war. Others claimed he had acted too softly. These critics believed that Kennedy should have invaded Cuba and ousted Castro.

2. Name the two Cuban crises that the Kennedy administration faced.

_____

_____

Crisis Over Berlin (pages 883–884)

How did the U.S. and Soviets try to ease tensions?

Cuba was not Kennedy's only foreign policy problem. In 1961, the president faced a growing problem in Berlin. The city was still divided. East Berlin was under Communist control. West Berlin was under the control of Great Britain, France, and the United States. By 1961, almost 3 million East Germans had fled into West Berlin.

Khrushchev threatened to block all air and land routes into West Berlin. Kennedy warned the Soviet leader against such action. As a result, Khrushchev changed his plan. He built a large concrete barrier along the border between East and West Berlin. It was known as the **Berlin Wall.** It prevented any more East Germans from fleeing to West Berlin.

Despite their battles, Kennedy and Khrushchev did attempt to reach agreements. They established a **hot line** between their two nations. This special telephone hookup connected Kennedy and Khruschchev. It allowed them to talk directly when a crisis arose. The two leaders also agreed to a **Limited Test Ban Treaty.** This treaty barred nuclear testing in the atmosphere.

3. Name two ways the U.S. and Soviet Union worked to ease tensions between them.

_____

_____

Name _____   Date _____

The New Frontier

TERMS AND NAMES

New Frontier The name given to Kennedy's domestic program

mandate An overwhelming show of support by voters

Peace Corps A program that enlisted volunteers to help in poor countries

Alliance for Progress A program that supplied aid to Latin America

Warren Commission The body that investigated the assassination of President Kennedy

BEFORE YOU READ

In the last section, you read about how President Kennedy dealt with explosive foreign matters.

In this section, you will read about Kennedy's domestic agenda and how his presidency—and life—was cut short.

AS YOU READ

Use this diagram to take notes about Kennedy's New Frontier programs.

PROGRAM	DESCRIPTION
deficit spending	government spends more than it has in order to boost economy

The Promise of Progress
(pages 885–888)

What were Kennedy's domestic plans?

President Kennedy called his domestic program the **New Frontier.** However, Kennedy had a difficult time getting Congress to support his program. Conservative Republicans and southern Democrats blocked many of his bills. These included bills to provide medical care for the aged, rebuild cities, and aid education.

One reason for Kennedy's difficulties was that he was elected by a small margin. As a result, he lacked a popular **mandate,** or a clear indication that the voters approved of his plans. Because he

lacked overwhelming support, Kennedy rarely pushed hard for his bills.

Kennedy did succeed with some proposals. To help the economy grow, the Kennedy administration used deficit spending. This occurred when the government spent more money than it received in taxes. Kennedy hoped that increased spending on defense would help boost the economy.

Kennedy also introduced the **Peace Corps.** This was a program of volunteers working in poor nations around the world. The purpose of this program was to decrease poverty *abroad.* It was also meant to increase goodwill toward the United States. The Peace Corps was a huge success.

People of all ages and backgrounds signed up to work for the organization. By 1968, more than 35,000 volunteers had served in 60 nations around the world.

Another program was the **Alliance for Progress.** This program gave aid to Latin American countries. One reason for this program ·was to keep communism from spreading to these countries.

In 1961 the Soviets launched a person into orbit around the earth. The news stunned America. A space race began between the United States and Soviet Union. President Kennedy pledged that the nation would put a man on the moon by the end of the decade. That goal was reached on July 20, 1969, when Neil Armstrong stepped onto the moon.

The space race affected American society in many ways. Schools taught more science. Researchers developed many new technologies. The space race also contributed to economic growth.

The Kennedy administration also tried to solve the problems of poverty and racism. In 1963, Kennedy called for a national effort to fight American poverty. He also ordered the Justice Department to investigate racial injustices in the South.

1. Name two successful programs of the Kennedy administration.

_____

_____

Tragedy in Dallas (pages 888–889)

Who killed President Kennedy?

On November 22, 1963, President and Mrs. Kennedy arrived in Dallas, Texas. Kennedy had come there to improve relations with the state's Democratic Party. Large crowds greeted the Kennedys as they rode along the streets of downtown Dallas. Then, rifle shots rang out. Kennedy had been shot. The president died about an hour later at a nearby hospital.

The tragic news spread across the nation and then around the world. Millions of Americans sat glued to their televisions over the next few days. They watched on live television as a gunman shot and killed the president's accused killer, Lee Harvey Oswald.

The events seemed too strange to believe. Many people wondered if Oswald had acted alone or with others. Chief Justice Earl Warren headed a commission to investigate the assassination. The **Warren Commission** determined that Oswald acted alone. However, many people continue to believe that Oswald was part of a *conspiracy.*

The assassination taught Americans that their system of government could survive an upset. Lyndon Johnson took office on Kennedy's death and promised to carry on his programs.

2. What did the Warren Commission determine?

_____

_____

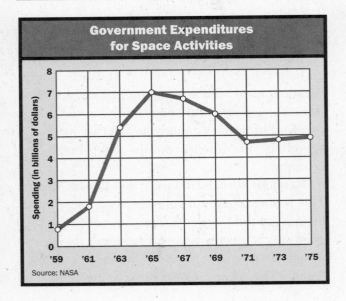

Government Expenditures for Space Activities

Spending (in billions of dollars)

'59 '61 '63 '65 '67 '69 '71 '73 '75

Source: NASA

Skillbuilder

Use the chart to answer these questions.

1. Between which two years was there a dramatic rise in government expenditures for space activities?

_____

2. How much was spent in 1965?

_____

The Great Society

BEFORE YOU READ

In the last section, you read about President Kennedy's domestic programs.

In this section, you will read about Lyndon Johnson's bold plan to reshape America.

AS YOU READ

Use this diagram to take notes about President Lyndon Johnson's Great Society programs.

TERMS AND NAMES

Lyndon Baines Johnson 36th president of the United States

Economic Opportunity Act Act that created numerous antipoverty measures

Great Society Name given to Johnson's domestic agenda

Medicare and Medicaid Health benefits for the elderly and poor

Immigration Act of 1965 Established new immigration system that allowed more immigrants into the U.S.

Warren Court The Supreme Court under Chief Justice Earl Warren

reapportionment The way in which states redraw their election districts

PROGRAM	DESCRIPTION
Economic Opportunity Act	Created antipoverty programs

LBJ's Path to Power; Johnson's Domestic Agenda (pages 892–894)

How did Johnson wage a "war" on poverty?

Lyndon Baines Johnson, a Texan, was Senate majority leader in 1960. Johnson was a skilled lawmaker. He demonstrated a great ability to negotiate and reach agreements. During the 1960 presidential campaign, Kennedy's advisers thought that Johnson would make the perfect running mate. They believed that Johnson's connections in Congress and his Southern background would help Kennedy's presidential chances. Kennedy asked Johnson to be his vice-presidential candidate. Johnson agreed. He helped Kennedy win important states in the South.

Upon Kennedy's death, Johnson became president. Under President Johnson's leadership, Congress passed two bills that President Kennedy had proposed. One was a tax cut to help stimulate the economy. The other was the Civil Rights Act of 1964.

Johnson then launched his own program—a "war on poverty." He worked with Congress to pass the **Economic Opportunity Act.** This law created youth programs, antipoverty measures, loans for small businesses, and job training. The law created the Job Corps youth training program and the VISTA (Volunteers in Service to America) program.

Johnson ran for president in 1964. He easily defeated his Republican opponent, Barry Goldwater.

1. Name two programs created by the Economic Opportunity Act.

_____

_____

Building the Great Society; Reforms of the Warren Court
(pages 895–898)

How did the Great Society and the Warren Court change America?

President Johnson had a grand vision for America. He called it the **Great Society.** Throughout his term, Johnson introduced legislation to help him create his Great Society. Among other things, these laws:

- provided federal aid for schools to purchase textbooks and library materials;
- created **Medicare and Medicaid** to ensure health care for the aged and poor;
- funded the building of public housing units and created the cabinet-level Department of Housing and Urban Development (HUD);
- lifted restrictions on immigration through the **Immigration Act of 1965**—which opened the door for many non-European immigrants to settle in the United States;
- required efforts to ensure clean water, through the Water Quality Act of 1965;
- offered increased protection to consumers, through the Wholesome Meat Act of 1967;
- established safety standards for automobiles and tires.

The wave of liberal reform that characterized the Great Society also affected the Supreme Court. Chief Justice Earl Warren took an active role in _promoting_ more liberal policies. The **Warren Court** ruled school _segregation_ unconstitutional. The court also banned prayer in public schools and strengthened the right of free speech.

The Warren Court also changed the area of congressional **reapportionment.** This is the way in which states redraw their election districts. The Court ruled that election districts within each state had to have roughly the same number of people in them. Because so many people lived in the cities, the court's ruling led to the creation of many new urban districts. As a result, political power shifted from the countryside to the cities.

The Warren Court strengthened the rights of people accused of crimes. The Court ruled police had to read suspects their rights before questioning them. These rights are known as Miranda rights.

2. Name one result of the Great Society and one result of the Warren Court.

_____

_____

Impact of the Great Society
(page 899)

How successful was the Great Society?

The Great Society and the Warren Court changed America. People disagree on whether these changes left the nation better or worse off than before. On one hand, Johnson's antipoverty measures helped reduce the suffering of many people. However, many of Johnson's proposals did not achieve their stated goals. Most people agree on one point: No president since World War II increased the power and reach of federal government more than Lyndon Johnson.

Eventually, some Americans began to question the increased size of the federal government. They also wondered about the effectiveness of Johnson's programs. Across the country, people became _disillusioned_ with the Great Society. This led to the rise of a new group of Republican leaders.

3. How did the Great Society affect the size of the federal government?

_____

_____

Glossary	CHAPTER 28 The New Frontier and the Great Society

abroad Outside of one's own country

conspiracy An agreement between two or more people to perform an illegal or evil act

conventional Using means other than nuclear weapons or energy; traditional

disillusioned Let down or disappointed

promote To contribute to the progress or growth of

recession A temporary decline in economic activity

segregation Separation, including by race

AFTER YOU READ

Terms and Names

A. Choose the letter of the term or name that correctly fits the description or definition.

_____ **1.** The direct communication link between the president and the Soviet leader set up in the 1960s was
  a. the flexible response.
  b. the hot line.
  c. massive retaliation.
  d. reapportionment.

_____ **2.** The New Frontier program created to offer economic and technical assistance to help Latin American countries was
  a. the Peace Corps.
  b. the Great Society.
  c. Economic Opportunity Act.
  d. the Alliance for Progress.

_____ **3.** The way in which states redraw election districts based on the changing number of people in them is called
  a. reapportionment.
  b. flexible response.
  c. the hot line.
  d. mandate.

_____ **4.** The Chief Justice of the Supreme Court who oversaw liberal court rulings was
  a. Richard Nixon.
  b. Barry Goldwater.
  c. Earl Warren.
  d. Robert Kennedy.

_____ **5.** This measure was not part of the Great Society.
  a. Medicare and Medicaid
  b. Immigrations Act of 1965
  c. flexible response
  d. Wholesome Meat Act of 1967

B. Write the letter of the name or term that matches the description.

a. Nikita Khrushchev

b. Peace Corps

c. New Frontier

d. flexible response

e. Medicare and Medicaid

f. Great Society

_____ **1.** The Soviet leader who squared off against President Kennedy during the Cuban crisis

_____ **2.** The strategy intended to broaden America's range of options during international crises

_____ **3.** The name for Kennedy's domestic and legislative programs

_____ **4.** The program in which U.S. volunteers provided assistance to developing nations of the world

_____ **5.** Programs that provided low-cost health insurance to the aged and poor

AFTER YOU READ (continued) *CHAPTER 28* The New Frontier and the Great Society

Main Ideas

1. Why did Kennedy have trouble getting much of his New Frontier legislation through Congress?

_____

_____

2. Describe the two international aid programs launched during the Kennedy administration.

_____

_____

3. How did the Great Society address the problem of poverty?

_____

_____

4. How did the Supreme Court strengthen the rights of people accused of a crime.

_____

_____

5. Why is the Great Society's legacy considered to be mixed?

_____

_____

Thinking Critically

Answer the following questions on a separate sheet of paper.

1. How important is a president's personality in his ability to lead? Consider how Kennedy's charm and mystique and Johnson's persuasive skills affected their success as presidents.

2. What do you see as the advantages and disadvantages of increasing the size and reach of the federal government?

CHAPTER 29 Section 1 (pages 906–913)

Taking on Segregation

BEFORE YOU READ

In the last section, you read about President Johnson's Great Society.

In this section, you will read how African Americans challenged the nation's policies of segregation and racial inequality.

AS YOU READ

Use this diagram to take notes on early battles of the civil rights movement.

INCIDENT	RESULT
Little Rock School Crisis	National Guard forces school to let in African Americans
Montgomery Bus Boycott	
Lunch counter sit-ins	

The Segregation System

(pages 906–908)

How did World War II help start the civil rights movement?

By 1950, most African Americans were still considered second-class citizens. Throughout the South, Jim Crow laws remained in place. These were laws aimed at keeping blacks separate from whites.

During the 1950s, however, a civil rights movement began. This was a movement by blacks to gain greater equality in American society.

In several ways, World War II helped set the stage for this movement. First, the demand for soldiers during the war had created a shortage of white male workers. This opened up many new jobs for African Americans.

Second, about 700,000 African Americans had served in the armed forces. These soldiers helped free Europe. Many returned from the war ready to fight for their own freedom.

Third, during the war, President Franklin Roosevelt outlawed racial *discrimination* in all federal agencies and war-related companies.

World War II had given American blacks a taste of equality and respectability. When the war ended, many African Americans were more determined than ever to improve their *status*.

1. **Name two ways in which World War II helped set the stage for the civil rights movement.**

_____

_____

Challenging Segregation in Court (pages 908–909)

What was important in the case of Brown v. Board of Education?

Even before the civil rights movement began, African-American lawyers had been challenging racial discrimination in court. Beginning in 1938, a team of lawyers led by **Thurgood Marshall** began arguing several cases before the Supreme Court.

Their biggest victory came in the 1954 case known as ***Brown v. Board of Education*** of Topeka, Kansas. In this case, the Supreme Court ruled that separate schools for whites and blacks were unequal—and thus unconstitutional.

2. What did the Supreme Court rule about separate schools for whites and blacks?

_____

_____

Reaction to the *Brown* Decision; the Montgomery Bus Boycott (pages 909–911)

Where did African Americans fight racial segregation?

Some Southern communities refused to accept the *Brown* decision. In 1955, the Supreme Court handed down a second *Brown* ruling. It ordered schools to desegregate more quickly.

The school desegregation issue reached a crisis in 1957 in Little Rock, Arkansas. The state's governor, Orval Faubus, refused to let nine African-American students attend Little Rock's Central High School. President Eisenhower sent in federal troops to allow the students to enter the school.

School was just one place where African Americans challenged segregation. They also battled discrimination on city buses. In Montgomery, Alabama, a local law required that blacks give up their bus seats to whites. In December 1955, Montgomery resident **Rosa Parks** refused to give her seat to a white man. Parks was arrested.

After her arrest, African Americans in Montgomery organized a yearlong *boycott* of the city's bus system. The protesters looked for a person to lead the bus boycott. They chose **Dr. Martin Luther King, Jr.,** the pastor of a Baptist Church.

The boycott lasted 381 days. Finally, in late 1956, the Supreme Court ruled that segregated buses were illegal.

3. Name two places that African Americans targeted for racial desegregation.

_____

_____

Martin Luther King and the SCLC; The Movement Spreads (pages 911–913)

Where did King get his ideas?

Martin Luther King, Jr. preached nonviolent resistance. He termed it "soul force." He based his ideas on the teachings of several people. From Jesus, he learned to love one's enemies. From the writer Henry David Thoreau, King took the idea of civil disobedience. This was the refusal to obey an unjust law. From labor organizer A. Philip Randolph, he learned how to organize huge demonstrations. From Mohandas Gandhi, King learned that a person could resist *oppression* without using violence.

King joined with other ministers and civil rights leaders in 1957. They formed the **Southern Christian Leadership Conference (SCLC)**. By 1960, another influential civil rights group emerged. The **Student Nonviolent Coordinating Committee (SNCC)** was formed mostly by college students. Members of this group felt that change for African Americans was occurring too slowly.

One protest strategy that SNCC ("snick") used was the **sit-in.** During a sit-in, blacks sat at whites-only lunch counters. They refused to leave until they were served. In February 1960, African-American students staged a sit-in at a lunch counter at a Woolworth's store in Greensboro, North Carolina. The students sat there as whites hit them and poured food over their heads. By late 1960, students had desegregated lunch counters in 48 cities in 11 states.

4. Name two people from whom Martin Luther King, Jr. drew his ideas.

_____

_____

Name _____ Date _____

The Triumphs of a Crusade

BEFORE YOU READ

In the last section, you read how African Americans began challenging the nation's racist systems.

In this section, you will read how civil rights activists broke down many racial barriers and prompted landmark legislation.

AS YOU READ

Use this diagram to take notes on the achievements of the civil rights movement.

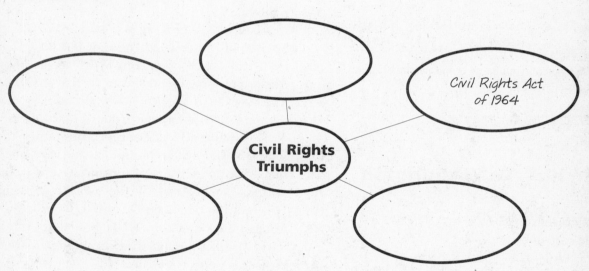

Civil Rights Act of 1964

Civil Rights Triumphs

Riding for Freedom (pages 916–917)

Who were the freedom riders?

Freedom Riders were protesters who rode buses with the goal of integrating buses and bus stations. In 1961, a bus of Freedom Riders was attacked in Anniston, Alabama, where a white mob burned the bus. Another instance occurred when a group of Nashville students rode into Birmingham, Alabama, where they were beaten.

Attorney General Robert Kennedy ordered a reluctant bus company to continue to carry the freedom riders. When freedom riders were attacked in Montgomery, Alabama, the federal government took stronger action. President Kennedy sent 400 U.S. marshals to protect the freedom riders. The Interstate Commerce Commission banned segregation in all travel facilities including waiting rooms, rest rooms, and lunch counters.

1. Name two ways the government tried to help the freedom riders.

_____

_____

Standing Firm (pages 917–920)

What happened in Birmingham?

Civil rights workers soon turned their attention to *integrating* Southern schools. In September 1962, a federal court allowed **James Meredith** to attend the all-white University of Mississippi. However, Mississippi's governor refused to admit him. The Kennedy administration sent in U.S. marshals. They forced the governor to let in Meredith.

Another *confrontation* occurred in 1963 in Birmingham, Alabama. There, King and other civil rights leaders tried to desegregate the city. Police attacked activists with dogs and water hoses.

Many Americans witnessed the attacks on television They were outraged by what they saw. Eventually, Birmingham officials gave in. They agreed to end segregation in the city.

The growing civil rights movement impressed President Kennedy. He became convinced that the nation needed a new civil rights law. Kennedy called on Congress to pass a sweeping civil rights bill.

2. **What was the outcome of the demonstrations in Birmingham?**

_____

_____

Marching to Washington
(page 920)

What did the Civil Rights Act of 1964 do?

President Kennedy's civil rights bill outlawed discrimination based on race, religion, national origin, and gender. It also gave the government more power to push for school desegregation. Civil rights leaders wanted Congress to pass the bill. So they staged a massive march on Washington, D.C.

On August 28, 1963, more than 250,000 blacks and whites marched into the nation's capital. There, they demanded the immediate passage of the bill.

Dr. Martin Luther King, Jr., spoke to the crowd. He called for peace and racial harmony in his now-famous "I Have a Dream" speech.

Several months later, President Kennedy was assassinated. Lyndon Johnson became president. He won passage in Congress of Kennedy's **Civil Rights Act of 1964.**

3. **Name two things the Civil Rights Act of 1964 did.**

_____

_____

Fighting for Voting Rights
(pages 921–922)

Where did workers try to register African Americans to vote?

Civil rights activists next worked to gain voting rights for African Americans in the South. The voting project became known as **Freedom Summer.** The workers focused their efforts on Mississippi. They hoped to influence Congress to pass a voting rights act.

Meanwhile, civil rights activists challenged Mississippi's political structure. At the 1964 Democratic National Convention, SNCC organized the Mississippi Freedom Democratic Party (MFDP). The new party hoped to unseat Mississippi's regular party delegates at the convention.

Civil rights activist **Fannie Lou Hamer** spoke for the MFDP at the convention. She gave an emotional speech. As a result, many Americans supported the seating of the MFDP delegates. However, the Democratic Party offered only 2 of Mississippi's 68 seats to MFDP members.

In 1965, civil rights workers attempted a voting project in Selma, Alabama. They met with violent resistance. As a result, Martin Luther King, Jr. led a massive march through Alabama. President Johnson responded by asking Congress to pass a new voting rights act. Congress passed the **Voting Rights Act of 1965.** The law *eliminated* state laws that had prevented African Americans from voting.

4. **Name two states where civil rights workers tried to register blacks to vote.**

_____

_____

Challenges and Changes in the Movement

BEFORE YOU READ

In the last section, you read about the triumphs of the civil rights movement.

In this section, you will read about challenges and changes to the movement and how it ultimately left a mixed legacy.

AS YOU READ

Use this diagram to take notes on the mixed legacy of the civil rights movement.

TERMS AND NAMES

de facto segregation Segregation by custom or practice

de jure segregation Segregation by law

Malcolm X African-American civil rights leader

Nation of Islam Group headed by Elijah Muhammad

Stokely Carmichael Leader of Black Power movement

Black Power Movement that stressed black pride

Black Panthers African-American group founded to combat police brutality

Kerner Commission Commission that reported on race relations in America

Civil Rights Act of 1968 Act that banned discrimination in housing

affirmative action Program aimed at hiring or including minorities

---

ACHIEVEMENTS	REMAINING PROBLEMS
full voting rights	high unemployment

African Americans Seek Greater Equality (pages 923–925)

What problems did African Americans in the North face?

The biggest problem in the North was **de facto segregation**—segregation that exists by practice and custom. De facto segregation can be harder to fight than **de jure segregation**—segregation by law. Eliminating de facto segregation requires changing people's attitudes rather than repealing laws.

De facto segregation increased as African Americans moved to Northern cities after World War II. Many white people left the cities. They

moved to suburbs. By the mid-1960s, many African Americans in the North lived in decaying urban slums. There, they dealt with poor schools and high unemployment.

The terrible conditions in Northern cities angered many African Americans. This anger led to many episodes of violence.

1. Name two problems African Americans in the North faced.

_____

_____

New Leaders Voice Discontent
(pages 925–927)

What did new leaders call for?

During the 1960s, new African-American leaders emerged. They called for more *aggressive* tactics in fighting racism.

One such leader was **Malcolm X.** Malcolm preached the views of Elijah Muhammad. Muhammad was the head of the **Nation of Islam,** or the Black Muslims. Malcolm declared that whites were responsible for blacks' misery. He also urged African Americans to fight back when attacked.

Eventually, Malcolm changed his policy regarding violence. He urged African Americans to use peaceful means—especially voting—to win equality. In February 1965, he was assassinated.

Another new black leader was **Stokely Carmichael.** He introduced the notion of **Black Power.** This movement encouraged African-American pride and leadership.

In 1966, some African Americans formed a political party called the **Black Panthers.** The party was created to fight police brutality. They urged violent resistance against whites. Many whites and *moderate* African Americans feared the group.

2. Name two new civil rights leaders.

_____

_____

1968—A Turning Point in Civil Rights
(pages 927–928)

Who was killed in 1968?

In April 1968, a gunman shot and killed Martin Luther King, Jr., in Memphis, Tennessee. Many leaders called for peace. But anger over King's death led many African Americans to riot. Cities across the nation erupted in violence.

A bullet claimed the life of yet another leader in 1968. In June, a man shot and killed Senator Robert Kennedy. Kennedy was a strong supporter of civil rights. The assassin was a Jordanian immigrant. He allegedly was angry about Kennedy's support of Israel. Kennedy had been seeking the Democratic nomination for president when he was killed.

3. Name two of the nation's leaders killed in 1968.

_____

_____

Legacy of the Civil Rights Movement
(pages 928–929)

Why is the legacy of the civil rights movement considered mixed?

Shortly after taking office, President Johnson formed a group known as the **Kerner Commission.** The commission's job was to study the cause of urban violence. In March 1968, the commission issued its report. It named one main cause for violence in the cities: white racism.

What, then, did the civil rights movement achieve? The movement claimed many triumphs. It led to the passage of important civil rights acts. This included the **Civil Rights Act of 1968.** This law banned discrimination in housing.

The movement had also led to the banning of segregation in education, transportation, and employment. It had also helped African Americans gain their full voting rights.

Yet many problems remained. Whites continued to flee the cities. Throughout the years, much of the progress in school integration reversed. African Americans continued to face high unemployment.

The government continued steps to help African Americans—and other disadvantaged groups. During the late 1960s, federal officials began to promote **affirmative action.** Affirmative-action programs involve making special efforts to hire or enroll minorities.

4. Name one goal the civil rights movement achieved and one problem that remained.

_____

_____

Glossary

aggressive Inclined to move in a hostile or angry manner

boycott A protest against something by refusal to buy or use it

confrontation To face with hostility and anger

discrimination The act of regarding someone as different due to various features, including race

eliminate To get rid of; remove

integrate To unify; to open to all races

moderate Mild, calm, reasonable

oppression The state of being kept down, or treated poorly

status The legal condition of a person

AFTER YOU READ

Terms and Names

A. Write the letter of the term that best answers the question.

a. **Fannie Lou Hamer**

b. *Plessy* v. *Ferguson*

c. **Stokely Carmichael**

d. **Malcolm X**

e. **Civil Rights Act of 1968**

f. *Brown* v. *Board of Education*

_____ **1.** What Supreme Court case declared segregation in schools unconstitutional?

_____ **2.** Who urged African Americans to fight back when attacked?

_____ **3.** Who spoke for the Mississippi Freedom Democratic Party in the 1964 Democratic convention?

_____ **4.** Who introduced the idea of Black Power?

_____ **5.** What was the legislation that banned discrimination in housing?

B. If the statement is true, write "true" on the line. If it is false, change the underlined words to make it true.

_____ **1.** The NAACP lawyer who argued the *Brown* v. *Board of Education* case in front of the Supreme Court was <u>Thurgood Marshall</u>.

_____ **2.** In 1957, Dr. Martin Luther King, Jr., was one of the founders of the <u>Student Nonviolent Coordinating Committee</u>.

_____ **3.** In September 1962, <u>James Meredith</u> was the first African American to attend the University of Mississippi.

_____ **4.** Segregation that exists by practice and custom, not by law, is <u>de jure segregation</u>.

_____ **5.** The <u>Black Panthers</u> was a political party formed to fight against police brutality in the ghetto.

AFTER YOU READ (continued)   *CHAPTER 29*   Civil Rights

Main Ideas

1. How did the Montgomery Bus Boycott begin?

_____

_____

2. Describe Martin Luther King, Jr.'s "soul force."

_____

_____

3. What were the different objectives of the freedom rides and Freedom Summer?

_____

_____

4. What did Malcolm X preach?

_____

_____

5. What challenges continued to face the nation in the area of civil rights?

_____

_____

Thinking Critically

Answer the following questions on a separate sheet of paper.

1 A civil rights activist once said, "You can kill a man, but you can't kill an idea." How did the civil rights movement prove this?

2 What civil rights achievement do you consider most important? Explain your answer.

CHAPTER 30 Section 1 (pages 936–941)

Moving Toward Conflict

TERMS AND NAMES

Ho Chi Minh Leader of North Vietnam

Vietminh Communist group led by Ho Chi Minh

domino theory Eisenhower's explanation for stopping communism

Dien Bien Phu Major French outpost captured by the Vietminh

Geneva Accords Peace agreement that split Vietnam in two

Ngo Dinh Diem Leader of South Vietnam

Vietcong Communist rebel group in South Vietnam

Ho Chi Minh Trail Network of paths running between North and South Vietnam

Tonkin Gulf Resolution Resolution that allowed President Johnson to fight in Vietnam

BEFORE YOU READ

In the last section, you read about the legacy of the civil rights movement.

In this section, you will read how the United States became involved in Vietnam.

AS YOU READ

Use the diagram below to take notes on the important Vietnam-related events during the following years.

1946 War begins between French and Vietminh.

1957

1954

1965

America Supports France in Vietnam (pages 936–938)

Why did the U.S. get involved?

Vietnam is a long, thin country on a *peninsula* in southeast Asia. From the late 1800s until World War II, France ruled Vietnam. The French treated the Vietnamese badly. As a result, the Vietnamese often rebelled. The Communist Party in Vietnam organized many of the rebellions. The group's leader was **Ho Chi Minh.**

In 1941, Japan conquered Vietnam. That year, the Vietnamese Communists combined with other groups to form an organization called the **Vietminh.** The Vietminh's goal was to achieve independence for Vietnam. In 1945, Japan was defeated in World War II. As a result, the Japanese left Vietnam. The Vietminh claimed independence for Vietnam.

However, France wanted to retake control of Vietnam. French troops moved back into the country in 1946. They conquered the southern half of Vietnam. The Vietminh took control of the North. For the next eight years, the two sides fought for control of the entire country.

The United States supported France during the war. America considered the Vietminh to be Communists. The United States, like other western nations, was determined to stop the spread of communism. President Eisenhower explained his country's policy with what became known as the **domino theory.** Eisenhower compared many of the world's smaller nations to dominoes. If one nation fell to communism, the rest also would fall.

The Vietminh defeated the French. The final blow came in 1954. That year, the Vietminh conquered the large French outpost at **Dien Bien Phu.**

Several countries met with the French and the Vietminh to negotiate a peace agreement. The agreement was known as the **Geneva Accords.** It temporarily split Vietnam in half. The Vietminh controlled North Vietnam. The anti-Communist nationalists controlled South Vietnam. The peace agreement called for an election to unify the country in 1956.

1. For what reason did the United States support France in the war?

The United States Steps In
(pages 938–940)

Who were the Vietcong?

Ho Chi Minh ruled North Vietnam. **Ngo Dinh Diem** led South Vietnam. When it came time for the all-country elections, Diem refused to take part. He feared that Ho would win. And then all of Vietnam would become Communist.

The United States supported Diem's decision. The U.S. government provided aid to Diem. America hoped that Diem could turn South Vietnam into a strong, independent nation. Diem, however, turned out to be a terrible ruler. His administration was *corrupt*. He also refused to allow opposing views.

By 1957, a rebel group had formed in the South. The group was known as the **Vietcong.** It fought against Diem's rule. Ho Chi Minh supported the Vietcong from the North. He supplied arms to the group along a network of paths that ran between North and South Vietnam. Together, these paths became known as the **Ho Chi Minh Trail.**

John Kennedy became president after Eisenhower. Kennedy continued America's policy of supporting South Vietnam. He, like Eisenhower, did not want to see the Communists take over Vietnam.

Meanwhile, Diem's government grew more *unstable*. The Vietcong rebels were gaining greater support among the peasants. The Kennedy administration decided that Diem had to step down. In 1963, military leaders overthrew Diem. Against Kennedy's wishes, they executed Diem.

Two months later, Kennedy himself was assassinated. Lyndon Johnson became president. The growing crisis in Vietnam was now his.

2. Who were the Vietcong fighting?

President Johnson Expands the Conflict (pages 940–941)

What was the Tonkin Gulf Resolution?

South Vietnam did not improve after Diem's death. A string of military leaders tried to rule the country. Each one failed to bring stability. Johnson, however, continued to support South Vietnam. The president was determined to not "lose" Vietnam to the Communists.

In August 1964, Johnson received reports of an incident in the Gulf of Tonkin off North Vietnam. A North Vietnamese patrol boat allegedly had fired torpedoes at a U.S. destroyer. President Johnson responded by bombing North Vietnam.

He also asked Congress for special military powers to stop any future North Vietnamese attacks on U.S. forces. As a result, Congress passed the **Tonkin Gulf Resolution.** The resolution granted Johnson broad military powers in Vietnam. In February 1965, President Johnson used his new power. He launched a major bombing attack on North Vietnam's cities.

3. What did the Tonkin Gulf Resolution grant President Johnson?

CHAPTER 30 Section 2 (pages 942–947)

U.S. Involvement and Escalation

BEFORE YOU READ

In the last section, you read how the United States became involved in Vietnam.

In this section, you will read about the war America fought in Vietnam.

AS YOU READ

Use this diagram to take notes on why the United States had trouble fighting the Vietcong.

TERMS AND NAMES

Robert McNamara Secretary of defense under Johnson

Dean Rusk Secretary of state under Johnson

William Westmoreland Commander of U.S. troops in Vietnam

Army of the Republic of Vietnam (ARVN) The South Vietnamese military forces

napalm Gasoline-based explosive

Agent Orange Chemical that destroyed jungle land

search-and-destroy mission Tactic in which U.S. troops destroyed Vietnamese villages

credibility gap Situation in which the U.S. public no longer believed the Johnson administration

Vietcong used hit-and-run ambush tactics.

U.S. Inability to Win an Easy Victory

Johnson Increases U.S. Involvement
(pages 942–943)

Who supported Johnson's decision to send U.S. troops to Vietnam?

In 1965, Johnson began sending U.S. troops to Vietnam to fight the Vietcong. Some of Johnson's advisers had opposed this move. They argued it was too dangerous.

But most of the president's advisers supported sending in troops. They included Secretary of Defense **Robert McNamara** and Secretary of State **Dean Rusk.** These men believed that America had to help defeat communism in Vietnam. Otherwise, the Communists might try to take over other countries.

Much of the public also agreed with Johnson's decision. Many Americans believed in stopping the spread of communism.

By the end of 1965, the United States had sent more than 180,000 troops to Vietnam. The American commander in South Vietnam was General **William Westmoreland.** Westmoreland was not impressed by the **Army of the Republic of Vietnam (ARVN)** as a fighting force. He asked for even more troops. By 1967, almost 500,000 American soldiers were fighting in Vietnam.

1. Name two groups that supported Johnson's decision to use troops in Vietnam.

_____

_____

Fighting in the Jungle (pages 944–946)

Why did the war drag on?

The United States believed that its superior weaponry would lead to a quick victory over the Vietcong. However, several factors turned the war into a bloody *stalemate*.

The first factor was the Vietcong's fighting style. The Vietcong did not have advanced weapons. As a result, they used hit-and-run *ambush* tactics. The Vietcong struck quickly in small groups. They then disappeared into the jungle or an elaborate system of tunnels. These tactics frustrated the American troops.

The second factor was the Vietcong's refusal to surrender. Throughout the war, the Vietcong suffered many battlefield deaths. However, they continued to fight on.

The third factor was the American troops' inability to win the support of the Vietnamese peasants. In fighting the Vietcong, U.S. troops ended up hurting the peasants as well. For example, U.S. planes dropped **napalm,** a gasoline-based bomb that set fire to the jungle. They did this to expose Vietcong tunnels and hideouts. They also sprayed **Agent Orange.** This was a leaf-killing chemical that destroyed the landscape. Both of these weapons wounded villagers and ruined villages.

American soldiers also turned the peasants against them by conducting **search-and-destroy missions.** During these missions, soldiers destroyed villages they believed supported the Vietcong.

The frustrations of fighting the war caused the *morale* of American soldiers to sink. Soldiers endured great hardships, especially prisoners of war captured by the North Vietnamese.

2. Name two reasons why the U.S. failed to score a quick victory against the Vietcong.

_____

_____

The Early War at Home
(pages 946–947)

How did the war affect Johnson's domestic programs?

The number of U.S. troops in Vietnam continued to increase. So did the cost of the war. As a result, the nation's economy began to suffer. In order to pay for the war, President Johnson had to cut spending for his Great Society programs.

By 1967, many Americans still supported the war. However, the images of the war on television began to change that. The Johnson administration told the American people that the war was going well. But television told the opposite story. Each night, Americans watched the brutal scenes of the war on their television screens. This led to a **credibility gap** in the Johnson administration. A growing number of people no longer believed what the president was saying.

3. How did the war affect Johnson's Great Society?

_____

_____

_____

Skillbuilder
Use the graph to answer the questions.

U.S. Military Personnel in Vietnam*

536,000

Troops (in thousands) — 600, 500, 400, 300, 200, 100, 0

1963 '64 '65 '66 '67 '68 '69 '70 '71 '72

*Year-end figures
Source: *Satistical Abstract of the United States, 1985; Encyclopedia America*

1. What year saw the largest number of U.S. forces in Vietnam?

_____

2. Between which two years was there a dramatic drop in the number U.S. troops in Vietnam?

_____

CHAPTER 30 Section 3 (pages 948–953)

A Nation Divided

BEFORE YOU READ

In the last section, you read about America's war effort in Vietnam.

In this section, you will read about how the United States became divided over the war in Vietnam.

AS YOU READ

Use this diagram to take notes on the beliefs and actions of the New Left organizations.

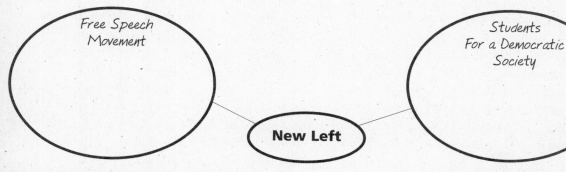

The Working Class Goes to War
(pages 948–950)

Who fought the war?

Most soldiers who fought in Vietnam were called into combat under the country's Selective Service System, or **draft.** Because the war was growing unpopular, thousands of men tried to avoid the draft.

One of the most common ways to avoid the draft was to attend college. Most men enrolled in a university could put off their military service.

Many university students during the 1960s were white and financially well-off. As a result, a large number who fought in Vietnam were lower-class whites or minorities. Nearly 80 percent of American soldiers came from lower economic levels. Thus, Vietnam was known as a working-class war.

Early on, a high number of African Americans served and died in Vietnam. During the first sever-al years of the war, 20 percent of American soldiers killed were black. Blacks, however, made up only about 10 percent of the U.S. population. This situation prompted protests from many civil rights leaders, including Martin Luther King, Jr. Many African-American soldiers also endured racism within their units.

The U.S. military in the 1960s did not allow women to serve in combat. However, nearly 10,000 women served in Vietnam as army and navy nurses. Thousands more volunteered in the American Red Cross and the United Services Organization (USO). This organization provided entertainment to the troops.

1. Name two groups of Americans who did most of the fighting early on in Vietnam.

_____

_____

The Roots of Opposition
(pages 950–951)

What were the New Left groups?

By the 1960s, American college students had become politically active. The growing youth movement of the 1960s was known as the **New Left.** The group took its name from the "old" left of the 1930s. That movement had tried to push the nation toward socialism. The New Left did not call for socialism. However, it did demand sweeping changes in American society.

One of the better known New Left groups was **Students for a Democratic Society (SDS).** This organization called for greater individual freedom in America.

Another New Left group was the **Free Speech Movement (FSM).** This group was formed at the University of California at Berkeley. It grew out of a fight between students and administrators over free speech on campus. FSM criticized business and government institutions.

The strategies of the SDS and FSM eventually spread to colleges throughout the country. There, students protested mostly campus issues. Soon, however, students around the nation found one issue they could protest together: the Vietnam War.

2. Name two New Left groups.

_____

_____

_____

The Protest Movement Emerges
(pages 951–953)

How did the hawks and doves differ?

Across America, college students rose up in protest against the war. They did so for various reasons. The most common reason was that the conflict in Vietnam was a civil war between the North and South. Thus, the United States had no business being there. Others believed that the war kept America from focusing on other parts of the world. Still others saw the war as morally *unjust*.

In April 1965, SDS helped organize a march on Washington, D.C. About 20,000 protesters participated. In November 1965, a protest rally in Washington drew about 30,000 protesters. Eventually, the antiwar movement reached beyond college campuses. Small numbers of returning veterans protested. Musicians took up the antiwar cause. Many protest songs became popular.

By 1967, Americans were divided into two main groups. Those who wanted the United States to withdraw from the war were called **doves.** Those who supported the war were called **hawks.** Other Americans took no stand on the war. However, they criticized doves for protesting a war in which U.S. troops were fighting and dying.

3. Briefly explain the positions of the hawks and doves.

_____

_____

_____

Skillbuilder

Use this cartoon to answer the questions.

1. Who is the person pictured on the poster?

_____

_____

2. Which group do you think designed it, the hawks or the doves?

_____

_____

A parody of a U.S. World War I poster.
Credit: Peter Newark's American Pictures

1968:
A Tumultuous Year

BEFORE YOU READ

In the last section, you read how the Vietnam War divided America.

In this section, you will read about the shocking events that made 1968 one of the most explosive years of the decade.

AS YOU READ

Use this diagram to take notes on the shocking events of 1968.

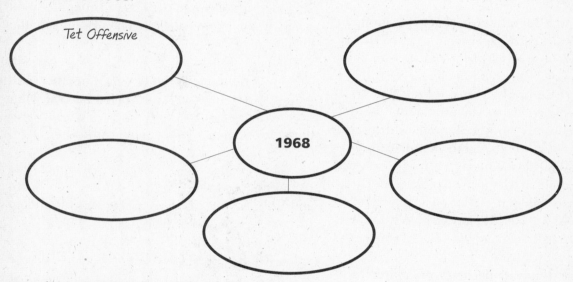

The Tet Offensive Turns the War

(pages 954–956)

How did the Tet offensive affect America?

January 30 was the Vietnamese equivalent of New Year's Eve. It was the beginning of festivities known as Tet. During the Tet holiday in 1968, a week-long *truce* was called. Many peasants crowded into South Vietnam's cities to celebrate the holiday.

However, many of the peasants turned out to be Vietcong rebels. The rebels launched a massive attack on nearly 100 towns and cities in South

Vietnam. They also attacked 12 U.S. air bases. The attacks were known as the **Tet offensive.** The offensive lasted for about a month. Finally, U.S. and South Vietnamese forces regained control of the cities.

General Westmoreland declared that the Tet offensive was a major defeat for the Vietcong. From a military standpoint, he was right. The Vietcong lost about 32,000 soldiers during the attacks. The United States and South Vietnam lost only 3,000 soldiers.

However, the Tet offensive shattered America's confidence in the war. The enemy now seemed everywhere. Many Americans began to think that the war was unwinnable. The Tet offensive also shocked many in the White House. **Clark Clifford** was the president's new secretary of defense. After Tet, Clifford decided that America could not win the war.

The Tet offensive also hurt President Johnson's popularity. By the end of February 1968, nearly 60 percent of the public disapproved of Johnson's handling of the war. In addition, nearly half the country said it had been a mistake to send troops to Vietnam.

1. How did the Tet offensive affect Johnson's popularity?

_____

_____

Days of Loss and Rage (pages 956–957)

Which events shocked the nation?

Even before the Tet offensive, an antiwar group in the Democratic Party had taken steps to *unseat* Johnson. The group looked for someone to challenge Johnson in the 1968 primary election. They asked **Robert Kennedy,** a senator from New York. Kennedy declined. However, Minnesota senator **Eugene McCarthy** agreed. He would run against Johnson on a *platform* to end the Vietnam War.

McCarthy surprised many people by nearly beating Johnson in the New Hampshire Democratic primary. Suddenly, Johnson appeared politically weak. As a result, Robert Kennedy declared himself a presidential candidate. The Democratic Party was now badly divided.

President Johnson decided to address the nation on television. He announced that he would seek peace in Vietnam. Then he declared that he would not seek reelection as president. The country was shocked.

In the days and months ahead, several more incidents stunned the nation. On April 4, a gunman killed civil rights leader Martin Luther King, Jr. Two months later, an assassin gunned down and killed Robert Kennedy.

Meanwhile, antiwar protests continued to rock college campuses. During the first six months of 1968, almost 40,000 students on more than 100 campuses held demonstrations.

2. Name two events that shocked Americans in 1968.

_____

_____

A Turbulent Race for President
(pages 957–959)

What happened in Chicago?

In August 1968, the Democrats met in Chicago for their presidential convention. There, they would choose a presidential candidate. In reality, Democratic leaders had already decided on the candidate: Vice-President **Hubert Humphrey.** This angered many antiwar activists. They favored McCarthy.

About 10,000 antiwar protesters came to Chicago. Some protesters wanted to pressure the Democrats to create an antiwar platform. Others wanted to voice their opposition to Humphrey. Still others wanted to create violence to *discredit* the Democratic Party.

Violence eventually erupted at a downtown park away from the convention hall. There, police moved in on thousands of demonstrators. They sprayed the protesters with Mace. They also beat them with nightsticks. Many protesters fled. Others fought back.

The violence in Chicago highlighted the Democrats' division. The Republicans were more unified. They nominated former Vice-President Richard Nixon for president.

Nixon campaigned on a platform of law and order. He also assured the American people that he would end the Vietnam War. Nixon's campaign was helped by the entry of a third-party candidate, **George Wallace.** Wallace was a former governor of Alabama. He took many democratic votes away from Humphrey. In November, Nixon won the election. It was now up to him to resolve the Vietnam crisis.

3. Name two reasons that protesters came to Chicago for the Democratic convention.

_____

_____

CHAPTER 30 Section 5 (pages 960–967)

The End of the War and Its Legacy

BEFORE YOU READ

In the last section, you read about the explosive events that occurred in 1968.

In this section, you will read how the Vietnam War ended and what effect the war had on America.

AS YOU READ

Use this diagram to take notes on the important dates and events relating to the end of the Vietnam War.

TERMS AND NAMES

Richard Nixon President of the United States, elected 1968

Henry Kissinger Nixon adviser who helped negotiate an end to the war

Vietnamization President Nixon's plan for ending America's involvement in the war

silent majority Those mainstream Americans who supported Nixon's policies

My Lai Site of massacre of Vietnamese civilians by American soldiers

Kent State University Site of protest where National gaurd killed four students

Pentagon Papers Government documents that showed the government had no real plan for leaving Vietnam

War Powers Act Act that forbids the president from mobilizing troops without Congressional approval

```
┌─────────────────────────┐   ┌─────────────────────────┐
│       August 1969        │   │       June 1971          │
│ The first 25,000 troops  │   │                          │
│ return home.             │   │                          │
└─────────────────────────┘   └─────────────────────────┘

    ┌─────────────────────┐       ┌─────────────────────┐
    │     April 1970      │       │     March 1973       │
    │                     │       │                      │
    │                     │       │                      │
    └─────────────────────┘       └─────────────────────┘
```

President Nixon and Vietnamization (pages 960–961)

How did Vietnamization work?

Richard Nixon pledged to end American involvement in the Vietnam War. With National Security Adviser **Henry Kissinger,** he came up with a plan to end the war. Their plan was known as **Vietnamization.** It called for the gradual withdrawal of U.S. troops and for the South Vietnamese to do more of the fighting. By August of 1969, the first 25,000 U.S. troops had returned home. Over the next three years, the number of American troops in Vietnam dropped from more than 500,000 to less than 25,000.

Nixon, however, did not want to lose the war. So as he pulled American troops out, he ordered a massive bombing attack against North Vietnam.

Nixon also ordered that bombs be dropped on the neighboring countries of Laos and Cambodia. These countries held a number of Vietcong bases.

1. Name both aspects of the Vietnamization plan.

_____

_____

Trouble Continues on the Home Front (pages 962–963)

Which events weakened support for the war?

To win support for his war policies, Nixon appealed to what he called the **silent majority.** These were *mainstream* Americans who quietly supported the president's strategy. Many Americans did support the president. However, the war continued to divide the country.

In November of 1969, Americans learned of a shocking event. U.S. troops had massacred more than 100 unarmed Vietnamese in the village of **My Lai.** In April 1970, the country heard more upsetting news. President Nixon announced that U.S. troops had invaded Cambodia. They had tried to destroy Vietcong supply lines there. Upon hearing of the invasion, colleges exploded in protest.

A protest at **Kent State University** in Ohio turned tragic. To restore order on the campus, the local mayor called in the National Guard. Some students began throwing rocks at the guards. The guards fired into a crowd of protesters. Four students were killed.

Nixon's invasion of Cambodia cost him public support. It also cost him political support. Members of Congress were angry that he had invaded Cambodia without telling them. As a result, Congress repealed the Tonkin Gulf Resolution. This had given the president the freedom to conduct war policy in Vietnam on his own.

Support for the war declined even further in June of 1971. That month, a former Defense Department worker *leaked* what became known as the **Pentagon Papers.** These documents showed that the past U.S. presidents had never drawn up any plans to withdraw from Vietnam.

2. Name two incidents that weakened support for the war.

_____

_____

America's Longest War Ends
(pages 964–965)

Who won the war?

1972 was a presidential election year. To win reelection, Nixon believed he had to end the Vietnam War. Nixon called on Henry Kissinger, his adviser for national security affairs. Kissinger negotiated a peace settlement with the North Vietnamese. In October 1972, Kissinger announced that peace was close at hand. A month later, Nixon was reelected president.

However, the promised peace in Vietnam did not come. South Vietnam objected to the proposed peace settlement. As a result, the peace talks broke down. Nixon responded by ordering more bombings against North Vietnam.

Eventually, the peace talks resumed. In January 1973, the warring parties signed a peace agreement. By the end of March, the last U.S. combat troops had left. For America, the Vietnam War was over.

Shortly after America left, the peace agreement collapsed. North and South Vietnam resumed fighting. In April 1975, North Vietnamese troops captured the South's capital, Saigon. Soon after, South Vietnam surrendered to North Vietnam.

3. What happened to South Vietnam after America left?

_____

_____

The War's Painful Legacy
(pages 965–967)

How did the war affect America?

The Vietnam War cost both sides many lives. In all, about 58,000 Americans died in Vietnam. Another 303,000 were wounded. Vietnamese deaths topped 2 million.

After the war, Southeast Asia continued to experience violence and unrest. The Communists imprisoned hundreds of thousands of South Vietnamese. In Cambodia, a communist group known as the Khmer Rouge took power in 1975. They attempted to transform the country into a peasant society. In doing so, they killed many government officials and intellectuals. The group is believed to have killed as many as 1 million Cambodians.

In the United States, the war resulted in several policy changes. In November 1973, Congress passed the **War Powers Act.** This law prevented the president from committing troops in a foreign conflict without approval from Congress. In a larger sense, the war made Americans less willing to become involved in foreign wars. The war also left many Americans with a feeling of mistrust toward their government.

4. Name two ways in which the war affected Americans.

_____

_____

Glossary   CHAPTER 30   The Vietnam War Years

ambush A surprise attack

corrupt Dishonest or immoral

discredit To damage in reputation

leak To reveal secret information

mainstream Representing the commonly occurring attitudes, values and practices of a group

morale Attitude or spirit

peninsula A land area surrounded on three sides by water

platform A declaration of one's beliefs or principles

stalemate A situation in which both sides are stuck; a deadlock

unjust Violating principles of justice or fairness; unfair

truce A temporary halt of fighting

unstable Unsteady, weak

AFTER YOU READ

Terms and Names

A. Write the letter of the best answer.

_____ **1.** Which of the following gave the U.S. president broad military powers in Vietnam?

    a. Vietnamization

    b. Pentagon Papers

    c. War Powers Act

    d. Tonkin Gulf Resolution

_____ **2.** Which of the following revealed the U.S. had no plans for ending the war as long as the North Vietnamese continued to fight?

    a. Vietnamization

    b. Pentagon Papers

    c. War Powers Act

    d. Tonkin Gulf Resolution

_____ **3.** What organization called for greater individual freedom in America?

    a. Free Speech Movement

    b. Students for a Democratic Society

    c. hawks

    d. doves

_____ **4.** Who ran as a third-party candidate in the 1968 election?

    a. George Wallace

    b. Eugene McCarthy

    c. Hubert Humphrey

    d. Robert McNamara

_____ **5.** What law prevented the president from committing troops in a foreign conflict without the approval of Congress?

    a. Tonkin Gulf Resolution

    b. Pentagon Papers

    c. War Powers Act

    d. Geneva Accords

AFTER YOU READ (continued)   CHAPTER 30   The Vietnam War Years

B. Write the name or term that best completes each sentence.

Robert McNamara

New Left

silent majority

domino theory

Robert Kennedy

Eugene McCarthy

1. The idea that countries on the brink of communism were waiting to fall one after the other was called the _____.

2. An adviser to President Johnson who supported the sending of troops to Vietnam was _____.

3. The _____ was the term given to the growing youth movement of the 1960s.

4. _____ decided to join the 1968 Democratic race for president after seeing the surprising results in the New Hampshire primary.

5. President Nixon made a special appeal to the _____ to win support for his war policies.

Main Ideas

1. How did the Tonkin Gulf Resolution lead to greater U.S. involvement in Vietnam?

_____

2. Name three reasons why U.S. troops had difficulty fighting the Vietcong.

_____

3. Why were many African-American leaders opposed to the Vietnam War?

_____

4. Why was the Tet offensive considered the turning point of the war?

_____

5. What was one immediate and one more lasting impact of the Vietnam War on America?

_____

Thinking Critically

Answer the following questions on a separate sheet of paper.

1. How did the division at home over the war demonstrate America's long-held belief in freedom of expression?

2. Do you agree or disagree with the War Powers Act? Explain your answer.

Name _____ Date _____

Latinos and Native Americans Seek Equality

TERMS AND NAMES

César Chávez Leader of the farm workers movement

United Farm Workers Organizing Committee Union that fought for farm workers' rights

La Raza Unida Latino political party

American Indian Movement (AIM) Group that fought for greater reform for Native Americans

BEFORE YOU READ

In the last section, you read about the end of the Vietnam War.

In this section, you will read about how Latinos and Native Americans fought for greater equality.

AS YOU READ

Use the following diagram to take notes on the goals and tactics of the Latino and Native American movements.

GROUPS	GOALS	TACTICS
Latinos	better working conditions	formed farm workers union
Native Americans		

The Latino Presence Grows
(pages 974–975)

Who are Latinos?

Latinos are Spanish-speaking Americans. During the 1960s, the Latino population in the United States tripled—from 3 million to more than 9 million.

During this time, the nation's Mexican American population grew. Many were *descendants* of Mexicans who stayed on the land that Mexico surrendered to the United States in 1848. Others were the children and grandchildren of the Mexicans who arrived after Mexico's 1910 revolution. Still others came as temporary laborers during the 1940s and 1950s. Mexican Americans always have made up the largest group of Latinos.

About a million Puerto Ricans have lived in the United States since the 1960s. Most Puerto Ricans have settled in the Northeast, especially in New York City.

Many Cubans also settled in the United States during the 1960s. They had fled Cuba after the Cuban Revolution in 1959. Most Cubans settled in or near Miami.

Thousands of Salvadorans, Guatemalans, Nicaraguans, and Colombians immigrated to the United States after the 1960s. They came to escape political *persecution* and poverty at home. Wherever they settled, many Latinos experienced poor living conditions and discrimination.

1. Name two groups that make up the Latino community.

_____

_____

Latinos Fight for Change

(pages 975–977)

Which groups fought for change?

In the 1960s, Latinos began to demand equal rights and respect. One such group was Mexican-American farm workers. These men and women worked on California's fruit and vegetable farms. They often worked long hours for little pay.

César Chávez was the group's leader. Chávez believed that the farm workers should organize into a union. In 1962, he helped establish the National Farm Workers Association. In 1966, Chávez merged this group with a Filipino agricultural union. Together, they formed the **United Farm Workers Organizing Committee** (UFWOC).

California's grape growers refused to recognize the farm workers union. As a result, Chávez called for a nationwide boycott of grapes. His plan worked. In 1970, the grape growers finally signed contracts with the UFWOC. The new contracts guaranteed union workers higher pay and granted them other benefits.

Latinos also wanted greater recognition of their culture. Puerto Ricans demanded that schools offer classes taught in their native language. In 1968, Congress passed the Bilingual Education Act. This law funded *bilingual* and cultural programs for students who did not speak English.

Latinos began organizing politically during the 1960s. Some worked within the two-party system. Others created an independent Latino political movement. José Angel Gutiérrez, for example, started **La Raza Unida** (the United People Party). The party ran Latino candidates and won positions in city government offices.

2. Name two organizations that fought to promote the cause of Latinos.

_____

_____

Native Americans Struggle for Equality

(pages 977–979)

What problems did Native Americans face?

Native Americans, like Latinos, are a diverse group. However, despite their diversity, most Native Americans have faced similar problems. These problems include high unemployment rates, poor health care, and high death rates.

During the 1950s, the Eisenhower administration tried to solve some of these problems. The government thought that introducing Native Americans to more aspects of mainstream culture would help them. As a result, the government moved Native Americans from their reservations to the cities.

The plan failed. Most Native Americans who moved to the cities remained very poor. In addition, many Native Americans refused to mix with mainstream American society.

Native Americans wanted greater opportunity to control their own lives. In 1961, representatives from 61 Native American groups met to discuss their concerns. They demanded the right to choose their own way of life.

In 1968, President Johnson responded to their demands. He created the National Council on Indian Opportunity. The council's goal was to make sure that government programs reflected the needs and desires of Native Americans.

Many young Native Americans were not satisfied with the government's new policies. They wanted greater reform. They also wanted it more quickly. As a result, some young Native Americans formed the **American Indian Movement (AIM).** This organization demanded greater rights for Native Americans. At times, the group used violence to make its point.

Meanwhile, Native Americans won greater rights through the court system. Throughout the 1960s and 1970s, they won legal battles that gave them greater education and land rights.

3. Name two problems that Native Americans faced.

_____

_____

CHAPTER 31 Section 2 (pages 982–986)

Women Fight for Equality

BEFORE YOU READ

In the last section, you read how Latinos and Native Americans fought for greater rights.

In this section, you will read how the nation's women also attempted to improve their status in society.

AS YOU READ

Use this diagram to take notes on the successes and failures of the women's movement.

SUCCESSES	FAILURES
Government declares all-male job ads illegal	ERA is defeated

A New Women's Movement Arises (pages 982–984)

How did the women's movement emerge?

The theory behind the women's movement of the 1960s was **feminism.** This was the belief that women should have economic, political, and social equality with men.

The women's movement arose during the 1960s for several reasons. First, a growing number of women entered the work force. In the workplace, many women received less pay than men—even for the same job. Many women saw this as unfair.

Second, women had become actively involved in both the civil rights and antiwar movements. These movements led women to take action on behalf of their own beliefs. In addition, many men in these groups refused to give women leadership roles. As a result, many women became more aware of their *inferior* status.

In 1963, **Betty Friedan** published *The Feminine Mystique.* This book expressed the discontent that many women were feeling. Friedan's book helped to unite a number of women throughout the nation.

1. Name two factors that helped launch the women's movement.

_____

_____

The Movement Experiences Gains and Losses (pages 984–985)

What were the movement's successes and failures?

In 1966, several women including Betty Friedan formed the **National Organization for Women (NOW).** The group's goal was to more actively pursue women's goals. NOW pushed for more child-care facilities. It also called for more educational opportunities.

The organization also pressured the federal government to enforce a ban on *gender* discrimination in hiring. The government responded by declaring that male-only job ads were illegal.

Women also attempted to gain political strength. In 1971, Journalist **Gloria Steinem** helped found the National Women's Political Caucus. This group encouraged women to run for political office.

In 1972, Congress passed a ban on gender discrimination in higher education. As a result, several all-male colleges opened their doors to women. In 1973, the Supreme Court's decision in the case *Roe* v. *Wade* granted women the right to choose an abortion.

The women's movement also met with some failure, such as with the **Equal Rights Amendment (ERA).** The ERA was a proposed *amendment* to the U.S. Constitution. It would have outlawed government discrimination on the basis of sex. One prominent ERA opponent was **Phyllis Schlafly.** Schlafly called the ERA the work of *radical* feminists.

In addition, the women's movement angered many of the nation's *conservatives.* In response, these conservatives joined together to form a movement known as the New Right. This movement emphasized traditional social, cultural, and moral values. Throughout the 1970s, the New Right gained support for its social conservatism.

2. Name one success and one failure of the women's movement.

_____

_____

The Movement's Legacy (page 986)

What was the movement's legacy?

In 1977, the ERA was close to being passed, but the New Right gained strength. In 1982, the ERA went down to defeat.

But the influence of the women's movement could be seen in the workplace as more women started careers instead of staying home with their children. In 1970, 8 percent of all medical school graduates and 5 percent of law school graduates were women. By 1998, those numbers had risen to 42 and 44 percent respectively. Women also made political gains as many ran for and were elected to office.

3. Cite two examples of how the women's movement helped women improve their standing in society.

_____

_____

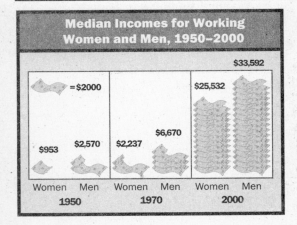

Median Incomes for Working Women and Men, 1950–2000

= $2000

$953 $2,570 $2,237 $6,670 $25,532 $33,592

Women Men   Women Men   Women Men
1950   1970   2000

Skillbuilder

Use the graph to answer the questions.

1. How much more did the average woman make in 2000 than she did in 1970?

_____

2. How much less did the average woman make than the average man in 2000?

_____

Culture and Counterculture

TERMS AND NAMES

counterculture Movement whose members sought to drop out of mainstream society

Haight-Ashbury Community in San Francisco that attracted many hippies

the Beatles British rock group that helped popularize rock 'n' roll

Woodstock Massive outdoor concert that demonstrated rock 'n' roll's popularity

BEFORE YOU READ

In the last section, you read about the women's movement that emerged in the United States in the 1960s.

In this section, you will read about the emergence of the counterculture movement—and how the nation reacted to it.

AS YOU READ

Use this diagram to take notes on how the counterculture affected America

IMMEDIATE EFFECT	LONG-TERM EFFECT
Mainstream America blamed it for decline of traditional values.	Rock 'n' roll became a part of mainstream culture.

The Counterculture (pages 987–988)

What characterized the counterculture?

During the 1960s, many young people adopted values that differed from those of mainstream society. These Americans were part of a movement known as the **counterculture.**

The movement was made up mostly of white middle-class youths. Members of the counterculture were known as "hippies." Many hippies shared some of the beliefs of the New Left. They took part in demonstrations against the Vietnam War. However, a majority of hippies chose to turn their backs on America. They wanted to establish a new society based on peace and love.

The main characteristics of the hippie culture were rock 'n' roll, colorful clothes, and the use of drugs. Many also chose to live in large groups called communes. Many hippies moved to San Francisco's **Haight-Ashbury** district. This community was popular mainly because of the availability of drugs.

After a few years, the counterculture movement began to decline. Some aspects of the movement became violent. Many urban communes grew dangerous. The widespread use of drugs also led to the decline of the movement.

More than anything else, hippies eventually found that they could not survive outside mainstream America. They needed money to live. For many, this meant returning to mainstream society—and getting a job.

1. Name two characteristics of the counterculture.

_____

_____

_____

A Changing Culture (pages 989–990)

How did the counterculture affect America?

The counterculture movement collapsed after only a few years. However, some aspects of it had a lasting effect on mainstream culture.

The movement affected the worlds of art and fashion. The 1960s saw the rise of popular, or pop, art.

One celebrated pop artist was Andy Warhol. His work was characterized by bright, simple, commercial-looking images such as portraits of soup cans and other icons of mass culture. These images were repeated to look mass-produced as a criticism of the times. They implied that individual freedoms had been lost to a "cookie-cutter" lifestyle.

The most lasting legacy of the counterculture movement was its music. Rock 'n' roll continues to be a popular form of entertainment. Perhaps the most influential band was **the Beatles.** The British group took America by storm and helped rock music become part of mainstream America.

A dramatic example of rock 'n' roll's popularity was an event known as **Woodstock.** This was a massive outdoor rock concert in upstate New York. It occurred during the summer of 1969. More than 400,000 people attended—far more than expected. For three days, popular bands and musicians performed. Despite the crowd, however, the festival was peaceful and well organized.

The counterculture movement affected Americans' social attitudes as well. The American media began to address the subjects of sex and violence. Before this time, few Americans discussed these topics.

2. Name two areas of society affected by the counterculture.

_____

_____

The Conservative Response

(page 991)

Why did mainstream America attack the counterculture?

In the late 1960s, many mainstream Americans criticized the counterculture. They blamed the movement for the decline of traditional American values.

Some conservative groups called the movement a threat to law and order. They also accused members of the counterculture of being *immoral.*

Mainstream America's anger toward the counterculture affected the country's political scene. In 1968, the Republicans nominated Richard Nixon as their presidential candidate. Nixon ran on a platform of law and order, and conservative values. His ideas appealed to many voters. As a result, Nixon won the election. He then set the nation on a more conservative course.

3. Cite two reasons why Americans criticized the counterculture.

_____

_____

Glossary   CHAPTER 31   An Era of Social Change

amendment A revision or change

bilingual Presented in two languages

conservative Cautious, traditional, against change

descendant An offspring; someone derived from an ancestor

gender Relating to male or female

immoral Evil; characterized by bad behavior

inferior Lower, lesser rank

persecution The act of oppressing or treating badly

radical Extreme, carried to the furthest limit; promoting change

AFTER YOU READ

Terms and Names

A. If the statement is true, write "true" on the line. If it is false, change the underlined word or words to make it true.

1. _____ In the 1970s, La Raza Unida fielded Latino candidates and won positions in several city governments.

2. _____ A major opponent of the Equal Rights Amendment was Betty Friedan.

3. _____ Phyllis Schlafly helped found the National Women's Political Caucus.

4. _____ A popular British band, the Beatles, helped propel rock 'n' roll into mainstream America.

5. _____ Young Native Americans formed a group known as ERA, which helped fight for Indian rights.

B. Write the letter of the name or term that matches the description.

a. counterculture

b. Woodstock

c. César Chávez

d. National Organization for Women

e. American Indian Movement

_____ **1.** The person who organized Mexican-American farm workers

_____ **2.** A sometimes violent Native-American rights organization

_____ **3.** An organization created to pursue the goals of the women's movement

_____ **4.** A movement made up of white middle-class youths, who were fed up with mainstream America

_____ **5.** A massive outdoor concert in 1969 that highlighted rock's popularity

AFTER YOU READ (continued)   **CHAPTER 31** An Era of Social Change

Main Ideas

1. Name the different ways in which Latinos fought for greater equality.

_____

_____

2. Why did President Eisenhower's Native American plan fail?

_____

_____

3. What achievements did the women's movement make?

_____

_____

4. Why did the counterculture decline?

_____

_____

5. How did many Americans view the counterculture? How did this view affect the nation's political scene?

_____

_____

Thinking Critically

Answer the following questions on a separate sheet of paper.

1. How were the Latino and Native American movements similar? How were they different?

2. A stereotype is a generalization made about a group. What stereotypes do you think hippies and mainstream Americans made about each other? Why?

CHAPTER 32 Section 1 (pages 1000–1007)

The Nixon Administration

BEFORE YOU READ

In the last section, you read about the counterculture.

In this section, you will learn about President Nixon and his attempts to move the country in a more conservative direction.

AS YOU READ

Use the web below to take notes on the major policies of President Richard Nixon.

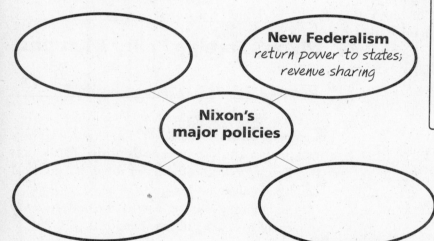

New Federalism
return power to states; revenue sharing

Nixon's major policies

Nixon's New Conservatism
(pages 1000–1002)

How did Nixon pursue conservative policies?

President **Richard M. Nixon** wanted to turn the United States in a more conservative direction. He tried to decrease the power of the federal government. Nixon's plan was called **New Federalism.** Its goal was to give federal power to the states.

Nixon introduced **revenue sharing.** The federal government usually told state and local governments how to spend their federal money. Under revenue sharing, state and local officials could spend their federal dollars however they saw fit with few limits.

Nixon also wanted to reform welfare. He supported the **Family Assistance Plan** (FAP). Under this plan, every family of four with no income would receive a payment of $1,600 a year, and could earn up to $4,000 more a year. But this plan failed to pass Congress.

When Nixon first took office, he cooperated with Congress. But he soon refused to spend money that Congress wanted to spend on programs that he did not like. Federal courts ruled that Nixon's action was unconstitutional. They ordered that Nixon spend the money on the programs.

Nixon also followed "law and order" policies to stop riots and antiwar protests. He used the Central Intelligence Agency (CIA) and the

Internal Revenue Service (IRS) to harass people. He created an "enemies list" and had the CIA and IRS target people on this list. The list included liberals and other opponents of his policies.

1. What conservative programs did Nixon support?

Nixon's Southern Strategy
(pages 1002–1004)

What was the Southern strategy?

Nixon wanted to make sure he would get reelected in 1972. To achieve this, he used what he called a **Southern strategy** to win the support of Southerners.

To attract white voters, Nixon tried to slow school desegregation. But the Supreme Court ordered the administration to move more quickly. Nixon also opposed the extension of the Voting Rights Act of 1965. But Congress extended the act.

Nixon believed that the Supreme Court under Chief Justice Earl Warren was too liberal. During his presidency, four justices, including Warren, left the Court. This gave Nixon an opportunity to appoint more conservative justices.

2. How did Nixon hope to win Southern support?

Confronting a Stagnant Economy (pages 1004-1005)

What is stagflation?

One of the biggest problems facing Nixon was a weak economy. Between 1967 and 1973, *inflation* and unemployment increased. This situation is known as **stagflation.**

Stagflation had several causes. Unemployment increased because *trade competition* increased. This made it harder for Americans to sell their goods overseas. The nation also had trouble finding jobs for millions of baby boomers who reached working age.

Inflation increased for two main reasons. First, more government spending on social programs and the war in Vietnam raised prices. The second cause

was the nation's need for foreign oil. The United States received much of its oil from the Middle East. Many of these countries belonged to a *cartel* called **OPEC (Organization of Petroleum Exporting Countries).** During the 1960s, OPEC gradually raised oil prices. Then, in 1973, a war broke out, with Israel against Egypt and Syria. The United States sent military aid to Israel.

The OPEC nations sided with Egypt and Syria. They stopped selling oil to the United States. This led to problems in the United States. Between the fall of 1973 and March 1974, motorists faced long lines at the gas stations. Some factories and schools closed. When OPEC started selling oil to the United States again, the price had *quadrupled.*

3. How did OPEC affect the U.S. economy?

Nixon's Foreign Policy Triumphs
(pages 1005–1007)

What is realpolitik?

Nixon's main foreign policy adviser was Henry Kissinger. Kissinger based his foreign policy views on a philosophy known as **realpolitik.** This meant that Kissinger dealt with other nations in a practical and flexible manner. Kissinger believed it was practical to ignore a country that was weak. But it was important to deal with strong nations.

Realpolitik was a change from the policy of containment. Nixon and Kissinger changed U.S. relations with Communist countries. They called their policy **détente.** This policy was aimed at easing Cold War tensions.

In 1972, Nixon visited Communist China. Before this, the United States had refused to recognize the Communist government. Three months later, Nixon went to the Soviet Union. Nixon and the Soviet leader signed the **SALT I Treaty.** This five-year agreement limited nuclear weapons. Nixon's successes in foreign affairs helped him win reelection.

4. How did Nixon try to ease Cold War tensions?

Watergate: Nixon's Downfall

BEFORE YOU READ

In the last section, you read about President Nixon's approach to politics and the Cold War.

In this section, you will learn about the Watergate scandal.

AS YOU READ

Use the diagram below to take notes about the causes and effects of the Watergate scandal.

TERMS AND NAMES

impeachment The constitutional process for removing a president from office

Watergate Scandal that forced Nixon to resign

H. R. Haldeman Adviser to Nixon

John Ehrlichman Adviser to Nixon

John Mitchell Attorney general and director of Nixon's campaign

Committee to Reelect the President Nixon's campaign committee

Judge John Sirica Judge in the trial of the Watergate burglars

Saturday Night Massacre Nixon's firing of Justice Department officials, including the special prosecutor investigating Watergate

causes

- Imperial presidency

Watergate scandal

effects

- Nixon resigns

President Nixon and His White House (pages 1008–1009)

What was Watergate?

In 1974, the House Judiciary Committee voted to recommend the **impeachment** of—the bringing of formal charges against—President Richard Nixon. The cause was the **Watergate** scandal which was an attempt to *cover up* a burglary of the Democratic National Committee (DNC) headquarters.

By the time Richard Nixon became president, the executive branch had become powerful. Nixon expanded the power of the presidency. He confided in a small group of very loyal advisers. These advisers included **H. R. Haldeman,** chief of staff; **John**

Ehrlichman, chief domestic adviser; and **John Mitchell,** the attorney general. These men helped Nixon get reelected. They also shared Nixon's desire for power. This would lead Nixon and his advisers to cover up their role in the Watergate burglary.

1. Define Watergate scandal.

_____

_____

The Drive Toward Reelection (pages 1009–1010)

What was the CRP?

Nixon campaign aides were determined to win the 1972 election. They hired five men to raid

Democratic party offices in the Watergate complex in Washington, D.C. The men were caught photographing files and placing wiretaps on phones. The press soon discovered that the group's leader, James McCord, was a former CIA agent. He was also an official of a group known as the **Committee to Reelect the President** (CRP). John Mitchell, who had been attorney general, was the CRP's director.

Nixon and his staff tried to hide the link to the White House. Workers shredded evidence. Nixon and his staff asked the CIA to urge the FBI to stop its investigations into the burglary.

The Watergate burglary was not a big issue in the 1972 election. Only two reporters kept on the story. In a series of articles, the reporters found information that linked members of the administration to the burglary. The White House denied any connections.

2. Why did the CRP order the burglary of the Democratic National Committee headquarters?

_____

_____

The Cover-Up Unravels (pages 1010–1012)

How did Nixon get caught?

After Nixon's reelection, the cover-up began to unravel. In January of 1973, the Watergate burglars went to trial. All of the burglars except James McCord changed their pleas from innocent to guilty. McCord was found guilty by a jury. The trial's *presiding* judge, **Judge John Sirica,** believed that the burglars did not act alone. Then in March 1973, McCord sent a letter to Sirica, stating that he had lied under oath. He also stated that the White House was involved in the cover-up.

Soon the public interest in the Watergate burglary increased. In April 1973, three top Nixon aides resigned. The President then went on television and denied any cover-up. He announced that he was appointing Elliot Richardson as the new attorney general. He authorized Richardson to appoint a *special prosecutor* to investigate Watergate.

In May 1973, the Senate began its own investigation of Watergate. The Senate hearings were televised live. In the hearings, one of Nixon's aides said that Nixon knew about the cover-up. Then it was revealed that White House meetings had been tape-recorded. The Senate committee demanded the tapes. Nixon refused to release them.

Court battles over the tapes lasted a year. Archibald Cox, the special prosecutor, took the president to court in October 1973 to get the tapes. Nixon refused and ordered Richardson to fire Cox. In what became known as the **Saturday Night Massacre,** Richardson refused the order and resigned. The deputy attorney general also refused and resigned. Solicitor General Robert Bork finally fired Cox. But his replacement, Leon Jaworski, was determined to get the tapes.

3. What did Nixon do during the investigation?

_____

_____

The Fall of a President (pages 1012–1013)

How did Nixon's presidency end?

In March 1974, a grand jury charged seven Nixon aides with *obstruction of justice* and *perjury*. Nixon released more than 1,250 pages of taped conversations. But he did not release the conversations on some key dates. In July 1974, the Supreme Court ordered the White House to release the tapes.

Three days later, a House committee voted to impeach President Nixon. If the full House of Representatives approved, Nixon would go to trial in the Senate. If Nixon was judged guilty there, he would be removed from office. When the tapes were finally released, they proved that Nixon had known of the cover-up. On August 8, 1974, before the impeachment could happen, Nixon resigned.

Watergate produced distrust about the presidency. A poll taken in 1974 showed that 43 percent of Americans had lost faith in the presidency. In the years after Vietnam and Watergate, Americans developed a deep distrust of government officials.

4. Why did President Nixon resign from office?

_____

_____

The Ford and Carter Years

TERMS AND NAMES
Gerald R. Ford 38th president
Jimmy Carter 39th president
National Energy Act Law that aimed to conserve energy
human rights Rights and freedoms that all people should enjoy
Camp David Accords Agreements between Israel and Egypt
Ayatollah Ruhollah Khomeini Iranian religious leader who led the revolution against the Shah of Iran

BEFORE YOU READ

In the last section, you learned about Watergate.
In this section, you will read about the presidencies of Gerald Ford and Jimmy Carter.

AS YOU READ

Use the time line below to take notes on the major events of the Ford and Carter administrations.

1974 Helsinki Accords

1974

1981

Ford Travels a Rough Road; Ford's Foreign Policy
(pages 1016–1018)

What did Ford do as president?

Gerald R. Ford replaced Richard Nixon as president. Ford was likable and honest. But he lost public support when he *pardoned* Nixon.

The economy had gotten worse by the time Ford took office. Ford invited the nation's top economic leaders to the White House to discuss what to do. Ford promoted a program to slow inflation by encouraging energy conservation. This program failed. Ford then pushed for higher interest rates. This triggered the worst recession in 40 years.

In foreign affairs, Ford relied on Henry Kissinger, the secretary of state. Ford continued talks with China and the Soviet Union. In 1974, he participated in a meeting in Helsinki, Finland. There, 35 countries, including the Soviet Union, signed the Helsinki

Accords. These were agreements that promised greater cooperation between the nations of Europe.

1. What did Ford do about the economy?

_____

_____

Carter Enters the White House (page 1018)

Why did Carter get elected?

Ford ran for election in 1976 against Democrat **Jimmy Carter.** Carter ran as an outsider, or someone apart from Washington politics. Carter promised he would never lie to Americans. Carter won a close election with this message.

Carter stayed in touch with the people by holding "fireside chats" on radio and television. But Carter did not try to reach out to Congress. He refused to take part in deal-making. As a result, he angered both Republicans and Democrats in Congress.

2. Why did Carter win the 1976 presidential election?

_____

_____

Carter's Domestic Agenda
(pages 1018–1020)

How did Carter try to fix the economy?

Carter believed that energy policy should be his top priority. He signed the **National Energy Act.** It placed a tax on gas-guzzling cars. It removed price controls on oil and natural gas. It also funded research for new sources of energy.

But in 1979, violence in the Middle East caused another shutdown of oil imports. High prices made inflation worse. Carter tried voluntary price freezes and spending cuts, but these measures did not stop inflation.

Other changes in the economy caused problems in the 1970s. Greater *automation* meant fewer manufacturing jobs. Competition from other countries cost American jobs, too. Many companies moved their factories from the Northeast to the South and West. They were looking for lower energy costs and cheaper labor.

3. How did Carter try to solve the nation's economic problems?

_____

_____

A Human Rights Foreign Policy
(page 1021)

How did human rights affect Carter's foreign policy?

Carter tried to follow moral principles in his foreign policy. He believed the United States should promote **human rights.** Human rights are freedoms and liberties like those listed in the Declaration of Independence and the Bill of Rights.

Carter cut aid to countries that violated the rights of their people. He supported a treaty with Panama to give control of the Panama Canal to that country. Carter signed a nuclear arms treaty—called SALT II—with the Soviets. The treaty was opposed by the Senate. But when the Soviets invaded Afghanistan, Carter refused to fight for the treaty. It was never ratified.

4. What was Carter's foreign policy based on?

_____

_____

Triumph and Crisis in the Middle East (pages 1022–1023)

What did Carter do about the Middle East?

In 1978, Carter arranged a meeting between the leaders of Egypt and Israel. The two nations had been enemies for years. After several days of talks, Carter and the two leaders reached agreements known as the **Camp David Accords.**

In 1979, Muslim fundamentalists and their leader **Ayatollah Ruhollah Khomeini** overthrew the *shah* of Iran. In October of 1979, Carter allowed the shah to enter the United States for cancer treatment. This angered the revolutionaries. On November 4, 1979, they took control of the American embassy in Tehran, Iran's capital, and took 52 Americans *hostage.* They demanded that the United States send the shah back to Iran in return for the hostages.

Carter refused. A long standoff followed. Carter could not get the hostages released. They were held for 444 days. The hostages were freed just minutes after Ronald Reagan was inaugurated president on January 20, 1981.

5. Name one success and one defeat in the Middle East for Carter?

_____

_____

Environmental Activism

BEFORE YOU READ

In the last section, you learned about President Ford and President Carter.

In this section, you will see how Americans addressed their environmental concerns.

AS YOU READ

Use the web below to take notes about important events for the environmental movement in the United States.

TERMS AND NAMES

Rachel Carson Environmentalist crusader in the U.S.

Earth Day Annual day to celebrate the environment

environmentalist Person who actively tries to protect the environment

Environmental Protection Agency (EPA) Federal agency formed to decrease pollution

Three Mile Island Site of a nuclear plant that released radiation into the air

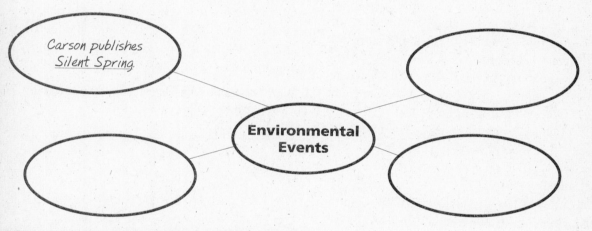

Carson publishes *Silent Spring.*

Environmental Events

The Roots of Environmentalism
(pages 1026–1027)

What is environmentalism?

Concern for the environment was increased by the 1962 book *Silent Spring,* written by **Rachel Carson.** That book argued that *pesticides* were poisoning food and killing birds and fish. *Silent Spring* sold nearly half a million copies within six months.

Carson's book was an awakening to many Americans. President Kennedy set up a committee to investigate the situation shortly after the book's publication. It took several years, but Carson's work helped to outlaw the use of DDT, a harmful pesticide, in 1972.

1. How did *Silent Spring* encourage environmentalism?

_____

_____

_____

Environmental Concerns in the 1970s (pages 1027–1031)

What were the key environmental issues of the 1970s?

On April 22, 1970, Americans celebrated **Earth Day** for the first time. Earth Day became a yearly event to highlight environmental issues.

Richard Nixon was not an **environmentalist**— someone who takes an active role in protecting the environment. But he did recognize the nation's concern over the environment. In 1970, he created the **Environmental Protection Agency (EPA).** This agency had the power to regulate *pollution* caused by *emissions* standards and to conduct research.

Nixon also signed the 1970 Clean Air Act. This law required industry to reduce pollution from factories and automobiles. Other new laws to protect the environment also passed.

In 1968, oil was found in Alaska. Oil companies began building a pipeline to carry the oil 800 miles across the state. The discovery of oil and the construction of the pipeline created many new jobs and increased state revenues.

But the pipeline raised concerns about Alaska's environment and the rights of Alaska's native peoples. In 1971, Nixon signed the Alaska Native Claims Settlement Act. This law gave millions of acres of land to the state's native tribes.

In 1978, President Carter set aside 56 million more acres in Alaska as national monuments. In 1980, Congress added another 104 million acres to Alaska's protected conservation areas.

In the 1970s, some people believed that nuclear energy was the energy of the future. They believed that it was cheap, plentiful, and safe.

Others opposed nuclear energy. They warned that nuclear plants were dangerous to humans and the environment. These people also feared accidents and nuclear waste.

On March 28, 1979, the concerns of opponents of nuclear energy appeared to come true. An accident caused one of the nuclear reactors on **Three Mile Island,** in Pennsylvania, to release *radiation* into the air. An investigation showed that workers at the plant had not been properly trained. It also showed that some safety measures were not taken. Afterwards, the government strengthened nuclear safety regulations.

2. What did the government do after the accident at a nuclear reactor on Three Mile Island?

_____

_____

A Continuing Movement (page 1031)

Have the goals of the environmental movement changed?

The debate over the environment continues today. The struggle is between proponents of economic growth and conservationists. Environmental regulations sometimes block economic development and cause a loss of jobs for workers. Though there is conflict, it is clear that environmental concerns have gained increasing attention and support.

3. What issue faces Americans today regarding the environment?

_____

_____

Environmental Progress in Los Angeles Region

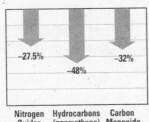

Ozone-Alert Episodes

Air Pollution Reduction, 1976–1990

Number of Days: 1977 = 121, 1986 = 80, 1996 = 7

Nitrogen Oxides −27.5%, Hydrocarbons (nonmethane) −48%, Carbon Monoxide −32%

Source: California Air Resources Board

Skillbuilder

Use the charts to answer these questions.

1. How many days in 1996 did people in Los Angeles face ozone-alert episodes?

_____

2. How much did carbon monoxide pollution decrease in Los Angeles between 1976 and 1990?

_____

Glossary

automation Making things with machines rather than people

cartel An organization that controls enough of the production of an item to set the price

cover up To hide or conceal

emissions Something that is given off or sent out

hostage A person held captive in an attempt to bargain for political or financial demands

inflation A steady increase in prices of consumer goods

obstruction of justice Preventing legal work from proceeding

pardoned Excused or forgave

perjury Lying under oath

pesticides Chemicals used to kill insects and rodents

pollution Waste or harmful material

presiding Holding a position of authority

quadrupled Made four times greater

radiation Possibly dangerous energy that is sent into the air

shah Ruler of Iran before the 1979 revolution

special prosecutor Lawyer appointed to investigate public officials

trade competition Competition from other nations to sell goods

AFTER YOU READ

Terms and Names

A. Write the letter of the term that best answers the question.

a. John Sirica

b. environmentalist

c. realpolitik

d. Jimmy Carter

e. stagflation

f. Gerald Ford

_____ **1.** What is the foreign policy in which nations deal with each other in a practical and flexible manner?

_____ **2.** What is the economic term that refers to the double problems of rising inflation and unemployment?

_____ **3.** Who was the judge in the trial of the Watergate burglars?

_____ **4.** Who was the president who based much of his foreign policy on human rights?

_____ **5.** Who is a person who takes an active role in advocating measures to protect the environment?

B. Write on the blank the name or term that best completes each sentence.

Earth Day

Saturday Night Massacre

Rachel Carson

revenue sharing

Camp David Accords

1. Through Richard Nixon's plan of _____, state and local governments were allowed to spend their federal dollars however they saw fit within certain limitations.

2. When Archibald Cox sued to obtain Nixon's tapes, Nixon set off the _____, by ordering the attorney general to fire Cox.

3. President Jimmy Carter negotiated the _____ between Israel and Egypt.

4. The book *Silent Spring*, written by _____, prompted Americans to address environmental issues.

5. On April 22, 1970, thousands of communities celebrated the first _____ by having some type of environmental awareness activity.

AFTER YOU READ (continued)   CHAPTER 32   An Age of Limits

Main Ideas

1. How did Nixon try to help the economy?

_____

_____

2. What were the effects of the Watergate scandal?

_____

_____

3. How did Ford handle the economy?

_____

_____

4. Describe one success and one failure of Carter's foreign policy?

_____

_____

5. What happened at Three Mile Island?

_____

_____

_____

Thinking Critically

Answer the following questions on a separate sheet of paper.

1. What do you think were President Nixon's successes? What were his failures?

2. How did Rachel Carson's book *Silent Spring* contribute to the environmental movement?

A Conservative Movement Emerges

BEFORE YOU READ

In the last section, you read about the environmental movement.

In this section, you will learn about the growth of the conservative movement leading up to 1980.

AS YOU READ

Use the web below to take notes about conservatives and their political beliefs.

TERMS AND NAMES

entitlement program Program that guarantees benefits to particular people

New Right Alliance of conservative groups to support conservative ideas

affirmative action Programs that required special consideration for racial and ethnic minorities and women

reverse discrimination Discrimination against whites to make up for past discrimination against others

conservative coalition Alliance of business interests, religious people, and dissatisfied middle-class voters to support conservative candidates

Moral Majority Organization formed to fight for traditional values

Ronald Reagan 40th president

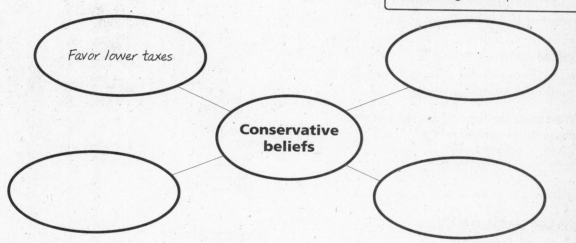

The Conservative Movement Builds (pages 1036–1038)

Why did conservatism grow?

American conservatism had been gaining support since Barry Goldwater's run for the presidency in 1964. Many people were questioning the power of the federal government.

Many Americans resented the cost of **entitlement programs.** These are programs that guaranteed benefits to particular groups. By 1980, one out of every three households was receiving benefits from government programs. Americans were unhappy paying taxes to support these benefits.

Some people also became frustrated with the government's civil rights policies. The Civil Rights Act of 1964 was meant to end racial discrimination. But over the years, some court decisions extended the act. Some people opposed laws that increased minority opportunities in employment or education. During the 1970s, right wing, grass-roots groups emerged to support single issues. Together these groups were known as the **New Right.** Among the causes they supported were opposition to abortion and school busing, blocking the Equal Rights Amendment, and supporting school prayer.

Many in the New Right were critical of **affirmative action.** This was the policy that required employers to give special consideration to women, African Americans, and other minority groups.

The New Right called this **reverse discrimination,** discrimination against white people and specifically white men.

Right-wing groups tended to vote for the same candidates. These voters formed the **conservative coalition.** This was an alliance of some intellectuals, business interests, and unhappy middle-class voters.

Members of the conservative coalition shared some basic positions. They opposed big government, entitlement programs, and many civil rights programs. They also believed in a return to traditional moral standards.

Religious groups, especially Christian fundamentalists, played an important role in the conservative coalition. Some of these groups were guided by television preachers. Some of them banded together and formed the **Moral Majority.** They interpreted the Bible literally. They also believed in absolute standards of right and wrong. The Moral Majority criticized a decline in national morality. They wanted to bring back what they saw as traditional American values.

1. What basic positions did members of the conservative coalition share?

_____

_____

Conservatives Win Political Power (pages 1038–1039)

Why was Reagan popular?

The conservatives found a strong presidential candidate in **Ronald Reagan.** He won the 1980 nomination and chose George Bush as his running mate.

Reagan had been a movie actor and a spokesman for General Motors. He won political fame with a speech for Barry Goldwater during the 1964 presidential campaign. In 1966, Reagan was elected governor of California. He was reelected in 1970.

In the 1980 election, Reagan ran on a number of issues. Supreme Court decisions on abortion, the teaching of evolution, and prayer in public schools all upset conservative voters. Reagan also had a strong anticommunist policy.

Reagan was an extremely effective candidate. High inflation and the Iranian hostage crisis also helped Reagan. Reagan easily won the 1980 election. The election also gave Republicans control of the Senate.

2. What factors helped Reagan win the presidential election in 1980?

_____

_____

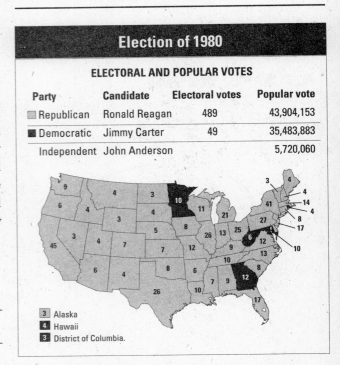

Election of 1980

ELECTORAL AND POPULAR VOTES

Party	Candidate	Electoral votes	Popular vote
Republican	Ronald Reagan	489	43,904,153
Democratic	Jimmy Carter	49	35,483,883
Independent	John Anderson		5,720,060

3 Alaska
4 Hawaii
3 District of Columbia.

Skillbuilder

Use the map to answer the questions

1. Did Ronald Reagan win more than 50% of the popular vote?

_____

2. Name three states that Jimmy Carter won.

_____

_____

CHAPTER 33 Section 2 (pages 1040–1044)

Conservative Policies Under Reagan and Bush

TERMS AND NAMES

Reaganomics Reagan's economic policies

supply-side economics Economic theory that tax cuts will increase jobs and government revenues

Strategic Defense Initiative Proposed system to defend the United States against missile attacks

Sandra Day O'Connor First woman Supreme Court justice

deregulation The cutting back of federal regulation of industry

Environmental Protection Agency Agency established in 1970 to fight pollution and conserve natural resources

Geraldine Ferraro Democratic vice-presidential candidate in 1984

George Bush Reagan's vice president elected president in 1988

BEFORE YOU READ

In the last section, you saw how conservative power grew before the presidential election of 1980.

In this section, you will read how President Reagan put in place conservative policies.

AS YOU READ

Use the chart below to take notes on the effects of Reaganomics.

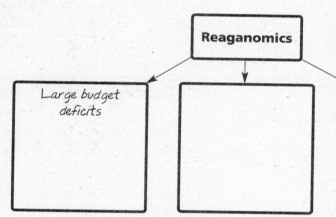

"Reaganomics" Takes Over
(pages 1040–1042)

What was Reaganomics?

Reagan tried to reduce the size and power of the federal government. He wanted to make deep cuts in government spending on social programs. He convinced Congress to lower taxes. This approach was called **Reaganomics.**

Reaganomics depended on **supply-side economics.** This theory said that cutting taxes would motivate people to work, save, and invest. More investment would create more jobs. More workers would mean more taxpayers, which would cause government *revenues* to increase.

Reagan also increased military spending. Between 1981 and 1984, the Defense Department

budget almost doubled. In 1983, Reagan asked the country's scientists to develop a defense system that would keep Americans safe from enemy missiles. The system became known as the **Strategic Defense Initiative,** or SDI.

The economy grew. Interest rates and inflation rates dropped. Government revenues, however, did not increase as much as Reagan hoped. So the federal government ran up huge budget *deficits.* During the Reagan and Bush years, the size of the government debt more than doubled.

1. What was the main idea of Reaganomics?

_____

_____

Judicial Power Shifts to the Right (page 1042)

What kind of judges did Reagan and Bush nominate?

Regan nominated Antonin Scalia, Anthony M. Kennedy, and **Sandra Day O'Connor** to fill seats in the Supreme Court left by retiring judges. O'Connor was the first woman appointed to the Court. Reagan also nominated Justice William Rehnquist to the position of chief justice.

President George Bush later made the Court more conservative when he nominated David H. Souter to replace the retiring justice William Brennan. He also nominated Clarence Thomas to take the place of Thurgood Marshall. In many decisions, the Court moved away from the more liberal rulings of the previous 40 years. The Court restricted a woman's right to an abortion, put limits on civil rights laws, and narrowed the rights of arrested persons.

2. What was the result of Reagan's and Bush's appointments to the Supreme Court?

_____

_____

Deregulating the Economy
(page 1043)

What was deregulation?

Reagan tried to reduce the power of the federal government through **deregulation.** Reagan removed price controls on oil and gas. He deregulated the airline industry and ended government regulation of the savings and loan industry.

Reagan also reduced environmental regulation. He cut the budget of the **Environmental Protection Agency** (EPA). He ignored requests from Canada to reduce acid rain. Reagan appointed opponents of environmental regulation to oversee the environment.

James Watt, Reagan's secretary of the interior took many actions that were questioned by environmentalists. He sold millions of acres of public lands to private developers, allowed drilling for oil and gas in the continental shelf, and encouraged timber cutting in national forests.

3. What actions did James Watt take that hurt the environment?

_____

_____

Conservative Victories in 1984 and 1988 (pages 1043–1044)

Who won the elections of 1984 and 1988?

By 1984, Reagan had the support of conservative voters who approved of his policies. These voters helped Reagan win the 1984 election. He defeated Democrat Walter Mondale. Mondale chose Representative **Geraldine Ferraro** of New York as his running mate. Ferraro became the first woman on a major party's presidential ticket.

In 1988, Vice-President **George Bush** ran for the presidency. He won the Republican nomination. The Democrats nominated Massachusetts governor Michael Dukakis.

During the campaign, Bush built on Reagan's legacy of low taxes by saying, "Read my lips: no new taxes." Most Americans saw little reason for change. George Bush won the election with 53 percent of the popular vote and 426 electoral votes.

4. What did the presidential elections of 1984 and 1988 show about the mood of the country?

_____

_____

_____

Name _____   Date _____

Social Concerns in the 1980s

BEFORE YOU READ

In the last section, you read about the conservative policies of Reagan and Bush.

In this section, you will learn about the social problems that existed in the 1980s.

AS YOU READ

Use the chart below to take notes about social issues during the 1980s and how Americans responded to them.

TERMS AND NAMES

AIDS (acquired immune deficiency syndrome) Fatal disease with no known cure, that became a U.S. and world-wide epidemic

pay equity Situation in which women and men receive equal pay for equal work

L. Douglas Wilder Nation's first African-American governor

Jesse Jackson Civil rights leader and presidential candidate

Lauro Cavasos Appointed secretary of education by President Reagan

Dr. Antonia Coello Novello Named Surgeon General by President Bush

SOCIAL ISSUES	AMERICANS' RESPONSES
Drugs	• Prosecute users and dealers • Antidrug education

Health, Education, and Cities in Crisis (pages 1045–1047)

What problems did Americans face in the 1980s?

A scary health issue that arose in the 1980s was **AIDS (acquired immune deficiency syndrome).** The disease is caused by a virus that destroys the *immune system* that protects people from illness. Most of the victims of AIDS were either homosexual men or *intravenous* drug users who shared needles. Many people also contracted AIDS through contaminated blood transfusions.

AIDS began spreading throughout the world possibly as early as the 1960s. It quickly became an epidemic in the U.S. and threatened much of the public blood supply.

Another issue that concerned Americans was abortion. In the 1973 *Roe* v. *Wade* decision, the Supreme Court said women had the right to have an abortion. Opponents of legalized abortion described themselves as "pro-life." Supporters of legalized abortion called themselves "pro-choice."

Battles over abortion rights often competed for attention with concerns over rising drug abuse. The Regan administration declared a war on drugs. Reagan supported laws to catch drug users and drug dealers.

Education remained an important issue. In 1983, a report entitled *A Nation at Risk* criticized the nation's schools. The report showed that

American students' test scores *lagged* behind those of students in other nations. Many people agreed that the nation's schools were not doing a good job. But they did not agree on solutions.

The nation's cities were also in crisis. Many poor and homeless people lived in cities. Budget cuts had eliminated earlier federal programs to aid the cities. Welfare payments to the poor had not kept up with rising prices.

1. How did Americans respond to the problems of the 1980s?

_____

_____

The Equal Rights Struggle
(pages 1048–1049)

Did women's lives improve in the 1980s?

Women continued to try to improve their lives. Women's groups were unable to get the Equal Rights Amendment ratified. But more women were elected to Congress.

By 1992, nearly 58 percent of all women had entered the work force. But women still earned only 76 cents for every dollar a man earned. New divorce laws and social conditions increased the number of single women heading a household. Many of these women lived in poverty.

Women's organizations and unions called for **pay equity.** This was an idea to make sure that women would earn the same pay as men doing the same work.

Under the pay equity system, jobs would be rated according to the skills and responsibilities they required. Employers would set pay rates to reflect each job's requirements. Women also called for benefits to help working mothers.

2. What political losses and gains did women have in the 1980s?

_____

_____

The Fight for Rights Continues
(pages 1049–1051)

How did minority groups fight for their rights?

Members of many minority groups achieved greater political power during the 1980s. Hundreds of communities had elected African Americans to serve in public offices. In 1990, **L. Douglas Wilder** of Virginia became the first African-American governor in the United States. The Reverend **Jesse Jackson** ran for the Democratic presidential nomination in 1984 and in 1988.

But the income gap between white Americans and African Americans was larger in 1988 than it was in 1968. In addition, Supreme Court rulings further limited affirmative action.

Latinos became the fastest growing minority group during the 1980s. Like African Americans, Latinos gained political power during the 1980s.

In 1988, President Reagan appointed **Lauro Cavasos** secretary of education. In 1990, President Bush named **Dr. Antonia Coello Novello,** to the post of Surgeon General.

Native Americans faced cuts in federal aid. Some opened casinos on their reservations to earn money. Asian Americans made economic advances but did not gain much political power.

Asian Americans were the second fastest growing minority in the United States during the 1980s. In 1976, an organization called Asian Women United (AWU) was founded to help Asian American women.

During the 1970s and 1980s, homosexual men and women worked for laws to protect their rights. By 1993, seven states and 110 communities had outlawed discrimination against homosexuals.

3. What were some political and social gains made by Latinos during the 1980s?

_____

_____

Name _____ Date _____

Foreign Policy After the Cold War

TERMS AND NAMES

Mikhail Gorbachev Last leader of the Soviet Union

glasnost Gorbachev's policy of openness in discussing problems in the Soviet Union

perestroika Gorbachev's policy of reforming the economy in the Soviet Union

INF Treaty Treaty to reduce nuclear weapons

Tiananmen Square Place in Beijing where Chinese protesters demonstrated against the Communist government

Sandinistas Communist rebel group that took power in Nicaragua

Contras Rebel forces supported by Ronald Reagan to overthrow the Sandinistas

Operation Desert Storm The 1991 U.S. attack on Iraq to force the Iraqis out of Kuwait

BEFORE YOU READ

In the last section, you learned about some of the social issues Americans faced in the 1980s.

In this section, you will see how American foreign policy changed after the Cold War.

AS YOU READ

Use the chart below to take notes about U.S. foreign policy in different regions of the world.

MIDDLE EAST	LATIN AMERICA	EUROPE
U.S. refused to sell arms to Iran.		

The Cold War Ends (pages 1054–1056)

What ended the Cold War?

In March 1985, **Mikhail Gorbachev** became the leader of the Soviet Union. He started talks with the United States to lessen Cold War tensions. Gorbachev thought this would allow the Soviets to cut their military spending. It would also let them reform their economy.

Gorbachev supported *glasnost* (openness in discussing social problems) and *perestroika* (economic *restructuring*) in the Soviet Union. He let private citizens own land. He also allowed more free speech and held free elections.

Talks led to the **INF Treaty** (Intermediate-Range Nuclear Forces Treaty). Reagan and Gorbachev signed the treaty in December 1987. The Senate ratified it in May 1988.

The weakness of the economy and Gorbachev's reforms led to the collapse of the Soviet Union. All the republics that were in the Soviet Union became independent nations. Then they formed a loose confederation called the Commonwealth of Independent States.

The collapse of the Soviet Union ended the Cold War. In January 1993, Russia and the United States signed the START II treaty. This treaty cut both nations' nuclear weapons by 75 percent.

Communists were knocked from power throughout Eastern Europe. Germany reunited. Other Eastern European nations *enacted* democratic reforms.

Students in China demanded freedom of speech. In April 1989, protesters held marches to voice their demands. The marches grew into large demonstrations in Beijing's **Tiananmen Square.** The Chinese military crushed the protesters. Soldiers killed hundreds of them and arrested others. People all over the world watched these actions. They were upset by what they saw.

1. What events in the Soviet Union led to the end of the Cold War?

_____

_____

Central American and Caribbean Policy (pages 1057–1058)

How did the United States act toward its neighbors?

In 1979, **Sandinista** rebels overthrew the Nicaraguan government. President Carter sent aid, as did the Soviet Union and Cuba. In 1981, President Reagan charged that the Sandinista government was Communist. He supported the **Contras,** a group trying to defeat the Sandinistas. After years of conflict, a peace agreement was signed and free elections were held in 1990.

Reagan sent U.S. troops to Grenada in 1983. He feared its government had ties with Cuba. The U.S. troops overthrew the pro-Cuban government. They set up a pro-American government in its place.

In 1989, President Bush sent more than 20,000 U.S. troops to Panama. He wanted to overthrow

Panamanian dictator Manuel Noriega. He also wanted to arrest him for *drug trafficking.* Noriega was taken by the American military. They took him to Miami. He was tried, convicted, and sentenced to 40 years in prison.

2. How did the United States influence affairs in Grenada?

_____

_____

Middle East Trouble Spots
(pages 1058–1061)

How did the United States act toward the Middle East?

In 1983, terrorists linked to Iran took some Americans hostage in Lebanon. Reagan condemned Iran. He called on U.S. allies not to sell Iran weapons for its war against Iraq.

Three years later, the American people found out that Reagan was breaking his own policy. Some of his staff had sold missiles to Iran. They were trying to free the hostages in Lebanon. Also, some of the profits from the sale were sent to the Contras in Nicaragua. These illegal activities were called the Iran-Contra affair.

In the summer of 1987, Congress investigated Iran-Contra. Some of Reagan's staff were convicted of crimes in the scandal. In 1992, President Bush pardoned some of these people.

In 1990, Iraq invaded Kuwait. On January 16, 1991, with the support of Congress and the United Nations, President Bush launched **Operation Desert Storm** to fight Iraq and to free Kuwait.

The United States and its allies staged air strikes against Iraq. On February 23, they also launched a ground attack. On February 28, President Bush announced a cease-fire. The Persian Gulf War was over. Kuwait was freed.

3. What was the purpose of Operation Desert Storm?

_____

_____

Glossary		**CHAPTER 33** The Conservative Tide
deficits Shortages or shortfalls	**immune system** Part of the body that fights off illness	**restructuring** Reform or reorganization
drug trafficking Delivering illegal drugs	**intravenous** Through the veins	**revenues** Monies received or gained
enacted Made into law	**lagged** Fell behind	

AFTER YOU READ

Terms and Names

A. If the statement is true, write "true" on the line. If it is false, change the underlined word or words to make it true.

_____ **1.** An <u>entitlement program</u> is one that guarantees benefits to particular people.

_____ **2.** <u>Reaganomics</u> led to an increase in the national debt.

_____ **3.** President Reagan nominated <u>Sandra Day O'Connor</u> to the position of Chief Justice of the Supreme Court.

_____ **4.** The <u>pay equity</u> system was proposed by unions and women's rights organizations to close the income gap that left so many women poor.

_____ **5.** The actions of Iraq against Kuwait led the United States and its allies to start the <u>Strategic Defense Initiative</u>.

B. Write the letter of the best answer on the line.

_____ **1.** Which of the following was an alliance of conservative groups that opposed liberal programs?
   a. the New Left
   b. the New Right
   c. affirmative action
   d. Silent Majority

_____ **2.** The theory that tax cuts would increase government revenues was called
   a. affirmative action.
   b. entitlement programs.
   c. supply-side economics.
   d. reverse discrimination.

_____ **3.** The first woman to run on a major party's presidential ticket was
   a. Sandra Day O'Connor.
   b. Anita Hill.
   c. Peggy Noonan.
   d. Geraldine Ferraro.

_____ **4.** What was the policy that was intended to correct the effects of discrimination in the employment and education of minority groups and women?
   a. affirmative action
   b. pay equity
   c. entitlement program
   d. deregulation

_____ **5.** What was the policy set up by Mikhail Gorbachev that called for openness in discussing social problems in the Soviet Union?
   a. perestroika
   b. affirmative action
   c. glasnost
   d. reverse discrimination

AFTER YOU READ (continued)   **CHAPTER 33** The Conservative Tide

Main Ideas

1. Why did Reagan win the election of 1980?

_____

_____

2. Name two key policies of Reaganomics.

_____

_____

3. Define deregulation.

_____

_____

4. Name two gains made by women in the 1980s.

_____

_____

5. What caused the collapse of the Soviet Union?

_____

_____

Thinking Critically

Answer the following questions on a separate sheet of paper.

1. What were two goals of the conservative movement in the late 1970s?

2. How did the conservative policies of the Reagan and Bush administrations affect women and minority groups in the 1980s?

CHAPTER 34 Section 1 (pages 1066–1074)

The 1990s and the New Millennium

TERMS AND NAMES

William Jefferson Clinton 42nd president

H. Ross Perot Texas billionaire who was a third-party candidate in 1992 election

Hillary Rodham Clinton First Lady and health-care reformer

NAFTA Trade agreement between Canada, Mexico, and the United States

Newt Gingrich Speaker of the House of Representatives

Contract with America Republican plan for political reform

Kenneth Starr Independent counsel who investigated Clinton

Al Gore Clinton's vice-president, and Democratic candidate in 2000 election

George W. Bush 43rd president of U.S.

BEFORE YOU READ

In the last section, you learned about American foreign policy at the end of the Cold War.

In this section, you will read about Bill Clinton's presidency.

AS YOU READ

Use the time line below to take notes about the major events of Clinton's first term.

1993 Congress approves NAFTA	**1995**
1994	**1996**

Clinton Wins the Presidency; Moderate Reform and Economic Boom
(pages 1066–1068)

What was the important issue in the 1992 election?

Governor **William Jefferson Clinton** of Arkansas was the first member of the baby-boom generation to win the presidency. Clinton defeated President George Bush and Texas billionaire, **H. Ross Perot** in the election. Bush's popularity, which was sky-high after the Gulf War, fell as the economy went into a recession. Clinton convinced voters he would move the Democratic Party to the political center by embracing both liberal and conservative programs.

Clinton tried to reform the nation's program for health care insurance. He appointed First Lady **Hillary Rodham Clinton** to head the team creating the plan. Congress never voted on the plan after

Republicans attacked its promotion of "big government." Clinton was more successful in balancing the budget. The economy began to produce surpluses for the government and the economy boomed.

1. Why did George Bush's popularity fall after the Gulf War?

_____

_____

_____

Crime and Terrorism (pages 1068–1069)

Where did terrorists attack?

Terrorism and violence raised Americans' fears during the 1990s and in the first years of the 2000s. In 1993, foreign terrorists exploded a bomb at the World Trade Center in New York City. In 1995, an American terrorist named Timothy McVeigh exploded a bomb at the Federal building in Oklahoma City. The bomb killed 168 men, women, and children.

School violence also plagued the nation. In 1999, two students at Columbine High School in Colorado killed 12 and wounded 23 classmates and a teacher before killing themselves.

In 2001, the worst attack on the United States in its history took place. Foreign terrorists hijacked airplanes and flew them into the World Trade Center and the Pentagon outside Washington, D.C. The explosions leveled the World Trade Center and severely damaged the Pentagon. Approximately 4,500 people died in the attacks.

2. What buildings were the target of two terrorist attacks?

New Foreign Policy Challenges; Partisan Politics and Impeachment
(pages 1069–1071)

Why was President Clinton impeached?

In the 1990s, the major foreign policy problem was in Yugoslavia where Serbs embarked on a murderous policy of "ethnic cleansing" first in Bosnia, then in Kosovo. The United States and NATO launched air strikes against the Serbs forcing them to back down.

Free trade was a goal of the Clinton administration. In 1994, the **North American Free Trade Agreement (NAFTA)** was signed into law by President Clinton. It provided for free trade between the United States, Mexico, and Canada. Critics of free trade opposed American actions by protesting at meetings of world trade groups in Seattle, Washington, and Quebec City, Canada.

President Clinton developed political troubles beginning in 1994 when the Republicans gained control of both houses of Congress. **Newt Gingrich,** who became speaker of the house, led the Republicans. The Republicans used a document they called the **Contract with America** to oppose President Clinton.

Clinton won reelection in 1996 even though he was being investigated by **Kenneth Starr,** the independent counsel appointed by the federal court. Starr began investigating Clinton's involvement in a land deal. He then investigated whether Clinton had lied under oath in questioning about an improper relationship with a young White House intern. The House approved two articles of impeachment against the president even though a majority of Americans approved of Clinton's job performance. The Senate trial that followed in 1999 failed to convict Clinton and he remained in office. The impeachment trial left bitter political partisanship for the remainder of Clinton's term in office.

3. Why was President Clinton impeached?

The Race for the White House; The Bush Administration Begins Anew (pages 1072–1074)

What was controversial about George W. Bush's election as president?

The candidates in the 2000 election were Vice-President **Al Gore,** the Democratic candidate, and Texas Governor **George W. Bush,** the Republican candidate. There was confusion on election night over who won the state of Florida. Gore had won the popular vote. But whoever won Florida would win a majority of the electoral votes and the election.

Both sides sent lawyers and spokespeople to Florida to try to secure victory. Bush held a slim lead. A confusing ballot in one county caused many likely Gore voters to cast votes for other candidates. Gore's representatives called for a recount, while Bush's representatives opposed the recount. The battle moved to the courts. On December 12, more than a month after Election Day, the U.S. Supreme Court ruled 5-4 to stop the recount. As a result, Bush won Florida and the presidency.

In his first six months in office, Bush signed into law a large tax cut. He faced opposition over environmental decisions. In May, Republican Senator Jim Jeffords of Vermont, unhappy with the conservative direction of Bush's policies, left the party. As a result, control of the Senate passed from the Republicans to the Democrats, creating further legislative problems for the new president.

4. How was the election of 2000 decided?

The New Global Economy

BEFORE YOU READ

In the last section, you learned about the presidencies of Bill Clinton and George W. Bush.

In this section, you will read about the economic issues that Americans faced at the end of the 20th century.

AS YOU READ

Use the web below to take notes about the major changes that occurred in the U.S. economy at the end of the 20th century.

Loss of manufacturing jobs

Changes in the Economy

The Shifting American Economy (pages 1075–1077)

What changed for American workers?

There was good news and bad news about the economy between 1993 and 2000. Millions of new jobs were created. By 2000, the unemployment rate had fallen to the lowest it had been since 1970. But wage inequality between upper-income and low-income Americans also grew.

There was an increase of jobs in the service sector. The **service sector** is the part of the economy that provides services to people. By 2000, nearly 80 percent of American workers were teachers, medical professionals, lawyers, engineers, store clerks,

waitstaff, and other service workers. The largest growth in the service sector came in jobs that paid low wages. These included jobs such as sales clerks and janitors.

Many companies **downsized**—reduced staff in order to cut costs. They hired temporary workers to replace full-time staff. This had serious *consequences* for the workers. Most temporary workers had lower wages, little job security, and few benefits. This led many workers to feel insecure about their jobs.

Manufacturing jobs declined sharply in the 1980s and 1990s. The loss in jobs in manufacturing led to a drop in union membership. Workers with high-paying jobs saw no need to join unions. Workers with low-paying jobs were too worried about losing their jobs to join unions.

Workers in high-tech fields such as computers, made up about 20 percent of the work force. These new high-tech jobs demanded that workers have special skills. Most workers who had high-tech jobs earned high salaries.

By the 1990s, some people who had creative ideas about computers made fortunes. **Bill Gates** was one of these people. He founded Microsoft, a computer *software* company. By 2000, he had assets of more than $60 billion. This made him the wealthiest man in the world.

High-tech business traded on the **NASDAQ** (National Association of Securities Dealers Automated Quotation System) exchange grew rapidly. These Internet businesses called **dotcoms** created fortunes for their founders. But the stocks of these businesses were terribly overvalued, and beginning in 2000 the NASDAQ fell sharply. Despite the decline, new industries such as web security, and wireless communication had been founded.

1. What were three changes in the workplace in the United States during the 1990s?

_____

_____

_____

Change and the Global Economy (pages 1078–1079)

What is the global economy?

Improvements in transportation and communication allowed people, goods, and information to move around the world faster than ever. One of President Clinton's major foreign policy goals was to expand trade.

In 1994, the United States joined other nations in signing a world trade agreement called **GATT** (General Agreement on Tariffs and Trade). GATT lowered tariffs. It also set up the World Trade Organization (WTO). This organization was created to settle trade disputes.

Many people believed that GATT would be good for the U.S. economy. But many American workers feared they would lose their jobs. They thought it would help companies make products in countries where wages were low.

Many low-wage American jobs were lost as a result of NAFTA. But exports to Canada and Mexico increased. By 1997, there were 300,000 more jobs in the United States than there had been in 1993.

Developing nations also offered some businesses the chance to avoid laws on the environment. For example, in Mexico, many assembly plants dumped dangerous chemicals on Mexican soil.

2. In what ways did President Clinton try to expand trade?

_____

_____

Persons Employed in Three Economic Sectors*			
Year	Farming	Manufacturing	Service Producing
1900	11,050	7,252	6,832
1950	6,001	18,475	20,721
2006 (projected)	3,618	24,451	111,867

*Numbers in millions

Sources: *Historical Statistics of the United States, Colonial Times to 1970;
Statistical Abstracts of the United States, 1953, 1954, 1999*

Skillbuilder

Use the table to answer the questions.

1. What sector of the U.S. economy has seen the greatest increase in workers?

_____

_____

2. How many more people are expected to be employed in manufacturing than in farming in 2006?

_____

_____

CHAPTER 34 Section 3 (pages 1082–1087)

Technology and Modern Life

BEFORE YOU READ

In the last section, you saw how the American economy changed in the 1990s.

In this section, you will learn how technology has changed Americans' lives.

AS YOU READ

Use the chart below to take notes on the technological changes described in this section and how these changes have affected your life.

CHANGES	EFFECTS
Information superhighway	• Internet • e-mail

The Communications Revolution (pages 1082–1084)

How have new technologies affected communications?

President Clinton wanted to create an **information superhighway.** This would be a computer *network* that would link people around the world. The network would link cable, phone, and computers to provide entertainment and information.

Clinton appointed Vice-President Gore to oversee the government's role in creating the information superhighway. They wanted private *entrepreneurs* to build the network. But they believed the government should protect people's rights to use it.

Most people took part in the information superhighway through the **Internet,** a worldwide computer network. By 2000, experts expected that 97 million Americans regularly used the Internet to send e-mail—electronic notes and messages.

New technologies let many Americans **telecommute,** or work out of their homes instead of going to an office every day.

The changes in communications caused the growth of many communications companies. Congress passed the **Telecommunications Act** in 1996 to make sure people would receive good service. The law allowed telephone and cable companies to enter each others' industries. One of the results of the law was an increase in *mergers*. This cut the number of competing companies.

Congress passed the Communications Decency Act as part of the Telecommunications Act. Congress called for a *"V-chip"* to be placed in television sets. This computer chip would allow parents to block TV programs that they do not want their children to see.

The communications industry liked the Telecommunications Act. But some people believed that the law allowed a small number of people to control the media. Civil rights activists thought the Communications Decency Act limited free speech. Parts of these laws were struck down in court.

1. How did the Internet and cable television affect Americans?

_____

_____

Scientific Advances Enrich Lives
(pages 1084–1087)

How does technology affect daily life?

In addition to telecommunications, great progress was made in robotics, space exploration, and medicine. Visual imaging and artificial intelligence were combined to provide applications in industry, medicine, and education. Flight simulators helped train pilots. Doctors have been able to better explore within the body. Architects and engineers have used virtual reality to build visual models of buildings and structures.

In space, *Pathfinder* and *Sojourner* transmitted live pictures from the surface of Mars. Shuttle missions began building the *International Space Station (ISS)*. The Hubble Space Telescope was used to discover new planets.

Enormous progress was made in the field of biotechnology. The Human Genome Project announced in 2000 that it had mapped the genes of the human body. Molecular biologists hoped this genetic map of DNA would help them to develop new treatments for inherited diseases. But the applications of this new information or "biotechnology" was controversial. Many people were concerned about animals that were cloned from single cells. The use of **genetic engineering,** the artificial changing of the molecular biology of organisms' cells to alter an organism, aroused concern. Scientists used genetic engineering to alter food crops like corn. Consumer groups resisted the practice, and it was restricted in some places.

Applications of technology helped medical progress. New treatments for cancer and AIDS helped many patients. The use of magnetic resonance imaging (MRI) helped doctors with medical diagnoses.

Environmental concerns rose through the decade. People looked for ways to reduce the use of fossil fuels and the production of acid rain. Americans also improved recycling efforts.

2. What were some important technological advances in the United States?

_____

_____

_____

CHAPTER 34 **Section 4** (pages 1088–1093)

The Changing Face of America

BEFORE YOU READ

In the last section, you learned about the ways technology affects modern life.

In this section, you will read about the changes facing Americans at the start of the 21st century.

AS YOU READ

Use the web below to take notes about the changes occurring in the United States.

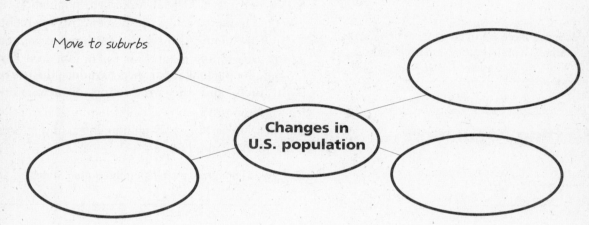

Urban Flight (pages 1088–1090)

Why did people move to suburbs?

Between 1950 and 1970, America experienced a pattern of **urban flight,** where Americans left the cities and moved to the suburbs. By 2000, after years of decline, some major cities had increased their population or slowed the rate of decline.

There were several causes of urban flight. Overcrowding in cities was one. Overcrowding helped cause increased crime and decaying housing. Many city dwellers who could afford to, moved to the suburbs for better schools and safer neighborhoods. Cities lost taxes and downtown shopping districts lost business to suburban malls.

By the mid-1990s, people began to return to the city. In a process known as **gentrification,** they bought and rehabilitated old houses and neighborhoods. Neighborhoods came back, but low-income residents were *displaced* by rising housing costs.

Many suburban workers commuted to the city for work. But suburbs competed for business and industry. Suburbs offered tax breaks to get business to locate there and then saw their tax revenues decline as a result.

1. How did urban flight change the nation's cities?

_____

_____

_____

The Aging of America (pages 1090–1091)
How will aging affect America?

The 2000 census revealed that Americans are getting older. The median age, 35.2 years, was two years older than the median age in 1990. The cause was simple: people were living longer and the large baby boom generation was getting older. This trend put pressure on programs for the elderly. Social Security was stressed because there were fewer younger workers paying into the system and retirees were living longer.

In 1996, three workers made Social Security contributions to support every retired person. But experts expect that by 2030, there will be only two workers to support each retired person. Social Security will begin to pay out more than it takes in. As a result, some people want to reform the Social Security system.

2. **How does the increase in the number of elderly people affect Social Security and Medicare?**

_____

_____

The Shifting Population (pages 1091–1093)
How has immigration affected America?

Changes in Mexico's economy have spurred illegal immigration from Mexico to the United States. The 2000 census showed how immigration was changing the face of one state, California. By 2001, California had become a majority minority state, with ethnic minorities making up more than half its population. Throughout the decade, illegal immigration grew with immigrants from Mexico, Central America, and Haiti arriving every month. By 2001, between 5 and 6 million illegal immigrants lived in the United States. In California, opposition to illegal immigration resulted in the passage of a law known as **Proposition 187.** This law cut all education and non-emergency health benefits to illegal immigrants. Proposition 187 was ruled unconstitutional. It helped inspire Hispanic immigrants, who saw themselves as targets of the law, to become more politically involved.

Native Americans continued to struggle. In 2001, about 32 percent of Native Americans lived below the poverty line. During the 1990s, Native Americans strived to improve their lives through building casinos and using the courts to gain greater recognition for their tribal ancestry and land rights.

Between 1970 and 1995, the population of the United States increased from 204 million to more than 280 million. Much of this increase was because of immigration. Most of these immigrants came from Latin America and Asia.

Experts believed that immigration would change the ethnic and racial makeup of the United States. They predicted that by 2050, *non-Latino whites* will make up 53 percent of the population, down from 74 percent in 1996. They expect the Latino population to increase from 10 percent of the population in 1996 to 25 percent in 2050. The Asian-American population is expected to increase from 3 percent to 8 percent. The African-American population is expected to increase from 12 percent to 14 percent.

In 1994, almost two-thirds of Americans wanted to cut back immigration. Some people feared that immigrants took jobs away from Americans born in the United States.

Another problem was illegal immigration. By the early 1990s, about 3.2 million illegal immigrants came to the United States.

3. **How is immigration changing the United States?**

_____

_____

America in a New Millennium (page 1093)
What challenges do Americans face in the 21st century?

America entered the 21st century with several concerns, old and new. For example, environmental concerns have become a global issue and have gained importance. Poverty is a major concern, as is curbing acts of terrorism that threaten Americans both at home and abroad.

4. **What challenges faced Americans at the turn of the 20th century?**

_____

_____

Name _____ Date _____

consequences Effects, results

developing nations Countries that are building industries

displaced Moved or forced from the usual place

entrepreneurs People who use their own money to create a new business

manufacturing Making goods such as automobiles

merger Joining together of separate business entities

millennium A period of 1,000 years

network Group of connections

non-Latino whites Ethnically "white" people who are not Latinos

software Programs that make computers work

terrorism Use of violence to create political change through fear

V-chip Computer chip to allow parents to prevent children from watching some TV shows

AFTER YOU READ

Terms and Names

A. Write the letter of the name or term that matches the description.

a. urban flight

b. GATT

c. telecommute

d. NAFTA

e. Internet

_____ **1.** Agreement that ended trade barriers between the United States, Canada, and Mexico

_____ **2.** Treaty that lowered tarrifs and set up the World Trade Organization (WTO)

_____ **3.** A worldwide computer network

_____ **4.** When Americans left the cities and moved to the suburbs

_____ **5.** To use new communications technology to work from home

B. Write the name or term that best completes each sentence.

genetic engineering

downsize

Hillary Rodham Clinton

gentrification

service sector

1. President Clinton appointed _____ to head the task force on health care.

2. The 1990s saw a decrease of jobs in manufacturing and an increase in jobs in the _____.

3. The fixing up of old city neighborhoods is called _____.

4. The use of _____ to alter food caused concern in the 1990s.

5. Companies that tried to cut costs would often _____ their staffs.

AFTER YOU READ CHAPTER 34 The United States in Today's World

Main Ideas

1. What was the Contract with America?

_____

_____

2. Why did some American companies downsize?

_____

_____

3. Describe two ways that technology changed people's lives in the 1990s.

_____

_____

4. How did urban flight affect cities?

_____

_____

5. How will the Human Genome project help people?

_____

_____

Thinking Critically

Answer the following questions on a separate sheet of paper.

1. Describe three ways that the U.S. economy changed by the end of 1990s.

2. What are some possible effects of the American population?